Nudity

Dress, Body, Culture

Series Editor **Joanne B. Eicher**, *Regents' Professor, University of Minnesota*

Books in this provocative series seek to articulate the connections between culture and dress, which is defined here in its broadest possible sense as any modification or supplement to the body. Interdisciplinary in approach, the series highlights the dialogue between identity and dress, cosmetics, coiffure, and body alterations as manifested in practices as varied as plastic surgery, tattooing, and ritual scarification. The series aims, in particular, to analyse the meaning of dress in relation to popular culture and gender issues and will include works grounded in anthropology, sociology, history, art history, literature and folklore.

ISSN: 1360-466X

Previously published titles in the series

Nudity
A Cultural Anatomy

Ruth Barcan

Oxford • New York

First published in 2004 by
Berg
Editorial offices:
1st Floor, Angel Court, 81 St Clements Street, Oxford OX4 1AW, UK
175 Fifth Avenue, New York, NY 10010, USA

Berg is an imprint of Oxford International Publishers Ltd.

Library of Congress Cataloging-in-Publication Data
Barcan, Ruth.
    Nudity : a cultural anatomy / Ruth Barcan.
        p. cm. — (Dress, body, culture)
    Includes bibliographical references and index.
    ISBN 1-85973-872-9 (cloth)
  1. Body, Human—Social aspects. 2. Body, Human—Symbolic aspects.
3. Nudity—Social aspects. 4. Sex symbolism. I. Title. II. Series.

    GN298.B37 2004
    306.4—dc22

                                                            2004003082

British Library Cataloguing-in-Publication Data
A catalogue record for this book is available from the British Library.

ISBN   1 85973 872 9

Typeset by JS Typesetting Ltd, Wellingborough, Northants.
Printed in the United Kingdom by Biddles Ltd, King's Lynn.

www.bergpublishers.com

Contents

Illustrations

Acknowledgements

This book has been a while in the making, and there are many people who have come for the ride and who share my joy at its arrival. To them, at last, I have an answer to the oft-posed question, "How's the nude book coming along?"

First and foremost, I would like to thank the research assistants who worked on this project for their considerable help on what was at times tricky territory: Cath Barcan, Kristen Davis, Chris Fleming, Erin Helyard, Jay Johnston, Belinda Morrissey, Katrina Schlunke and Craig Williams. I would most especially like to thank the intrepid Linda Barcan, who proved herself to be a researcher of extraordinary capability. Stuart Ferguson provided expert help with translation from German, and Karen Entwistle and Tim Haydon were both an enormous help in tracking down copyright permissions. I am grateful for the generosity of copyright holders in granting permissions. I am grateful to the College of Arts, Education and Social Sciences at the University of Western Sydney (UWS) for financial assistance with production costs. Patrick Terrett generously helped with image production.

Interviews were carried out as part of two studies funded by the University of Western Sydney, Hawkesbury, Australia: the first was an F.G. Swain New Researcher Award, and the second, an Internal Research Grant. I would like to express my sincere gratitude to the University's Research Office, especially Lorraine Bridger, for their support of this quirky project. The University of Western Sydney also accorded me two periods of study leave, without which the book could never have been completed. I would like to express my gratitude to UWS, and to the two departments who welcomed me during those periods of leave – the Department of English at the University of Newcastle, NSW, and the Faculty of Humanities and Social Sciences at the University of Technology, Sydney. I made regular use of the library collections of the University of Sydney and the University of Western Sydney, whose staff I thank, and made highly useful visits to the British Library in London, the Bibliothèque nationale in Paris, and the American Nudist Research Library at Cypress Cove, Florida.

A number of people acted as expert readers for sections of the manuscript, and I am very grateful for their comments. I would like to thank those who have helped provide a necessary disciplinary corrective to my more daring excursions into transdisciplinarity, as well as those who egged me on into unknown territory: Bernie Curran, John Frow, Helen Gilbert, Jane Goodall, Sara Knox, Simon Ryan, Fiona Mackie and the late Godfrey Tanner, a true gentleman and scholar. Thanks to my dear father, Alan Barcan, for his scholarly input and his support.

This project arose during the brief but productive life of the New Humanities Transdisciplinary Research Group (NHTRG) at the University of Western Sydney, Hawkesbury. Though the inevitable university restructure saw the end of this flourishing little group, in its few years it provided an open, rigorous and adventurous forum in which to try out ideas. I would like to thank my NHTRG colleagues for their intellectual stimulation and their receptivity.

Most especially, I would like to thank the wealth of people from all walks of life who shared their insights about nakedness in interviews. To all of them I owe a deep debt of gratitude. All participants' names are pseudonyms, with the exception of several well-known interviewees. The project team interviewed, among others: beauticians, teachers, a mortician, nudists, a stripper, magazine editors, "Home Girls and Blokes," an anatomy lab technician, a porn-maker, a manufacturer of genitally correct dolls, tattooists, a retoucher, nursing mothers, event organizers, nurses, medical students, psychologists, police officers, masseurs, radiographers, artists, photographers, photo-lab operators, models and even users of urinals. I greatly appreciate the ways in which their ideas have enriched my understanding and their voices have added to the text. Moreover, over the years, myriads of friends and acquaintances have told me anecdotes and handed me "nude snippets" of all imaginable kinds. I gratefully recognize the contribution they have made to the book.

This book has been a labour of love over many years. I have never lost interest in the richness of nakedness as metaphor, concept and experience, and I am grateful that Berg Publishers have been happy to share that enthusiasm. Throughout, they have been encouraging, efficient and easy to work with, and I would like to thank them; especially Kathryn Earle, Joanne Eicher, Caroline McCarthy, Ken Bruce and the anonymous readers for their useful comments, intellectual support and practical assistance.

And speaking of love, I acknowledge my wonderful family and my dear partner Mark Higgs, who have been unstinting in their support of me, unwavering in their enthusiasm for this project, and a constant source of both stimulation and comfort. I dedicate this book to them, and to our brand new daughter Sophia, whose timelines paralleled those of this book in a difficult but rich intertwining.

R.B.

What is often being argued, it seems to me, in the idea of nature is the idea of man.

Raymond Williams, "Ideas of Nature"

Introduction

One of the early chapters of Anatole France's quietly devastating satire on modernity and civilization, *Penguin Island* (1909), is entitled "The First Clothes." *Penguin Island* is a fable about a group of penguins baptized mistakenly by a doddery saint. Since baptism is a rite signalling the shift from the natural state to the social order – and thus a rite specifically about *humanness* – the baptized penguins present God and His assembly of saints with a dilemma that can be resolved only by transforming the penguins into humans. God is initially reluctant to do this, but finds Himself trapped by the logic of His own doctrines. On rolls this logic, inexorably: the newly transmogrified penguins must next be clothed. "Since they have been incorporated into the family of Abraham," sighs the saint, "these penguins share the curse of Eve, and they know that they are naked, a thing of which they were ignorant before" (France 1909: 43). Once the penguins are clothed, they start to lose all modesty. The novella depicts clothing as the first human hypocrisy, to be followed by a train of others: property, wealth, class and war. Human morality, it seems, is based on hypocrisy, vanity and violence. The Devil, in the form of a monk, carries off the first clothed penguin and rapes her: "Then the penguins felt as if the sun had gone out" (France 1909: 48).

This fable tells us a number of things about nudity: first, it replays the familiar moral argument that it is clothing and not nudity that provokes desire, and that modesty comes into existence only with the category of sin. Nudity (like modesty) does not precede clothing; rather, it comes into being with the invention of clothing. The story also follows a long tradition in seeing clothing as a form of alienation from a primordial unselfconsciousness, a means by which people differentiate themselves from others. In short, clothing is part of the sad story of "civilization." The fable also recognizes that both clothing and nudity are bound up in a quite primal way with the fundamental ordering categories of societies – especially gender and rank (or class) – and with the power, politics and pleasures of sex. Most profoundly of all, it recognizes that nudity is a human category, for the penguins, while ever they remained birds, were not naked.

I have chosen this episode as a kind of exemplary tale because it captures many of the themes and arguments of this book, which aims to clothe with detail its central argument – that the categories of clothing and nakedness are bound up with a fundamental ambiguity about the nature of human existence, and have thus repeatedly been used as indices of humanness, its others and its hierarchies. Because of its supposed "naturalness," nudity has been a powerful metaphorical vehicle for dividing up humans into categories. Most fundamentally, it has divided the non-human from the human, and has divided humanness into "types" or gradations: male/female; civilized/savage; sane/insane; normal/deviant and so on. Consumer culture too has its own modes of nudity that help construct types of person: "heroes," "ordinary people," "glamorous people," "celebrities," and so on. Nudity is "natural," but nature is, paradoxically, never enough. The natural state is, in fact, *unnatural*, if we accept that there have never been human societies in which the body has remained totally unclothed, decorated or adorned. Humans may be naturally naked, but we have used clothing to define our kind (especially to differentiate ourselves from animals), and to differentiate ourselves from each other. Depending on whether one is thinking of humans as essentially naked (a "natural" truth) or as always clothed (a social "truth"), nakedness can be a noble or a degraded state. The possible meanings of the naked body are structured by particular religious, symbolic and visual traditions. This book explores some elements of the Western tradition, focusing on two metaphysical traditions underpinning Christianity – Platonic and Jewish – that have, broadly speaking, helped produce the meaning of nakedness. These traditions have left the West with a complex legacy of "positive" and "negative" meanings of nudity. Given their importance to the European colonists, they have also played a significant role in structuring the post-settlement experiences of nudity of indigenous peoples.

Nudity is caught up in a web of contradictions and paradoxes. Despite the knowingness and even cynicism of much contemporary consumer culture, a glimpse of flesh, or indeed, even the *mention* of nudity, still can, in the right contexts, incite a smile, a nervous giggle or even outrage. Nudity is both big business and mundane fact of embodiment, the staple of the porn industry and an obstacle at school gym classes. Our society's attitudes, rules and conventions around nudity are riddled with contradictions, complexities and disavowals; as Erving Goffman put it, our attitudes to body exposure are a set of "jumbled attitudes and rationalizations" (Goffman 1965: 50).

To study nudity is to enter this manifold terrain. It is to ask questions about the mundane (do you wrap a towel around yourself when you come out of the shower?) and, at the same time, to enter mythical, philosophical or moral domains. It is also to pose questions about the modern experience of the body more generally, since our experiences of and responses to nudity are, in many ways, more broadly legible as the legacy of a longstanding somatophobic metaphysics that has translated, for many of us, into a more subtly somato-phobic embodiment. Magnus Clarke, author of a classic study of Australian nudism, put it less kindly (and less accurately) when he claimed that "there are still individuals for whom the body is a mysterious and unexplored expanse of flesh which hangs from their necks" (Clarke 1982: 220).

Uneasiness with nudity is, in part, related to unease about sex. The etymology of the words "naked" and "nude" has nothing to do with sex, but in the popular imagination the link is almost automatic. As the author of a 1968 report on the public image of nudism commented, many people continue to "link the words nudity and sex as readily as they would link knife to fork" (quoted in Clarke 1982: 212). But the automatic association between sex and nudity can itself be treated as a phenomenon. This book also explores nudity in some of its "other" guises – mundane, technical or professional. As we will see, different professions create their own interesting relations to the naked body.

But of course, there are many connections, both obvious and subtle, between nudity, sex and eroticism. In the case of consumer culture, for example, nudity usually operates at least in part as a sign for sex. But sex itself is neither self-contained nor simple. It can, for example, operate as a mode of discipline by which "correct," "ordinary," "deviant" or privileged versions of masculinity and femininity are constructed. In tracing the connections between nudity and sex, then, my interest has often been to see how sex is bound up in larger questions, especially the formation and regulation of identity, both individual and collective. The naked body is a site of *ambivalence*, both personally and collectively. It may be a site for ambivalence about the beauty or sufficiency of one's own body. More abstractly, though, the regulation of nudity often occurs in the shadow of hidden ambivalence about what it is to be human.

A commonsense link exists, too, between nakedness and universality, which is no doubt why many popular books about nakedness start with paradigmatic tales from myth or folklore, such as Adam and Eve, Lady Godiva and *The Emperor's New Clothes*. Nudity calls up fantasies of universality, for it is true that every human being on the planet has a naked body. But to speak of the universality of nudity is to say everything and nothing, for the meanings and experiences of nudity differ markedly between contexts. The use of nudity as a *sign* of universal humanity is, however, highly significant culturally, and it continues unabated.

Nakedness, then, is not just a modern metonym for sex; it is a deeply important cultural idea and a significant metaphor. When it turns up in religious, philosophical or mythical tales (such as the ones mentioned above), it is connected not only to sex but also to a broad range of moral, philosophical or theological issues. In *Penguin Island*, for example, nudity serves as a metaphor for humanness. The Adam and Eve story can likewise be read as a parable about the simultaneous birth of many of the things that have been imagined to define human identity (mortality, difference from God, sinfulness, self-consciousness, the seeking of knowledge) or human society (the social necessity of clothing, the mortification of the body and of femininity). In this one tale are combined social, psychological, moral, biological, theological and cultural definers of humanness. The Genesis story has at its heart a lament, that distinctive humanness should be born from sin, separation and loss.[1]

So when these stories connect nakedness with sex, they do so within this larger moral and philosophical context. The stories of both Adam and Eve and Lady Godiva affirm the link between nakedness and sex within a larger exploration of power and knowledge. They explore both the positive and negative meanings of nudity, and the sex that they link with nudity is morally ambiguous and highly metaphorical, signifying both self-knowledge and forbidden knowledge, innocence and guilt, high moral purpose and shame, justice and punishment. Both tales see sexual knowledge as inseparable from other forms of knowledge and from questions of identity and justice. In *The Emperor's New Clothes*, the grand themes of self-knowledge, identity, power and rank recur, and nakedness again appears as a metaphor for our shared humanity. All these stories, and others like them, suggest that the body, knowledge and categories of humanness (like gender, rank and age) are primally and inextricably intertwined. Nudity and sex are linked together, but sexuality is itself embedded in larger questions about subjectivity, power and human identity.

Studies of Nudity

There have been many academic studies of "the nude," but very few of nudity. I have seen only one study whose central aim is to theorize or conceptualize nakedness itself, Paul Ableman's (1982) *Anatomy of Nakedness* (republished in 1984 as *The Banished Body*), and one detailed study of nakedness as a metaphor in a particular context, Judy Kronenfeld's (1998) *King Lear and the Naked Truth*. Karl Toepfer's (1997) detailed historical study of nakedness in pre-World War Two German body culture also moves usefully beyond historical case studies to bring the naked body into a theorization of modernity. But such studies are rare. I initially found this lacuna quite surprising; how could it be that a physical state shared by all human beings, and so saturated in customs, conventions and taboos, could have been all but ignored in academic literature? Perhaps it is simply because it is very hard to know what *can* be said of nudity-in-general, since naked bodies take their meaning from particular contexts.

Despite the difficulty in discussing nudity *per se*, I believe that there is something to be gained from situating particular naked states and practices within larger historical and conceptual contexts. Perhaps, too, the lacuna is itself symptomatic, to the extent that it can be seen as imbricated in one of the subtler manifestations of Cartesianism: the devaluation of bodily experience and embodied knowledge. If this is so of bodily knowledge generally, perhaps we should not be surprised to find a conceptual gap around the supposed degree-zero of human embodiment, nakedness.

It's not of course that there are no studies of naked bodies; there's an enormous literature on the nude in fine art and on pornography, to take two obvious examples. There exists, too, a strong feminist counter-response to canonical treatment of the nude, emanating from both theoreticians and art practitioners. But most studies of nakedness, even politicized studies, focus on representation, whether from the perspective of an implicitly masculinist visual arts tradition (the nude in photography, sculpture or painting) or from feminist cultural criticism (e.g. debates about pornography or "the male gaze"). The focus on representation reflects the difficulty in speculating about embodiment, especially in historical studies. It also reflects, though, the devaluation of experience, especially bodily experience, as both basis and object of academic knowledge within some areas of the humanities. A few books do engage with everyday practices of nakedness. Margaret Miles (1989) has written a study of the religious meanings and experience of female nakedness in medieval times (*Carnal Knowing*), in which she undertakes the difficult task of trying to speculate about the relationship between representation and embodiment in a historically remote period. Though its medieval subject matter means that it cannot move much outside the realm of speculation in regard to female embodiment, it is quite remarkable in its insistence that nakedness is a gendered bodily experience and not just a fact of representation. Another example is Anne Hollander's (1993) *Seeing Through Clothes*, a sweeping and conceptually rich study of the role of fine art in generating modes of perception of bodies and clothing in everyday life. Studies of nudism have also had to engage with questions of embodiment. Nudist literature has continued unabated since it first flourished in Europe and the US in the 1920s and 1930s, and there have been one or two isolated attempts from within the academy to write about nudism outside of either the pro-nudist or the deviance paradigm (e.g. Clarke 1982; Toepfer 1997). For the most part, though, texts about the nude body don't explicitly or systematically connect with speculation about nude embodiment – what it actually looks and feels like to be nude in different contexts. This book addresses questions of meaning, representation and discourse, but also strives to connect such questions with actual embodied practices and with "everyday" people's attitudes to and experiences of nakedness.

Within the social sciences, nudity has been a staple topic for empirical investigation. But the sociology and criminology of the 1960s and 1970s (and sometimes the 1980s and even the 1990s) tended to relegate practices of nakedness, including nudism, to criminal, social or psychological deviance. Within psychology, nudity has frequently been a site for the definition and regulation of norms of psychological and developmental health. Many psychological studies use nakedness as a taken-for-granted category, responses to which can serve as indicators of psychosocial "normalcy" and can be used as the basis for regimes of psychiatric or medical treatment. To my mind, such approaches, while they might be clinically useful, are not conceptually rich, imprisoning fascinating cultural practices within impoverished categories like exhibitionism or deviance.

This book differs from these traditions in a number of ways. Primarily, it does not assume nudity to be a taken-for-granted category, but asks questions like "what *counts as* nudity in a given context?" It explores in particular the metaphorical meanings of nudity and their relationship to embodied existence. It tries to explore both what nudity might mean (to the self or to others) in a given context, and also what it feels like, how it is experienced, drawing on ethnographic research to help answer these questions. In exploring the cultural meanings and experiences of nudity, this book often takes positivistic research as *itself* symptomatic of an unacknowledged but reverberating cultural legacy – the tendency to assume an automatic link between nudity and sex, and the deployment of nudity as a means of categorizing different "types" of people (criminals, perverts, deviants and "normal" people).

It goes without saying that this book can deal with a limited number of examples of naked practices, representations or experiences. There are two different dimensions to this qualifier. The first is simply one of scale; I have had to select particular examples of nude practices and have chosen to make a broad, "horizontal" study of numerous examples rather than a detailed, "vertical" study of only a few, largely because I have seen so few books attempt to situate particular practices of nakedness in a broad context and thus to draw together particular kinds of otherwise invisible connections.[2] The second qualifier is more fundamental and is a qualitative rather than a quantitative limit. That is, when I speak of the cultural meanings of nudity in the modern West, I am speaking only of a particular (though vast and rich) system of meaning – the Judeo-Christian tradition. The book makes no claim to encompass the full diversity of cultural codes in operation in any global, multicultural society. On the contrary, its explicit focus is the Judeo-Christian tradition and its enduring impact within contemporary Western consumer cultures. As a middle-class white Australian from an English-speaking background, this is the hegemonic cultural field with which I am most familiar and that has produced my way of seeing the world. I can make only limited or general claims about the experiences or meanings of nudity even in relatively historically congruent cultural systems (including the US and some European countries), let alone in systems of meaning in operation in my country for thousands of years before white occupation. I can, however, begin to ask questions about how dominant fashion codes establish a norm that puts pressure on non-Anglo bodies to implicitly Anglicize themselves (e.g. by hair removal), or about the ways in which the naked bodies of indigenous people have been forced to signify with European semiotic systems. This study frequently discusses race – indeed, it sees race as a key element in the deployment of nakedness as a cultural category – but it does not claim to *enter* the experiential or hermeneutic world of indigenous people or people from non-English-speaking backgrounds. On the contrary, it looks at the importance of Judeo-Christian traditions in structuring hegemonic relations to the nude body (and considers their relation to marginal, deviant and resistant forms of embodiment).[3]

Perhaps the most important influence on this book has been an essay by Mario Perniola (1989), "Between Clothing and Nudity." In this essay, Perniola analyses two distinct metaphysical traditions that have been major factors behind the ambiguity of nudity in the modern West: the Judaic and the Greek. According to Perniola, the Judaic tradition envisaged transcendent divinity as clothed or veiled, and hence nudity as a loss or deprivation, a distancing from the Godhead – the state of slaves, prostitutes, the damned or the mad. The Greek tradition, on the other hand, represented in Platonic metaphysics as well as in athletic and sculptural practice, saw nudity as the state of the ideal human figure. Each of these traditions was complex and had its own internal contradictions. Moreover, the two traditions have interwoven, with the result that nudity is ambiguous and multivalent both as metaphor and physical state. In countries settled or colonized by Europeans, such as the US and Australia, European ambivalence about nakedness was made more complex by contact with indigenous cultures, which had their own meanings for the naked body. Today, immigration, globalization and the liberalizing effects of consumer culture have produced a complex cultural field in which nudity can mean many different things.

Underlying the many case studies in this book is an interest in the metaphorical richness of nudity and the possible relationships between metaphors and bodily experience. The book's aims are dual: to shed critical light on a range of common, but sometimes subterranean, cultural practices, and to extricate nudity from the confines of the reductive hermeneutic frame in which it is all too often understood. It is a study of "nude practices," in that it sees representation as a reflection of and influence on bodily experience and not as a world apart from the body. Moreover, it aims to restore a hint of the importance of senses other than the visual to our everyday experience and understanding of the world. Methodologically and stylistically, the book moves between a number of registers of language and across a broad range of cultural activities, finding that the mundane practices of everyday people's lives are as worthy of exploration as more traditional sites of study, such as the nude in fine art. For better (and, inevitably, for worse) it is radically transdisciplinary. My disciplinary raids have been tactical rather than exhaustive or conventional, but I hope they have always been respectful.

This book is divided into two halves. The first half (Chapters 1 and 2) comprises broad studies of the place of nudity in some Western philosophical, religious and literary traditions. In particular, these chapters explore how nudity and clothing are always bound together in a productive dialectic. Two major factors account for this. The first is a fundamental ambiguity in the nature of human existence: humans are originally naked (for however brief a moment) and yet clothing and/or body ornamentation is a social inevitability. It can thus equally truly be said of humans that they are essentially naked or essentially clothed, and nudity can equally well be seen as a natural state and an exceptional – even deviant – one. The second major pull between clothing and nudity in the Western tradition can be seen as the historical elaboration of this tension: that is, the interplay of the "positive" and "negative" meanings of nudity that we have inherited from the Greek and Hebrew traditions. I argue that nudity's multivalence, and especially its metaphorical association with the degree-zero state of the human, have made it a category easily mobilized in struggles over what constitutes "the human." Chapter 1 focuses on the dialectic between clothing and nudity, and the struggles at the borderlines between nudity and clothing, and between the human and the non-human or the less-than-human. Chapter 2 studies the positive and negative meanings of nudity as a metaphor, arguing that ultimately, nudity functions in the West as a metaphor for the lack of metaphor, a paradox that makes it an unstable and hence powerful cultural idea and bodily state.

The second half of the book looks at how these complexities have played themselves out in particular instances. In particular, it focuses on "types" or "modes" of humanness and their relation to categories of identity. Chapter 3 looks at how the potentially negative meanings of nudity allow it to be used as a marker of undesirability. The chapter focuses on the role of nakedness in constructing ideas of mess, savagery, deviance and perversion. Chapter 4 studies the rather more mixed fortunes of nudity in contemporary consumer culture, where nudity's relatively automatic association with sex and liberation – but also its metaphorical meaning of lack – make it a useful marketing tool. I explore a number of different modes of nudity in consumer culture: satirical, heroic, celebrity, glamour and homemade nudity. I argue that the "nothingness" of nudity, as well as taboos in photographic representation, help make nudity an ideal vehicle for the production of heroicized, glamorized and satirical images, and that such genres are increasingly blurred in postmodern visual culture. This represents a contemporary dynamic between the traditional "all" or "nothing" of nudity.

Throughout this study, it will be seen that clothing, too, is complex, and that our attitudes to it are often contradictory. Oddly, both nudity and clothing have been considered obscene, corrupt or moral; they can *both* be "positively or negatively valenced" (Kronenfeld 1998: 7). A critique of clothes can be traced back at least as far as the Adam and Eve tale, which construes clothes as both innocent and corrupt. In philosophical and moral discourses, clothing has been imagined as both covering up obscenity and as constituting a form of corruption in itself. It is paradoxically both superfluous and essential, just as nudity is both innocent and obscene. The critique of clothing is often displaced onto *fashion*, in the form of a (dubious) opposition between clothing (need, necessity) and fashion (unnecessary, luxuriant, vanity). Such are the paradoxes of clothing and nudity.

Throughout the book, I am interested in both the power and the instability of the clothing/nudity opposition, the way this opposition is often aligned with other crucial binary divisions, and the way that these categories play out in understandings of the human. All the chapters investigate different types and activations of binary oppositions. Chapter 1 looks at the nudity/clothing dialectic in relation to philosophical understandings of what it means to be human, focusing on clothing as a prevailing metaphor for language and sociality itself. Chapter 2 turns to primal moral divisions – the most basic division into "good" and "bad," or the attainment and non-attainment of the prize of humanness. Chapter 3 looks at how the moral categories associated with nakedness have worked in relation to the production of specific types: savage/civilized; pervert/sane; deviant/proper, via a study of Australian Aboriginality, nudism and flashing, among other things. I argue that nudity functions paradoxically as the "unnatural natural." Chapter 4 looks at categories and styles of personhood in consumer culture, with particular emphasis on contemporary forms of the opposition between celebrity and "ordinariness." Threading through all chapters is an interest in the relationship between metaphorical traditions and lived bodily experience. My interest in both symbolic traditions and everyday embodied life is reflected in the two major kinds of research that have gone into this book: cultural theory and ethnographic research. The latter has profoundly enriched my understanding of what nakedness means, is and can be in modern Western societies.

Whatever it is, the nude body is never naked, if naked means stripped of meaning, value and political import. The processes in which bodies (or parts of bodies) are rendered visible or invisible are profoundly social and profoundly political. This book uses an empirical base to produce what I hope is a small contribution to a study of the politics of the person, of everyday practices and of powerful institutions. Given the scale of my topic, it goes without saying that the book will be full of gaps; it can make no claims to completeness or even representativeness. I have tried, however, to write a book that makes connections, asks questions, invites speculation, and opens up, rather than covers, a field.

Notes

1. For a recent, more positive, reading of Genesis, see Senchuk (1985) and Hanson (1993).

2. I have published more detailed studies elsewhere (see Barcan 1999, 2000, 2001, 2002a, 2002b, 2004).

3. Even the term "Western" required qualification. "The West" is, in a sense, a fiction, but a useful one for my purposes. I am using it to refer to cultures that are majority English-speaking, based on the Judeo-Christian tradition, and now largely consumer cultures. My reference points are predominantly the UK, the US and Australia, though readers may well see parallels elsewhere in certain instances. Some of the analyses (e.g. the sections on nudism) hold good for European countries outside the UK; others do not. My use of the term "West" does not include Westernized cultures outside the Judeo-Christian tradition, such as Japan.

4. It is one of my regrets that funding restrictions prevented me from carrying out a planned series of interviews with Aboriginal people to investigate their attitudes towards nakedness.

The Nudity/Clothing Dialectic

In Virginia Woolf's 1928 novel *Orlando*, which tells the story of a seventeenth-century youth who lives through four centuries and who changes sex in the process, the narrator reflects on the power of clothes to create identities: "[T]here is much to support the view that it is clothes that wear us and not we them; we may make them take the mould of arm or breast, but they mould our hearts, our brains, our tongues to their liking" (Woolf 1977: 117). Clothes, in other words, maketh the man; indeed, what they make is the difference *between* man and woman. A few paragraphs later, however, we are offered the reverse hypothesis: "The difference between the sexes is, happily, one of great profundity. Clothes are but a symbol of something hid deep beneath" (p. 117). And then, a third hypothesis, presented seemingly as an extension of the second, but really closer to the first: all human beings contain some mix of the two sexes, and throughout our lives, we move between the two poles of maleness and femaleness. Clothes are what keep this vacillation in check, a kind of stable identity label: "In every human being a vacillation from one sex to the other takes place, and often it is only the clothes that keep the male or female likeness, while underneath the sex is the very opposite of what it is above" (p. 118). In just over one page, then, we have three theories of sexed identity, with three corresponding theories (and metaphors) of clothing: sexed identity is socially constructed; sexed identity is intrinsic and unchanging; sexed identity is, in fact, so variable as to be a pretence.

We see here in miniature an age-old philosophical debate about identity, organized around two conceptual extremes: cultures make identity or, conversely, cultures reflect identity. Clothing functions here as a metaphor for all social and cultural institutions and practices – not only gender roles, but also moral systems, laws, economics or political systems. At either end of this continuum, the naked body must implicitly be understood differently – as either the neutral, raw material out of which identities are fashioned according to social circumstances, or the authentic self that social circumstances allow to shine forth in particular ways.

The concerns of this chapter are primarily philosophical. Its theme is humanness itself, in relation to the opposition between nakedness and clothing. Why might this opposition have something to teach us about humanness? Because of the biological fact that we are all born naked and the cultural fact that all human societies cover, ornament or adorn their bodies, both clothing and nudity can equally well be imagined as "primal." The naked state can seem a little less than human, while clothing can nonetheless seem superfluous to bare necessity. The dialectic between nakedness and clothing is thus a potent cultural site for a tussle between sameness and difference, between the idea of the universality of our shared primal nakedness and the diversity of the forms our bodies take in culture.

Both clothing and nakedness can serve as a metaphysical foundation. According to Mario Perniola, a metaphysics of clothing characterized Egyptian, Babylonian and Hebrew traditions. That is, clothing was given an absolute value as an index of humanness, conceived of in opposition to animality:

> Clothing prevails as an absolute whenever or wherever the human figure is assumed to be essentially dressed, when there is the belief that human beings are human, that is, distinct from animals, by virtue of the fact that they wear clothes. Clothing gives human beings their anthropological, social and religious identity, in a word – their being. From this perspective, nudity is a negative state, a privation, loss, dispossession. (Permiola 1989: 237)

In the Old Testament tradition, says Perniola, God "clothed" the earth in the process of creation ("Thou coveredst [the earth] with the deep as with a garment": Psalm 104.6) and is Himself veiled (in splendour, glory, perfection):

> Bless the Lord, O my soul. O Lord my God, thou art very great; thou art clothed with honour and majesty. Who coverest thyself with light as with a garment: who stretchest out the heavens like a curtain . . . (Psalm 104.1–2)

The Greek tradition, on the other hand, saw nudity (rather than clothing) as the absolute value. Thus, two of the traditions most fundamental to Christian modernity – the Hebrew and the Greek – have left the (post)Christian West the contradictory legacy of nakedness as loss of full humanness (the province of slaves, the destitute, the mad) and as the epitome of glorious humanness.

Of course, whichever principle (nakedness or clothing) is taken as a foundation, neither can fully escape the other. Nakedness and clothing work dialectically, both within and between metaphysical systems. Nor does this dialectic operate in isolation, for it takes its place among a welter of other binary oppositions. Western metaphysics is based on a whole system of such binary oppositions. As the work of Jacques Derrida has highlighted, these oppositions are valued, hierarchized and occasionally reversible in meaning or value. The boundaries and borders that separate them are blurry, changeable, and culturally laden.

This fundamental insight from Derrida is the bedrock of much contemporary cultural theory. Bryan Turner's (1996: 66) version of a list of classic Western binary oppositions (and there are many other lists) is as follows:

Private	*Public*
Gemeinschaft	Gesellschaft
desire	reason
female	male
informal	formal
affectivity	neutrality
particularity	universality
diffusion	specificity
hedonism	asceticism
consumption	production

This list is meaningful vertically as well as horizontally. Moreover, many other binary pairs can be suggested, such as "white/black," "civilized/savage" or "adult/child." Feminists such as Hélène Cixous (1981: 90) have produced versions that highlight the operations of gender:

Activity/passivity,
Sun/Moon,
Culture/Nature,
Day/Night,

Father/Mother,
Head/heart,
Intelligible/sensitive,
Logos/Pathos.

Form, convex, step, advance, seed, progress.
Matter, concave, ground – which supports the step, receptacle.

Man
———
Woman

The second term in each of these oppositions is frequently denigrated or devalued in the "official" public sphere, and people who embody these characteristics are often materially disadvantaged. The devalued term is nonetheless often subject to romanticization or idealization, particularly within domestic, private or feminized discourses (since these are, after all, already the devalued terms in the public/private opposition).

Nakedness and clothing can take their place among the binary oppositions that constitute the sense-making categories for Western thinking about human identity. A list of relevant binaries might look something like this:

nakedness	clothing
natural	cultural
unchanging	changeable
invisible	visible
truth	lies
pure	corrupt
human nature	human society
pre-, non-, antisocial	social

These terms are valued according to context, blurry at their edges, and occasionally reversible. As we will repeatedly see, the valuation depends on the context, and on whether the nakedness is metaphorical or actual, represented or corporeal.

To such lists of oppositions, we could also add an aesthetic binary – beautiful versus ugly. This is an important consideration in a study of nudity, since the themes of nature and beauty are crucial not only to the fine arts, but also in a colonial context. Kobena Mercer (1990) has observed that European racism always had an aesthetic dimension; blackness was understood as the ugly negation of white beauty. "Distinctions of aesthetic value" have, he argues, "always been central to the way racism divides the world into binary oppositions in its adjudication of human worth" (Mercer 249). So when nakedness is considered the ugly Other to beautiful clothing, or when it is split internally into the beauty of nudity versus the ugliness of nakedness, then we should be alert to the likelihood of a submerged racial politics.[1]

Woven in to such politics is always, somewhere, a theory of nature. Historically, the word "nature" has acted, in the words of Arthur Lovejoy (1960: 69), as a "verbal jack-of-all-trades." Ideas of nature have undergone so many historical changes, and have interwoven with each other so much along the way, that it is now a slippery term and concept indeed, between whose connotations it is easy to slip imperceptibly, "pass[ing] from one ethical or aesthetic stand to its very antithesis, while nominally professing the same principles" (p. 69). Hence, in part, some of the slipperiness of nakedness itself, that "natural" state. When understood as God's handiwork, "nature is superior to culture or art;" when understood as fallen, perverted or weak, nature (and hence nakedness) is "inferior to culture, art or discipline, which are understood as supplementing or rectifying the lack" (Kronenfeld 1998: 17). Perhaps the best word to sum up this modern confusion is *ambivalence* to both nature and nakedness (and, if not to clothing *per se*, then often to fashion).

This chapter is a study of the primal opposition between nakedness and clothing. The first half of the chapter examines how these two terms function dialectically, a word that suggests not only their interrelationship but also their permeability as categories. Then follows a limit case – hair, which can be imagined as a little like clothing but also as a sign of nakedness. I then examine the splitting of nakedness itself into a binary opposition, the well-known distinction in fine arts between the naked and the nude. The second half of the chapter considers how the two terms nakedness and clothing have functioned in philosophical debates about identity, society and language, considering in particular where femininity is placed in such debates. This leads me, finally, to a consideration of the very idea of the human and its others.

A Dialectic of Concealment and Revelation

Any binary opposition creates questions of both taxonomy and relation – in other words, what belongs in each category, and how the two categories might relate to each other. In the case of the opposition between nudity and clothing, this amounts to questions about what actually *counts* as a piece of clothing or as exposure, as well as questions about the movement from nudity to clothing or vice versa. In this section, both questions will be considered.

Pasi Falk (1994: 45) has claimed that "the fundamental concept-historical starting point for any examination of the historicity of the human body is . . . the relationship between the body and something else: the body as opposed to or distinct from something else." In thinking of the naked body, that "something else" will most often be the clothed body. Classicist Larissa Bonfante (1989: 544) lists five conventionally cited functions of clothing: protection from the elements; a means of distinguishing tribes or classes; protection from shame; source of aesthetic pleasure (e.g. decoration or sexual attraction); and apotropaic functions (turning away the effects of sorcery, the evil eye or hostile spirits). This list spans five major and interconnected domains of human life: the physical, the cultural or aesthetic, the social, the psycho-logical and the religious. Clothing has received considerable attention in the anthropological, historical, aesthetic and psychological literatures, among others. Not only is it enormously variable culturally, but also it is conceptually complex. Unsurprisingly, there are many paradoxes and inversions to be found in literary or philosophical rhetoric around clothing and nakedness. To take just two examples: we commonly find nudity figured as a form of clothing, or clothing imagined as something that wears *us*. Moreover, clothing itself involves what Jennifer Craik (1994) calls a dialectic of concealment and revelation.

Clearly, clothing (that necessary superfluity) is no simple beast. Its definition, functions and limits are called into question all the time as part of the regular taxonomic work of all culture, such as in decisions, both implicit and explicit, about which garments count as clothes. Adornments – jewellery, a necktie, a watch – are obvious examples of liminal clothes. Swimwear is another classic example of borderline clothing. It is, as Craik (1994: 136) puts it, "a form of underclothing worn in public," which is why it was until quite recently decorated with belts and modesty skirts:

> [I]n order to distinguish swimwear from underwear, designs . . . emphasised tailoring and accessories such as belt, buttons and buckles to reinforce the public respectability of swimming, and remove it from the private, erotic associations of lingerie. (Craik 1994: 146)

Writer Angela Carter (1982) goes further, considering many forms of clothing – furs, evening dresses, ball gowns, jewellery and lingerie – to be "non-garments," since their function is primarily ritual. Seeing them as items of conspicuous consumption rather than of concealment or protection, she compares them to luxury "non-foods" like ice-cream (Carter 1982: 97–8).

There are clothes whose function is paradoxical rather than marginal, their primary function being to make the body look naked. Many, like the body-stocking, false genitals or breasts, or even the merkin used occasionally in sex work, are theatrical devices. Others, like "nude" make-up or "nude" stockings, belong to the everyday world. A number of elite fashion designers have played with making clothing that simulates nakedness, and have made "nude" outfits – flesh-coloured shoes, dresses, jackets, handbags, stockings and make-up. In 1995, a *Harper's Bazaar* fashion editor was sent out to test some of these outfits. She described her feelings of panic, initially, turning later to a feeling of power as she imagined what the men around her must be imagining (Jackson 1995). Clothes masquerading as flesh, she found, were highly erotic even when they covered much of her real flesh. In its own way, such clothing is also theatrical, highlighting clothing as a form of public performance. Angela Carter (1982: 85) considers this to be a barely sublimated function of *many* forms of garments and fabrics; leather, suede and velvet, for example, are "profoundly tactile" fabrics that "mimic nakedness" and invite the touch.

The question of what counts as clothes is by no means frivolous; it can have profound consequences. For example, European explorers didn't always consider the body ornamentation and coverings worn by Australian Aborigines to be "clothing." Considering Aboriginal people to be undressed was part and parcel of a more general colonial understanding of Australia as "uninhabited," "unimproved," still to be civilized. Today, judgements about what counts as clothing are also crucial to judicial or policing decisions; inappropriate clothing can see one ejected from public spaces, and there are categories of person and action based around insufficiency of dress (flashing, streaking, exhibitionism, offensive behaviour, indecent exposure and so on). The place of nakedness in the policing of race and of "correct" behaviour is the subject of Chapter 3, which looks at the categories of savage, criminal and pervert.

Individuals (as well as the law) constantly make judgements about what is or isn't "clothing" and what is or isn't "decent." Think of the expression "Are you decent?" meaning "Are you dressed?" "Decency," though, is not really a question of the amount of exposed flesh, but rather of the liminality of some forms of clothing, especially lingerie, nightwear, underwear and swimwear. A bikini top may cover far less than a bra, but be less "rude." In contemporary Australia, one could never wear just a bra to, say, a shopping centre, while one could usually get away with wearing a bikini top, provided certain other conditions were met: it would probably need to be a beachside centre, one would need to be wearing shorts and not a bikini bottom, and it couldn't be a highly exclusive shopping area. It also goes without saying that one would need to be female, unless one were a performer in a school holiday play at the shopping centre. The status of clothes is partly a matter of the materials of which they are made. Transparency is one indicator, but even then, not a simple one. The opaqueness of fabric is part of the legal definitions of "decency" in most US states, and yet a solid white bra is still less acceptable in public space than a crocheted bikini top. Clothing constitutes a highly complex continuum or matrix; there is no simple opposition between being clothed and being naked. There is, rather, a whole complex matter of being sufficiently or appropriately clothed, and that is context- and code-driven rather than being intrinsic to the piece of clothing. It is a dynamic or dialectic rather than a question of absolutes. In particular legal circumstances, though, a specific body part can be considered almost intrinsically indecent. For example, in almost every public context except medical and occasionally theatrical circumstances, the penis is by definition indecent. Its exposure in public space – especially if intentional, and especially if the penis is erect – is an almost automatic matter of legal indecency. This is sometimes true of breasts, although the codes are more variable and (at this juncture) more contestable. For example, a number of Northern American and Canadian test cases have been fought on the question of whether breasts are intrinsically indecent, usually in explicit comparison with the male chest.

The dialectic nature of clothing and nudity means that "covering up" can have paradoxical effects, as can be seen in a debate in both fine arts and sexology about modesty poses. Seymour Howard, for example, wrote an essay about a number of modesty devices in fine art. He argued that devices such as the fig leaf, while they manifestly aim to "cloa[k] the charged generative centers of our bodies and being" (Howard 1986: 293), nonetheless still function as representations or cultural equivalents *of* the genitals, and actually serve to identify the source of male and female powers. He points out that the form of the fig leaf that adorns many classical sculptures "repeat[s], in simplified contours, precisely those of the phallus, testicles, and pubes, which [it] ostensibly replace[s] and conceal[s]" (Howard 1986: 289). As John Langdon-Davies (1928: 50) put it, "It is quite certain that Adam assumed the fig leaf, not in order to hide his shame, but in order to draw attention to something of which he was proud."

For Howard (1986), the female equivalent of the fig leaf is the so-called pudica pose, in which the woman modestly covers her genitals with her hand. Sexologist Havelock Ellis considered the pudica pose to be the stylized representation of a widespread and instinctive defensive posture – woman's "natural" response to the unwanted sexual advances of a male (Ellis 1937: 38–9). Howard (1986), conversely, conceives of it as a veiled sign of power. Of its supposed prototype, Praxiteles' Cnidian Venus (*c.* 350 BC), Howard (1986: 291) argues that "the hand that seems modestly, unselfconsciously to cover the exposed goddess of love . . . in fact points to the source of her powers." So for Howard, concealment is also always an act of sublimated revelation. But Kenneth Clark's reading of the same statue keeps concealment and revelation separate; indeed, it attributes them to different aesthetic cultures: "[T]he luxuriant sensuality of the form is modified by the Greek sense of decorum, so that the gesture of Venus' hand, which in eastern religions indicates the source of her powers, in the Cnidian modestly conceals it" (Clark 1956: 74). Howard, relying on theories of archetypes, sees all such poses as subtle signs of female power; Clark, as an art historian, sees different aesthetic traditions as producing different meanings for the pose.

The intuition that concealment is often more erotic than full revelation is a commonplace. Nudists, for example, constantly claim that swimwear is more tantalizing or erotic than full nakedness. The same can be said of lingerie, or of elements of costume such as the traditional pasties (nipple caps), which fetishize as much as conceal the stripper's nipples. The doubleness of these "tiny glittering cones of modesty to which [US] State authorities resolutely clung," (as Wortley (1976: 71) rather ambiguously put it), makes a mockery of the laws that required them in order to protect "decency."

But the dialectic between clothing and undress put into play so effectively in striptease is far more than an interplay between visibility and invisibility. Like all live performance, striptease puts the mutual dependence of nudity and

clothing into greater flux than more static arts like sculpture or photography. Although Roland Barthes (1973: 92) stressed the aestheticization of the stripper's nudity and hence saw the nudity revealed in striptease as ultimately chaste, other commentators see the *movement between* nakedness and concealment as at the heart of eroticism. Mario Perniola (1989), for example, speaks of this movement as a "transit," arguing that neither clothing nor nudity is erotic when it prevails as an absolute value; only the movement or transit between them is erotic. Similarly, Jennifer Blessing (1997: 47) sees striptease as an institutionalization of the transitional state between the (supposed) artifice of clothing and the (supposed) purity of nudity. Striptease makes use of the tactic of delay in order to prolong this transitional state. As an icon of Australian striptease told us of her routines in the 1970s:

> In those days we wore clothes on stages. If I was doing a twenty minute spot I had more clothes than you'd need for a weekend. I used to wear ten G-strings! Sometimes two bras, gloves, a gown, a hat, a shawl. Stuff to take off – that was the tease.

Striptease is far too complex and varied a practice in its own right for one to generalize too much. Suffice to say that there are many different kinds of striptease and that all kinds work with their own dialectic of dress and undress. For my purposes here, I am interested only in noting that many commentators see paradoxical elements at its heart, since it is based on the interplay of offering and denying, of both provoking and satisfying desire.

Whatever else it may do, striptease actually problematizes nudity as much as simply revealing it. It reminds us, perhaps, that nakedness is not self-evidently the same as exposure, either experientially or conceptually. Bareness and nudity are not the same thing; bare flesh is not always naked. Can an elbow be nude? Or a face?[2] What about bald heads? Or feet? We talk about "bare" feet, but never about "nude" or "naked" feet; nor do we talk about a "nude" head. Not all parts of the body can, it seems, *be* "naked." This is a cultural matter. In eighteenth-century England, the wig was an emblem of male authority, and the man who had lost his wig was a figure of fun, "rather like the man who has lost his trousers" (Pointon 1993: 176). In those times the word "naked" could, in fact, be used of bald heads, whereas nowadays we tend to think of nakedness as a temporary state; otherwise we use a different label, like baldness. To take another example, the medieval expression "naked as my nail" (i.e. fingernail) has completely faded from usage; we don't, nowadays, tend to think of our fingernails as able to be "naked." Likewise with another, very old and now obsolete expression dating from the year AD 725, the "naeced tunge" ("naked tongue"), meaning a tongue thrust out or exposed. To take a more metaphorical example, the English expression "the naked eye" arose after the invention of optical technologies (the *Oxford English Dictionary's [OED]* first citation is 1664).

The English language reflects the continuum between nakedness and being clothed in quite complex ways. There's no single noun for the state of wearing clothes as there is for the state of undress; we can describe a person as being clothed, or wearing clothes, but there's no such word as clothedness or dressedness (I have, just once, seen the word "unclothedness"). Mid-twentieth-century words like "toplessness" suggest that we can conceive of the state of semi-undress, but perhaps being clothed is so unquestionable that it's almost inconceivable *as concept.*[3] Contrast this with Irene Watson's (1998: 2) statement that she has found no word in any of the Australian indigenous languages to describe nakedness.

Although in modern times we think of nudity as simply the state of being without clothes, this is an unsatisfactory definition, and in any case a recent one, since the English word "naked" could at one time mean wearing only an undergarment. For example, the *OED* gives the following citation, dating from 1761: "The streets were . . . filled with naked people, some with shirts and shifts on only, and numbers without either." In the language of the fine arts, too, "nude" does not always mean totally naked. Paintings designated as "nudes" almost always include semi-clad or lightly draped bodies, including those covered by *draperie mouillée.* In a number of US states even the penis covered in an opaque fabric is legally "nude" if it is erect.[4]

The absoluteness of the term "nakedness" has been the source of debate in both biblical and classical scholarship, in the form of disagreements about translations from Latin and Greek. Scholars have traditionally assumed that biblical usage of the Greek word *gymnos* usually implies some form of clothing. For example, the *New Catholic Encyclopedia* cites only two possible moments when a biblical description of nakedness seems likely to mean total nakedness (Mark 14:52 and Acts 19:6), both of them New Testament translations of *gymnos.* It also glosses Old Testament (OT) usage as almost always meaning wearing only a loincloth, or ill clad, since "the ethical spirit of the OT insisted on the personal decency of the one who was to approach Yahweh (*Ex* 20.26)" (Montalbano 1967: 559). This encyclopedia interprets the Christian commandment to clothe the "naked" as an injunction to clothe the "ill clad." Christian nudists, seeking to rebuff the anti-nudist sentiments of their conservative counterparts, have also entered such debates (see Robinson website). In classical scholarship too, standard reference texts have translated both the Greek *gymnos* and the Latin *nudus* as "scantily clad." Such translations appear to be compromised, the result more of prudery and assumption than accurate scholarship, for these words do in fact appear to have meant completely naked (see Sturtevant 1912; Mann 1974). This interpretation of *gymnos* and *nudus* was originally advanced by a Dutch scholar, Gisbert Cuypert, and remained, apparently, unquestioned thereafter, thus "sav[ing] modern prudery many a serious shock" (Sturtevant 1912: 324).[5] Even related historical facts (like whether Greek boxers and wrestlers were completely nude) appear to have been compromised. Such revisionism has had its popular counterparts too, as in British Prime Minister W. E. Gladstone's attempt to argue that it was impossible that nakedness could have been tolerated in Homeric Greece.[6] As one classicist put it curtly, though, "there is no point in trying to make the Greeks 'nice'" (Mann 1974: 178).

There are not only philological but also conceptual issues surrounding the idea of degrees of nakedness. Can one undressed body be "more naked" than another? When we interviewed a beautician about depilatory practices, she said that shaving makes the body "more naked." The idea that something can be more or less naked doesn't make grammatical sense; "naked" and "nude" are adjectives without comparative or superlative forms, except, perhaps, in the hyperbolic marketing language of soft porn, where magazine covers sport headlines like: "The Sexiest and Nudest Celebrities on the Planet" or "Nicole Kidman Naked. Castro's Niece Ultra-Naked." Despite this grammatical fact, many colloquial expressions do implicitly recognize clothing and nudity as terms on a continuum. In their emphasis on the totality of the nude state, such expressions as "not a stitch on," "stark naked" or "total nudity" imply that there are degrees and kinds of nudity and dress.

The idea of nakedness as a gradation has been important to theatre and theatre studies. Karl Toepfer (1996) argues that nudity is always conceptually troubling in the theatre because the revelation of truth that we associate with nudity must conflict with the obvious artificiality of theatre. Toepfer argues that in theatrical performance, nakedness is experienced to greater or lesser degree depending on how it is imbricated in textuality, especially speech. Seeming "more naked" is not only is about how visible the genitals are, but also has got something to do with speech. The body is more than an object revealed to sight; it is known to us through all our senses. Thus, the performer's voice, for example, as well as the content of their speech, can influence audience perceptions of how naked a performer is:

> [T]he voice is as much a part of the body as any organ, and the capacity of a body to speak means that a completely *unclothed* body, with genitals exposed, can become "more naked" or signify even greater vulnerability by speech emanating from it, speech addressed to it, or speech about it. The voice connects language to the body and even makes language a "part" of the body. (Toepfer 1996: 77)

Toepfer studies a number of postmodern theatrical performances and explores the factors that influence the audience's perception of "how naked" a performer is. Although the focus of his analysis is on theatrical performance, it has interesting implications for understanding everyday experiences of nakedness as well (for example, he discusses the importance of speech to one's experience of nakedness in everyday sexual encounters). For in everyday life generally we also regularly feel naked to greater or lesser degree.

In many academic discussions, the idea of nakedness as a variable bodily feeling is canvassed in relation to shame or embarrassment. For example, in a short discussion of nakedness, sociologist Erving Goffman (1965) attempts to think about shame not as an abstract or unchanging moral quality, but as a contextualized human experience. Goffman suggests that rather than thinking about nudity in terms of the parts of the body exposed or the degree of exposure, we should consider instead what he calls "the *orientational* implications of exposure" (Goffman 1965: 50, original emphasis). By this he means that states of dress or undress do not occur in a vacuum but take place in particular situations involving a whole complex of roles and actants. Social occasions call up or expect from us certain orientations. In the case of dress, what is relevant is not so much the type or degree of exposure, but whether or not that exposure is appropriate to the gathering and the social occasion; in other words, whether or not it demonstrates that the participant is *appropriately* involved in his or her context. Goffman takes the example of the "relative undress of décolletage at balls," reading it as an implicit acknowledgement that

> the participants are so tightly in step with the occasion as a whole, and so trustful of the good conduct of their socially homogenous circle, that they can withstand this much temptation to undue mutual-involvement without giving in to it. (Goffman 1965: 50)

In other words, implicit social codes both advertise and protect the "normative stability" (p. 50) of social groups.

Extrapolating from this, shame or embarrassment can be seen less as an *a priori* response to tabooed parts of the body than as a response to someone misreading or misjudging a particular set of roles, contexts and relationships. These things are embarrassing, says Goffman (1965: 52), because they are "symbols of alienation," external markers of our distance from a given context, expected roles, and the other participants in the occasion. This helps explain seeming paradoxes and inconsistencies, such as, to expand on one of Goffman's examples, the "minor relationship crisis" that occurs when a visitor to a house accidentally witnesses a resident of the house in disarray (p. 51). The visitor might actually see less of the resident's naked body than later in the evening when he attends a ball with her to which she wears a low-cut dress; what is embarrassing, then, is not so much the view of naked flesh, as the moment when the nature of their relationship and the bounds of their intimacy are publicly exposed and tested, and where the conservatizing moral codes of the group are tested and reaffirmed. This also allows us to understand how it is that we can sometimes feel naked even while dressed; if I wore my pyjamas to work I might be well covered but feel naked. I have attracted the gaze of others to my body, and have ruptured the seamlessness of social contexts and, in my alienation from others and from the context, have drawn attention to the constructedness of social relationships, roles and contexts, an action which may well leave me feeling isolated, and hence ashamed. As any woman who has worn a bikini to the beach without having shaved or waxed her bikini line can tell you, you do not have to actually *be* naked to feel shamefully exposed. Perhaps, then, since nudity exists only in its recognition by others, it is best defined as a psychological state – the state of feeling exposed. This is one interpretation of the paradigmatic Christian account. John Berger's reading of the Adam and Eve story focuses on nakedness as, to quote the title of his book, a way of seeing: "[Adam and Eve] became aware of being naked because, as a result of eating the apple, each saw the other differently. Nakedness was created in the mind of the beholder" (Berger 1972: 48). What this means is that nakedness is intersubjective; it could not exist without the gaze of the other.

But the modern philosophical preoccupation with vision often leads us to underestimate other factors important to our sense of our body in space. Bodyworker Stanley Keleman (1981), for example, places a great deal of importance on the role of uprightness in human being-in-the-world, seeing it as a property that distinguishes the human animal from most others, and that contributes distinctively to the nature and quality of human existence. Upright animals are more exposed and hence more vulnerable, but also more open to the possibilities engendered by unbounded space: "The front of us is an extended surface of contact and connection. This is what we present to the world" (Keleman 1981: 23). In public space, this extended surface is mostly kept covered. When it is exposed, our bodily comportment and sense of self are likely to change. As Elizabeth Grosz says (1994: 80), the body image marks this change: "subjects do not walk the same way or have the same posture when they are naked as when they wear clothing." Such a change may be only temporary. Regular and repeated public nakedness, however, must of necessity alter the body image more substantially, a possibility I have discussed with relation to female nudism (Barcan 2001). "Feeling naked" is thus a complex matter, calling into play such factors as the heightened perception of temperature and air movement, the loss of a familiar boundary between body and world, as well as the effects of the actual gaze of others and/or the internalized gaze of an imagined other.

Many currents in contemporary sociology and philosophy, from phenomenology to post-structuralism, might help us to move beyond the commonsense idea of nakedness and clothing as simple opposites. Judith Butler's (1990) concept of performativity, for example, has helped us to understand the body as something that we "make up."[7] Bodily comportment can be seen as consisting of a repertoire of coded practices of "self-formation and self-presentation" (Craik 1994: 5) that include gesture, posture and emotional display as well as clothing. Such approaches allow us to think less about nudity and being clothed as absolute states than about how we might "wear" our body as well as our clothes, and indeed, how our clothes and body might "wear" us, as Woolf (1977) suggested. Likewise, focusing on nakedness and "clothedness" as terms in a dialectic allows us to consider both the taxonomic question (what actually constitutes clothing in a given context) and phenomenological ones, like the experience of degrees of nakedness, or why one can be dressed but feel naked, and vice versa. Considering all three terms of the clothes-representation-body triangle as mutually constitutive allows one to pose the question of how representations feed into both perception and embodiment.[8] This is at the heart of Anne Hollander's (1993) intelligent study *Seeing through Clothes*:

> It is tempting to believe that people always feel physically the same and that they look different only because the cut of their garments changes – to subscribe to the notion of a universal, unadorned mankind that is universally naturally behaved when naked. But art proves that nakedness is not universally experienced and perceived any more than clothes are. At any time, the unadorned self has more kinship with its own usual dressed aspect than it has with any undressed human selves in other times and places, who have learned a different visual sense of the clothed body. It can be shown that the rendering of the nude in art usually derives from the current form in which the clothed figure is conceived. This correlation in turn demonstrates that both the perception and the self-perception of nudity are dependent on a sense of clothing – and of clothing understood through the medium of a visual convention. (Hollander 1993: xii–xiii)

This is a counter-intuitive and striking claim. I am not sure how legitimate it is to claim that because nudity is physically experienced in relation to a particular regime of clothing that nudity-and-clothing experiences are therefore more similar in any one era than nudity-nudity experiences across time. But still, unlocking the common-sense expectation that the body underneath the clothes is just a clothes-horse that feels the same whenever it is "liberated" is a sophisticated manoeuvre that recognizes both the conceptual and experiential relativity of both nudity and clothing. Hollander (1993: 90) argues that nudity and clothing are bound together; we perceive the "body-and-clothes unit." Indeed, even when we see naked bodies we still see the "implied absent clothing." Clothing thus structures our perception of nakedness.

A Limit Case: Hair as a Form of Clothing

Three damsels stood, naked from head to feet
Save for the glory of their hair.

William Morris, *Earthly Paradise*

Instrumental theories of the origin of clothing see it as a cultural supplement to the human body, made necessary by the increasing hairlessness of the evolving human body (Goldman and Goldman 1981: 166). Culturally, hair and clothing stand in complex and shifting relationship, for each of them can in some sense be considered both *of* the body and supplementary to it. Some of the early meanings of the word "naked" suggest that hair can be considered not only as a part *of* the organism, but also as a form of covering, a kind of bodily non-body. For example, "naked" could at one time mean "without hair," referring to both plants and animals. It could once mean "devoid of trees or vegetation", or (of water) "having no weeds," or (of trees) "bare of leaves or foliage." Today, hair is still often understood as a kind of covering over the body, as when one beautician told us that "In some countries the men like hair; they like their women fully covered." It can also, though, act as a sign of the body *bereft* of covering, as suggested by one French colloquialism for naked-ness – *à poil* (roughly, "down to one's hairs").

Hair has other paradoxical qualities: it is non-living yet organically renew-able, and it persists after death, which is why it is sometimes used as a memento (Synnott 1993: 122). It grows naturally yet is very visibly culturally fashioned. By such paradoxes, hair resembles clothing, which is itself cultural (supple-mentary, "unnecessary") and, perhaps, universal (socially necessary, an *a fortiori* component of "the human").[9] Neither fully culture nor nature, dead nor alive, hair can be both the epitome of the aesthetic (as in the cliché that a woman's crowning glory is her hair) and an abject, obscene thing. It is both innocence (covering, clothing) and obscenity (brute nature), civilization and savagery. On the head, hair is an important part of our individual and social identity. On the face and body, it can function culturally as both a necessary supplement to the pitifully denuded human body and an "unnecessary" protuberance – excessive, needing itself to be covered, trimmed or removed.

The idea that hair can function as a clothing equivalent or substitute has a long history in the West. St Paul claimed that woman's hair was "given her for a covering" (1 Corinthians 11:15).[10] Margaret Miles (1989) reports that medieval images of female saints sometimes depicted them as clothed in hair from head to ankle. The legend of St Mary of Egypt, for example, tells how she was so hirsute that she was mistaken for an animal. The Lady Godiva tale presumably draws on the Christian tradition of modest saintliness. Lady Godiva is clothed in hair and in her high moral purpose; she is somehow both naked and clothed.

The ambiguity of hair as both evidence of and protection from nakedness is particularly evident with pubic hair. Pubic hair has sometimes been seen as a form of modest covering for the nakedness of the genitalia and at other times as itself a naked obscenity. (The German word for pubic hair, *Schamhaar*, "shame-hair," suggests both these meanings.[11]) This means that both the absence and the presence of pubic hair can at times constitute obscenity. For example, one of the interviewees for this project ("Karen") worked as a model for an erotic photographer. On one occasion, she had recently shaved off her pubic hair, and the photographer wouldn't use her as a model, claiming that the absence of pubic hair would make the photographs pornographic. But pubic hair is itself often considered obscene, especially for women. The Ancient Greek aesthetic, in both art and life, often demanded pubic depilation for women (Bonfante 1989: 552). The display of pubic hair was an important element in Attic erotic painting (Kilmer 1982; Bain 1982). By and large, though, Greek antiquity bequeathed the West a representational norm of depilation for women and depiction, often in stylized form, for men. This Classical "divided convention . . . dictated the whole conception of nude beauty in the West until the twentieth century, a conception based on hair for men and hairlessness for women" (Hollander 1993: 137). What this absence of female pubic hair in fine art would have meant in earlier times for sheltered men encountering real women for the first time is anybody's guess. Scholars have speculated about such intimate matters in the case of Victorian writer and art critic John Ruskin, who married Effie Gray at age 28 but failed to consummate the marriage and eventually divorced her, stating in court that "though her face was beautiful, her person was not formed to excite passion. On the contrary, there were certain circumstances in her person which completely checked it" (in Danto 1994: 101). His wife lamented to her father that Ruskin "had imagined women were quite different to what he saw I was, and that the reason he did not make me his Wife was because he was disgusted with my person the first evening April 10th." Scholars have speculated that Ruskin, having (it is believed) seen no real woman naked and only the nudes of fine art, had been shocked by his wife's pubic hair and considered her a freak.[12]

Pubic hair's association with obscenity is so strong that its depiction is regulated by law. In Australia in the 1950s, only medical books were allowed to depict female pubic hair; even nudist (naturist) magazines had to retouch (i.e. airbrush) their photographs. In 1951, Ron Ashworth, editor of the nudist magazine *Australian Sunbather*, replied to readers' requests for unretouched photos:

> [The law] quite definitely states that no publication other than medical, can show hair on any part of a woman's body other than her head, nor can it show the organs of a male . . . [W]e in Australia have absolutely no need to break the law to popularise naturism. (quoted in Clarke 1982: 191)

Australian naturist magazines were obliged to retouch their photographs until 1972. In Britain, however, the laws were different, and the British magazine *Health and Efficiency* (even today a slightly more "cheeky" publication than its Australian counterparts) competed with British "girlie" magazines by depicting female pubic hair, which was, according to Magnus Clarke (1982: 154–5), still considered daring in the late 1960s, even in pornography. Clarke also reports that *Health and Efficiency* even introduced open-crotch shots, much to the disgust of many naturists, who felt that their ideals were being betrayed for commercial reasons (p. 155).

Legal anomalies put Australian naturist magazines at a commercial disadvantage. Australian law banned the publication of unretouched photographs, and yet allowed the importation of naturist magazines from elsewhere (including Britain and New Zealand) that showed pubic hair. In 1972, the magazine *Solar* argued to the NSW government that importation laws and obscenity laws were in contradiction, and won the argument (Clarke 1982: 214). The Secretariat of the NSW government replied:

> Following consideration by the State Advisory Committee on Publications, the Minister has determined that the publication *Solar* no. 54 shall not be the subject of proceedings under Section 5 or 16 of the Obscene and Indecent Publications Act. (Letter to nudist Elsa King, in Clarke 1982: 214)

What Clarke (1982: 156) calls "the pubic hair barrier" was broken in 1972, with the publication of the first unretouched photograph in *Solar*. Clarke's mini-history of the interrelated fortunes of naturist, "girlie" and pornographic magazines makes it clear that pubic hair is a highly labile cultural sign whose "obscenity" or "naturalness" is produced in relation to representations, themselves nowadays produced under conditions set down by law.

Pubic hair's hegemony in twentieth-century porn was brief. Now, the current aesthetic indubitably favours hairlessness in the body, certainly for women and increasingly for men. According to a survey of *Australian Playboy* carried out by one of the research assistants on this project,[13] the first evidence of obvious trimming of pubic hair is in 1986. Within two years, most pubic hair is obviously clipped and often in a neat line or stripe. By the 1990s, genital lips are clearly visible in most poses and the "stripe" shape continues. Prior to this, in the 1970s and early 1980s, there were no explicit shots of the genitals. Full bodily nudity was in itself the turn-on. Genitals were hidden by the pubic hair and many of the poses aimed to modestly conceal the genital area. Hair then, while itself daring in the 1960s, functioned also as a "cover" until the late 1980s, when the genital lips themselves become the new frontier of boldness.

From my research, it is clear that fashions in representation have marked effects on real bodies when it comes to pubic hair fashions, which are an especially interesting example, since they are learned mostly covertly. Magnus Clarke records that pubic depilation was practised by many nudist women in Australia in the 1950s, this despite the fact that, he believes, many of them were less keen on it than their husbands. Clarke (1982: 236) surmises that in this era it was associated more with medical than cosmetic practice, e.g. childbirth. He believes that depilatory practice was influenced by the laws requiring the absence of pubic hair in photographs. In support of this argument, Clarke (1982: 238) also notes that female pubic depilation declined in the nudist movement after 1972 (the "pubic hair barrier" year) to the point where it was almost entirely absent within the movement by 1982, the year of his study. Now, of course, it is an entirely different story, which further reinforces his argument, since fashions in representation have changed yet again. Popular adult magazines currently pronounce a unanimous aesthetic judgement. To take just one example, in a *People* magazine I surveyed, which contained probably a hundred or so images of naked women, not a single image of any kind (be it advertisement, cartoon, Home Girl or pin-up) showed a hairy genital area. Both female and male readers of tabloid magazines soon learn that "hair's just not acceptable . . . in this day and age," as one beautician put it.

Nowadays, it seems unarguable that pornography is the dominant source of such intimate fashions. The contemporary beauticians we interviewed all autonomously confirmed this hypothesis, as did a photo technician working for an adult magazine. All these interviewees believe that many heterosexual women fashion their pubic hair according to their partner's wishes, and that male tastes are themselves largely gleaned from sources like pornography and tabloid magazines. All the beauticians we spoke to believed that men ask their girlfriends to imitate the fashions displayed by the model in magazine porn: "[With] *Playboy* magazines they can see it – it's more of a turn-on and women just want to keep their husbands happy." Women often get full genital waxes for their wedding, at the request of their fiancé. Valentine's Day also produces particular requests, such as heart-shaped pubic hair. Women commonly ask for this as a surprise for their male partner, though the original source of this idea is harder to trace.[14] When it comes to full genital waxing – that is, total depilation of the genital area – women apparently have it done for three reasons: it's "cleaner," they feel "free," and their partners like it:

> We find that girls will have a girls' night and they'll all whisper and giggle to each other, "Oh, I had mine done and Brian loved it!" "Well, I'll have mine done and give him a surprise for his birthday!" That's going on a tremendous amount at the moment. ("Vera")

Despite the unpopularity in contemporary media theory of models that suggest that the media have too direct and unilateral an influence of ideals on practice, it seems that in the case of relatively covert practices like the shaping of pubic hair, the influence really is quite unsubtle. Representations seem to be primary in producing male and female desire, and intimate body maintenance practices are shared as pleasures and secrets between women until they eventually become norms.[15] With pubic fashions, this work is all the more powerful for being largely unseen or covert. This is especially obvious with full genital waxing, which in contemporary Australia is becoming increasingly common, for men as well as women. Most salons do it quite regularly, but few advertise it. (If they do so, it is likely to be under a euphemism, such as "Brazilian waxing.") Perhaps because of its association with porn, there is still an aura of disrespectability about this practice. One of the senior figures in waxing in Australia ("Vera") has invented a euphemism for the full genital wax: she calls it the Down-Under wax. According to this doyenne of waxing in Australia, full genital waxing was rarely practised even in the late 1990s – rarely offered or demanded – but she sees that changing rapidly:

> We've always done it but only discreetly. In other words we didn't advertise it. If anyone rang up, if they were rude or crude on the phone, we'd say, "No, we don't do it," because it depends on the attitude. If a guy was on the phone and said, "Would you do my balls?" we'd say "No, we don't," and that would be that because it's sort of a come-on in a way . . . Whereas today we actually advertise it. We put it on all our price lists and then we get a demand for it. But even so what happens now is people will come in for a bikini line and then they'll say, "Oh, I really wanted the whole lot done," and then we won't have the time to do the whole lot. So what we do now is when we're taking bookings involving the bikini, from now on all our operators say, "Is that just a normal bikini or do you want down-under waxing?" That's our normal request now.

This process is fascinating: the time schedules of a busy salon produce a linguistic formula that will in its turn produce effects on bodies.

In Chapter 3, I advance the proposition that body hair is currently seen as a kind of disgusting excess that needs to be "tidied up." I argue that hair can be considered a form of "dirt" in the sense used by cultural anthropologist Mary Douglas (1984), a culturally contaminating category. As I will discuss, hair is culturally and conceptually "dirty" because it is a borderline category between flesh and clothing. As a movable border between nudity and non-nudity, it is a site for the dynamic operations of other oppositions: male/female; hetero/homo; pre-pubescent/post-pubescent; Anglo/non-Anglo; sexual/non-sexual; human/animal; civilized/savage. Hair is, as Margaret Miles (1989) suggests, an index of social order, especially orderings of gender, race and age; leave it alone, and it rapidly grows into disorder. Hair is thus a kind of unnatural nature, a paradox that is the theme of Chapter 3. For now, the paradoxes are best encapsulated in this unedited response from one beautician:

Interviewer: Does removing hair make the body more naked?

Beautician: Yep. 'Cos the hair covers up a lot. So get rid of the hair and you're more naked. Cleaner. Cleanliness too, I think, is getting a big thing. 'Cos everything's to make you look more natural – well, they say natural, but if it was natural, you'd have the hair! [laughs] So that's the odd thing about it. Everyone's striving to look natural and not putting perms in their hair, not wearing make-up. We do make-ups all the time. "Can you just do me natural?" and I think, "Well, what are you here for? [laughs] Just go as you are." But they want the make-up done, but looking natural. They want their bodies to look natural but yet they want their hair off, 'cos they think no hair is natural. It's not. That is strange. Especially the make-up thing. When they say "just do it natural." They're paying \$25 to look natural. But I don't say it; I just think it.

This example highlights not the naturalness of nature, but rather its status as an intensely cultural artefact: a shifting line whose placement legitimizes or delegitimizes certain forms of social practice. In the next section, we look at how ambivalence about the "natural state" has produced a split even within the category of nakedness itself.

The Naked and the Nude

It is a central contradiction in European art that its celebration of the human form should involve subsuming the particularities of its subjects in the depersonalising idea of the nude, rendering her – in the name of humanism – an object.

Angela Carter, *Nothing Sacred*

The nude lies on architraves, holds up portals, ministers to great achievers in the streets of cities from London to Vienna to New York, and we are rarely asked to care for what she is feeling, rather to feel better because of what she makes us feel.

Marina Warner, *Monuments and Maidens*

In 1883, controversy erupted in Melbourne over the display of a painting of a naked woman, known affectionately as "Chloe," by French artist Jules Lefebvre. Ongoing Sabbatarian protests at the Melbourne Art Gallery's decision to open on Sundays were intensified once it was discovered that "Chloe" was to be exhibited. Much of the correspondence that ensued in *The Argus* newspaper displaced the issue of the Sabbath in favour of heated arguments about the propriety of "Chloe." The stark differences demonstrate the fierceness of the contradictions around the naked body in a clothed society. Here is a selection:

Would any of the gentlemen trustees permit a nude picture of their daughter or sister to be hung there; and if not, why any one else's daughter? (Russell 1883)

Can it be right that a mother cannot take her young daughters to a public gallery, never to speak of her sons, without feeling her cheeks tingling with shame at such an exhibition? ("A Mother" 1883)

It seems to me that the picture has a strictly and positively moral tendency in promoting the cause of matrimony. The artist shows us (I write as a bachelor) what a really beautiful thing a young maiden is . . . [I]f anything can fire the incipient sparks of affection into such a flame of love as shall induce a young man to go straight away and commit matrimony, it is the sight of "Chloe." ("T.P.I." 1883)

It seems to me that a picture which teaches us so clearly to admire the perfect work of the Creator in its highest aspect, free from all taint of our lower attributes and appealing strongly to our mind and soul, must have a purifying and ennobling effect. ("A Woman" 1883)[16]

Under what circumstances can an undressed body be considered "ennobling?" To answer this, we shall turn to a particular concept within fine art theory – the opposition between nakedness and nudity.

As we have seen, the opposition between body and clothing has been roughly understood as corresponding to a division between nature and culture; fine arts, though, has elaborated a distinction even *within* the category of undress, one that divides nudity itself up into "natural" and "unnatural" (i.e. aestheticized) nudity. In this famous opposition between nakedness and nudity, the nature/culture divide is redoubled within the domain of the undressed body, producing an opposition between "natural nudity" (i.e. nakedness) and "cultural nudity." In classical art, "naturalness" is not highly valued; nature is, rather, understood as raw material in need of purification, "cleaning up," or perfection. Both nature and subjectivity are evacuated from the naked model as s/he is transformed into an idealized object, the nude.

Before studying this distinction, it is useful to consider the etymology of the words themselves. The word "naked" comes from the Old English "nacod," and is related to similar words in the West Germanic family of languages: German, Old Frisian and Old Norse. It's an older word than "nude" and could refer to animals as well as people. In Middle English, it could also mean "without protection" or "defenceless." The word "nude," on the other hand, is of Latin origin, from *nudus*, meaning "bare." According to the *OED*, it entered the language in late Middle English. Up until the mid-seventeenth century it was an adjective meaning "mere," "plain," "open" or "explicit." From the mid-sixteenth century it could be used as a verb; "to nude" someone of something meant to deprive them of something. The term entered aesthetic vocabulary in the early eighteenth century, as a noun ("a nude") and by the middle of that century the genre was established enough for the expression "the nude" to have come into use. "Nude" came to be used adjectivally with reference to people only in the middle of the nineteenth century.

Over the last few centuries, the common literal meanings of the words "naked" and "nude" have diminished, even while their figurative meanings have remained rich and varied. Moreover, terms that could once refer to much of the world have come to refer mostly to humans. The word "naked" could once be used of most of the natural world, animate or inanimate (for example water, wind, rock, ground, fields, plants, animals, fish, seeds, fire) as well as of inanimate objects such as boats, rooms, walls or timber. Of animals, it could mean "without saddle," or without skin or hair. In this latter sense, it could be used of a human, plant or animal. The obsolete verb "to nake" meant to bare or strip,[17] including to unsheathe a sword. The word "nude" entered the language rather later than the word "naked" and has a more limited range of meanings, the greatest proportion of which refer specifically to humans, often to women. In other words, the usage with which we are almost exclusively familiar today belongs to the era of industrialization, aesthetic realism, urbanization. Nonetheless, it too could once be used of inanimate objects, and even landscapes (though not, it seems, of animals). In the nineteenth century, it could mean bare, without furniture, ornament or decoration, as in such expressions as "a nude valley" or "a nude room." It also had a legal sense (from as early as the sixteenth century) as an adjective referring to statements or promises that have not been formally attested or recorded. I believe that this gradual linguistic retraction needs to be understood alongside changes to the understanding of the place of humans in the world, whereby humanness was increasingly understood (and lived) as a separation from the world of nature.

As with many other pairs of Anglo-Saxon and Latin words, an implicit relation to rank and hierarchy remains. Latinate words were associated first with the Roman conquerors and later with the invading Norman nobility, with the result that words of Anglo-Saxon or Germanic origin often have connotations that are more crude, vulgar, coarse or down-to-earth than their Latinate equivalents. For a century and a half after the Norman conquest of England, "the supremacy of Norman French and Latin seems [to have been] total" (McCrum et al. 1986: 74). French had "social and cultural prestige," and Latin was the language of religion and learning (p. 75). English later made a comeback, such that "[e]ven among the educated classes it seems clear that French had become an *acquired*, not a natural, language (p. 77, original emphasis). Hundreds of years later, the Latinate word "nude" still carries the connotation of something sophisticated achieved through culture, rather than something organic.[18]

In art criticism, the distinction between "naked" and "nude" has a particular meaning, most famously discussed by Kenneth Clark (1956) in his book *The Nude: A Study in Ideal Form*. Put simply, Clark's opposition is this: nakedness is the "raw" human body, the human body without clothes. Nudity results when the artist works on that raw material. Thus, the nude is not a subject of art but a form of art (Clark 1956: 3). John Berger (1972: 53) glosses it thus: nakedness is a starting point and the nude is "a way of seeing." Nakedness is imperfect and individual; the nude is ideal and universal. Nakedness is nature; nudity, culture. The artist's work de-particularizes the model's nakedness, lifting it into ideality. This is one of the reasons that nudity has been understood as functioning like a form of dress:

> Surely nudity, as distinguished from nakedness, is our most subtle and sophisticated sort of clothing or covering for the genitalia. Like the pose projected onto the mirror or photograph, which reflects an ego-preferred imago – or cosmetics and masks, which create kindred personae for society – nudity serves as an aestheticizing gloss, a product of will and reason transforming the god-given nakedness of us hairless apes, who have precious few ambient-specific markings. (Howard 1986: 292)

Clark's opposition takes up Aristotle's conception of ideal art as the perfection of imperfect nature: "Art completes what nature cannot bring to a finish. The artist gives us knowledge of nature's unrealised ends" (Clark 1956: 9). But the nude should not be totally removed from nature, Clark argues. It should arouse in us the desire to perpetuate ourselves, and it should connect back to other kinds of human experience: "harmony, energy, ecstasy, humility, pathos"

(p. 7). So the nude is not a sublimation of nature, but an elevation, avoiding the "two evils of sensuality and aestheticism" (p. 21). The body is something we must both "accept" and "superintend" (p. 63). Clark's idealism is thus not puritanical. For Clark, ideality is not asexuality; the ideal artwork can hold a high degree of eroticism "in solution" (p. 6). Clark's reverence for ideality is not a cold formalism that disdains the body: "The rhythm of our breathing and the beat of our hearts are part of the experience by which we measure a work of art" (p. 23), he claims. But his valuation *is* based on an unequivocal hierarchy of mind over body, an idealist universalism, and the structural conflation of heterosexual male desire with desire-in-general.

The male nude was the basis of art training from the fifteenth century until the mid-twentieth century (Walters 1978: 7), and the idealizing tradition is at the heart of classical art training. One characteristic book is Arthur Thomson's (1964) *Handbook of Anatomy for Art Students*, first published in 1896. One photo in this text shows a female model holding a miniature Greek-style statue of a nude female, into whose image, she is, presumably, to be transformed. In some of Thomson's descriptions one can hear echoes of Clark's "disillusion and dismay" at the pitiful flesh that cannot live up to the ideal into which it will be transformed by art (Clark 1956: 4). The following description of female buttocks, for example, amply demonstrates the gap between real model and ideal form:

> When in the female fat is present here in undue amount it imparts a clumsy and ungainly appearance to the limb, particularly in certain positions, and models which [*sic*] display this tendency to any marked extent should be avoided. A slight fulness, however, below the trochanters is not unpleasant, as it conduces to a more rounded form of the limb and gives a better outline to the outer side of the thigh. The student should be warned against the ungainly forms which are dependent on the undue accumulation of fat in the region overlying the iliac crest. This is particularly liable to occur in female models past their prime, and imparts a grossness to the form at variance with the delicacy and refinement displayed in earlier life. (Thomson 1964: 271)

Note how the living model is referred to as an object ("which"). Nakedness must undergo "a severe formal discipline . . . if it is to survive as art" (Clark 1956:133).

Underneath such descriptions is an idea of a singular, universal body, an idealized composite of the "best" features of real bodies.[19] For example, after a lengthy discussion of pelvic obliquity, the author remarks: "The artist will of course be guided in his selection of models by reference to these points, avoiding, as far as possible, extreme conditions [i.e. women or men with sharply oblique pelvises], and recognizing that the most pleasing results are obtained when the average is represented" (Thomson 1964: 264). Differences between living bodies are to be imagined as aberrations or exceptions to this abstract idea of a putatively "universal" body; ageing, blemishes and so on are conceived of as deviations from an ideal rather than equally typical variations within a field.

A nineteenth-century version of the naked/nude opposition was that between the "nude of commerce" and the "nude of art." This distinction began in the 1860s and was unashamedly moralistic:

> The nude has something of the purity of little children who play naked together without minding at all. The *undressed*, on the contrary, always reminds me of the woman who shows herself for forty *sous* and specialises in "artistic" poses. (quoted in Stuart 1996: 102).

The assumptions underlying this opposition remain largely unchanged. Even today, a range of similar attributes can still threaten to devalue nudity: adulthood (as opposed to childhood nudity); contemporaneity (as opposed to classicism); movement (as opposed to stasis); live performance (as opposed to representation); particular subjects (as opposed to "universal" or allegorical subjects); commodification (as opposed to non-commercialized nudity); and nudity as labour (as opposed to product). These are just some of the criteria that will help determine whether a naked body will be considered decent. The point is, of course, that such distinctions are rarely clear-cut; nudity can rarely contain its potential wealth of meanings. The case of the nineteenth-century showgirl makes this clear. Because of decency regulations, she wore a body-stocking and adopted static poses rather than performing an active strip. Her nakedness, though "raw" and "unredeemed," was thus held in check, but only precariously:

> [T]he nude showgirl was a continual cause for consternation. Her erotic cavortings, her calculated immodesty and costumes that framed and displayed her erogenous zones, meant that for many she epitomised the "nude of commerce." To them she was the body unredeemed by any aura of spirituality, or polite distance. Instead she was available, and overtly sexual, with unpleasant connotations of vulgarity and money. (Stuart 1996: 103)

When it comes to non-white showgirl, the quality of her nudity was even more liminal (for white spectators), as Andrea Stuart (1996) argues in her study of black nineteenth-century showgirl Josephine Baker.

The Victorian theatrical entertainment known as *tableaux vivants* involved often titillating imitations of "high art" nude paintings (Blessing 1997: 50).

This suggests another submerged element in the nude/nakedness opposition: that of social class. It is permissible for the high art nude to arouse desire – indeed, Kenneth Clark insists that it *must* – but too overt a display of eroticism "cheapens" the artwork. Clark (1956) argues that the nude must hold its eroticism "in solution." It must arouse us,[20] but its affective content must be kept in check by form. An appreciation of form over emotional content serves as a marker of class or education, as the French sociologist Pierre Bourdieu's (1984) study of taste made abundantly clear. Bourdieu found that in the hierarchies of taste characteristic of modern French society, aesthetic "sophistication" involves the downplaying of emotionality or sentimentality of response, accentuating instead form and technique over content.

Feminist Critiques of Clark

The hierarchized oppositions on which the naked/nude binary relies have been challenged, especially by feminists. Clark's distinction is both subtly and unsubtly gendered. In harking back to Aristotle, he adopts some of the contradictions regarding the body that characterized Greek thought. The ideal nudity of the Greeks took the young male body first and foremost as its model for ideal beauty, and beauty was not linked to passive ornamentation but to virtue and power. Men exercised and studied nude in the *gymnasia*; female nudity, though, was mostly frowned upon in practice. In philosophical discourse, meanwhile, "body" was usually subservient to "mind." While Plato, for one, characterized virtue as equally available to both sexes and all ages, he saw the body as a lower faculty threatening to divert the soul from its higher purposes. Elizabeth Spelman (1982) characterizes Plato as contradictory in this regard. As a "psychophile," he saw all souls as equal, but as a "somatophobe," he was led to make misogynist statements, as he saw women's life of the body as characteristic of all the venal temptations that could drag the soul down (Spelman 1982: 119). Such paradoxes help explain why female nudes could function as allegories of virtues even while actual female nudity could be frowned upon. There was, according to Margaret Walters (1978: 39), "an impassable gulf between the power of the goddesses, and the narrow, limited lives of real Greek women."

Clark's (1956) discussion likewise implies a gap between a supposedly universal ideal (which the female nude can exemplify) and the actual life of the flesh. Although Clark discusses male as well as female nudes, his crucial distinction between the nude and the naked implicitly deals with a male artist and a female model (Miles 1989: 13–16). Although there are obvious historical reasons for this, the result is that his devaluing of nakedness is by implication displaced especially onto *female* nakedness and/or that nakedness itself becomes a feminized term. Moreover, for Clark, there is something abject about nakedness:

> It is widely supposed that the naked human body is in itself an object upon which the eye dwells with pleasure and which we are glad to see depicted. But anyone who has frequented art schools and seen the shapeless, pitiful model which the students are industriously drawing will know that this is an illusion ... A mass of naked figures does not move us to empathy, but to disillusion and dismay. (Clark 1956: 3–4)

(Note, again, the "which;" the living model has been turned into an object.) The classical nude, on the other hand, is perfect, unblemished; it abolishes the "wrinkles, pouches and other small imperfections" of the body (Clark 1956: 4).

For Clark, art provides "the most complete example of the transmutation of matter into form" (p. 23). He approves of this desire to perfect, seeing it as part of the Greek legacy to modern culture (p. 9). He uses terms like "purification," discipline" and "subordination" to describe the processes by which "the unruly human body" (p. 64) is perfected in art. Lynda Nead (1992), whose systematic critique of Clark's opposition underpins her book *The Female Nude*, comments on this Aristotelian denigration of (female) flesh. Ultimately, she argues, the distinction between form and matter, the ideal and the actual (Nead 1992: 14–15), on which the nude/naked binary reposes is both gendered and hierarchical, and the process of idealization is a metaphor for containment and control of "the feminine." The gendering of the distinction can clearly be seen in Albrecht Dürer's woodcut, *Artist Drawing a Reclining Nude* (1538) (Figure 1.1), in which the male artist works over the raw female material, and transforms nature into art, matter into form. That these male and female principles are opposites is made clear by the symmetrical composition. The woman's lush curves are contrasted with the draughtsman's phallic implements and dagger. The fierce concentration in his eyes and the glinting sharpness of his dagger remind us, as in the *Penguin Island* story (France 1909), of the violence that lurks as potential below the orderings of gender and sex implied in this opposition.

The gendering of the undressed body in painting is complex. On the one hand, "body" is a feminized term in the Western philosophical tradition and nakedness is the feminized opposite to nudity. And of course, most nudes in art are females. On the other hand, the male body can subtly stand in for "the" body, since the conceptual and linguistic assumption of a generic Man implicitly treats the "normal" body as male, and the female body as an exception, the marked term. The idealizing tradition thinks of actual bodies

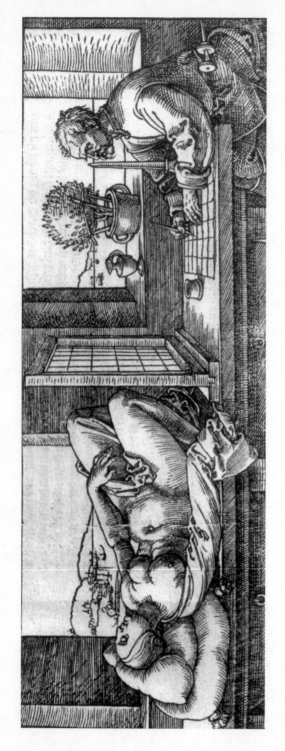

Figure 1.1 Albrecht Dürer. *De Symmetria Partium Humanorum Corporum*, 1532. Commonly known as "Artist Drawing a Reclining Nude."

as imperfect, variable versions of an ideal, and this hierarchy can easily be imagined in gendered terms. In Thomson's (1964) *Handbook of Anatomy*, for example, the female body is frequently imagined as a less able male body. For example, the surface depressions where the pectoral muscles sink under the deltoids "are absent in the female, or, if present, are very much softened on account of the quantity of fat and the feebler muscular development" (p. 134). The index to this handbook also makes it clear that maleness is assumed as the norm. It clearly constructs the female as the marked term, with entries like "Thorax, female" or "Groin, furrow of, in female" or "The flank, length of, in female." The most striking example of this assumption about "the" body is in the index entry for breasts, which reads, in an initially bizarre rupture of common-sense and alphabetical expectations:

Breasts, male
—— female

This text isn't a lone example. Nead's (1992) brief critique of a more recent art instruction book, Douglas Graves' (1979) *Figure Painting in Oil*, points out another example where the female breast is explicitly seen as a variant of the male chest. She criticizes the book for the way it "reproduces the notion that the female body is simply that which is added to the male body" (Nead 1992: 53). This notion goes back a long way; Renaissance artists often used male models even for female figures (Walters 1978: 7).

The creation of nudes from the bodies of naked women is not only a historical or high art practice; it's also very much the operation performed on a daily basis in popular magazines, via digital manipulation. Nowadays, all magazines, be they women's or men's, glamorous or homely, doctor many of their images to turn the blemished, wrinkled, shadowed faces and bodies of their subjects into smooth, unbroken, reflective surfaces. This transformation of real to ideal now routinely occurs not only with glamour shots of stars and models, but also with the images of "ordinary people" that adorn the covers of many magazines. In the case of adult magazines, the transformation is effected for both aesthetic and censorship reasons. To get some insight into these practices, we interviewed a man ("Ben") working as a digital retoucher for a major Australian magazine publisher. As he described it, idealization involves more erasure than addition – the removal of redness, shaving rashes, scars, tattoos, stretch marks, birthmarks and pubic hair (though it can also involve augmenting breasts and lips, or lengthening legs). In effect, it involves removing traces of the lived body, of time, experience, process, ageing. This brings real bodies in line with current ideals – part of the strange and insidious process by which people are encouraged to model themselves on bodies that never existed in the first place. With adult magazines, there's also a censorship dimension to this practice, since current regulations for the "Unrestricted" category in Australia forbid "sexualized nudity." What sexualized nudity means in practice is always difficult to judge. It's a combination of subject matter (e.g. no depiction of intercourse) and poses (no hands near the genital area) along with other, less definable, implied attitudes and looks. Certain rules, however, are clear-cut. There must be no erections, no "pink" flesh, no visible orifices, no realistic depictions of female genitals. The retouchers are thus constantly engaged in turning pink flesh tan and in sealing up orifices. Popular tabloid pornography depicts labia as creases rather than gaps or folds. The language used in the profession to describe this practice is (to me) quite horrifying. Staff speak unironically of "healing" women. "Heal to a single crease," "lose dangleberries" and "lose giblet" are examples of instructions from an art editor on a marked-up page of a popular adult magazine.

Ben himself disliked the whole process, and critiqued the censorship rules that ironically help produce what he saw as a form of symbolic violence against women:

> We would love to let these women go on to the news-stands as they are. There's no internal desire to chop women up so that they look a certain way. The Censorship Board forces us into these types of changes. When I started working with this type of stuff . . . what got to me was the way they chop women up. I was horrified that we were creating this perception of what women looked like. That still remains my biggest thing with it, that we actually create an image of women which is unattainable. Everything else is aspirations . . . but no women could achieve this for herself. What does a woman think when she sees these magazines, is what I want to know now?

Censorship laws thus paradoxically help create a regime of images in which unreal expectations about women's bodies are perpetuated, often with quite shocking results:

> Men write us letters: "Where can I find a woman like that? . . . And can I come and work on your publication because you find the best women? My girlfriend doesn't look like that." And worse than that, we find 18-year-old boys complaining how their 18-year-old girlfriend doesn't look like that.

Ben reported that some editors replied to such letters without admitting that the images are fabrications.

Another job of a retoucher is to create what are known in the trade as "smoos." A "smoo" is a completely fabricated image of labia, constructed usually from armpits or the back of the leg, where creases are neater, rounder, hairless – in short, far better than actual genitals. Such bodily fragments are cut and pasted onto the genital area, thus replacing the shadowy, ill-defined, imperfect labia with the perfect simulacrum; the imitation surpasses the inferior reality and thereby offends neither Censorship Board nor the aesthetic sensibilities of a magazine readership trained to admire such "perfection." Ben and I discussed this current aesthetic and its relation to the fine art tradition. I explained Clark's (1956) distinction to him, and he agreed that current practices could well be understood in the light of this enduring valorization of a de-particularized, universalized, sealed-off nudity over the seemingly inferior, vulnerable and flawed nakedness of actual bodies.

Perfected media images evacuate the signs of experience and history from a face and body. In advertising, the flawless face of the non-celebrity model has as little history and subjectivity as possible, since its role is to solicit you towards a commodity – indeed, since it functions as a commodity itself. This is why feminists like Annette Kuhn (1985) have followed John Berger (1972) in seeing the glamour aesthetic of modern advertising and pornography as an extension of the objectifying and idealizing tendencies behind the idea of the (female) nude:

> A glamorous image of a woman (or an image of a glamorous woman) is peculiarly powerful in that it plays on the desire of the spectator in a particularly pristine way: beauty or sexuality is desirable exactly to the extent that it is idealised and unattainable. (Kuhn 1985: 12)

"The transition from naked to nude," she says, "is also the transformation of woman into object" (Kuhn 1985: 11). In this she draws on Berger's central argument, that the European nude tradition (and its modern media descendants) are key components of a complex visual regime that constructs women as spectacle, even to themselves, in what Laura Mulvey (1975: 11) famously called woman's "*to-be-looked-at-ness.*" Despite subsequent feminist revision of these propositions, including by Mulvey herself, women's cultural positioning as object of the gaze remains an insight of crucial importance to feminism. Nonetheless, even such well-established feminist readings are not uncontentious and have often been received with hostility. For example, the cover story of the British magazine *Art Review* in September 1997 was "The Nude: Is it a Victim of Feminist Claptrap?" This feature article attacked feminist art critics and "the new puritans of Political Correctness" from whom "the nude" was in need of defence (Ashbee 1997: 56).

So what are the various forms of feminist response to the naked/nude opposition? There is, of course, a wide range of feminist positions regarding the complex politics of aestheticization. On the one hand, some feminists critical of glamour aesthetics have condemned Clark's (1956) preference for ideality over rawness in favour of a celebration of "the naked." These objections come not only from academics. As we will see in Chapter 4, over recent years there has been an explosion of interest in "homemade" nakedness; many sated media consumers have come to prefer the erotics of amateurism to the slick professional masquerade. Yet the gender politics of a preference for amateurism are not necessarily clear-cut either. For example, Jennifer Blessing (1997) critiques Barthes' (1973) discussion of striptease, in which he avows a preference for the amateur over the slick nudity of the professional striptease artist. His preference is, she claims, attributable to a fear of female mastery that leads him to find performances of female "lack" more pleasing.[21]

For my purposes, I would like to delineate two basic feminist approaches to the nude/naked binary – revaluation and rejection – along with a third approach, which is an extension of the former.

Revaluing the Binary: The "Other" Body

> Even in depictions in which the author or painter intended to present a "reformed" body, . . . I will seek the contours of the other body, the body formed and informed by the life of the subject.
>
> Margaret Miles, *Carnal Knowing*

Objectification is not always, or simply, a "bad thing." That naked or semi-naked female bodies have been able to represent high ideals – like justice, liberty or love – is important. Nonetheless, not all feminists are interested in divine perfection; some prefer celebrations of mess to ideals of purity.[22] So it is that a number of commentators and critics have accepted the basic terms of Clark's (1956) opposition, but have disagreed with his valuing of them. John Berger, for example, accepts the distinction between nakedness as physical state and nudity as a conventionalized way of seeing, but he subjects these terms to a feminist critique:

> To be naked is to be oneself.
> To be nude is to be seen by others and yet not recognized for oneself. A naked body has to be seen as an object in order to become a nude. (Berger 1972: 54)

The nude is a naked body on display, and this display, this disguise, can never be discarded: "The nude is condemned to never being naked. Nudity is a form of dress" (Berger 1972: 54). Almost all paintings of naked women in the European oil tradition are, says Berger, nudes. There exist only some hundreds of exceptions, paintings in which the artist's "personal vision" of the model is so strong that he knows himself to be an outsider, and "he cannot deceive himself into believing that she is naked for him" (pp. 57–8). The painter is bound to the woman *in relationship*, and thus he cannot objectify her:

He cannot turn her into a nude. The way the painter has painted her includes her will and her intentions in the very structure of the image, in the very expression of her body and her face. (Berger 1972: 58)

Berger wants to describe a relation of equals rather than a relationship of subject to object. Nonetheless, in his analysis the relationship is still ordered around the male painter's perception, since it is the strength of "the painter's personal vision of the particular women he is painting" that leaves no room for another spectator. And it is still a relationship based on male desire; these paintings are, says Berger, "paintings of loved women." "The painter's vision binds the woman to him so that they become as inseparable as couples in stone" (p. 57), he says.

Another example of the critique of nudity can be found in a poem by Robert Graves (1965), "The Naked and the Nude." Graves figures nakedness as above reproach, but nudity as "bold" and "sly." Making use of a longstanding trope that we will discuss in more depth later in this chapter, he equates nudity with trickery, rhetoric and sham piety. While showiness and slyness often win out in this world, the honesty of nakedness will triumph in the next:

> The naked, therefore, who compete
> Against the nude may know defeat;
> Yet when they both together tread
> The briary pastures of the dead,
> By Gorgons with long whips pursued,
> How naked go the sometime nude!

> (Graves 1965: 19–24)

In my interview with the photographic model Karen, I enjoyed hearing her suddenly and quite spontaneously use (but revalue) Clark's distinction:

I like the difference between the word "nude" and "naked." "Nude" sounds to me more proper, more sanctioned, maybe artistic, like paintings and things. And then the word "naked" to me is much more earthy. And I really like the sound of "naked" better – like that sort of comes from my body, whereas "nude" comes from my mind.

In response, I summarized Clark's argument, and suggested that it has been seen by feminists as highly gendered. She replied:

So for him, then, nudity becomes something finer. Nakedness is more base. [*I say that it's like the raw material*]. Yeah. So in a way I agree with him. But I've got a *preference* for the raw material [*laughs*]. You know, I don't think you can improve on it.

In Miles' (1989) terms, Karen is choosing to value the body as home of feeling, memory, subjectivity, experience, over the emptied, perfected, universalized body of the nude.

Miles herself isn't particularly interested in retaining the nudity/nakedness opposition. Her position on Clark is informed by a feminist desire to reclaim the subject in the object, to "seek the contours of the other body, the body formed and informed by the life of the subject" (Miles 1989: 16). Miles sees in Clark's praise of idealized bodies a preference for a body "from which the subjectivity, along with moles and lumps, has been elided" (Miles 1989: 14). She says: "At the same moment when the naked body was 're-formed' to render it pleasingly balanced and proportioned without blemishes, it lost its ability to express the personal character of the person whose body it is" (Miles 1989: 14). In this, she implicitly aligns herself with Berger's (1972) and Kuhn's (1985) critique of the objectifying operations of the nude genre, seeing the idealizing operations of nudity as inherently misogynist, since they delete the female subject of a painting and replace her with a function – the role of, in Clark's words, representing "a far wider and more civilising experience" (Clark 1956: 6).

Although Berger's (1972) *Ways of Seeing* doesn't itself move beyond looking at representation, it certainly opens the way for speculation about the effects of representation on the lives of women. Berger's insight about the role of representation in constraining women to think of themselves as spectacle, as object of a (male) gaze, opens up enormous questions about women's embodied life, even if *Ways of Seeing* doesn't pursue these vigorously. Berger does seem to want to make space for thinking about bodily experience; he recognizes not just the lifelessness of the nude, but also the fact that real-life nakedness differs even from the nakedness in those paintings that he calls "naked" rather than nude, and whose abilities to capture the woman's will and intentions he celebrates. "In lived sexual experience," he states, "nakedness is a process rather than a state" (Berger 1972: 60). In this book, though, I argue that nakedness is as complex a process in *all* forms of bodily experience, not just the sexual.

Re-valuing and Extending the Binary

Berger's (1972) account focuses on nakedness in relation to the act of seeing or being seen. But nudity and nakedness can also be considered in relation to other senses. To both invert and extend Clark's binary, that is, to value nakedness over nudity and to consider both of them as embodied experiences, is a doubly feminist operation, since it involves not only a restitution of the denigrated feminine term ("naked"), but also the invocation of a "feminine" form of knowing ("feeling"). One's feeling of nakedness doesn't always need the immediate gaze of another to be activated; that gaze has already been internalized, and the body image habituated to the experience of envelopment and enclosure. I discussed this possibility with Karen, who feels "much more exposed" when standing up. This can occur even in the absence of other people; Karen described being in the bathroom one morning and suddenly "feeling quite naked. Which sounds funny. I was really very conscious of the fact that I wasn't wearing anything."

When Karen speaks of the distinction between nudity and nakedness, she relates it to her own bodily experience. Of being posed for erotic photos, she says: "For some of the time I felt like I was nude, rather than naked. Because I was being *arranged*." For some of the photos she was asked to masturbate, "and then I was being more naked than nude." In other words, for Karen, nudity and nakedness are not just conceptually different, but are different qualities of lived experience. Clark's distinction gives little sense of what it feels like to be naked, even though he deplores asceticism and understands the Greek ideal as reflecting "pleasure in the human body" (Clark 1956: 48). Even many feminist responses to Clark, though they tell us plenty about what nakedness means, culturally, speak little of its phenomenal qualities. Karen, on the other hand, talks warmly and wisely about the lived experience of her body. She talks about *feeling* naked and *feeling* nude. I found the following discussion remarkable for its nuanced understanding of the different qualities of nakedness:

> I get more liberated every year . . . I feel much more comfortable now than when I was younger. Actually more comfortable with my nakedness now than when I was younger. My body is different. You know, in some ways it's not as perfect as it used to be when I was a teenager, but I really like it so much more than I used to. And also the work that it's done. You know, just the fact that I've carried two babies. You know, I look at my belly and it's sort of very very soft and slightly wrinkled, because it's been so huge a couple of times. I just feel very loving because of what my belly's done. And it's the same with my breasts. You know, they're nowhere near as firm as they used to be, and yet I think, well they've suckled two children. So I look at it differently. I look on my body as something that's worked for me, and given me a gift. Whereas when I was a teenager I just saw it as my body . . . So I suppose now my nakedness is a richer experience than it used to be. I've actually got more comfortable inside my skin than I used to be.

I wonder when the process of actually *feeling* naked starts to happen. One can only assume that birth must be a violent physiological shock for the baby: expelled out of the dark, warm, enclosed womb into the open play of air and light onto the skin; the first passage of air through the nasal cavities; the first opening of the eyes to light; reliance on the arms of another to stop toppling through space; the first full extension of the body in this space. (And yet, we remember none of this consciously.) But would this exposure feel like vulnerability? It's hard to know. Baby care books frequently claim that a newborn feels vulnerable and exposed without clothes after the enclosure of the womb, and only gradually learns to be comfortable with post-natal nakedness. Slowly, though, a *differential* experience of exposure and enclosure must begin. If we think of a newborn baby as a bundle of sensations, an organism taking in, processing and making primal meanings of sensations across its entire body well before it begins to acquire language, then we would have to assume that this differentiating process begins very early. The process of wearing nappies begins to experientially code the baby's genital areas as somehow different from the rest of its body. The genital area – encased, enwrapped, contained – is experientially different well before its cultural ramifications have been called explicitly into play within a symbolic order. Perhaps, then, the infant brought up within a culture that uses (indeed enforces) nappies feels clothed, and therefore naked, in this area of its body from a very early age. Perhaps nakedness can be as much a way of *feeling* as of seeing.

Rejecting the Binary: Post-structural Feminism

Another form of feminist critique has been a rejection of the nude/naked binary altogether, as in the work of Lynda Nead (1992). As we have seen, Nead is critical of Clark's (1956) opposition. She is also, though, critical of Berger's (1972) attempts to render it more female-friendly. For Nead, what is left undisturbed in Berger's critique of Clark is "the implication that the naked is somehow freer from mediation, that it is semiotically more open and represents the body liberated from cultural intervention" (Nead 1992: 15). Although, as we will see in Chapter 2, there is a long metaphorical convention to support Berger's contention that "to be naked is to be oneself," and although many nudists would agree with him on that, ultimately, of course, such an idea is hard to sustain philosophically. As Nead makes clear, the naked/nude distinction relies on the concept of a body outside of or prior to representation. For that reason, I do not adhere to it in this book. Except when the distinction is itself a phenomenon to be discussed, I use the words "nude" or "naked" interchangeably. However, one need not completely abandon the idea of a "natural" body or of being "oneself;" instead, I see naturalness and unselfconsciousness as genuine bodily and subjective *experiences*. There are some modes of inhabiting our body that *feel* more real, more natural, than others. To acknowledge this is not to essentialize experience. It is simply to take bodily experience seriously, and to ask questions about what might produce such experiences. It also allows us to politicize our understanding of bodily feelings

– to note that not all people experience their body as "theirs" or as "natural" (or at least, not in all situations), and that what "feels natural" will vary not only between people but also across the different contexts of a single life. "Feeling natural" is a political and an ideological matter.

Clothing, Language and "The Human"

We turn now to the question of how nudity and clothing have been implicated in philosophical and theological debates, which will lead us to further consider the politics of naturalness. Putting nakedness at the centre of an idea of the human is not new. The Bible places shamed nakedness at the beginning of human society and construes the act of clothing as the fundamental starting point of an alienated human culture. The story of the Fall can be read as exploring a discomfort with both nudity *and* clothing. For a thinker such as Thomas Carlyle, whose work we will explore in depth shortly, disgust at clothing and at nakedness are inseparable, for it is human beings' exceptional nakedness that makes them dependent on the rest of nature to cover their pitiable state. Thus both nudity and clothing pay testimony to human need.

Even though the Eden myth is arguably hostile to the body, it nonetheless places the body at the centre of things. As Marina Warner (1985: 294) says of the Adam and Eve tale: "From the imagined start of human experience in the West, human identity is inseparable from the theme of the personal body and self-consciousness as a physical creature." So while it is often said that Western knowledge has increasingly come to be rational and disembodied, it is worth remembering the centrality of the body to the foundational myths of the Western tradition.

Ideas about the body sit at the core of any idea of human nature and human history. They therefore have some relation to all the qualities or properties that have been taken to be the mark of the distinctively human, such as the wearing of clothes, advanced reasoning capacity, a soul, labour, the aesthetic capacity, the capacity for emotion or morality, and language. (I am not, by the way, claiming that such properties *are* in any way simple markers of human distinctiveness; rather, that these are some of the hubs around which such commonsensical claims turn. Many social and cultural forms, from hard science to philosophy to popular entertainment, explore, research or play with these imagined frontiers of humanness.) These supposed linchpins of humanity are some of the grand recurring motifs in Western theological and philosophical debate, and it is therefore unsurprising that they have often been made to mirror, parallel or map onto each other. For example, the wearing of clothes has been taken as a sign of heightened morality; aesthetic capacity has been linked to the possession of a soul. My interest here is in a long tradition linking clothing and language, both of which have been seen as special properties of humans, and as distinctive and deep-rooted elements of sociality. The biblical tale, for example, brings body and language into relations of implicit homology. Over the centuries, this religious homology has been philosophically and theologically elaborated into an often metaphorical inquiry into the relationship between clothing systems and systems of language.

Clothing can be a fundamental metaphor within those philosophical systems, usually idealist or essentialist, that see the world as ideas (spirits, essences) clothed in form (content, matter). The metaphor can be found in passing, for example, in Descartes' *Second Meditation*, an extended reflection on the nature of mind, in which Descartes famously posits reason as the bedrock of identity and of humanness (*cogito ergo sum*: "I think, therefore I am"). He discusses the properties of a piece of wax (its whiteness, fragrance, shape and so on). Since these properties are changeable (for example when the wax is brought near to the fire), Descartes reasons that they cannot be of the essence of wax itself; they must be non-essential to it. So too for the mind that perceives the wax, which is also prone to errors. What then is the true nature of the wax, and which human faculty is best placed to apprehend this nature? At this point, Descartes has recourse to a metaphor of nakedness and clothing:

> [W]hen I distinguish the wax from its outward form, and as it were unclothe it and consider it in its naked self, I get something which, mistaken as my judgment may still be, I need a human mind to perceive. (Descartes 1970: 74)

This metaphor relies on the assumption of a true essence clothed in the transitory, changeable and misleading garb of the material world.

This kind of idealism has been fundamental to the Christian tradition, which often conceives of the human as a spirit clothed in body clothed in garments. Two biblical stories – Adam and Eve and the Tower of Babel – exemplify the idea of human culture as a secondary or fallen condition. In the first, clothing results from Adam and Eve's Fall, and symbolizes the moment of rupture from naked and unselfconscious truth. In the second story, also from Genesis, God proliferates languages as a means of divine retribution and control. The story starts with the claim that the earliest people (the descendants of Noah) originally spoke the same language and that all the different lineages could understand each other. Hoping never to be separated, these people decide to settle in one spot, beginning by building a tower of bricks. God, seeing in the tower a sign of human power, confounds them by mixing up their language and causing them to be scattered across the earth. Their city is never built. Genesis describes this act as a deliberate punishment for human over-reaching:

> And the Lord said, "Behold, the people is one, and they have all one language; and this they begin to do: and now nothing will be restrained from them, which they have imagined to do. Go to, let us go down, and there confound their language, that they may not understand one another's speech." So the Lord scattered them abroad from thence upon the face of all the earth: and they left off to build the city. (Genesis 11: 6–8)

The tale has generally been read as one human pride punished by a vengeful God. As a story about language, it evokes the mythical ideal of an originary unmediated communication that is ruptured by a chaotic descent into different languages. In this tale, the variety of human languages are instruments not of communication and understanding, but of misunderstanding and human division. Here we see an early and influential conception opposing the com-monsensical view of language as a vehicle or tool of communication, in favour of a view of language as something to be mistrusted – at the very least as prone to error and miscommunication, or worse, an active instrument of falsity, seduction or corruption. Many of the Ancient Greeks (notably Plato and Aristotle) came to mistrust the Sophists for this very reason, condemning their emphasis on persuasion over the search for truth. A contemporary philosophy like post-structuralism also inherits this mistrust, though it does not contrast it with an ideal of pure communication.[23]

These two falls – clothing and language – have become implicitly and explicitly intertwined and paralleled in the Christian tradition and post-Christian philosophy. The Adam and Eve story instigates clothing as a primary metaphor for duplicity, deception, and indeed language itself, which is understood as a sadly necessary alienation from the naked truth of God. Adam's fig leaf is, as the German writer Franz Werfel put it, "the first cultural document" (in Blumenberg 1998: 62). In the Christian tradition, this foundational metaphor of the Naked Truth veiled by the lie of language (or painted over with the artifice of rhetoric) is implicated in both an ontology of the individual and a wider view of human society. "Culture," writes Werfel, "begins precisely in that we have something to hide" (quoted in Blumenberg 1998: 62). Humans are understood as intrinsically untruthful, since they no longer present themselves in their "natural" state: "Can Truth, . . . in its 'natural' openness and thrust [*Andringlichkeit*], be in any way compatible with the nature of a 'clothed' human being?" (Blumenberg 1998: 62). For St Ambrose, a Milanese bishop at the end of the fourth century, clothing is the evidence that Adam and Eve's descendants continue to live in a state of deceit and concealment –

from each other and from God (Miles 1989: 93). Clothing is the first human gratification, a palliative response to the unpleasant emotion of shame:

> [Adam and Eve] added gratification so as to increase the idle pleasures of this world, sewing, as it were, leaf upon leaf in order to conceal and cover the organ of generation. (Ambrose, *Paradise*, quoted in Miles 1989: 93)

Ambrose parallels clothing and language, since they are both forms and evidence of corruption, as is, indeed, even nakedness itself, now that it has been despoiled:

> Whoever, therefore, violates the command of God has become naked and despoiled, a reproach to himself. He wants to cover himself and hide his genitals with fig leaves, making use, as it were, of empty and idle talk which the sinner interweaves word after word with fallacies for the purpose of shielding himself from his awareness of his guilty deed. (Ambrose, *Paradise*, quoted in Miles 1989: 93)

Like the layers of clothing that cover the now despoiled nakedness of fallen man,[24] the layers of idle talk are distractions from the truth of sin. Clothing and empty language are both forms of deceit – empty of truth, and actively misleading. Like clothing, idle or empty talk obstructs spontaneous and unmediated knowledge of the world. Untruthfulness is thus the fundamental state of postlapsarian humanity, a rupture of the "natural" human state of unselfconsciousness and oneness with God. Clothing (and in Ambrose's version even nudity itself) becomes a metonym of this rupture, symbolizing alienation from God and nature, and from the self, in the form of shamed self-consciousness. This is not just a matter of individual human ontology, but of the nature of human society, since in this reading, clothing is the primal instance of the symbolic order.

At its core, this theology engages with the long-held idea that human beings are fundamentally double. The idea of the human self as split in two was famously articulated by Plato in his doctrine of the Forms, and taken up by Christianity, which saw man as fundamentally divided between mortal body and eternal soul. Descartes secularized this split into a body/mind division via his conception of the body as a machine-like device subject to the laws of nature, and distinct from consciousness, "a distinctively modern version of the notion of soul" (Grosz 1994: 7). Onto this split is mapped a whole series of other, highly value-laden, qualities: naked/clothed; mortal/divine; animal/spirit; pitiful/noble. This tradition has lived on as a fundamentally ambiguously defined humanity. Philosophically, it is possible to understand this doubleness either as a fundamental duality in human nature or, nostalgically, as a movement away from a primal, unalienated, human nature to a second, derivative form. The various imagined definers of humanity (e.g. self-consciousness, morality, clothing, language, social institutions, tool-use) are also often layered onto one another. Particular philosophical streams then take up the question of relations between any of these supposed markers of humanity (e.g. the relationship between clothing and language, morality, or self-consciousness, or the relationship between language and tool use). Logically, both ways of understanding human nature as dual (the dialectic and the nostalgic) allow for ambiguities about the natural or proper state of humanness, as well as for moralizing about corruption of the "true" human state.

The philosophical homology most relevant here is an imagined relationship between clothing and language. In the Western tradition, both dualist and nostalgic conceptions of this relationship have been formulated. Over the centuries, writers and thinkers have explored most of the logical options that could bind clothing, nakedness and language use together. Four patterns recur. They can be summed up rather baldly as follows: first, nudity is pure, clothing is corrupt, language is corrupt; second, nudity is sinful, clothing is corrupt, and language is corrupt; third, nudity, clothing and language are all (potentially) sacred, but to different degrees; fourth, nudity is not a state to be idealized; language and clothing are both necessarily alienated and alienating, but they are nonetheless productive of human subjectivity and sociality. (A fifth possibility, that nudity is impure and clothing chaste, I take to be a moral rather than philosophical argument, and one too familiar to be of special interest here. The moral valuation placed on nudity is the subject of Chapter 2.) I will give a brief sense of the first three streams of argument, before turning my attention in greater depth to the fourth tradition, in which both clothing and language figure as metonyms of productive loss.

The first tradition, in which clothing figures as a sadly alienated result of either, variously, humankind's Fallen state or the needless and often hypocritical social dogmas that make clothing a false necessity, is fairly straightforward and needs little exemplification. The analogy runs as follows: just as clothing is a corruption of the natural human state of pure, naked embodiment, so too language(s) is/are a sad rupture from the imagined ideal of total communication among humans and between humans and God (as exemplified in the Tower of Babel story). Both clothing and language, insofar as they are the manifestations of human cultures, express and promote our alienation (from God and from each other). In particular, they divide us along gender, class and racial lines, since both clothing and language seat us into specifically valued and hierarchized social positions. We are forced to take up the pronoun "she" or "he," just as we are forced to wear the trappings of our sex, and are forced to "wear" a skin colour. Human society is thus built on alienation from God and between peoples, and on a division between the sexes and a mortification of female weakness. In the Christian tradition, gender and class have been understood in this way. As Miles (1989: 93) notes, clothing symbolizes "Eve's subjection to Adam; the first gender arrangements occurred simultaneously with the first clothing." This gender order is underpinned by violence. In the Adam and Eve story, the Fall brings eternal wrath onto the first Mother; in *Penguin Island* (France 1909) the first clothing provokes the first violence – a rape.[25] The Adam and Eve tale does not explicitly address questions of race, but the story of the Tower of Babel does, figuring language(s) as part of humankind's alienation from each other and from God. As we will see in the discussion of colonialism in Chapter 3, clothes have not only been a metaphor for social differentiation but also concretely functioned as instruments of racial domination.

For a radical, clothes can function as a powerful symbol of the hypocrisies and inequities enacted in the name of the social. An example of this is the early-twentieth-century satirist John Langdon-Davies, who saw nakedness as the true condition of humanness. For Langdon-Davies (1928), clothing is "corrupt" because it creates false distinctions between humans, the kinds of divisions and deceptions for which veils, masquerades and even make-up have long served as a symbol. In his book *Lady Godiva: The Future of Nakedness*, he satirizes the moralism, hypocrisy, self-interest and, above all, fear that have brought about the strange paradox by which "natural" nakedness could have become "an unnatural and vicious condition of the human body" (Langdon-Davies 1928: 12), and indeed, even a crime.

The second philosophical stream is perhaps best understood as a pessimistic extension of the first. It is exemplified by the quotations from St Ambrose given earlier. Not only are clothing and idle chatter metonyms of humankind's sinful state, as above, but even nudity itself is corrupt from the moment of Eve's primordial sin. Once nakedness knows itself, it is already too late; it has become corrupt. This idea of nakedness as already corrupt, since it was born out of sin, provides at least a part-explanation for the emergence and persistence of an otherwise perverse trope: that of nudity as a form of costume. Of course, pure comic inversion is at least one reason for it, as in popular locutions that figure nakedness as a form of dress ("in your birthday suit," "in Adam's garb"). But there is also a philosophical undercurrent. For example, St Ambrose distinguished two kinds of nakedness, each of which he imagined as a form of clothing: nakedness before sin (where Adam and Eve were clothed with the garments of virtue) and nakedness after sin (Miles 1989: 92). The trope of nakedness as a form of clothing, costume or masquerade will be discussed in more detail below.

In a third tradition, the implicit parallel between clothing and language is not part of a pessimistic lament for lost purity, but part of a conception of the self as layered rather than split. In his elegy *To His Mistress Going to Bed*,

John Donne reworks the old trope of the world as sacred text to consider women as a layered set of mysteries. Women's clothing and adornments are likened to mere pictures, or the cover of a book, while their naked bodies are the sacred text inside, for worthy readers only:

> Gems which you women use
> Are like Atlanta's balls, cast in men's views,
> That when a fool's eye lighteth on a gem,
> His earthly soul may covet theirs, not them.
> Like pictures, or like books' gay coverings made
> For laymen, are all women thus arrayed;
> Themselves are mystic books, which only we
> Whom their imputed grace will dignify
> Must see revealed.

(Donne 1971: lines 35–43)

Inside the covering we have not nakedness, but more text, but it is text of a different quality. Clothing is a mere adornment, mere pictures; nakedness is more sacred, a mystical text.

For post-structural thinkers, too, there is no lament for lost purity, since in post-structuralism, the very idea of a pure origin has become impossible. Neither nudity nor clothing can be corruptions, since there is no pure, universal, original state from which they can be deviations. Post-structuralist thought does not see nudity as the pure, natural bedrock of human embodiment. The analogy with language persists in post-structuralism via the key theoretical idea of "textuality," and in postmodernism via that of performance. Across the conceptual chasm that separates these contemporary theories from earlier philosophical and religious thought, contemporary motifs and metaphors for nudity still resonate with their forebears, though they sit on altogether different philosophical foundations. Nudity can still be imagined as a form of clothing – masquerade, veil, costume – but not in opposition to some putatively "real" bedrock of humanity. In anthropology, for example, nudity-as-clothing can appear as the category of "ritual nudity," in which the theorist analyses the way nudity can function as a kind of costume in ritual or magic (see, for example, Bonfante 1989). Some theorists of theatre or performance, especially postmodern theorists, have also been interested in nudity as costume or as textuality (see Toepfer (1996) on postmodern theatre, or Barthes (1973) on striptease). Everyday expressions also suggest homologies between the naked body and items of clothing (e.g. the term "sleeve" for a full-length arm tattoo). There may be, perhaps, a bodily experience that accompanies the paradoxical idea of the naked body as clothed. Can one sometimes wear one's nakedness like clothes? Although many of the nudists I interviewed would not find the concept of the costume of nudity appealing, so attached are they to the idea of nakedness as a total *shedding*, some of the people I interviewed who were involved in performance were quite comfortable with this idea. The photographic model Karen, for example, described how she had felt dressed when being photographed by an erotic photographer, since it was so clear that her naked body was being "arranged."

To sum up so far: for early thinkers, nakedness was often either a lost purity, perhaps irretrievably corrupted, and clothes a sad necessity. For postmodern thinkers, both nakedness and clothing are "impure," but in a new sense: they are culturally and historically produced and experienced. What I am calling the fourth tradition stands historically and conceptually somewhere in between, at a place of struggle and ambivalence about the nobility of the human body and human institutions. This tradition takes alienation as a given, but is still somewhat optimistic, since it sees both language and clothing as productive of the value of humanness. Whereas for many early theologians clothes were always already corrupt (an unconscious assumption that, incidentally, still permeates a lot of thinking about fashion, if not clothing *per se*), some later thinkers came to understand clothes more ambivalently. While they could still be seen negatively as evidence of human difference (and/or alienation from God), they could also be valued positively as evidence of human sociality and human distinctiveness. The symbolic order is thus productive (in that it enables subjectivity, communication, culture) but also inevitably alienated, in that it cannot replace the idea of unmediated intimacy with reality, and in that it is hierarchically and violently classed (and, modern commentators might add, gendered and racial).

The foremost exponent of this idea was the nineteenth-century writer Thomas Carlyle, in whose work we find the most systematic and sustained use of clothing as a metaphor not just for language but also for culture and its institutions more generally. The metaphor forms the basis for Carlyle's (1987) fictional work *Sartor Resartus* (which means "The Tailor Re-Tailored"). This work purports to be extracts from a German "clothes-philosopher" Professor Teufelsdröckh, edited and commented upon by an English editor for an English audience. *Sartor Resartus* depicts clothing not as a lamentable distancing from the Godhead but as part of the social trappings necessary for the housing of spirit, the prime instance of and metaphor for both the necessity and the fallibility of human systems. Clothing and culture are figured ambivalently rather than as simple corruptions of purer states.

Teufelsdröckh's starting point is the inherent duality of humankind – naked and clothed; pitiful and wondrous; mortal flesh and divine spirit. Clothes are by nature ambiguous. On the one hand, they are breeders of class and difference, and yet they are also an example of and metaphor for the valuable human systems in which spirit manifests itself. The doubleness of clothes comes from an inherent doubleness in humans themselves, who are, intrinsically, both naked and clothed. To recall a phrase used by Barthes (1972: 93) in his discussion of striptease, clothes are "superfluous yet essential." "To the eye of vulgar Logic, what is man?" asks Teufelsdröckh. "An omnivorous Biped that wears Breeches" (Carlyle 1987: 51). This definition assumes both nakedness and its inevitable corollary, clothing, to be a primal part of the definition of humanness. While clothes are not a natural human property "like the leaves of trees, like the plumage of birds" (p. 4), they are a kind of tool, and the human being is "a Tool-using Animal" (p. 32). Clothes are thus part of humanness, but they are evidence and example of human society rather than human nature. Humans may be naked, but *society* "is founded upon Cloth" (p. 41). Clothes, then, have made (socialized) humans out of (primal) Man: "Clothes gave us individuality, distinctions, social polity" (p. 32). Dissolve clothes and you dissolve civilization.[26] Both the "gold-mantled Prince" and the "russet-jerkined Peasant" (p. 45) are at base naked bipeds, but Cloth helps to cover this fact.

Teufelsdröckh depicts the human need for tailored clothing as pitiful and disgusting, especially in contrast to "self-tailoring" animals:

> The Horse I ride has his own whole fell: strip him of the girths and flaps and extraneous tags I have fastened round him, and the noble creature is his own sempster and weaver and spinner: nay his own bootmaker, jeweller, and man-milliner; he bounds free through the valleys, with a perennial rainproof court-suit on his body; wherein warmth and easiness of fit have reached perfection. . . . While I – Good Heaven! – have thatched myself over with the dead fleeces of sheep, the bark of vegetables, the entrails of worms, the hides of oxen or seals, the felt of furred beasts; and walk abroad a moving Rag-screen, overheaped with shreds and tatters raked from the Charnel-house of Nature, where they would have rotted, to rot on me more slowly! (Carlyle 1987: 44–5)

As in *Penguin Island* (France 1909), clothes are seen as ushering in a psycho-logical order (the invention of modesty and shame), and a social order (the invention of rank or class). (They also usher in a gender and race order, though *Sartor Resartus* doesn't discuss this.) But whereas for the author of *Penguin Island* this social order is inevitably corrupt and alienated, founded as it is upon difference, for Carlyle, the social, though divided and fractured, is an inevitable corollary of spirit's need to manifest itself. The wonder of wonders is that a human being is not just a pitiful naked wretch, but "also a Spirit, and unutterable Mystery of Mysteries" (Carlyle 1987: 45). Humankind, then, is spirit clothed in body clothed in cloth "clothed" in roles and institutions.

Underneath this world of "solemnities and paraphernalia" lies a "Naked World" (Carlyle 1987: 50).

Carlyle is a philosophical idealist, and *Sartor Resartus* is an implicit rejoinder from German Idealism to English empiricism or utilitarianism. It depicts flesh as a kind of wrapping or packaging of Spirit, a formulation that echoes both Plato's conception of the body as the covering of the soul and Erasmus' figuration of clothes as the body's body (this latter explicitly articulated in *Sartor*).[27] The human body is thus paradoxical; it is a symbol, and like all symbols, it both reveals and conceals. Through symbols, we experience the Infinite in the Finite; we look through things into Things (Carlyle 1987:155). Clothing makes Spirit manifest (by giving it form) but it also conceals (or clothes) naked Spirit (p. 166). In this, it is the Ur-type of all symbols, both embodying and covering Spirit. The body too is a form of clothing, the symbol or garment of God – "the Garment of Flesh . . . textured in the Loom of Heaven" (p. 51). This makes it the most fundamental of human symbols. But *all* the things of this world are symbols, in that they give form to spirit. As William Henry Hudson writes in an introduction to *Sartor Resartus*:

> Visible things are but the manifestations, emblems, or clothings of spirit. The material universe itself is only the vesture or symbol of God; man is a spirit, though he wears the wrappings of the flesh; and in everything that man creates for himself he merely attempts to give body or expression to thought. (Hudson 1908: x–xi)

There is nothing, then, that is not metaphorical, the whole universe being "but one vast Symbol of God" (Carlyle 1987: 166). All the manifestations of society – art, culture, government, language, institutions – can be considered symbols and thus a form of clothing. In sum, clothes are negatively figured as the consequence of the Fall of humankind, but also positively – as something to be rejoiced in, "a warm moveable House, a Body round thy Body, wherein that strange THEE of thine [sits] snug" (p. 46).

This ambivalence has made Carlyle an object of critique by both more radical and more nostalgic theorists. The former prefer a more politically straightforward mobilization of the metaphor of clothing as metonym of inequitable social divisions. Langdon-Davies, for example, castigates Carlyle for being the lukewarm son of St Paul – a "would-be iconoclast and rebel in thought" (Langdon-Davies 1928: 59), whose Idealism is a "triumph of Saul's haberdashery" (p. 59).[28] For although Carlyle is critical of the role of clothing in the production of social class, his philosophical idealism and his theology ultimately reconcile him somewhat to what he perceives as the inevitability of human inequity. His theological purpose is at least as important to him as a political one.

Carlyle's struggle brings him to a surprisingly modern conclusion, one that brings *some* aspects of his thought to a place not unlike post-structuralism, though with the crucial distinction that he remains an unqualified idealist. Finally, his insistence on the contingency of both clothing and nakedness and his fascination with the social and cultural manifestations of human existence lead him to a subtle understanding of symbolic processes. Carlyle's schema, despite his idealism, leads him to see clothes as exemplary symbols – symbols, in fact, of symbolization itself. Clothing is his metaphor for metaphor (in fact, a metonym of metaphor). What does this mean for nudity? Well, the logical corollary of Carlyle's schema (although he is so focused on clothing that he doesn't draw it) is that nakedness is a metaphor for the lack of metaphor. Carlyle's claim that there is nothing that is not metaphor, if extended to include nudity itself, would lead us to the very modern proposition (which is at the heart of this book) that nakedness too is a metaphor, and as social and cultural a phenomenon as clothing. This is very different from the realist position so common in everyday discourse – that nakedness is a pure, universally experienced, natural state. Moreover, the realization of nudity's metaphoricity allows one to analyse what this metaphor *does*, politically – in other words, to consider the politics of "nothingness." For nakedness' putative nothingness is a seeming bedrock on which battles for the "all" and the "nothing" of human existence can be fought.

Nudity as a "Nucleus of our Sense of Order"

George Lakoff and Mark Johnson (1980: 22) argue that metaphors reflect the most fundamental values of a society and are a key component of cultural coherence. We have just seen how nakedness and clothing have functioned as metaphors in debates about the very idea of the human. Freud, too, saw nakedness as fundamental – in his case, as core psychical material. In his lecture "Symbolism in Dreams," Freud (1963: 153) claimed that despite the wealth of symbolic material produced in dreams, there are relatively few concepts symbolized: the human body, parents, children, brothers and sisters, birth, death, nakedness, the house and sexual life. That nakedness should figure among this short and primal list shows how fundamental Freud took it to be.

Kenneth Clark also saw nakedness as pivotal. The subjects of art, he says, have often been unimportant in themselves and yet have been able to function as "nuclei, so to say, of ["men's"] sense of order" (Clarke 1956: 4). The naked body, though merely a point of departure for the artwork, is a nucleus "rich in associations" (p. 4), which, while they are transmuted by the artwork, are never entirely lost in it. Although a range of human passions are "held in solution" by the nude, the core human impulses that the nude transmutes are sexual-reproductive: "memories of all the things we wish to do with ourselves; and first of all, we wish to perpetuate ourselves" (p. 6). To paraphrase Clark, the human body, especially in its naked form, can most illuminatingly be thought of as a "nucleus of our sense of order." While there is much to question in Clark's account, it's important to note that he recognized the role of nakedness in expressing a society's sense of its core values. Clark's insight is that a subject of art (in this case the naked body) might be at the heart of a given society's sense of order. As we will see, though, Clark's conflation of one particular ordering of gender, sex and sexuality with a universal humanity is not inconsequential. This brings me to the question of veiling, nakedness and femininity.

Nudity and Femininity: The Masquerade

Although the theological and philosophical treatment of nakedness and clothing considered so far proceeds as though both were simply *human* states, it is of course the case that the meaning and significance of both nakedness and clothing has a great deal to do with gender. The philosophical unease with clothing is even more pronounced when it comes to *fashion*. While it is only since the Industrial Revolution that fashion has come to be understood so definitively as a marker of gender more than rank (Silverman 1986), it is indubitable that the "philosophic hostility" to fashionable dress (Hanson 1993: 229) has a gendered dimension to it. Karen Hanson argues that fashionable dress (as opposed to clothing *per se*) is disquieting for traditional Western philosophy, which is often rationalist, masculinist, and wary of both body and pleasure. Fashion is, she argues, associated with change, instability, surfaces, appearance and passivity. Philosophy's traditional "search for lasting truths and enduring values" has made it sceptical of all that is associated with the mundane, the corporeal and the transient (Hanson 1993: 231). The philosophical distrust of worldliness, transience and appearance is thus symptomatic of (and a major contributor to) a disdain for values and interests often deemed feminine. From make-up, to the masquerade, to the veil, femininity has often been associated with triviality, passivity, inauthenticity and vanity.

Many women say they feel "naked" without their make-up, and yet make-up has often been subject to moral denigration. Imagined as a form of clothing or mask, it has been regarded as a sign of inauthenticity. A long tradition sees make-up as part of the feminine repertoire of masquerade techniques, an artifice used to disguise authentic identity. Whereas in pre-modern or tribal societies facial decoration reflected group identity, in the modern West it functions as a marker of individual identity more than social emplacement, except, perhaps, in subcultural uses. Its use outside of ritual or theatrical contexts has by and large become restricted to women, which is partly why it has been subject to moral judgement: "Whereas body decoration is regarded as active and purposeful behaviour, the use of make-up and cosmetics is interpreted as passive and trivial behaviour" (Craik 1994: 153–4).

The masquerade, both as historical practice and as metaphor, has likewise been a cultural site in which the complexities of gender identity and desire have been played out in contradictory and politically uncertain ways. The costume-masquerade metaphor is linked to a traditional understanding of femininity as layers of clothes and veils. In this tradition, woman's "genius for finery" is inextricably linked to her derivativeness, to her "instinct for the *secondary* role" (Nietzsche 1973: 84, original emphasis). An important use of this metaphor as a way of understanding femininity is found in the work of psychoanalyst Joan Rivière, who imagined femininity itself as a kind of masquerade. In her essay "Womanliness as Masquerade," Rivière (1986: 35) argued that "women who wish for masculinity may put on a mask of womanliness to avert anxiety and the retribution feared from men." She describes cases of capable, intellectual women who nonetheless revert to "compulsive ogling and coquetting" (p. 37) in their relations with men, in order not to be found to possess a prohibited masculinity.[29] Womanliness is worn like a mask, "much as a thief will turn out his pockets and ask to be searched to prove that he has not the stolen goods" (p. 38). Rivière goes on to ask how this assumed womanliness differs from "genuine" womanliness, and concludes that "they are the same thing" (p. 38). Femininity consists precisely of a mimicry, a dissimulation of a fundamental masculinity (Heath 1986: 49).

French philosopher Luce Irigaray (1985: 133–4) agrees that femininity is a form of masquerade, since for a girl to become a "normal" woman, she must enter into male-constructed circuits of desire, and see herself via the desires and fantasies of men. Thus, women's experience of nakedness must differ from men's, since women's everyday performances of their gender are already so structurally convoluted, and since both female fashion and female nudity are strongly and particularly fetishized in the visual economies of the dominant culture. In a discussion of sexual difference and identity, Irigaray (1985) discusses what she calls "containers" or "envelopes" of identity. This is a metaphor used to express the idea that to have an identity, one needs a stable "container" or place that acts as the anchor or ground of identity. Woman, she argues, acts as a container or place for man. Her role as literal "container" for the embryo has been culturally enlarged into a further role of moral stability and stasis; she must be the stable originary point that allows man to move away, to act, to journey, without dissipating or losing his identity. But that function is not structurally reciprocated (though it may be reciprocated by particular men). Man does not, structurally, act as point of departure for woman's journey, nor as holding place awaiting her return. The holding function that stabilizes identity is structurally asymmetrical; woman, having no "proper" place of her own, cannot receive, but is condemned to be, structurally, a giver.

For Irigaray, woman is psychologically naked, for she has no place of her own, no container of identity:

> In the meantime, this ethical question comes into play in matters of *nudity* and *perversity*. Woman must be nude because she is not situated, does not situate herself in her place. Her clothes, her makeup, and her jewels are the things with which she tries to create her container(s), her envelope(s). She cannot make use of the envelope that she is, and must create artificial ones. (Irigaray 1993: 11, original emphasis)

"Man" provides a physical container for "woman" – the house he buys for her, or shuts her up in – but this is not the same as the fleshly container that woman is for man:

> He contains or envelops her with walls while enveloping himself and his things with her flesh. The nature of these envelopes is not the same: on the one hand, invisibly alive, but with barely perceivable limits; on the other, visibly limiting or sheltering, but at the risk of being prison-like or murderous if the threshold is not left open. (Iragaray 1993: 11)

Irigaray thus uses nudity as both exemplum and metaphor for woman's primal unsituatedness, and she sees fashionable dress as the things that hold her in place. Woman is provider first of literal and later of psychological shelter for the man, receiving in return a physical but not a psychological home from him. Woman must create her own "envelope" to give shape to her "naked" identity. Woman is naked; femininity is the veil or mask donned not so much to cover that nakedness as to actually give female subjectivity a form. The psychoanalytical theme of the masquerade is thus a reworking of longstanding metaphors of cloaking and nakedness in order to attempt to understand the psychical import of an asymmetrically gendered symbolic order.

Angela Carter's discussion of women's nakedness foreshadowed some of the terms of this debate, in particular, the idea that "woman" is made up of her accessories. Carter (1982: 103) writes scathingly of the "articles which will accessorise the nakedness of the pin-up, her erotic apparatus of beads, feathers, white stockings, black stockings, corsets, scarves, bodices, frilly knickers, [and] hats," which she sees as sanctioned by the tradition of the nude in fine art. Feminists have been uncertain whether to read the masquerade as a metaphor for women's inevitable subservience to a patriarchal gender order or as a site for possible subversions of it (see Craft-Fairchild 1993). Irigaray's intellectual and political project involves diagnosing the inequities and asymmetries in patriarchal structures and seeking in the hidden spaces of these structures the seeds of a feminine difference that can be excavated and celebrated. Carter (1982: 103), too, sees some advantages in women's disadvantages, some positive possibilities in woman's clouds of accessories. The real woman's nakedness lies hidden underneath the patriarchal invention of "the nude" and remains a hidden and untouchable source of connection to her own body: "Our relation to our own bodies is both more intimate and more abstract than that of most men to theirs" (p. 103). For Carter, while woman might be primally naked (in the sense that no automatic symbolic power attaches to her person), the positive side of this mystification of her body is that her symbolic power can never be stripped from her:

> Naked, a woman can never be less than herself for her value in the world resides more in her skin than in her clothes. Though, naked, she loses her name and becomes "a blue nude," "the bather," "woman dressing," "Suzie," "Gina," "Europa," "Eve," "Venus," this personal anonymity is the price of a degree of mystification of her naked body that means she can accede to a symbolic power as soon as her clothes are off, whereas a man's symbolic power resides in his clothes, indicators of his status. (Carter 1982: 103–4)

Carter asks us to imagine the different import of the story of *The Emperor's New Clothes* if its protagonist were a woman, surmising that the stripping away would be evidence not of her foolishness, but of her authority (as in the case of Lady Godiva).

There have been feminist attempts to rethink or revalue fashion and its relation to feminine identity. Phenomenologist Iris Marion Young (1990), for example, argues that some elements of women's experience of fashion do evade the oppressiveness of the way the gaze is structured in modern patriarchies. She describes the importance of the female bonding that can surround female fashion-play; the fantasy of "multiple and changing identities without the anxiety of losing oneself" (Young 1990: 185) that fashion play can engender; and the importance of touch (rather than just visuality) to the pleasure in clothing. Even within the realm of visuality, the question of oppression and passivity can be rethought. Kaja Silverman (1986), for example, argues that the historical importance of ostentatious display to upper-class and aristocratic men as well as to women proves that male subjectivity and sexuality need not be understood as necessarily stable and active, in contrast to the imagined fluidity, instability and passivity of female subjectivity. History reminds us that there have been formations in which certain male subjects have been as dependent for their identity on the gaze of the Other as women are currently envisaged as being (Silverman 1986: 143). Feminine display should therefore not always be understood as implying "women's subjugation to a controlling male gaze" (p. 139). Within philosophy, Karen Hanson (1993) has argued that although fashionable dress is often decried because of its role in games of social appearance, it need not be seen as passive, trivial or superficial. It is time, she says, that the philosophical disdain for worldliness and appearances be subjected to feminist revision. If fashion implies a self-conscious relation to one's body, why is such self-consciousness *devalued* in philosophy? After all,

> [s]elf-consciousness, it must be remembered, is generally an epistemological *advance*. One would need a special argument to show that the self-consciousness connected with an awareness of and interest in one's appearance is inherently retrograde. (Hanson 1993: 239, original emphasis)

Such a manoeuvre takes Hanson away from the nostalgia and lament that characterize so many discussions of the Eden myth. Rather, she reassesses self-consciousness as a positive value rather than a sad fall from blissful unself-consciousness, and argues that the primal tale of the birth of human society is due for a rereading:

> Even the Western myth that most clearly promotes nostalgia for the Eden before self-consciousness deserves a different reading by committed philosophers. When Adam and Eve eat from the tree of knowledge, their eyes *are* opened. They know they are naked, so they sew together the fig leaves and make aprons. When God subsequently adds to their wardrobe, making the coats of skins, his act of clothing is treated as – it *is* – a ceremony of investiture: accompanying the robing are God's solemn words, "Behold, the man is become as one of us, to know good and evil" (Genesis 3:22). (Hanson 1993: 239, original emphasis)

Hanson (1993) derives this rereading of clothing in the Adam and Eve tale from Dennis Senchuk (1985), who provocatively inverts the dominant reading of Genesis as the story of a Fall into humanness. Senchuk chooses, wilfully, to read the Eden story not as one of loss but as the story of a female-led uprising into the plenitude of rich human life.

But meanwhile, the tradition of seeing woman as her clothing, make-up, veils or mask, and the denigration of such devices, most commonly construes femininity as a fundamental dissimulation. The plain truth of masculine subjectivity is contrasted with the veiled mystery of feminine subjectivity, notoriously unknowable. Femininity is imagined as both inauthentic (a mimicry) and deceitful. Public reception of the nude dancer and spy Mata Hari is a case in point. The public regarded Mata Hari's nudity as evidence not of her openness but of her dangerous duplicity, a reading encouraged by her involvement in espionage and by "the dense web of lies, fabrications, and deceptions" of which her public image was made up (Toepfer, 1997: 25).

A misogynist strain of the biblical tradition certainly construed femininity as superficial, vain and deceitful, but nowadays, Western women and men tend to judge only certain *styles* of femininity as superficial, vain or inauthentic (those, for example, in which a woman can be deemed to place "too great" a reliance on clothes for identity). Modern Westerners are also perhaps used to displacing elements of the idea of deceit and/or inscrutability (although usually not vanity) onto their own Others – Middle Eastern women, whose veiling practices are often read as evidence, variously, of oppression, passivity, inscrutability or sexual mystique. It is not that veiling was absent from the Judeo-Christian heritage; indeed, the veiling of women was a feature of Roman, Greek and Jewish societies probably before it was taken up within Islam (El Guindi 1999: 148–50). It is rather that modernity has imagined itself as a great unveiling.

Within Western psychoanalytical theory, however, the metaphor of veiled femininity is still of importance, despite some philosophical attempts to rework it. If woman is primally naked, and femininity a form of dress, what happens when you strip away the veils? In a gesture that many feminists reject as essentialist (though, given the complexity of her work even this is not entirely certain), Luce Irigaray (1985) seeks traces of an authentic feminine bodily syntax that might be detectable underneath the veils. She seeks a residue of the "something else" that has not been (cannot be?) incorporated into the "system of values that is not hers" – that escapes the moment when the masquerade of femininity is congealed via the operations of the female Oedipus complex (Iragaray 1985: 134). She imagines this distinctive female mode as a form of language, discernible in women's suffering and laughter, and, if one knows how to hear it, in the language women use in psychoanalysis. She thinks it most obviously subsists in "the gestural code of women's bodies" (p. 134), what she calls a feminine bodily syntax. The latter is difficult to discern, however, since it has often been either paralysed or incorporated into the masquerade. Like Hélène Cixous (1981), who coined the term *écriture féminine*, Irigaray is interested in the attempt to (re)discover and (re)create a distinctive, bodily mode of feminine language.

While Irigaray seeks and detects residues of, if not an authentic femininity, then of something that has not been fully incorporated into the patriarchal masquerade of femininity, others might fear that if the accoutrements of femininity are stripped away, *nothing remains*. That is one possible interpretation of the sequence of photographs of model Veruschka (see Figure 1.2). This

Figure 1.2 Vera Lehndorff / Holger Trülzsch. "Mimicry Dress Art." What remains
when the trappings of femininity are stripped away? Peterskirchen
1973.

sequence plays with the common-sense idea that a stripping away of veils leads
to the revelation of an authentic woman underneath. In this case, the gradual
peeling back of the accoutrements of femininity reveals not a final nakedness,
but the nothingness of femininity outside of its patriarchal constitution. Is this
darkness a place of joyous escape, or a place of oblivion?

Nudity and Humanness

> [T]o be naked is to be so much nearer to the being a man, than to go in livery.
>
> Charles Lamb, "A Complaint of the Decay of Beggars in the Metropolis"

Having considered the specifics of feminine identity, I want to turn back to
the idea of humanity as a universal, for an idea of "the" human has its uses.
Considering humanness at its borders with the non-human can remind us quite
simply of the role that clothing (and hence nakedness) play in establishing the
borders of the human. Humanness is always defined *against* something,
whether implicitly or explicitly. In order to understand how nakedness is used
in contests over humanness, we need to look at what might lie outside the
category, that is, what the category of "human" might be including or keeping

at bay. The human has been defined in opposition to such categories as the divine, the animal, the monster, the ex-human (corpse or ghost), the machine and the thing. Recently, it has also been defined against the alien and various forms of "posthuman" entity. In the modern era, humanness has increasingly come to mean separateness from the rest of the living and non-living organisms and things around us. But borderlines are compelling, and many different ideals, fears or fantasies about human nature have continued to flourish in literature, the arts and sciences. Contemporary culture is fascinated by the borders of humanness, as evident in the explosion of belief or interest in such borderline or hybrid forms as cyborgs, artificial intelligence, aliens, angels, spirits or fairies. Ideas to do with the interconnections between humanity and other facets of the life-world are being (re)attested in myriad forms – from religious revival, to New Ageism, the Green movement, contemporary cosmology and cybernetics. Postmodernity is witnessing its own expansion in the category of the human, at its border with the machine, the divine, the animal and the alien.

Humanness has often been understood as morally ambiguous, depending on what it is being defined against. It can be seen as the attainment of an honourable state or as a pitiable reduction. "Pure Man" is both "the measure of all things" (Protagoras) and a "poor, bare, forked animal" (*Lear*), "the quintessence of dust" (*Hamlet*). When measured against the divine, humanness will mostly be subordinate, though a Romantic tradition sees it as richer, more emotionally and psychologically complex than divinity itself. For example, Hollywood films often tell the story of how machines or angels become human, and what they lose and gain in the transformation. They lose magical powers, omniscience, immortality (or non-mortality), but gain something romantically understood as more precious – a richly ambiguous emotional life.

It makes an interesting study to consider nudity at the edges of humanness – for example, where humanness borders animality. Nowadays, we don't, normally speaking, think of other living things, like plants, as being nude (or naked) outside of scientific discourse, where the word "naked" still carries this meaning (e.g. bird chicks can be described as "naked"). In everyday speech, if an animal loses its feathers or fur, we normally speak of it as having become "bald" rather than naked (as in the bald eagle). In our everyday way of thinking, animals are rarely thought of as being nude, even though you can buy blankets and saddles for your horse and coats for your dog. The use of the terms "naked" or "nude" for an animal is so unusual in everyday language that it is mostly found in satire or in humour. The two Matthew Martin cartoons reproduced here (Figures 1.3 and 1.4) demonstrate twin facets of nudity as an exclusively human category. In each case, humour is derived from the fact that the humanness of clothing (and therefore nudity) is being violated:

Figure 1.3

Figures 1.3, 1.4 Clothing animals can produce humour. The first cartoon refers to the popular children's figures "Bananas in Pyjamas." Matthew Martin. "Bananas in Pyjamas" and "Crocodile Undee".
© 1995 Matthew Martin. From David Dale and Matthew Martin (1995) *480 Words on Anything.* Sydney: Hodder & Stoughton.

in one case when a piece of fruit is seen as being naked; in the other, when a crocodile is wearing underpants. In fact, this is a staple joke of classic American animations: a bird is blown up, loses its feathers, and covers its nakedness with its wings. See also Figure 1.5. Clothing is, as Angela Carter (1982: 98) puts it, "anti-nature," used to distinguish between "beings under social restraint and beings that are not." This, she says, can be seen in any circus: "It is amazing what a number of non-garments – bridles, plumes, tassels – even the liberty horses wear, to show to what degree they have suppressed their natural desire to run away" (Carter 1982: 98).

Our ambivalence about humanness explains why to render animals human-like is sometimes comic, sometimes degrading, depending on the valuation of both animality and humanity in a given context. The elderly orang-utan in *Babe 2: Pig in the City*, who cannot flee to safety until he has dressed himself in his waistcoat and trousers, is depicted as sadly humanized; his natural animality has been corrupted by humanness. Like Adam and Eve, he knows he is naked, and is ashamed. A woman was banned from a Sydney café in 1999 for having spoon-fed a dog dressed in a pink bib; the newspaper characterized her as sad and degraded for having so misapprehended her dog's nature. (Honesty compels me to admit that she did also try to make her dog talk into her mobile phone, which may have been a worse offence against animality than the bib.) I recently saw a dog clothed in a rather expensive looking coat made of the fake black and white cow skin that is currently in ironic fashion. This was on the one hand a kind of sartorial joke – dressing the dog in the deliberately fake-looking garb of a different animal – but it also showed the role of clothes as markers of social distinction, even by proxy. Animals can also be dressed in order to cover *human* shame. For example, Marina Warner (1985: 310) reports that in a 1919 re-enactment of Lady Godiva's ride through Coventry, not only did Godiva wear leotards (as she still does in any re-enactment), but even the *horse* wore trousers!

When animals are given something of the human, comedy (and occasionally pathos) may result; when the border crossing works in the other direction, there may also be comedy (as when humans dress up as animals in theatre or pantomime). But when humans are seriously thought of or treated as animals it is no longer a matter for jokes. The imagined borderline between the human and the animal can be a grave matter indeed. In Chapter 3, we will look at how the clothing/nudity opposition can play a role in policing the borderlines of "full" humanness, when we consider the case of the savage.

Nakedness or clothing are less important, I think, at other borderlines, such as that between human and object. Nonetheless, there are a few, relatively politically uncharged, ways in which an implicit homology between the human body and designed articles can make objects seem naked or dressed. After all,

AFRICA EXPOSED

Figure 1.5 "Africa Exposed." South African Airways advertisement, 1990, using nudity as an anthropomorphic device. Griffin Advertising.

many objects are made (consciously or otherwise) to mimic the human body, which provides, if not the "measure of all things," then an implied model or scale for much of the built and designed environment. Buildings not only take the human body as their foundation (in the sense that the dimensions of usable buildings always imply a human scale and spatiality) but also sometimes mimic bodies, or parts of bodies, especially faces. Furniture, for example, has "legs" or "arms," screws have "heads," needles have "eyes." This underlying homology often remains submerged, but is sometimes explicitly called into play, either by designers or users. Can an object, nowadays, be naked? The cliché of the chair legs covered in Victorian times to protect modesty springs to mind. This is more than likely to be a piece of folklore (Ellen Jordan calls it a piece of "apocryphal Victoriana"). There is only one written reference to it,[30] and even in Victorian times it surfaced as a satirical joke. Nonetheless, one respondent to the *Victoria* Internet list where I have sourced a discussion of the phenomenon did claim first-hand experience of the custom:

> I can testify that in Yorkshire, England, well after W.W.II, my grandmother, born in the Victorian era, had stockings on all four legs of her dining table, though they were barely visible below the enormous table-cover. just as her own stockinged legs were barely visible below her long skirts. (Hargreaves, website, original punctuation)

My point here is not really the veracity or otherwise of the practice, which I leave to the specialists, but the more general one, that objects can be haunted by humanness and that they can, as a result, occasionally be "naked." The most psychically and politically charged example of objects haunted by humanness is, of course, the domain of visual images, which will be considered in Chapter 4.

The border between humanity and the divine is also relevant. It is one of the features of Christian modernity that it conceives of God, animals and humans as (more or less) ontologically distinct. The incarnation in human form of Christ is thus absolutely crucial, theologically. Leo Steinberg (1996) has famously argued that in Renaissance art the genitals of Christ (as infant and as crucified man) became an iconographic index of his full humanness. He argues that the nudity of the infant and dead Christ in Renaissance painting was not blasphemous, impudent or irreverent – rather, it was the solemn iconographic vehicle for arguing the Incarnation, evidence that Christ was indeed "complete in all the parts of a man." In other words, nudity was emblematic of his humanness. Renaissance art was characterized by the deliberate use of detail for symbolic rather than naturalistic purposes, so Christ's genitals, which, moreover, do not merely figure incidentally, but are actively foregrounded visually, cannot be understood as a naturalistic detail, all the more so as their appearance contradicts the Gospel account of the infant Jesus as wrapped in swaddling clothes by Mary. Such images were common (Steinberg (1996) claims that there are at least 1,000 extant examples, and he reproduces 300 of them) and Renaissance artists intended them reverently. While some elements of Steinberg's thesis have been controversial, and though even sympathetic commentators have considered his argument a little overstated, most have nonetheless agreed with his basic tenet (Warner 1985: 305; Miles 1989: 143).

Feminist medievalist Caroline Walker Bynum (1991), though admiring of Steinberg's work, nonetheless problematizes his argument somewhat, in ways that are useful to my question here of nudity as an emblem of humanness. She agrees with Steinberg that Christ's humanation is theologically crucial and that by "humanation" theologians often meant "enfleshing" (Bynum 1991: 90). However, she criticizes Steinberg for what she perceives as his own, politically loaded, reduction – the focus on Christ's penis to the exclusion of other indices of his humanation. She argues that even before the Renaissance (the focus of Steinberg's study) medieval theologians and mystics were describing and depicting encounters with Christ in deeply bodily ways, and that it is not his penis alone that emblematizes his full humanness. There is an abundance of medieval texts and images that highlight the bleeding body of Christ, often feminizing it, and even depicting his bleeding side as breast- or womb-like. The tales of Christian mystics, both male and female, sound to modern readers like erotic encounters, so vividly do they describe the swooning ecstasy of union with Christ: Christ breathing deeply into their mouths, Christ's tongue entering the mouth, Christ penetrating deep into their bodies (Bynum 1991: 86). By focusing on genitality, Bynum argues, Steinberg repeats the patriarchal error of mapping maleness onto humanness.

While the details of this particular debate belong to art history,[31] the underlying problem is relevant to our study, in that what is at stake is an idea of generic or universal Man, and the nature of "his" embodiment. The problem turns on the difference between defining humanness (against its non-human others) and trying to make one generalizations when thinking *within* the category of the human. This latter operation produces political effects because there is no one type of body that could logically stand in for all others. Bodily differences (in age, sex, race and so on) are not secondary variants of some putatively primal "type." Elizabeth Grosz (among others) has persuasively argued that it is more helpful (conceptually and politically) to think of "a field of body types" (Grosz 1994: 22) rather than of "the" body, since such factors as sex, colour, age and so on are not incidental characteristics – mere variants on a putatively neutral, "normal" "Body" – but are fundamental facts of different forms of embodiment:

There is no one mode that is capable of representing the "human" in all its richness and variability. A plural, multiple field of possible body "types," no one of which functions as the delegate or representative of the others, must be created, a "field" of body types – young and old, black and white, male and female, animal and human, inanimate and animate – which, in being recognized in their specificity, cannot take on the coercive role of singular norm or ideals for all the others. (Grosz 1994: 22)

If there is no singular "Body," it follows that there is no singular "nude." And yet, "the" nude is a common concept, especially in the fine arts, where it is frequently used to imply the *female* nude (whence the rejoinder implied in the title of Lynda Nead's (1992) feminist study, *The Female Nude*).

Over the course of my research into nudity, each of the binary oppositions nominated above by Grosz (young/old; male/female; human/animal; black/white; animate/inanimate) has emerged as profoundly relevant to an understanding of the cultural functioning of nudity as a category in a given context. Classicist Larissa Bonfante (1989) has constructed a very similar list for the ancient world:

In Classical antiquity . . . the contrast between the clothed and the naked human body was used to express some of the most basic contrasts of the human experience: God and man, human and animal, man and woman, public world and private life, wealth and poverty, admiration and pity, citizen and slave, civilization and barbarism, spirit and flesh, life and death, power and helplessness. (Bonfante 1989: 569–70)

In other words, the opposition between nakedness and clothing lies at the heart of unconscious assumptions about what is most essentially human. These fundamental divisions persist in the contemporary world. Even today, being "over"-dressed (e.g. the veiled Muslim) or "under"-dressed (e.g. the "slut" or the "primitive") affects one's place in the hierarchy of humanness.

The border between the human and the non-human has been understood to be blurry, and humanness has often been understood as a scale or gradation. The humanist concept of "Man" of necessity involves "a definition of the human species, or simply the human," that can easily lead to an "infinite process of demarcation between the human, the more than human and the less than human" (Etienne Balibar, quoted in Montag 1997: 286). A particular human attribute (whiteness, masculinity, heterosexuality) is universalized not by assuming that all humans share it, but by using it as a marker of the human against the non-human (or the less-than-human). As Warren Montag (1997: 287) puts it, this involves "adjusting the boundaries of the human species," such that those who do not share it are seen to be non-human or scarcely human. In other words, any idea of humanness involves not only a division between human and non-human, but also the implicit or explicit imaging of internal boundaries dividing humanity into "types" and/or gradations. To take just one infamous example, Darwin conceived of humanity as a gradual ascent from the "savage" to the European. Often, these divisions can be mapped onto each other, as Warner's summary of anthropologist Edward Ardener's work makes clear:

> [H]uman beings bond themselves together as a whole to distinguish between humanity and non-humanity, according to one set of criteria; but within human society itself, in the same way as men and women together look upon animals as different, we distinguish between men and women, and bond with our own sex to see the other as different. (Warner 1985: 281)

The result, as we saw at the beginning of this chapter, is that "types" of humans or attributes of humanity can map onto each other, as for example, in infamous clusters like female/black/child/animal/irrational. Close to the "edge" of a particular quality used to define humanness (reason, a soul, language, as well as more visible attributes like sex or skin colour), "types" appear and proliferate: the less-than-human, the more-than-human. As we will see, nudity has had a role to play in the deeply ideological and power-laden processes by which people find themselves divided into categories: most fundamentally of all, the human and the non-human, but also, male/female; adult/child; civilized/savage; ideal/abject; human/animal; human/machine; insider/outside; familiar/alien.

As a state shared by everyone, and one ambiguously understood as both a noble bedrock and a degraded form of humanness, nakedness is an ideal tool in the assertion of difference and domination. Larissa Bonfante points out, for example, that this was the case with the valorization of athletic nudity in ancient Greece: "As it developed, Greek nudity came to mark a contrast between Greek and non-Greek, and also between men and women" (Bonfante 1989: 543). Thus, it is wrong to idealize the Greek relation to nudity; as Margaret Walters (1978: 11) points out, "it is simply that their taboos [around nudity] differ from ours and are therefore harder for us to recognize." Walters notes not only the gendering of the Greek nude ideal, but also the fact that the Greeks were "acutely anxious about the aging bodies of either sex" (p. 11). The Greek ideal was partial, subtended by harsh exclusions, and no doubt hard on the men who had to live up to it.

It may seem strange that a word that connotes nothingness, simplicity or bareness can be so clothed in meanings. I suggest that it is precisely in the "nothingness" of nakedness – its ability to symbolize the raw human being, the human being outside culture, time and artifice – that profound cultural operations are performed. In the name of the degree-zero humanity, all sorts of boundaries can be drawn, exclusions made, bodies regulated and disciplined, and cultural work performed. In the next chapter, we will look at some of these questions, when we examine the moral implications of the metaphor of nudity.

Notes

1. Mercer (1990) cites George Mosse's contention that the very word "Caucasian" is based on this assumption of white beauty. Mosse states that Fredrich Bluembach introduced it as a term for Europeans in general, and that it came from Bluembach's belief that the slopes of the Caucasus mountains in eastern Europe were the original home of the most beautiful European species (Mercer 1990: 250).

2. I would have liked to be able to consider the question of the naked face more closely, but space does not permit. On the one hand, it would be interesting to consider the question in relation to countries in which the face is often veiled. Emmanuel Levinas' characterization of the face of the Other as a form of nudity would also need to be considered. I am also intrigued by William Ewing's original suggestion that the restrictive and concealing clothing of nineteenth-century Europe might in part account for that century's fascination with phrenology and physiognomy, "which tried to 'read' into [the face and head] the inner constitution" (Ewing 1994: 12).

3. The adjective "topless" has existed in English since the late sixteenth century, but only since the mid-twentieth-century has it been able to refer to a garment, a woman herself or a place (e.g. a topless dress, a topless model or a topless beach).

4. The Indiana Code 35–45–4–1 states: "'Nudity' means the showing of the human male or female genitals, pubic area, or buttocks with less than a fully opaque covering, the showing of the female breast with less than a fully opaque covering of any part of the nipple, or the showing of covered male genitals in a discernibly turgid state." South Carolina law uses a similar phraseology. See *The Rec.Nude Legal FAQ* website and Posner and Silbaugh (1996).

5. I haven't been able to discover when this error arose. Sturtevant sources it in Gisbert Cuypert's *Observationes* I.7, but he cannot state its date: "the book is inaccessible to me," he writes (Sturtevant 1912: 324). As Sturtevant himself wrote this in 1912, and as British Prime Minister Gladstone allegedly made similar claims, the error dates at least from the late nineteenth century.

6. Gladstone's comment was made in reference to the scene in *The Odyssey* in which Nausicaa and her maidens bathe the naked Odysseus. Paul Ableman (1984) quotes Gladstone (without, unfortunately, stating his source): "It is almost of itself incredible that habitually among persons of the highest rank and character, and without any necessity at all, such things should take place, and as it is not credible, so neither, I think, is it true" (quoted in Ableman 1984: 36). Gladstone's claim is also discussed by John Langdon-Davies (1928: 69ff.).

7. So too has Michel Foucault's (1984) concept of "technologies of the body," and its antecedent, Marcel Mauss' (1973) "techniques of the body."

8. This "clothes-representation-body" terminology is adapted from the phrase "clothes-art-body triangle" used by Carter Ratcliff on the back cover of Hollander's (1993) *Seeing Through Clothes*. I have extended it to refer to forms of representation apart from art.

9. Any claim about the universality of clothing depends, of course, on one's definition of clothing, especially on whether it includes ornamentation and body modification. This matter is discussed further in Chapter 3.

10. The King James Bible cites "veil" as an alternative translation. The translation cited in Miles (1989: 51) is that hair is a "natural garment." For a detailed analysis of Paul's discussion of hair in 1 Corinthians, see Derrett (1973).

11. Shame and modesty are entwined, as the following translations make clear: *Scham* (a feminine noun) means shame; *Shamhaftigkeit* means modesty; *die Schamteile* ("shame-parts") means genitals.

12. This story is repeated in Wendy Cooper (1971: 88). Cooper also cites an example from her own survey of a man who asked his female partner to shave her pubic hair, since he had always imagined women to be hairless (p. 88).

13. Thanks to Kristen Davis for carrying out this thankless task.

14. The 1960s fashion designer Mary Quant was an advocate of pubic hair fashioning, publicly discussing how her husband had cut hers into a heart shape. Quant believed that the demands of fashion would lead to the increasing exposure and fashioning of pubic hair (Cooper 1971: 116).

15. This may still be one arena where male desire has quite a shaping influence on female desire. Wendy Cooper (1971) believes so. Based on a survey of two hundred university students, she argues that in terms of pubic, leg and axillary (armpit) hair, women "seem willing to yield to male preference, as they do not where head hair is concerned. Perhaps this is simply because, while head hair is often on public display, body hair is a more private and intimate possession" (p. 116). Why men should have more influence on the "more private and intimate" parts of women is a question she does not discuss.

16. "Chloe" is now a Melbourne tourist attraction. It is housed in the Young and Jackson Hotel, opposite Flinders Street Station.

17. Derived, apparently, from the mistaken apprehension of the "-ed" ending of "naked" as a past participle (*OED*).

18. To give one example, a short story by Dany Falconer-Flint begins with a rumination on the contrast between the flavour of the two words:

Nude. *Nude.*
Newd.
A prissy word, that, thought Marge . . . Naked was nicer. And better still was skinny-dipping – now there was a word to conjure with, for daring and delight. While *newd* bathing always sounded as though there was rubber, fine as a condom, between the swimmer and the awkward glance. (Falconer-Flint 1992: 69, original emphasis)

Here we see the idea that nudity is a kind of glossy protective sheath, a coated, aestheticized nakedness.

19. Cf. Raphael's comment to Castiglione with regard to his *Galatea*, that he had been unable to find any one model who was sufficiently beautiful, but that he had used the best parts of several (Clark 1956: 109).

20. Clark universalizes spectatorship, taking the presumed responses of the educated heterosexual male spectator as a model for viewing-in-general. Clark's distinction is also limited in that he claims to be discussing a timeless and universal quality, even though as an art historian he is obviously well aware that the body type he admires as universally beautiful springs from a specific aesthetic canon.

21. Cf. a comment in Seymour Fisher's (1973) *Body Consciousness* and a discussion of it in Paul Ableman's (1984) *The Banished Body*. Fisher argues that striptease is reassuring because it reminds a clothed society that there is in fact a natural body underneath: "Watching someone undress, and seeing their body emerge intact from its ordeal by clothing, reassures us that the natural order is still operational" (Ableman 1984: 88). While this is an interesting argument, it fails to take account of the fact that striptease is a highly gendered practice (the recent existence of male strippers notwith-standing). Taken together with Blessing's (1997) comments about the reassurance provided by performances of female lack, we might reframe Ableman's comment and agree that indeed striptease does remind its (male) spectators that "the natural [gender] order is still operational."

22. One of the most famous feminist articulations of this discontent is the closing line of Donna Haraway's "Cyborg Manifesto:" "I would rather be a cyborg than a goddess" (Haraway 1991: 181). While the cyborg is not a messy figure in the way that nakedness has been construed as messy, postmodern feminism, which is interested less in purity than in hybridity, difference, boundary crossing and impurity, has taken it up as an exemplary metonym.

23. Nietzsche spoke of "the seduction of language" (*Genealogy of Morals*, quoted in Mansfield: 2000: 56). Derrida's idea that miscommunication is at the heart of communication can be seen as a descendant of this tradition.

24. Although I mostly follow contemporary protocols with regard to the generic or universal "man," I have occasionally used it when discussing theology, in order to leave visible the symptomatic conflation of men and universal man, which is precisely one of the salient points here. I am assuming that feminist interventions on this score are sufficiently entrenched as to obviate the need for the repeated use of "*sic*."

25. The idea that gendered violence underpins sociality accords with feminist social contract theory. A well-known example is Carole Pateman's (1988) feminist rereading of Freud's "fantastic" hypothesis in *Totem and Taboo* of the first human society, in which she argues that an act of gender violence or domination precedes and enables the first symbolic order.

26. This, by the way, appears to have been one of the assumptions and aims of the radical utopian sect the Adamites, at least in their fifteenth-century French manifest-ation. As well as banning clothes, they banned all manifestations of social structure, including labour, class, money, bureaucracy, the church and the military ("L'Utopie").

27. The Platonic conception of the relation between body and soul made its way into Christianity and Christian debate. It is taken up playfully by John Donne in his

elegy *To His Mistress Going to Bed*, in which the poet urges his mistress to undress, piece by piece:

> Full nakedness, all joys are due to thee.
> As souls unbodied, bodies unclothed must be,
> To taste whole joys.
>
> (Donne 1971: lines 33–5)

This is a secular (and tendentious) application of a religious trope (clothes are to the body what the body is to the soul) for altogether more worldly purposes.

28. Langdon-Davies (1928) was an advocate of nudism writing in the late 1920s, and there is possibly a fascinating (unconscious?) relation between his critique of clothing and a rising anti-Semitism. Is the figure of "the Jew" unconsciously invoked in his denunciation of clothing? The association of the profession of tailor with Jews, the Jewish metaphysics of veils described by Perniola, the figure of Saul, and some other elements of Langdon-Davies' reading of the Lady Godiva story suggest such a possibility, but it is one that I have not yet been able to explore. It would be a very complex matter, given, on the one hand, early nudism's contiguities with eugenics and, on the other hand, Hitler's denunciation and banning of it as corrupt, and Langdon-Davies' evident social progressivism.

29. Cf. Nietzsche's maxim (placed immediately before the one on finery): "When a woman has scholarly inclinations there is usually something wrong with her sexuality" (Nietzsche 1973: 83).

30. It is found in Frederick Marryat (1796–1848): "On being ushered into the reception room, conceive my astonishment at beholding a square piano-forte with four limbs. So that the ladies that visited . . . might feel in its full force the extreme delicacy of the mistress of the establishment . . . she had dressed all these four limbs in modest little trousers, with frills at the bottom of them!" See the discussion in the *Victoria* Internet list (http://www.indiana.edu/~victoria/discussion.html#vic), whence the quotation from Ellen Jordan comes. Thanks to Susan K. Martin for alerting me to this list.

31. Steinberg (1996) replies to Bynum (1991) in the second edition of *The Sexuality of Christ*, in an epilogue titled "Ad Bynum."

2

The Metaphor of Nudity

Question: "What is the dominant metaphor of the age? – any age?
Answer: "What that age accepts as literal."

Aphorism reported by Raymond Williams
Quoted in Liam Hudson, *Bodies of Knowledge*

"[W]hat is it all but Metaphors, recognised as such, or no longer recognised; still
fluid and florid, or now solid-grown and colourless?"

Thomas Carlyle, *Sartor Resartus*

In the previous chapter, we looked at the place of a metaphorics of clothing
and nudity in philosophical understandings of humanness, focusing especially
on the tradition paralleling clothing and language. We saw that each of two
poles of philosophical reflection (social constructionism and idealism) called
up a corresponding imaginary relation between the clothed and naked body.
This is not surprising, since a relationship with the body must necessarily be
at the core of human identity, and since language – that most cultural and yet
most basic of social institutions – is also, in the form of speech, a bodily experience. In this chapter, we turn to the metaphor of nudity in some of its other
guises. We will see that it has been crucial not just in abstract philosophical
ideas about culture, language and identity, but also as a lodestone in moral
categories. This chapter, then, looks at the proliferation of metaphorical
meanings of nudity, and their anchorage in the most primal cultural binary –
the division between good and bad.

In her study of female nakedness in early Christianity, Margaret Miles (1989:
xi) warns that what Julia Kristeva has called the inherent significance of the
human body cannot be understood outside of its particular historical and
cultural contexts. While this is of course true, it is nonetheless possible to paint
with broad brush strokes some of the persistent elements of a symbolic
tradition, in this case the Judeo-Christian tradition. In the modern West, this
tradition has been significantly modified by the influences of multiculturalism,
globalization and consumerism (among other things), but it is nonetheless a
legacy that resonates still in contemporary culture.

Idioms and Euphemisms

Any search in a library catalogue under the words "naked" or "bare" provides rapid and startling evidence that the metaphorical uses of nakedness far outweigh any literal studies; titles (often of novels) like *Naked Ambition, The Naked Truth* and *The Naked Ape* abound.[1] There exists a wealth of idiomatic and vernacular expressions for nakedness, a linguistic richness that suggests both a presence and an absence. By this I mean that the proliferation of idioms, colloquialisms and metaphors for nakedness signals the unspeakableness of nudity at the same time as it multiplies the ways of naming it. Holder's *(1995: passim) Dictionary of Euphemisms* records the following:

> As Allah/God made him; au naturel; in the skin; in the raw; to be in your naturals; to be in your birthday suit; to be in the garb of Eden; starkers; in the altogether; to be in nature's garb; to skinny-dip; to streak; to be in the state of nature; to wear a smile; zero; bollocky; bottomless

Similar conceits are to be found in other European languages: "*dans le costume d'Adam* (ou *d'Eve*)" ("in Adam's (or Eve's) dress"); "*dans le plus simple appareil*" ("in the simplest get-up"); "*nackt wie Gott mich geschaffen hat*" ("as naked as God made me"). To this list of euphemisms we might add some others: "full frontal," "not a stitch on," or the rather endearing Australian expression "in the nuddy." John Ayto's (1993: 155) book of euphemisms considers "nude" itself to be a kind of euphemism, a genteel alternative to "naked."

Broadly, these euphemisms can be seen to refer either to time (origins), body parts, or a bodily state. The origins alluded to can be natural (*au naturel*, "wearing only what Mother Nature provided"), biblical (Adam and Eve) or personal ("in your birthday suit"). Idioms referring to the body tend either to focus on particular fetishized body parts or to the entirety of the skin. Thus we find "in the bollock," "in your naturals" ("naturals" being an obsolete contraction of "natural parts," i.e. genitals), and "bottomless" (a term used of a woman, usually a waitress, to mean "fully naked," arrived at by extrapolation from the term "topless"), as well as "in the buff," "buck naked," "in the skin" and "skinny-dipping." Skin features regularly, which is not surprising, given the historical prevalence of images of the self as a series of layered containers. For example, Platonic and Christian metaphysics imagined the body as the clothing of the soul (Perniola 1989: 239). Imagining the self as comprised of sets of mutually enclosing "layers" necessarily draws attention to borders and hence to skin. In particular, it allows skin to be understood as a form of clothing, and clothing as a form of skin. In other words, skin can be understood as a canvas to be dressed up (as in ornamentation practices such as tattooing), and clothing can be understood as a second skin. Skin is thus a crucial border site in the shifting relation between nudity and clothing – a bodily site with great cultural, psychological and phenomenological import. Its cultural functions include acting as a marker of racial identity, regulating the opposition between the "inside" and "outside" of the body and, meta-phorically, acting like a kind of shell or clothing, holding the body in place.

Expressions for nudity often begin with the word "in," where perhaps one might have logically expected "out" (since being nude is being "out" of one's clothes). Why "in?" "In" usually suggests a state (e.g. "in a dream," "in a trance," "in a rage") or physical containment ("in bed," "in the bath" and so on). This formula constructs nakedness as a state significant in its own right, rather than simply the opposite of the clothed state. It also suggests that you are a participant in something outside of yourself, perhaps bigger than you (like being "in" a rage or "in love"). Many locutions construct nudity as a total state, the emphasis on completeness (e.g. "in the altogether" or "full frontal")[2] reminding us that there is an entire and complexly modulated continuum between being clothed and being naked – that, for example, there is a world of moral and experiential difference made by that last flimsy triangle of textile around the loins.

As we have seen, many of these idioms ironically or perversely see nudity as itself a form of clothing. Many are of Christian origin,[3] or else replay in the everyday domain some of the religious and philosophical debates about the relationship between body, soul and clothing that I discussed in Chapter 1: "Adam's suit," "your birthday suit," "the simplest trappings," "Eden's clothing" and so on). Another example is the delightful word "skyclad" (i.e. clad only by the sky), a term used especially of witches, and nowadays used by neo-pagans practising ritual nudity.

Metaphors

Marina Warner (1985: 295) states that in medieval religious art, "nudity is very rarely circumstantial, more frequently symbolic." Even today, nakedness is rich cultural terrain, both physically (since it is a privileged and often tabooed state) and metaphorically (since it is capable of bearing a wealth of often contradictory symbolic meanings). A distinction, though, between physical states and metaphors is misleading, based as it is on a false split between body and mind. In everyday embodied life (as opposed to specific representational traditions, such as the one to which Warner is referring), the distinction between the "circumstantial" and the "symbolic" is ultimately hard to sustain. For our bodies operate on metaphorical lines; they are a living metaphorics.

And anyway, metaphors themselves are not abstract ideas, or simply "poetical." As the title of Lakoff and Johnson's (1980) famous study reminds us, they are concepts "we live by." Lakoff and Johnson argue that metaphors are part of the everyday world, embedded not just in language but in our perception, our concepts and our activities:

> [H]uman *thought processes* are largely metaphorical . . . [T]he human conceptual system is metaphorically structured and defined. Metaphors as linguistic expressions are possible precisely because there are metaphors in a person's conceptual system. (Lakoff and Johnson 1980: 6, original emphasis)

Metaphors, then, are everyday, conceptual, systemic and, moreover, embodied and practised. Metaphors are deeply embedded; witness not only this sentence, in which the word "embedded" is itself part of spatial and cosmological metaphors, but even the word "metaphor" itself, whose etymology, derived from the Greek verb "to carry or transport across," is, after all, itself metaphorical.

One of the larger questions underlying this study of nudity, then, is the relationship of metaphor to lived bodily experience. What are the effects of language (metaphor, image) on our bodies and bodies on our language? Although I have begun by talking about metaphor and experience as though they were distinct, I hope that this book will gradually erode the false absoluteness of the distinction between concepts like the symbolic and literal, even if it does not have a coherent system with which to replace such a distinction. For, just as Jennifer Craik (1994: 4) can argue of clothing that it is "neither simply functional nor symbolic in the conventional senses," so we can say that in bodily life more generally, functions and meanings cannot be separated.

Margaret Miles begins her study of the meaning of female nakedness in early Christianity with an affirmation of "the bewildering array of meanings associated with naked bodies" in the Christian West:

> Naked bodies gathered meanings that ranged from innocence to shame, from vulnerability to culpability, from present worthlessness to future bliss in the resurrection of the body. (Miles 1989: xi)

Among this welter, Marina Warner's list of the four types of nudity distinguished by medieval theologians is a useful starting point:

> *nuditas criminalis*, or the nakedness of the sinner, a sign of vice; *nuditas naturalis*, the human condition of animal nakedness, which should inspire humility since man alone among the animals has no covering, no bark, feathers, fur or scales . . .; *nuditas temporalis*, the figurative shedding of all worldly goods and wealth and status,

voluntary or involuntary; and *nuditas virtualis*, symbolizing innocence, the raiment of the soul cleansed by confession, the blessed company of the redeemed in heaven and of Truth herself. (Warner 1985: 295)

Cruden's classic *Concordance to the Bible* lists six different biblical meanings of "naked:"

1) one altogether unclothed or uncovered; 2) such as have but few clothes on, having put off the greatest part of them; 3) one void of grace, that is, not clothed with the righteousness of Christ, and so is exposed to the wrath of God for his sins; 4) such as had heinously sinned, and were deprived of the favour and protection of God, and so might be easily surprised by their enemies; 5) one destitute of worldly goods; and 6) that which is discovered, known, and manifest. (Cruden 1848: 470)

One could produce a range of such taxonomies. At their heart, though, these taxonomies reflect a fundamental moral dichotomy produced by the internal subtleties of and the complex interactions between two of the major traditions that fed into Christianity and the Western philosophical tradition: the Hebrew and Greek. We have already mentioned Perniola's contention that at the heart of the Judaic tradition is a metaphysics of clothing: the veiled God who clothed the world and the robes of whose priests recall the "metaphysical pre-eminence" of clothing (Perniola 1989: 238). The God of the Old Testament is "essentially 'clothed,'" covering His power with veils when revealing Himself to a human world unable to bear the direct sight of God (p. 238): "You cannot see my face: for man shall not see me and live" (Exod. 33:20). Greek meta-physics after Plato, on the other hand, came to imply the importance of clear vision to the apprehension of the truth.

Neither tradition is, of course, reducible to a single metaphysical principle, as Perniola points out. Some Jewish thinkers (e.g. Philo of Alexandria) interpreted the Old Testament from a Greek perspective (Perniola 1989: 239). Larissa Bonfante also points out that while Hebrew tradition was "fundament-ally opposed to the institution of Greek athletic nudity," some Hellenized Jews, even while they may not have accepted the institution as a whole, attended the *gymnasia* because of the philosophical discussions that took place there (Bonfante 1989: 563). Perniola (1989) also considers medieval sects like the Adamites (who rejected clothes and other social institutions in the name of reclaiming an original relation to God) to represent a "grafting" of Platonism onto the Bible (though he claims that in general such a grafting did not go much beyond the metaphor of the naked truth). In Gnosticism, Perniola sees the reverse influence: in the adoption of the idea of a clothed truth visible only to a few initiates (p. 239), and of the stark duality between a "naked body, destined for perdition" and a "clothed spirit, destined for salvation" (p. 242).

The Greek ideal of nudity developed gradually, and was only ever a mainland phenomenon. Moreover, Bonfante (1989: 545) claims that the Greek word for sexual organs, *aidoia* ("shameful things"), and the Latin *pudenda* ("shameful") indicate that nudity was not always accepted, although these simple translations do not in fact do justice to the complexity of the value systems in which these words were embedded. In the ancient Near East, nakedness was a sign of wretchedness, shame and defeat, as it was in the Old Testament. Bonfante surmises that the first hints of nudity beginning also to signify virtuousness and beauty probably came in Athenian Geometric art and with Homer (*c*. 800 BC), in whom there is a mix of old and new attitudes to nudity (p. 549). Homer sometimes associates nakedness with shame. But as W. Thomas MacCary (1982) has observed, Homeric heroes are *gymnos* and shamed when they are armourless rather than when they are unclothed. Homer explicitly feminizes a hero rendered "naked" in this way. Losing one's armour means losing one's ability to fight, and hence being unmanned. Homer does occasionally describe the beauty of a naked slain man. The most unequivocal admiration of naked beauty, however, came with the *kouroi*, or heroic or divine statues of naked youths, which began to appear in the seventh century BC (Bonfante 1989: 549).

The tradition of ideal beauty is quite strongly gendered. As Marina Warner points out, the primary connotation of the naked bodies of warriors, athletes, gods and heroes in Greece, Rome and most neo-classical contexts was not exclusively erotic, whereas the revelation of the lower half of a woman's body almost always "mark[ed] the figure as a prime and exclusive object of desire" (Warner 1985: 313). In Attic art, naked women are usually prostitutes, and in everyday life, women's nudity was rare in public, usually serving ritual and occasionally athletic purposes (Bonfante 1989: 559). Female nakedness, in everyday life, but also in representation, was able to shock. Pliny reports, for example, that the total nakedness of Praxiteles' Aphrodite (later known as the Cnidian Venus) was considered a scandalous innovation (Warner 1985: 313). As these examples make clear, the Greek ideal was not open to all bodies; youthful, male, Greek, able-bodied citizens were its subjects, and even then, nudity's meaning was not simple.

For convenience, I am going to group the metaphorical associations of nakedness broadly into positive and negative meanings, without, however, wanting to freeze them into inert "categories." While on the one hand I want to demonstrate how the meanings of nakedness can be very fundamentally morally valued ("good" or "bad"), it is also crucial to note that the contradictory meanings and experiences of nakedness often coexist, inflect and infect each other to produce precarious, ambiguous or shifting moral valuations. Even the stock meanings of nakedness are really much more about *clusters* of meaning, shifting across time, valued differently according to context, and unevenly available to different kinds of bodies. This chapter aims simply to note some broad patterns that form a repertoire of meanings in relation to which contemporary experiences of nakedness take shape.

Taking these complexities into account, the Judaic and Greek traditions at the base of Christian metaphorics furnish the metaphysical basis for the two very broad groupings of symbolic meanings of nakedness: those associated with *presence* (authenticity, truth, origins, nature, simplicity) and those with *absence* (deprivation, degradation, vulnerability, exposure, punishment). These broad patterns interact with an ambivalence about human nature: bare humanness as positivity (pure origin, pure presence) and as *lack* of something positive (such as civilization, culture or divinity). Their interplay, along with influences from many other traditions, means that nudity can symbolize many different things – including quite precisely opposing terms (e.g. innocence and the lack of innocence; order or the threat of disorder), or similar qualities, valued differently according to context (e.g. nakedness as both naturalness and savagery). It also corresponds to a duality within conceptions of nature – as God's handiwork or as brutal and base.

"Positive" Associations of Nakedness

Simplicity, Lack of Artifice or Worldliness

One of the earliest (and now obsolete) meanings of the word "nude" comes from the mid-sixteenth century: "mere, plain, open, explicit" (*OED*). Although this usage has now faded, it persists analogously in the symbolics of the Christian renunciation of worldliness, epitomized in such figures as Job, Jerome, Mary Magdalene and Mary of Egypt (Warner 1985: 303). Divesting the body of clothing – stripping it back to its most "natural" or organic state – signified a lack of care for the vanities of the world. There are still some modern contexts in which the stripping off of clothes can carry the symbolic meaning bequeathed to it by the *nuditas temporalis*, especially within counter-cultures (the hippy musical *Hair* (1967) is one obvious example).

This tradition means that nudity is also a useful tool in personal or political protest (a connection I have studied in detail: see Barcan 2002a). In 1997, for example, a homeless man sat naked in the dock of Sydney's Central Local Court, where he was being charged for praying naked in St Mary's Cathedral. His courtroom action, which he said was a protest about not being allowed to have a shower, was reported with a brief unobtrusive paragraph in the newspaper (Anon. 1997b). His actions could be interpreted within the religious metaphorics by which (voluntary) nakedness symbolizes the stripping away of secular socialization, a repudiation of investment in the social world (Miles 1989: 81). The man himself both invited and abjured such an interpretation, telling police that it was his right to pray naked, but refusing to amplify this to the judge, saying instead: "I'm not really interested in discussing theology at the moment."

The tradition persists in remnant form in modern naturism (nudism), which first came into being as a health practice with strong ideological foundations, usually including anti-materialism. In contemporary Australia, the UK and the US, naturism has by and large mutated into a "lifestyle;" this is certainly the discourse used by the vast majority of nudists to describe their practice. Certainly, most nudists would be happy to espouse an unobjectionable principle of "simple living," but by this they often mean a kind of psychological simplicity (avoid stress; don't worry too much about what others think of you). I have seen no evidence that nudists are any more or less likely than the rest of the population to eschew material goods!

There are exceptions, though – people whose nudism sits squarely and self-reflexively at the heart of an anti-materialist philosophy. Kevin is one example. A man in his late middle age, he is a well-known figure at a long-running environmental festival, where he is to be found manning the gate, naked. Kevin was formerly a farmer and later an agricultural researcher, and his agricultural background has given him a clear awareness of the environmental ravages caused by the wool and cotton industries. His pleasure in driving the tractor naked as a young man gradually connected up to this larger picture, and he is now a committed nudist on philosophical grounds. Having seen first-hand the effects of wool and cotton (in the form of insecticides, irrigation, fertilizers, chemicals, land-clearing, erosion and fossil fuel use), Kevin sees wearing clothes as "an unnecessary intrusion on our environment." He now wears clothes only outside his home.

Nudity as Honesty, Openness

In Middle English, "naked" could mean "free from concealment or reserve; straightforward, outspoken" (*OED*). This literal sense persists faintly in a number of contemporary idioms, but is more strongly evident metaphorically, in common-sense or anecdotal associations between nudity and openness. Certainly, most nudists believe in the literalness of this connection. "Nudists have nothing to hide," they say. Seeing their own bodies as symbolic terrain, as embodiments of a certain ethical relation to the world, they are proud of their openness.

This common-sense association of nudity with openness, disclosure or honesty has been mobilized in some forms of psychotherapy. In the 1960s, for example,

Paul Bindrim experimented with nudity as a tool in psychotherapeutic "mara-thons" (intensive group workshops), seeing whether consensual nudity helped accelerate and sharpen psychological and emotional openness. He found that it did and, conversely, "that there was a growing tendency to disrobe as emotional intimacy and transparency developed between the group members" (Bindrim 1968: 180). Nudity, he found, enhanced "authenticity and inter-relatedness" (p. 181) and worked against the individualizing and privatizing tendencies encouraged by modern social relations.

I asked a participant in similar contemporary workshops (Karen, whose views on nakedness were mentioned in Chapter 1) whether she believed that physical nudity encourages honesty. "I don't think it follows," she replied. "I think it *can*, but it doesn't have to." I asked whether she had observed any correlation between privacy and clothing at a sexuality workshop she had attended. She saw it as a complex matter:

> Certainly the people who kept their clothes on appeared to be more private in their talking as well. I'm glad you used that word "private," because it sort of implies that you can choose to be open or you can choose to be private. Being private doesn't mean that you're not open . . . They may be open but decided that at this point they wanted to be private. So yes, I think there is a correlation between being clothed and being private, but whether there's a correlation between being naked and being open, I don't know. For some reason I don't feel as sure about that.

The assumption of a link between psychological and bodily openness has been tested experimentally (see, for example, Sussman 1977). In one such experi-ment, in the US in 1973, a group of psychologists aimed to see whether there was indeed any correlation between bodily and psychological "cover-ups:" that is, whether "those people who talk openly about their problems and exhibit their thoughts and feelings in group sessions are prone to display their bodies or, under favorable circumstances, to be fond of their nudity" and, conversely, whether "those who do not reveal themselves are sexually modest and cover their body carefully" (Ehrentheil et al. 1973: 363). The researchers wondered whether "people who are willing to disclose the secrets of their soul may also be willing to disclose the secrets of their bodies, even if the people to whom they reveal their soul are not identical with those to whom they display their bodies" (p. 367). They found that the conjecture was confirmed for men, but not for women. The researchers discovered that comfort with bodily disclosure was more common among the highly educated, those under 40, and in men.

Their study is, however, as interesting for its own extraordinary assumptions and blindspots as it is for its findings. For example, in the process of differentiat-ing "normal" body display from clinical exhibitionism, Ehrentheil et al. (1973:

363) have recourse to the following definition of being "fond" of nudity or display: "The normal tendency of many people to enjoy nudity or at least showing their legs in miniskirts or their breast form in tightly fitting sweaters." This definition is doubly remarkable: first, because it makes no distinction between the state of nakedness and the wearing of (arguably) sexually provocative clothing; and second, because the definition of body display is so distinctly feminized. The experiment, setting out to see whether men and women had similar attitudes to their own undress, crudely assumed the deep-seated idea that women reveal and men watch, as evident in questions from their specially designed "Body Display Rating Scale:"

E1 Do you like it if young women are wearing miniskirts   Yes/No

E2 (for females) I like to wear low cut evening and summer
dresses   Yes/No

(for men) I like it when my wife (girlfriend) wears low cut
evening and summer dresses   Yes/No

E3 (for females) I don't like tight fitting sweaters because
they show my form   True/False

(for men) I don't that like my wife (girlfriend) wears tight
fitting sweaters because they show her form   True/False

(Ehrentheil et al. 1973: 364)

Men's attitudes to their *wife's* clothing were assumed to be indicative of their *own* exhibitionist tendencies! Bodily display of the man's own person was deemed to be irrelevant (impossible?), and his attitudes to his own body were revealed through his wife's. I linger over what is, thirty years on, an obviously crude study merely in order to signal how deep-seated the assumptions about male and female nudity can be. In this study, women's bodies were understood in contradictory ways: they were assumed to be viable indicators of their husbands' psychology and less reliable indicators of their own. Paradoxically, male nudity appeared only as an absence.

The metaphorical association of nakedness with openness or honesty makes sense only in relation to a parallel association between clothing and conceal-ment. Only against such a tradition can nakedness mean "without artifice." The metaphor of the cover is, as we have seen, an old one. Plato's conception of the body as a kind of occasionally obstructive "layer" covering the soul still persists in subtle ways, but increasingly alongside another conception and experience of the body – that of the body as a means of expression of the individual person. In this more recent conception, the body is not a cover but a revelation (of the soul, the individual, the personality). It thus "acquires a new duality: that of the *outer manifestation* (expression) and the *inner being*" (Falk 1994: 53, original emphasis). In Pasi Falk's terms, the modern body is both a "shell and a means of expression" (p. 53). In the Platonic conception it is still an "outside" (the covering of the soul); in the modern conception it can be taken to symbolize or express the soul or inner self, especially in contrast to the clothed self, which is more readily legible as the workings of an "external" culture. Perhaps, then, the modern experience of nakedness is inherently contradictory: the naked body can figure as both "inside" and "outside."

In fact, though, there is no single modern experience of nakedness, just as these metaphors for the self do not work in the same way for all kinds of people. While Falk's analysis points us towards historical changes in the metaphorical understanding of the relation between body and soul, feminist psychoanalysis can also be useful for understanding how not all forms of human subjectivity may be function as core identities that can be subsequently "dressed up" or "clothed" in different ways. For example, as we saw in Chapter 1, when we discussed the metaphor of the masquerade, femininity has been understood to function as a set of veils under which there is no stable "naked" identity. The potential for a hidden gender and racial politics within the seemingly universal metaphor of nakedness as honesty is made clear when one contrasts the metaphor of naked honesty with a potential opposite – that of duplicitous veiling or covering.

Veiling is a varied and complex phenomenon, and it is well outside the scope of this book (and my expertise) to investigate its complexities (for a detailed study of veiling, see El Guindi 1999). The salient point for my analysis here is that the modern West has taken it up as a *sign* or *metaphor* for mystery, secrecy, sexual allure, submission, oppression, passivity (or repression) and, sometimes, deception, in contrast to the metaphor of nudity as openness, honesty and truth. Moreover, it has appropriated it as a *feminized* signifier (despite the existence of an occasional real-life practice of masculine veiling in the Arab world) – duplicity, passivity, secrecy and submission being, in the misogynist strain of the Christian tradition, the fundamental condition of femininity. It can thus also be put to work against feminized Others. For a current, highly political, mobilization of the veil as a sign of dangerous duplicity and/or inscrutable mystery, we need look no further than its widespread use, post September 11, as a sign of a nebulously conceived Islamic threat to the West.

The entire nudity/clothing dialectic is replete with paradoxes, and the nudity-openness/clothing-secrecy configuration is no exception. There exists, for example, a longstanding paradox according to which nudity (or openness) can itself be the best form of disguise. "If you want to hide your face, go completely naked," runs the adage (quoted in Guillois and Guillois 1989: 149). It is found, for example, in William Congreve's play *The Double-Dealer* (1694), where the double-crossing character Maskwell claims that the best way to deceive people is not so much to lie as to speak truth but conceal your duplicitous motives:

> No mask like open truth to cover lies,
> As to go naked is the best disguise. (V.i.89–90)

This is the opposite of the masquerade tradition alluded to by the name "Maskwell," in which clothing is donned to disguise identity. This paradox is detectable in Karen's response to a question about whether the correlation made proudly by nudists between bodily and emotional openness necessarily holds good. Did she believe, as many nudists do, that once you've revealed all, you have nothing to hide? Is the nudists' naked body a symbol of their honesty?:

> Well, I think it *could* be a symbol for their honesty or it could be a cover. I think you
> could be honest with your body but not necessarily honest with your communication.
> I think you can almost hide behind your nakedness. You can give the impression of
> being an open person just because you take your clothes off, but I don't think you
> have to be. (Karen)

What is fascinating here is that, in speaking of a "cover," Karen has unconscious recourse to a variant of the same metaphor that she is problematizing – proof indeed of how deeply embedded this metaphor is. Then again, it was already there in my question, since I asked if the body *symbolized* honesty. The important question of whether the naked body "is" honest or *symbolizes* honesty brings us back to Carlyle, who saw the body as a form of symbolization. As we saw in Chapter 1, this can be extrapolated into an argument that nudity too must therefore symbolize, rather than reflect, its own naturalness. Nudity is symbolically charged, even when that symbolic meaning is, precisely, its own nothingness.

Innocence, Humility and Childhood

Since the body can be seen both as matter (i.e. an impediment to the soul) and as a *reflection* of the soul, it follows that nudity will have a complex and paradoxical relationship to most moral categories. Innocence, for example, figures in many of the classic tales involving nakedness: Adam and Eve, Lady Godiva, *The Emperor's New Clothes*, and even *Penguin Island* (France 1909). In *The Emperor's New Clothes*, only the (innocent) child can recognize the emperor's nudity. The emperor's physical nakedness is matched by the spiritual/emotional nakedness of the child; being without guile, the child both sees and speaks the naked truth without concealment.

In the Christian tradition, nudity functions doubly, as metaphor both for innocence and the lack of it. Nudity both "is" and *ought* to be innocent; it "was" innocent (before the Fall), but is no longer. In the archetypal Christian story for the doubleness of nudity, that of Adam and Eve, self-conscious nudity comes into being only at the moment that innocence is lost: "And they were both naked, the man and his wife, and were not ashamed" (Genesis 2:25). The Old Testament narrative is already informed by the postlapsarian experience: the fact that one can discuss the lack of shame means that writer and audience now already take the tie between nudity and shame as a given. Nakedness is, then, a state of mind as well as a bodily state; it is brought into being by (shamed) self-consciousness. The following quotation from the Gnostic Gospel of Thomas, dropped from the modern Bible, equates nakedness, innocence, childhood and true seeing:

> Jesus said, "When you disrobe without being ashamed and take up your garments and place them under your feet like little children and tread on them, then [will you see] the son of the living one, and you will not be afraid." (II, 2.37 in Lambdin 1996: 130)

Lady Godiva is a secular descendant of this tradition. Her goodness and innocence protect her from the gaze of Peeping Tom. However, once a painter tries to represent such naked innocence within a particular set of visual codes, other (or submerged) meanings almost inevitably attach themselves; witness the scandal provoked in Victorian England by Edwin Landseer's 1865 painting of Lady Godiva (see Smith 1996: 55, 109). Nonetheless, as an imagined (rather than painted) figure, Lady Godiva is the heir of a Christian tradition in which nakedness can symbolize both goodness and innocence: the *nuditas virtualis* of the medieval taxonomers.

Naturists are particularly keen on the association between nakedness and innocence. They understand naturism as morally, physically and psychologically healthful, and as a return to the childhood state: "You were born a naturist," proclaims the advertising slogan of the Katikati naturist park in New Zealand; "I wasn't born with a suit on. Were you?" nudists commonly ask. They explicitly refute the equation between nakedness, shame and sin so prevalent in our culture. "Nude ain't rude" is a popular nudist slogan. Kevin, the environmentalist nudist at the greenie festival, puts up posters like that shown in Figure 2.1. He also enjoys challenging religious proselytizers who come to his suburban home. Greeting them naked at the door, he asks provocatively, "Aren't I good enough as God made me?"

Figure 2.1 Poster at environmental festival, 1998. Reproduced with permission.

It is less likely that religious evangelists would be shocked if the naked figure greeting them at the door were a young child. In Western culture, the nakedness of children carries an important symbolic and moral weight and is largely understood to be innocent. Since we are all born naked, nudity has come "naturally" to be associated with the infant and the young child.[4] Freud, for example, noted that childhood is the only time that modern Westerners are seen "in inadequate clothing both by members of our family and by strangers – nurses, maid-servants, and visitors; and it is only then that we feel no shame at our nakedness" (Freud 1953: 244).

As subjects-in-process, children are somewhat exempted from the taboo on public nakedness. The cultural belief in their innocence, asexuality and closeness to nature means that they transfer the quality of innocence onto their nakedness. This exemption from taboos associated with adulthood is always precarious, of course, and must be limited by other cultural conventions, particularly spatial rules. In Western cities, even young children cannot, in general, be nude in urban or public space. They may be nude at the beach, or at other people's houses – in other words, in places coded as natural or domestic (and hence feminized). But, generally speaking, they really shouldn't be nude at a shopping centre or on the bus. Their nakedness is acceptable when it does not overflow too much into the public sphere.

There is another axis to this ambiguity. It's not just that the nakedness of children is spatially constrained, but also that the category of "child" is itself not watertight, especially in modern Western societies, where rites of passage from childhood to adulthood have become less formal or ritualistic. In a discussion of child photography and the law, Anna Douglas (1994) casts the "problem" of childhood rather dramatically: she labels childhood "a Molotov cocktail for our time." The question, "What is a child?" logically focuses on persons understood as on the border between childhood and adulthood – the pre-pubescent and the adolescent. Their ambiguous personhood poses particular moral and legal conundrums, as we see in the contemporary fears surrounding paedophilia, adolescent sexuality or child criminality. The moral ambiguity of nudity means that nudity can be innocent but that, conversely, innocence must be protected *from* nudity. Children, who are in general given more leeway to be nude than adults, must nonetheless be protected *from* nudity. Criminal codes thus frequently make adult criminal nudity a greater offence if committed in front of children.[5]

In a society concerned in particular about the potency of *images*, it is not surprising that much of this concern extends to images of naked children. Photographs of naked children are as old as the medium itself. Nude child portraiture was an established practice in high society; even some British royalty were photographed nude in the 1920s and 1930s (Townsend 1996: 10). Chris Townsend argues that within thirty years of the birth of photography, three "types" had evolved: the nude child as "erotic subject, aestheticised innocent (often with a concealed erotic sub-text), or victim" (p. 9). Now the ambiguities have become especially fraught, and once-acceptable genres have becomes criminal. In Britain, the Protection of Children Act (1978) legislates against indecent photographic images of children, but does not define "indecency" (p. 10). This Act has, according to Townsend (1996), mainly trapped innocent parents and unwary nudists. Nudists are mostly all too aware of this danger, however, and many nudist magazines contain advertisements for nudist photo processors. But nudism has had its own share of genuine scandals, and it is hard for anyone to get a reasonable fix on the problem amid the hysteria.[6]

In such a climate, concerns spread rapidly. There is, for example, an increasing uneasiness about children's exposure to the nudity of adults. This concern is in part prompted by increasing knowledge of and publicity about the operations of paedophiles. But unease about adult nudity in front of children is also a logical corollary of the increasing relegation of nudity to the private sphere and the cultural invention of childhood as a time of asexual innocence, and it is thus not a recent anxiety. Even in the late 1980s, before the explosion of popular discourse about paedophilia, academic psychologists could report that "a frequent concern" of parents was the "potential harm to their child" that might be caused by exposure to the nudity of parents, siblings or friends (Lewis and Janda 1988: 349). Indeed, Freud's dramatization of the "primal scene" constructs parental nudity and sexual activity as a shock to the young child, albeit a universally experienced and "necessary" one. Researchers since Alfred Kinsey have reported that unselfconscious parental nudity has been uncommon in the US (Lewis and Janda 1988: 350). In academic disciplines, this unease has been visible in the proliferation of studies of the "effects" of adult nudity on children. Studies reassuring parents that appearing naked in front of their children will not have "adverse long-term effects" and could even be beneficial appear in psychological journals and medical magazines. Over the twentieth century, the state gradually extended its right to intervene directly into the family and into matters once considered private, a right that is of quite complex moral value (simultaneously extending the reach of human rights and threatening civil liberties). Recent strenuous popular debate about paedophilia will no doubt increase the legislative reach of the state. One politically active nudist told me, for example, that in some states of the US, legislation is currently being prepared that will render it illegal for an adult to be naked in front of a child (although I have been unable to source or confirm this claim). Moreover, the general privatization and sexualization of the body might also conceivably lead to a breakdown in the association between childhood nakedness and innocence. My students (and some of the interviewees in this study) report cases of neighbours complaining about toddlers playing naked in suburban gardens. Nudist Internet newsgroups also record similar stories. The alt.nudism.moderated newsgroup, for example, has carried discussions of a number of cases that suggest that tolerance of the nudity of children may be diminishing. A Californian man described two incidents in which his toddlers were asked to cover up – one when they were playing topless in the soapy water as he washed his car (and they were instructed by a 4-year-old girl to cover up because her father and 1-year-old brother could see them) and the other when his 3-year-old daughter was playing outside without a top and his neighbour sent over his son to say he should put a top on her. The mostly North American respondents chimed in with other stories and with theories about the causes of an increase in prudery – media images, moral panic over paedophilia, American puritanism, even the spread of socialism into the US. The author concluded as follows:

> Really, when I start to think about what goes on in these persons' minds I think they have some pretty twisted ideas. Later on I will have to start a thread on where we should move to get away from weirdoes like this. (Mike)

In an article about the pedagogical functions of public art in Renaissance Florence, Christopher Fulton (1997) argues that "the city's youth represented the hope for the future" and that "their conduct and demeanor reflected the city's moral condition" (p. 33). Perhaps children and youth are often are asked to bear the symbolic burden of representing a society's moral state back to itself. Images of children and youth can function as mirrors to an adult society eager to verify its own moral state. This might help explain not only why representations of children can be subject to idealization, but also why both the effect of images *on* youth and the representation of youth *in* images can become concentrated sites of social unease and regulation.

Nakedness and Freedom

> It's fun to be free
>
> Advertising slogan, Katikati Naturist Park, New Zealand

In many stories, such as those of Adam and Eve and Lady Godiva, nakedness is linked to self-assertion or rebellion. In societies in which there is a legislated taboo on public nudity, the naked body is an effective weapon in political protests (see Barcan 2002a). Moreover, the nude protestor is aided by the longstanding symbolic equation between nakedness and freedom. In this trope, we can trace yet another recurrence of the Platonic analogy of the body as clothing: the body is to the soul what clothes are to the body. To be stripped of one's clothes thus can (in certain contexts) signify a foreshadowing of the ultimate freedom, when the soul throws off the shackles of the body and re-enters its pure state.

Freedom can be imagined to reside not only in an anticipated future but also in retrospection, in revisiting the childhood state and regaining some of its lost pleasures. Adulthood mostly means the loss of the privilege of public nudity – except in strictly circumscribed conditions or as a subversive possibility. Do human beings experience this as a loss? Freud certainly thought so. In his discussion of the typical dream of feeling embarrassed at being naked in public, he conjures up a quite vivid picture of the freedoms of childhood nakedness:

> We can observe how undressing has an almost intoxicating effect on many children even in their later years, instead of making them feel ashamed. They laugh and jump about and slap themselves, while their mother . . . reproves them and says: "Ugh! Shocking! You mustn't ever do that!" Children frequently manifest a desire to exhibit. One can scarcely pass through a country village in our part of the world without meeting some child of two or three who lifts up his little shirt in front of one – in one's honour, perhaps. (Freud 1953: 244)

Freud reads the story of Adam and Eve as a collective myth about the loss of this Paradise, a utopian shame-free nakedness that is lost when we are expelled from childhood into adult life and its attendant tasks (and pleasures) of sexual life and cultural activity. The dream of public nakedness thus involves an element of wish-fulfilment, for, in Freud's words, "we can regain this Paradise every night in our dreams" (Freud 1953: 245).

Nudists, of course, argue that we don't have to wait till night to be free. Again and again, they report that the pleasure attained from nudism is "freedom." Nudism promotes both a lack (of self-consciousness about the body) and a positivity (the pleasures of sun and water on bare skin), both of which nudists consider to aid their experience of freedom. In general, nudists are reluctant to see this pleasure as inflected by social factors like gender, race or class, though of course in practice they are well aware that, for example, it is harder to attract women into nudism than men. While it is clear that male and female social nudity each have their own kinds of risk and pleasures, the humanist gauntlet thrown down by nudists has been a productive challenge for me, both intellectually and experientially.[7]

In linking nudity to freedom, most nudists try to avoid too explicit a discussion of the relation of sex to liberation, preferring to stress the non-sexual aspects of the public nudity involved in nudism. Nonetheless, dominant cultural narratives continue to link nudity to sex and sex to liberation. The consumerist equation between nudity, sex and liberation associates bodily pleasure with consumer goods, and construes purchase as a moment of self-assertion. In the process, both nudity and sex are reinscribed as "naughty" pleasures. The supposed hedonism of contemporary consumerist imagery thus continues to imply and reproduce an underlying asceticism. Consumerism's evolutionary narrative of liberation is still tied to the necessity of an originary repression. Consumerist discourse promises us the liberated body but needs a belief in or experience of a "repressed" or constrained body so that its promise of freedom-through-purchase can take effect. In consumerism, liberation is not so much actual as imminent – just one (more) purchase away.

Of course, contemporary bodies are neither more nor less "free" than earlier bodies – at least, not in any simple way. Likewise, attitudes to nudity are neither more "liberated" nor more "repressed" in any simple way than those of earlier times. The history of nudity (or clothing) in the West is not a simple linear tale either of increasing repression (humans becoming more and more alienated from their "natural state") or of liberation (humans becoming progressively more permissive or free), though both of these discourses can commonly be heard.

The idea of our increasing liberation from an earlier repression is, according to the philosopher Michel Foucault, a grand twentieth-century discourse purveyed not just in popular culture but also in academic disciplines like history, sexology, and psychology. "A great sexual sermon" has, he claims, been preached by both populists and experts over the last few decades (Foucault 1984: 7). Paradoxically, this sermon noisily affirms our sexual repression: "By what spiral did we come to affirm that sex is negated?" wonders Foucault. "What led us to show, ostentatiously, that sex is something we hide, to say it is something we silence?" (p. 9). Foucault's work alerts us to a central paradox around contemporary discourses about sexuality: that our society noisily affirms the repression of sex, that it "speaks verbosely of its own silence" (p. 8). He questions the received modern truth about sex: that the rise of industrial society and the institution of the bourgeois family ushered in an era of sexual repression from which we are only just now beginning to extricate ourselves. From Foucault's fundamental paradox – the contemporary mania for speaking about our inability to speak about sex – we can extrapolate to thinking about some of the contradictions surrounding nakedness in contemporary culture: nudity is encouraged, even demanded, in certain contexts, but also regulated and prohibited. It is imbricated in discourses of both liberation and repression. Nakedness is popularly taken to be self-evidently "about" sexuality, and sexuality itself is assumed to be struggling against the forces of repression and regulation.

Foucault argues that it is more complex than that – that we have witnessed neither the simple "liberation" promised by consumer culture nor the top-down oppression theorized in traditional Marxism, but rather, a fundamental shift in the nature of power. In *Discipline and Punish*, Foucault (1979) argues that there has emerged a new form of subjectification, one based on the internalization of disciplinary power rather than subjection to external, spectacular power. The new form of subject and the new mode of subjectification constitute, according to Foucault, the dominant forms of personhood in late modernity and their hallmark is the transformation of external surveillance into the more powerful, because seemingly apolitical, regimes of *self*-surveillance. Such changes are inevitably interconnected with changes in actual bodily behaviour. Foucault considers that bodies have become more heavily policed, more (self)-regulated, and ultimately more "docile" under this new regime. In this, he indirectly echoes the work of German sociologist Norbert Elias (1994), whose book *The Civilizing Process* argued that the "embarrassment threshold" has increased rather than decreased over the centuries. Although Elias' study was written in the 1930s, it can still shed light on postmodernity; it can help us see that while postmodernity has certainly brought about the end of a certain form of privacy (which it nonetheless fetishizes and relentlessly pursues), actual bodily behaviours have, in another way, perhaps become even more private, individualized or shame-laden.

Elias (1994) characterizes modern bodily comportment as narrower, less diverse and more strictly regulated than medieval corporeality. While it is important to note that late modernity is very different again from Europe in the late 1930s when Elias was writing, his arguments nonetheless give rise to a more embodied understanding of contemporary changes to privacy. In particular, they can provide a way of understanding the limits of contemporary sexual liberationist discourses. For while it is true that moral liberalization does indeed bring about forms of bodily liberation, it need not necessarily signal a liberation of the body more generally. On the contrary, the obsessive recurrence in consumer culture of discourses of sexual liberation points rather to what Elias diagnosed as the increasing *narrowness* in the range of publicly acceptable modes of bodily behaviour. Consumer culture is prone to reducing "body" to "sex." In celebrating "the body," it is less likely to celebrate, say, breathing, digestion, defecation or sleep than to celebrate beauty, health, vigour or fitness – all conceived of as both producing and resulting from a "liberated" sexuality. It is for this reason that, unlike the more sanguine analyses of resistance and pleasure that characterized much post-1980s cultural studies, I tend to celebrate only rather modestly the modes of bodily freedom that consumerism has undoubtedly brought into being. While the proliferation of, for example, advertising billboards depicting semi-naked people might indeed be read as indicative of some form of bodily liberation we must remember that first, only some types of bodies are accorded this privilege, second, "the body" is far more than just its sexual aspects, and third, there are big differences between actual permissible bodily practices and regimes of representation. In truth, the whole concept of bodily "liberation" is problematic.

Nonetheless, Elias' work makes it clear just how restricted contemporary canons of acceptable public bodily behaviour are, when contrasted with medieval ones. In the modern world, you and I are likely to be ashamed if we snore or if our stomach rumbles at a meeting; if we are women, we cannot walk topless into a shop, and are likely to feel shame if we do not wear a bra in public, or if our legs or underarms are hairy. We have definitely lost some of the wider tolerance of the body that was inevitable for our medieval fore-bears. There is no cause, though, for an unreflective lament for a lost plenitude or a lost innocence, for the picture is more complex than that. To take just two examples, in some ways we can be far *less* conscious of our bodies than our forebears, thanks to the benefits wrought by modern medicine, which allows us to block out or remedy much bodily pain. Or again, while consumer culture relentlessly purveys a narrow range of "acceptable" body types, the democratic liberalism that is one of the concomitants of consumerism also generates forms of body tolerance impossible in earlier times – such as the human rights discourses that recognize the different needs of the bodies of the disabled, or the elderly, or women, or children. We must be cautious, then, of both evolutionary and devolutionary assumptions.

Nakedness, Nature and "Naturalness"

As we have seen, many of the idiomatic expressions for nakedness refer, often ironically, to nudity as the "natural" state. No matter how problematic this idea of "nature," it's nonetheless still worth emphasizing how fundamental nakedness is. One of the very few things shared by every human being on the planet is that we are all born naked, though of course, this is a brief moment and we ourselves don't remember it. Nonetheless, it has proven crucial to one idea of the human – the idea that nakedness is "natural," and that clothing is "one of the most distinctly social habits that [has] evolved" (Crawley 1965: 47).

As we have seen, though, nudity too is a social habit, and not only in regard to the strong taboos in all cultures that regulate the nature and extent of exposure. Nudity is more subtly social in that even the very definition and experience of nudity are produced in specific contexts. What a body can or will become in a given culture is greatly dependent on the repeated mundane tasks it will be called upon to perform. Naked bodies are not the raw material with which subjects perform these tasks or on which culture performs its work; they are actively *made within* their context:

> It is crucial to note that th[e] different procedures of corporeal inscription do not simply adorn or add to a body that is basically given through biology; they help constitute the very biological organization of the subject – the subject's height, weight, coloring, even eye color, are constituted as such by a constitutive inter-weaving of genetic and environmental factors . . . [The naked body] is still marked by its disciplinary history, by its habitual patterns of movement, by the corporeal commitments it has undertaken in day-to-day life. It is in no sense a natural body, for it is as culturally, racially, sexually, possibly even as class distinctive, as it would be if it were clothed. (Grosz 1994: 142)

Nonetheless, the idea that the naked body is culture stripped away to pure nature holds strong, especially among nudists. The perceived link between nudity and nature is evident in the alternative name for nudism – naturism – and slogans like "Nude is natural." As we will see in Chapter 3, however, nudity must inevitably be a paradoxical form of "naturalness" in a predominantly clothed society.

Nudity, Authenticity and Truth

The *OED* defines "the naked truth" as meaning "the plain truth, without concealment or addition." Its first citation for this expression comes from

1585. The symbolic association of nakedness with truth is obviously both old and widespread, for this expression (and similar ones like "the bare facts") exists in many European languages: French, German, Norwegian, Spanish and Italian to name just a few. William and Mary Morris give an unsatisfyingly vague account of the allegorical origins of the figure of Naked Truth as deriving from an "old fable:"

> Truth and Falsehood went swimming together in a stream. Falsehood came out of the water first and dressed in Truth's clothing. Truth, not wanting to don the garments of Falsehood, remained naked. (Morris and Morris 1988: 402)

This tale is symptomatic rather than originary, already implicated in, rather than generative of, a metaphysics of clothing and nudity. Its metaphysical foundations can be more clearly pinpointed. Perniola sees the metaphor of the naked truth as having begun with Plato, who conceived of Ideas or forms as in the light rather than the shadows: "From this foundation, the entire process of knowledge becomes an unveiling of the object, a laying it entirely bare and an illumination of all its parts" (Perniola 1989: 238). Perniola records one hypothesis that sees in the Greek word *theorein* (to look at, contemplate), a metaphor of "careful or exact seeing, that is, the metaphysical ability to see beyond all robes, veils and coverings through to the thing itself in its exact particulars" (p. 239).

The metaphor found its way into visual culture. In classical Greek statuary, the nude body symbolizes the Platonic ideal, of which our bodies are replicas (Perniola 1989: 239). This Greek representational practice "rest[ed] on [Platonic] metaphysical premises" (p. 239). In the European visual art tradition, allegorical figures representing Truth have frequently been naked or lightly draped females (one of the positive guises of adult female nakedness). In contemporary film, nudity sometimes functions as a revelation of the truth of a character's sex. Frances Bonner (1998) discusses "exposure" shots in cross-dressed films, shots in which the truth of a character is revealed to an ideally unsuspecting audience, via anatomical exposure. Bonner argues that once a shot of breasts would be enough to guarantee a character's femaleness; now, full-frontal nudity or a brief glimpse of the genitals is deemed necessary. Bonner sees such shots as following the old requirement put in place by the British Lord Chamberlain that drag shows be completed with "an undressing, a revelation of 'true' sex," including removal of the wig (Bonner 1998: 272). There's also a longstanding nudist joke about "real blondes," which relies simultaneously on two traditional ideas – female duplicity and the honesty of the naked truth (see Figure 2.2).[8]

The most detailed study of this metaphor has been carried out by Hans Blumenberg (1998),[9] who has traced its implicit and explicit use by a range of

Figure 2.2 "Well, well! A true blonde." Old postcard purchased at a french nudist resort. Paris: Editions Lyna. Série "Boules" 820/1.

theologians and European philosophers. Blumenberg argues that in much Christian theology, the metaphor appeared as a way of expressing utter exposure to the eyes of God. Religious genres like the confession make use of the trope of spiritual nakedness. "What is there in me that could be hidden from You, O Lord, to whose eyes the depths of man's conscience is bare, even though I did not confess it?" exclaims St Augustine (1986: 186) in his *Confessions*; "I might hide You from myself, but not myself from You." The title of this book of the *Confessions*, "The Examined Life," recalls Perniola's (1989: 239) contention that Platonic conceptions figured the search for truth as a process of careful or exact seeing. Rousseau likewise begins his *Confessions* with the trope of the human soul laid bare before God, a spiritual nakedness that prefigures one's ultimate nakedness at the scene of the Final Judgement:

> I propose to set before my fellow-mortals a man in all the truth of nature; and this man shall be myself . . . I will present myself, whenever the last trumpet shall sound,

before the Sovereign Judge with this book in my hand, and loudly proclaim, "Thus have I acted; these were my thoughts; such was I." (Rousseau 1935: 3–4)

In Chapter 3, we will see an Aboriginal argument about nakedness that is not dissimilar. Irene Watson (1998) argues that Aboriginal culture, people, law and the land itself were naked before white colonization. Just as Rousseau did, she presages the day when this naked truth will once again be revealed, and the current cycle of history will be at an end.

According to Blumenberg (1998: 64), in modernity the trope of the naked truth has frequently been used as a mode of attacking any social system believed to be based on or to promote false distinctions between human beings. We have already seen that Anatole France (1909) used clothing as the primal human hypocrisy in his novel *Penguin Island*. Blumenberg finds the metaphor in thinkers as different as Marx, Montaigne, Pascal and Kierkegaard. It appears, for example, in Marx's *Communist Manifesto* as a repeated topos of stripping away or unveiling. The bourgeoisie have stripped away the roles that held feudal society together as a seemingly "natural" set of relations between inferiors and superiors. Marx (1988) imagines such ties in terms of the particular forms of clothing worn by each social group. The bourgeoisie have stripped traditional social roles away, leaving the naked truth of human relations for all to see. Naked self-interest has become the new currency. The following passage shows the sustained use of a metaphor of the tearing away of veils, to reveal naked self-interest at the heart of human relations under capitalism:

> The bourgeoisie, wherever it has got the upper hand, has put an end to all feudal, patriarchal, idyllic relations. It has pitilessly torn asunder the motley feudal ties[10] that bound man to his "natural superiors," and has left remaining no other nexus between man and man than naked self-interest, than callous "cash payment." It has drowned the most heavenly ecstasies of religious fervour, of chivalrous enthusiasm, of philistine sentimentalism, in the icy water of egotistical calculation. It has resolved personal worth into exchange value . . . In one word, for exploitation, veiled by religious and political illusions, it has substituted naked, shameless, direct, brutal exploitation.
>
> The bourgeoisie has stripped of its halo every occupation hitherto honoured and looked up to with reverent awe. It has converted the physician, the lawyer, the priest, the poet, the man of science, into its paid wage-labourers.
>
> The bourgeoisie has torn away from the family its sentimental veil, and has reduced the family relation to a mere money relation. (Marx 1988: 57–8)

This is a naked truth that is in no way honourable or desirable.

For other philosophers, clothing (so obviously subject to fashion and difference) is a patent demonstration of the fact that social differences are a product of the human imagination. Pascal, for example, laughed at Montaigne's idealistic wish for others to be as attached to bare, unadorned truth as he himself claimed to be (*Essais*, Bk 1, see Blumenberg 1998: 65). According to Pascal, humans are attached to show, appearance and falsity, which he sums up in the word imagination: "Imagination decides everything; it makes beauty, justice, and happiness, which is the world's all in all" (quoted in Blumenberg 1998: 63). Pascal believed that in the great battle between reason and the imagination, the latter would always prove the stronger, since reason could never fully conquer imagination, while imagination could easily drive reason away completely. To develop this point, he discussed the role of clothing in persuading us of truth, describing the elaborate costumes worn by those wanting to deceive the world into believing that they are the possessors of truth – like lawyers, judges and doctors. "We cannot even see an advocate in his robe, with his cap on his head, without an enhanced opinion of his ability," claims Pascal (quoted in Blumenberg 1998: 63). Although Pascal doesn't explicitly make use of the metaphor of the naked truth, he draws on it implicitly, by arguing that the elaborate costumes of the privileged hide the fact that they have, in fact, no special powers (a possibility, incidentally, explored in *The Emperor's New Clothes*). The following exemplification is, as Blumenberg argues, indebted to the metaphor of truth as naked and unadorned:

> Our magistrates have fully recognized this mystery. Their red robes, the ermine in which they wrap themselves like furry cats, the halls in which they administer justice, the fleur-de-lis, and all their solemn apparel are most necessary; and if physicians had not their cassocks and their mules, and lawyers their square caps and their robes four times too wide, they would never have deceived the world, which cannot resist these imposing appearances. If lawyers dispensed true justice and physicians possessed the true art of healing, they would not need square bonnets; the majesty of their art would itself command sufficient respect. But since their arts are only imaginary, they have to adopt these vain devices that strike the imagination, . . . and so, in short, they inspire respect. (Pascal, quoted in Blumenberg 1998: 62–63)

Not all authorities rely on costume alone to sustain their privilege, says Pascal. Those backed up by brute force, like soldiers and kings, may wear the elaborate costumes, but they have real as well as symbolic power to sustain their hegemony. Kings have no need of disguise.

For the gloomy Christian philosopher Kierkegaard (1958), writing, one might note, in the cold climate of Scandinavia, clothing is a comforting necessity (as it was for Carlyle (1987), for whom it kept the self "snug" in a shell). Clothes are, for Kierkegaard, a necessary salvation from the starkness, exposure and vulnerability of the bare truth:

> What would be the use of discovering so-called objective truth, of working through all the systems of philosophy and of being able, if required, to review them all and show up the inconsistencies within each system; . . . what good would it do me to be able to explain the meaning of Christianity if it had *no* deeper significance *for me and for my life*; – what good would it do me if truth stood before me, cold and naked, not caring whether I recognised her or not, and producing in me a shudder of fear rather than a trusting devotion? (Kierkegaard 1958: 44, original emphases)

In this extract, the naked truth is a cold, stark reality disconnected from embodied, connected human life. This kind of nakedness, truthful or otherwise, is not the desirable condition of humanness. The philosophical quest ceases to be the pursuit of an absolute, objective, "naked" truth, but of a truth that can make life liveable and meaningful for the individual, and that is an understanding of God's express purpose for one's self: "[T]he thing is to find a truth which is true *for me*, to find *the idea for which I can live and die*" (p. 44, original emphases).

Throughout these various uses of the metaphor of the naked truth, then, we see once again a fundamental discomfort (often theologically derived) with the ambiguous state of the "natural" human – as either a wretch in need of clothing and/or a naked being for whom no veils or clothes are necessary. Although the female form has been dignified in this tradition (as in the allegorical statues of *Nuda Veritas*), we must note that woman's traditional characterization as skilful at make-up, clothing and adornment takes its meaning in relation to this theological/philosophical suspicion of clothing.

The increasing modern suspicion of the possibility or even the desirability of finding a naked truth can be seen being played out in relation to techniques of photographic representation. Technologies of mechanical reproduction, especially photography, have traditionally carried with them the cultural fiction that they re-present reality accurately or truthfully. This assumption means that images of nakedness carry a doubly weighty cultural baggage around authenticity and truth. But nudity and naked images can equally well be used in the reverse. As we saw in Chapter 1, the trope of nudity as masquerade, deception or lie both relies on and problematizes the traditional equation between nudity and truth. Its power derives precisely from the cultural centrality of the equation between nakedness and truth. Alongside a belief in the indexicality of photography there has run an awareness of it as a cultural artefact (trick photography is as old as the medium itself). Makers of images have of course been especially aware of their artificiality. Filmmaker Sergei Eisenstein apparently taught his students that the medium of film works to make lies, using the example of a camera showing a keyhole, zooming in, then cutting to a shot of a woman in the bath. The keyhole is in a door in Frankfurt, he said, and the woman is in a bath in Moscow. Nakedness here reveals not the truth but a lie, and the inversion is a comment on the powers of modern technology.[11]

It is no accident that Eisenstein should have chosen an image of nakedness to give impact to his point. Nor is it accidental that debates about the possibilities and ethics of digital manipulation of images, in their turn, have done the same. The rupturing of the age-old nexus between nakedness and truth functions well as an affirmation of the iconoclastic powers of any new reproduction technology.

One example came in 1993, when a digitally altered photograph of outspoken Australian politician Jeff Kennett appeared amid great controversy on the front cover of a magazine. The photo, which purported to depict Kennett nude at a public meeting, was captioned "Unreal, Jeff," and accompanied an article about the changes being wrought by digital technologies to photography's traditional status as index of the truth. It is no coincidence that the journalist chose to use the nude body – traditionally the index of the bare truth, the real thing – to make the point that photography's relationship to the real is undergoing a profound shift. Kennett was distinctly unimpressed, and threatened to sue. The magazine's editor Anne Summers said that the Premier had no basis for legal action since "he was not being held up to ridicule, he was not being defamed and nothing had been done to detract from his reputation" (Anon. 1993). There was no privacy issue since there was never any claim that the photograph was genuine. Nor was the issue one of improper display causing moral offence to the public, since the doctored photograph included a digitally added head in the crowd in front of the groin area. Rather, the issue became whether there was something inherently damaging about a representation of something that never took place and/or anything inherently defamatory about nakedness itself.

In this incident, manipulation was itself the offence – the offence of tampering with the naked truth. It is interesting to note that censorship practices reverse the usual moral valuation; censorship in fact *demands* the manipulation of naked truth for moral reasons. Whereas digital or other forms of manipulation are often themselves seen as dangerous because they jeopardize truth, in cases where truth itself is understood to be dangerous (as with some kinds of nakedness), digital manipulation is seen as salutary. In the Kennett incident, digital manipulation is figured as a form of deceit in which the naked truth is jeopardized just as the indexicality of the sign is jeopardized; in the case of censorship, it is the naked truth itself that is construed as dangerous, and digital manipulation is a form of safeguard. The airbrushing of genitals is an exception to the rule that rupturing the indexical status of the photo is dangerous.

The reversal of the taken-for-granted assumption that the naked body reveals truth is a good way to generate both shock and humour. An example came in the British TV series *A League of Gentlemen*, in which all the principal characters, male and female, were played by three male actors. In one episode, we discover that an eccentric married couple have a monthly "Nude Day." Both characters are initially shown in "modest" poses: the husband is seated in an armchair with a newspaper placed strategically over his lap, the wife is standing with her back to the camera. Eventually, though, "she" turns to reveal her full-frontal nudity to the camera. Her breasts are a moulded chestpiece like a flesh-coloured suit of armour; her genitals are covered by an enormous bush of pubic hair – long enough, we realize, to hide the actor's penis behind it. Her nakedness is especially striking because of its patent artificiality. On reflection, too, we might start to think that the actor's penis could have been concealed in other ways, without the need for such a preternaturally long beard of pubic hair. Perhaps the hair has been designed subtly to *look as though* it's hiding a penis. It is intended to throw us into confusion. No wonder the shock is comic, as so many contradictory categories – truth, concealment, authenticity, fake, male, female, hair as revelation, hair as covering – are offered us simultaneously.

Nakedness can symbolize not only the truth of the matter but also the truth of the self – psychological authenticity. The metaphor of stripping away implies an authentic self clothed in cultural baggage or social roles. John Berger (1972: 54) put it this way: "To be naked is to be oneself . . . To be naked is to be without disguise." This is how it has often been understood in psychoanalysis, except that psychoanalysis's focus on symbolization makes it more alert to the possibility that nudity might function as a *metaphor* for naturalness. Nakedness figures most prominently in psychoanalytic discussion in the form of debate about the common dream of being naked. Unlike Freud, who saw the dream of nakedness as emanating from repression and producing anxiety, Erich Fromm speculated that the dream of being naked may represent "the wish to be one's natural self" (quoted in Myers 1989: 118), and that the embarrassment experienced in the dream reflects social disapproval of the wish to be authentic. Thus, whereas for Freud the repression dealt with in this dream was that of the infantile desire to exhibit, for Fromm, the latent content centres on a more traditional interpretation of nakedness – as emblem of truth, in this case the truth of ourselves. Whereas Berger equates nakedness with *being* oneself, psychoanalysis would suggest, rather, that nakedness functions as a *symbol* for the absence of disguise.

And yet, as a discipline, Freudian psychoanalysis was prone to setting itself up as the revealer not of symbols but of the naked truth. This, at least, is Jacques Derrida's claim, in his exploration of Freud's (1953) discussion in *The Interpretation of Dreams* of the typical dream of being naked. Derrida (1987) claims that Freud understood psychoanalysis as a process of denudation, unveiling, or revelation. This is evident, he says, from Freud's use in this passage of the term *Einkleidung* ("clothing") for the secondary content that hides the naked truth of latent content, and in his use of *The Emperor's New Clothes* as the exemplary instance of the dream of nakedness. Psychoanalysis claims to strip back secondary psychical elaborations (or "manifest content") such as dreams or symptoms to reveal their latent content, in all its nudity. For Freud, underneath all secondary material, finally, lies an unbearable (and hence repressed) truth – that of the universally shared Oedipal material. Freud reads the dream (and *The Emperor's New Clothes*) as universally "about" the infantile desire to exhibit one's nakedness, a desire that must be repressed as the child grows up. In other words, Freud's psychoanalysis reveals not just the naked truth, but truth *as* nakedness (Derrida 1987: 415). For Derrida, it is no coincidence that Freud uses *The Emperor's New Clothes* as his own exemplary tale, since it is a perfect allegory for psychoanalysis, whose core business is revelation via analysis of the deceptive "garments" that both hide and reveal an underlying nudity. In Derrida's words, the story is about

> a nudity *and* a garment that are both invisible, in the form of a cloth visible for some and invisible for others, a nudity both apparent and exhibited. The same material hides and shows . . . the truth of what is present without a veil. (Derrida 1987: 418, original emphasis)

The dream or symptom is simultaneously a hiding and a showing – it can be stripped away to reveal a naked truth, but, for a post-structuralist critic such as Derrida, that revealed truth must always be another layer of cultural "clothing," the universal garment of the Oedipal story. Underneath the text-clothing lies not nudity, but more text(ile).[12]

It may seem as though Derrida's insightful reading of the metaphor of the naked truth goes well beyond its most commonsensical usage. And yet, the paradoxes of this metaphor continue to be commonly played out, even if they are rarely articulated with such relentless sharpness. Any medium (whether it be narrative, theatrical or visual) that attempts to *represent* nudity-as-truth contains the seeds of this paradox, whether it be acknowledged or not.

In the modern era, the idea that nakedness reveals the psychological truth of an individual began to be explored in painting. Anne Hollander (1993: 175) sees nineteenth-century painters like Courbet and Eakins as opening up a new terrain, wherein the nude could begin to become a serious subject, and not an object, in art. Their work began to eschew the obligatory classical references and to situate the nude in "significant surroundings drawn from the experience of everyday domesticity rather than in landscape and drapery" (p. 173). It foreshadows the twentieth century's "enlarged and complicated" (p. 175) sense of the place of sexuality in identity; such artists start to perceive and give expression to an "expanded psychic dimension for nudity" (p. 176). Modern painters like Hopper or Lucian Freud participate in the exploration of an inner life, and use nudity, especially in domestic settings or dream landscapes, as one vehicle for the expression of this new understanding of interiority.

Some kinds of naked images more than others can seem to approach the psychological truth of the person. We will explore this in detail in Chapter 4, when we discuss the recent explosion of interest in "homemade," "authentic" images of naked people by consumers who feel sated with the highly glossy nudes of advertising, magazine and film culture. The question of how much of the "real" person is revealed in a naked image is especially interesting when it comes to celebrity nudity, since the celebrity is the exemplary contemporary instance of a dual form of personhood: both particular and universal; individual and representative; irreplaceable and allegorical. We will see, then, that even while the philosophical elaboration of the metaphor of the naked truth might seem quite arcane, its core paradoxes are commonly played out in vernacular ways – as in the common late-modern oscillation between thinking of the self as an authenticity to be revealed and a performance to be played with.

"Negative" Connotations of Nakedness

As we have seen, the Christian tradition often used nakedness in a positive sense – as the stripping away of attachment to worldly things. In general, though, according to Margaret Miles, its symbolic valency was more often negative: "The mark of powerlessness and passivity, nakedness was associated with captives, slaves, prostitutes, the insane, and the dead" (Miles 1989: 81). Many of the negative connotations of nakedness can be seen as the flipside of the positive ones. Furthermore, the same attribute can be negative when applied to one group of people and positive when applied to another (e.g. the innocence of children versus that of "savages").

Nakedness and Exposure

The underside of nakedness as metaphoric truth or honesty is nakedness as exposure: the forced or unwilling revelation of the self. The literal exposure of one's body involves a symbolic dimension, and nakedness can itself symbolize other forms of revelation.

The relationship between bodily exposure and dreams of nakedness was discussed by Freud in *The Interpretation of Dreams*. Freud considered the possibility that dreams of being naked were caused by literal bodily exposure.

He outlined the major findings of biologically based (i.e. non-religious, non-superstitious) investigations into the cause(s) of dreams, dividing them into four possible sources: "(1) external (objective) sensory excitations; (2) internal (subjective) sensory excitations; (3) internal (organic) somatic stimuli; and (4) purely psychical sources of stimulation" (Freud 1953: 22). Many scientists, he says, explain dreams of nakedness in relation to categories one and/or four – these dreams occur, they say, when our bedclothes fall off at night (p. 24). The external stimulus (and/or internal somatic recognition of it) "causes" the dream. While he doesn't actually discount such interpretations, characterizing them as "plausible" (p. 38), Freud sees such theories, especially that of internal somatic stimuli, as weak, or at least incomplete. He claimed that somatic stimuli play a role only where they support the ideational content of a dream's psychical content, but otherwise not (p. 237). He is, of course, far more interested in the "great gap" left by these four categories: the latent rather than manifest psychical content of dreams. Freud was more interested in the symbolic rather than literal associations of nakedness with exposure.

Nakedness can be used as a metaphor for psychological exposure. The vernacular expression "getting caught with your pants down" associates the "honesty" of nudity with the feeling of guilt. It implies unreadiness – the idea that we prepare ourselves for the public gaze. To adopt the dramaturgical metaphor of Erving Goffman (1965), if social life can be thought of as a set of "presentations of self" in which we make use of available settings, props and symbols to play our socially sanctioned roles, then getting caught with our pants down represents being caught "off-stage," unprepared.

In biblical terms, nakedness signifies utter exposure to the gaze of God. As we have seen, this is part of its association with truth, which can be both an honourable state of authenticity or a threatening state of vulnerability: "Neither is there any creature that is not manifest in his sight: but all things are naked and opened unto the eyes of him with whom we have to do" (Hebrews 4:13). In Revelation, nakedness is used to symbolize spiritual unreadiness (and shame), when the sixth angel foreshadows the coming of God: "Behold, I come as a thief. Blessed is he that watcheth, and keepeth his garments, lest he walk naked, and they see his shame" (Revelation 16:15). The motif of nakedness before God links the metaphor of nudity with intimate genres like the religious confession and the diary. Here is an example from Kierkegaard's (1960) diary, in which he uses the metaphor of nakedness to evoke and compare a bare landscape (the heath), a condition of mind (disciplined self-reflection) and the human condition of total visibility before God:

> The heath must be especially influential in developing strong minds; here all lies
> naked, bared before God, and here the multifarious diversions have no place, the

many odd nooks and crannies in which our minds can hide and whence it is often hard for serious purpose to collect the scattered thoughts. Here the mind must close in upon itself, definitely and exactingly. "Whither shall I flee from Thy presence?" one could ask in truth here on the heath. (Kierkegaard 1960: 33)

This kind of exposure is linked to both truth and vulnerability (and as such, can actually not be seen as either "positive" or "negative" in any simple way).

Nakedness as a Sign of Sin and Criminality

There are, though, much less equivocal meanings of nakedness, such as the cluster in which it can function as a sign of sin or criminality. In biblical usage, the term "nakedness" is associated with incest or other forms of unlawful liaison. Cruden's (1848) *Concordance* glosses the repeated use of "nakedness" in Leviticus (e.g. "And thou shalt not uncover the nakedness of thy mother's sister, nor of thy father's sister" 20:19) as meaning a shameful, unlawful or incestuous relationship (Cruden 1848: 470). In the Adam and Eve story, sin either calls nakedness into being or changes its meaning forever (depending on which theologian one follows). St Augustine has a quite precise theory on this, at least, if one can believe Havelock Ellis's interpretation of Augustine's (1998) discussion of Eden in Book 14 of *The City of God* (*De Civitate Dei*): he claimed that there were no erections before the Fall. Nakedness became indecent only after this "shameless novelty" first occurred (discussed in Ellis 1937: 6). This theory, however, "fails to account for modesty in women," as Ellis matter-of-factly points out.[13]

As we have seen, centuries of misogynist Christian theology have meant that a naked female figure still "easily communicates sin, sex, and evil" (Miles 1989: 125). Allegorical figures for Lust, for example, have often been depicted naked. In the Middle Ages, with the general uptake of Aristotelian biology, which understood woman as a biologically inferior man, an earlier Christian ambivalence about the apportioning of blame between Adam and Eve gave way to a less unequivocal understanding of woman as morally culpable. The human condition of vulnerability to sickness, ageing and mortality was construed as a punishment for Eve's disobedience. Eve transferred her sinfulness not only onto all womankind, but also onto flesh itself, which she metonymically represents. This heritage encourages us to see female flesh as the epitome of the weakness, vulnerability, temptation and mundanity it accords flesh more generally. Eve's naked body represented her seductive power over Adam. As the authors of the *Malleus Maleficarum*, a fifteenth-century treatise on witches, declare: "Woman is beautiful to look upon, contaminating to the touch, and deadly to keep" (quoted in Polinska 2000: 50). Such beliefs, translated into visual culture, meant that "[n]ude female bodies become a visual sign of wickedness and decadence" (p. 51). Some medieval representations show the "good" woman in clothes and the "bad" woman (e.g. the prostitute) naked or part-naked (p. 52). Both written and visual accounts of witchcraft (e.g. the *Malleus Maleficarum* and the woodcuts of Hans Baldung Grien) imagine witches naked, despite the fact that naked covens were not a historical reality (Warner 1985: 300). Miles (1989: 138) argues that Baldung's witches, by dint of their iconographic association with Eves and maidens, "imply that witch-craft is nothing more than an extreme instance of endemic female vice and folly."

The importance of religious subjects and contexts to the Western fine art tradition meant that the ambivalence or even hostility towards naked adult female bodies became a part of mainstream visual culture. Indeed, Margaret Miles, in her analysis of works such as Tintoretto's 1560 painting *Susanna and the Elders*, claims that in sixteenth- and seventeenth-century visual culture "it was impossible to paint a naked female body in such a way that it symbolized innocence" (Miles 1989: 124). The mortification of female nakedness in Western art has been remarkably persistent. Victorian culture was obsessed with the figure of the prostitute. In Victorian fine art, the fight to extricate the female nude from its association with immorality took the form of, among other things, large-scale theoretical debates about the relationship of art and morality, conflicts over particular genres ("the nude") or pictorial codes (e.g. the use of colour) and of institutional battles about the use of female models and the suitability of female artists painting nudes (see Smith 1996). Moral and aesthetic discourses are still often in conflict, even today.

Female flesh is, then, "occupied territory" (Tickner 1978: 239), and it is scarcely possible to imagine how it might be seen and experienced anew.[14] The question of how it might be possible for radically different conceptualiza-tions and experiences of femininity to emerge is the perpetual challenge for feminism, whose foundations must always be paradoxical, proceeding "as if it were possibly to negate a history of negation" (Braidotti 1994: 189). One of the questions posed throughout this book is how different representational codes and practices affect each other, and what effects they have on women's and men's actual experiences of their body, particularly their naked body. It is, however, by no means always or only adult female nakedness that is "dangerous." First, to the extent that *all* flesh is devalued or problematized in the Western tradition, almost all nudity has the potential to be seen as morally dangerous.

Moreover, there are significant differences between the meanings a live naked body can carry and those produced in art or other forms of representa-tion. While the legacy of the classical tradition includes many positive meanings of male nudes, the fine art tradition more generally has bequeathed rather more ambiguous, precarious or double-edged meanings to female nudity. When it comes to the lived body, however, such valuations are almost reversed. In modern times, the nakedness of real-life male bodies in public space is much more "dangerous" than that of female bodies. The naked female body may still be considered morally dangerous (seductive, tempting, likely to lead one astray), but it is less likely to be construed as quite so literally deviant or criminal as is the naked male body in public. A naked female body on the streets is more likely to be seen as in danger rather than dangerous.

This is an obvious point given the normalization of male violence and the normalization of female nudity as an object for scrutiny, whether salacious or "aesthetic." Both norms mean that public male exposure is far more likely than female exposure to be considered deviant or criminal. This also gives it greater potential than the female body for use as a weapon or a protest vehicle. Flashing, for example, is an almost exclusively male activity, and one that has the power to shock and alarm far more than female exposure.[15] Even in contexts sympathetic to (indeed encouraging of) public exposure, such as the nudist resort, the body of the unaccompanied male is still subtly suspect, while that of the female is not. Historically, most nudist clubs banned single males, and some still do. Even in those clubs or resorts where single men are allowed, there is a subtle self-consciousness experienced by some men, as they are forced, in a sense, to embody their own innocence or good intentions. Male violence and its interrelations with aggressive sexuality have rendered even the "natural" male body always prone to suspicions of ill-intent.

The perceived moral, social or psychological power, even dangerousness, of nudity is evident in the (presumably) universal regulation of nudity by taboos and laws. Taboos recognize and activate nudity as something with strong psychological and/or social power. From early times, nudity has been widely used for magic – to ward off danger, paralyse enemies, or strengthen one's own magic. It has also had ritual and religious functions. In some religious traditions, one can be deemed to need protection from one's *own* nudity. In traditional Catholic teaching, for example, the eye could not roam over one's own body (Crawley 1965: 48). Havelock Ellis also cites anthropological claims about a similar teaching in ancient Islam: "The Sunna [customary law] prescribes that a man shall not uncover himself even to himself, and shall not wash naked" (Julius Wellhausen, quoted in Ellis 1937: 20). John Langdon-Davies reports a close friend telling him how as a child at the convent school she was made to have her bath in a chemise, in order that she not see her own body, and to likewise protect "the delicate sensibilities of her Guardian Angel" (Langdon-Davies 1928: 13–14). Ellis (1937: 34) reports a personal communication from an elderly lady who claimed never to have looked at her own nakedness in the whole of her life, because it frightened her, though this style of claim is hard to verify.

The modern social contract deems that one has a right to be protected from the nudity of others. Women and children have been deemed to be in special need of protection from adult nudity (even though children are also accorded greater freedom to *be* nude, and women, as carers, have traditionally had closer contact with certain kinds of naked bodies: infants, sick or elderly people). Women and children have been considered more vulnerable to its powers, a "weakness" whose positive guise is "feminine modesty." Havelock Ellis considered modesty to be an "emotion" that developed at puberty, and one that was so fundamental a part of femininity as to constitute "the chief secondary sexual character of women on the psychical side" (Ellis 1937: 1). Discourses of natural modesty and of protection often have a regulatory function. For example, in Victorian England, the codes of bourgeois femininity prevented female artists from exhibiting nudes and joining life classes, where female nudity would be on display. Such beliefs helped keep the art scene and its markets under male control (Smith 1996: 37–8). Historically, the discourse of protection applied not just to images agreed to be erotic or pornographic, but also to fine art, where idealist aesthetic discourses did battle with moral discourses. Attempts to bring aesthetic rather than moralistic discourse to bear on female nudes were part of a modernizing governance project of the late nineteenth century. Discourses of moral improvement through art accompanied the rise of public galleries and museums.

But the aesthetic discourse doesn't always "take," even today. For example, in 1990 there was a small local scandal around a painting of the tourist icon The Three Sisters (a famous rock formation in the Blue Mountains, west of Sydney). The painting depicted the three rocks as sculpted women, with big round breasts, a little in the style of an Indian temple. One of the members of the Blue Mountains City Council, hoping that the local council might buy and display the painting, enthusiastically unveiled it at a council meeting. Amid uproar, one of the local aldermen protested in the following terms: "He said that while he was usually leading the charge for this sort of thing when it was men only, he was affronted to have it displayed 'where women and children can see it'" (Anon. 1990: 1). This is a moment where the aesthetic discourse *failed* for moral reasons.

But there are other, more overtly political, reasons why the aesthetic discourse might fail. Feminist Doreen Massey (1994), for example, begins her analysis of the gendering of space with the recollection of visiting a European art gallery in her late teens with two male companions and experiencing it as an alienating and demeaning space:

[The paintings] were pictures of naked women painted by men, and thus of women seen through the eyes of men. So I stood there with these two young friends, and they looked at these pictures which were of women seen through the eyes of men, and I looked at them, my two young friends, looking at pictures of naked women as seen through the eyes of men. And I felt objectified. This was a "space" that clearly let me know something, and something ignominious, about what High Culture thought was my place in Society. (Massey 1994: 186)

Massey recounts that she lost the subsequent argument with her friends, who accused her of being "silly."

Massey's critique began with a bodily feeling of unease, and is an example of a discourse around nudity that would see itself as politically rather than morally based. As many liberal feminist commentators have pointed out, though, feminist critiques of image practices can often find themselves (unexpectedly) aligned with critiques coming from a more conservative moral position. A common interlinking of the moral and the political occurs in relation to pornography, where the aesthetic discourse has the least purchase of all. That many women experience porn as oppressive is commonly documented. Andrea Dworkin and Catherine MacKinnon are two thinkers who claim that pornography represents the wholesale, industrialized and commodified use of nudity as a weapon. While their position has been roundly critiqued by feminists of other intellectual and political persuasions, their conception of nude images as an assault on women by an oppressive patriarchy is one way of accounting for the otherwise strange-seeming fact that in contemporary Australia, women can still be deemed in need of "protection" from images of female bodies (the persistence of a discourse of feminine modesty is another). Women certainly can experience such images as an affront or an assault, especially in the case of pornographic images. In this case it is not necessarily or only that women are considered as in need of protection from nudity *per se*; women are also (implicitly) being protected from having to see the surface manifestations of a patriarchal organization of vision, corporeality and sexuality. Like many women, I am often grateful that I do not have to confront in my daily life certain distressing symptoms of a fundamentally inequitable social system. Nonetheless, I cannot help but wonder about the ultimate (i.e. long-term) value of such protective devices. To the extent that this "protection" both permits and helps shield a patriarchal ordering of bodies and perception, it is arguable what service this combination of paternalist control and liberal consumerism plays in changing the sexual status quo. However, these are far larger questions than I seek to explore here. My point here is mainly to emphasize the contradictions surrounding representations of female nakedness specifically, and to note the possibility that both images and live practices of nakedness can function as weapons, and can be deemed criminal or immoral.

Nudity and Sex

The examples above demonstrate the persistence of a strong set of discursive connections between nudity, sex and immorality. The mental association between nudity and sex is almost automatic for contemporary Westerners. It is, after all, the utter foundation of the multimillion dollar pornography industry, and of Hollywood. It also underpins high art traditions like that of the European nude, despite the disavowals of idealist forms of art criticism. Even conservative art historian Kenneth Clark requires of the nude that it have the power to arouse desire (in the heterosexual male spectator); indeed, he sees this as essential to its artistry.

Mario Perniola claims that the metaphysical richness of the Christian tradition has made possible a wealth of erotic possibilities in the figurative arts. He argues that, because it drew on both the Hebrew tradition of the "glorious garment" (Perniola 1989: 237) and the classical one of the naked truth, Christianity "made the consummate representation of eroticism possible in the figurative arts" (p. 243). This is because it introduced a hitherto undeveloped dynamic between concealment and revelation, whose force could work in two directions: evoking either the putting on or the taking off of garments. At the base of this argument is Perniola's belief that eroticism in art relies on the possibility of movement, or what he calls "transit" (p. 237). In other words, eroticism results from the *relation between* clothing and nudity rather than from either clothing or nudity as "absolute value." For him, the classical Greek nude had nothing to do with eroticism, since it embodied not a transit but an absolute value – that of the ideal human form. Likewise, no such transit was understood to form part of the Hebrew metaphysics of clothing. It is not until the modern era, according to Perniola, that the possibility for transit within Hebrew and Greek culture was discovered (p. 242).

If one accepts Perniola's definition of eroticism as a movement rather than a stable state, then the visual tradition of later Christianity can be understood as suffused with erotic potential, despite the theological links between sex and sin and the plethora of moral precepts about sexual behaviour. Christianity's complex metaphysical underpinnings make it an ideal vehicle for tensions and pulls rather than absolute states. The dual Judaic and Greek heritage, for example, means that over the centuries, art depicting Christian themes or stories has had two erotic vectors: not only the familiar erotics of undressing, but also an erotics of dressing. Perniola (1989: 243ff.) sees the erotics of undressing as most developed in the Reformation and in Mannerism, and the erotics of dressing in the Counter-Reformation and the Baroque.

The erotics of undressing relies on the idea that stripping away brings one closer to something authentic, hidden, true. The erotics of dressing, on the other hand, derives from the biblical comparison of the body to a garment or robe. This comparison allows one to envisage nudity as the endpoint not of a process of stripping, but of dressing. The naked body is not a deprivation but an incarnation – an em-bodying (dressing) of spirit. Being incarnate "is the consequence of a process of enclothing, materialization, personification" (Perniola 1989: 251). Perniola gives two key examples of this erotics: the first is the use of drapery, especially in Baroque work; the second, which will be discussed in the next section, is the idea of the body itself as a form of garment. In Baroque art, clothing, with its folds, crevices and movements, can seem less to cover a body than to resonate with the presence of the body. For Perniola, both erotic trajectories eventually find their limits in stasis. He argues, for example, that the corpse can be depicted in such a way as to freeze out all possibility of movement or return and hence all eroticism. Where this occurs, the erotics of undressing has been pushed to its limit. The erotics of dressing has its limits too, his key example being the ideal nude. Unlike Clark, Perniola sees the nineteenth-century academic nude as so formalist as to have frozen its erotic possibilities in "a sepulchral immobility" (p. 252).

Perniola's definition of eroticism seems to me to be useful, in that it posits eroticism as a dynamic rather than a state. This might help give a philosophical reason, for example, for the common-sense nudist wisdom that nudism isn't sexy. It might also give us a hint as to why so many euphemisms for nudity begin with the word "in" – locking nudity safely away as state rather than process. But Perniola has nothing to say about the power relations of that dynamic. What is the relationship between eroticism and, say, objectification? Does a transit imply any particular form of subject–object relations? It is all very well to define eroticism as a movement, a transit, rather than an assemblage of pleasing bodies or body parts, but discussions of eroticism and representation cannot ignore the question of gendered visual pleasure (at least, feminists believe so). Tellingly, Perniola speaks of "eroticism" generally, but all the *images* reproduced for his essay (barring, interestingly, a crucified Christ and a skeleton on the gibbet) are of naked *women*, and Madonnas, Venuses and female saints are the mainstays of his discussion. His brief discussion of Greek male statuary does mention the "classical male nude's sex appeal" (p. 243) but his argument refuses its erotic value, since he claims that the Platonist idealism underpinning the classical nude "precludes forever erotic transit" (p. 243). The gender problem is bound to arise, eventually, with any theory based on an idea of "the" body. Perniola's essay has been of inestimable value to my own study, but those searching for a political critique need to look elsewhere.

One of the merits of Perniola's study, though, is that it doesn't read nudity as an inevitable sign of sex or the erotic. To refuse this simple equation today is, however, to push against the grain of an almost automatic popular assumption, in which we can often detect the surprisingly strong persistence of an association between nakedness, sex and sin. The reception of the nudist movement in Australia makes for one interesting example of a practice attempting to refigure Christian suspicion of the body, often by recourse to an imagined prelapsarian state of unselfconsciousness. In Australia, where nudism is still seen by and large as a minority, if not perverse, activity, the nudist movement is presented with a particular bind. Longstanding accusations about orgies and sexual perversion have led the official voices of nudism to protest its innocence – some say too vigorously. In its efforts to disassociate itself in the public eye from sex, the nudist movement speaks long and hard of the innocence of nudism; as a result, some now denounce this rhetoric (and/or the movement) as puritanical! Early Australian naturists, particularly those who had the difficult job of running the gauntlet of Australian obscenity legislation by publishing nudist magazines, sometimes found themselves approaching the values of early Christian asceticism (in which nakedness symbolized innocence and industry) or even, indeed, the most puritanical discourses of conservative Christianity. A leading figure in early Australian naturism, Ron Ashworth, echoed both in an editorial in the *Australian Sunbather* in 1946, in which he called sex "an evil" that could lead a girl to prostitution. Even while it extolled the Edenic purity of the naked body, then, nudist discourse could also continue to draw on the association between sex, death, illness and nakedness, in the tradition of Genesis.

Among teenage girls, the equation between nudity, sex and immorality still appears to be fairly strong. A physical education (PE) teacher we interviewed told us that if a girl was comfortable with her own nudity in the school changing-room, this would be negatively interpreted as a sign of "sluttishness" rather than positively as a sign of confidence or unselfconsciousness. One of my students told our class that having large breasts was enough for her to be labelled both stupid and a "slut" at her high school.

There are, of course, contexts in which the association between nudity and sex has been cause for celebration. A whole cluster of twentieth-century theories and movements have aimed to disrupt or reinterpret the negative aspects of the Judeo-Christian legacy. Counter-cultural, personal development, New Age and nudist movements, among others, have drawn ammunition from the development of progressivist theories such as sexology, feminism, queer theory, psychology and psychoanalysis to seek out non-moral arguments about nudity and sex. Progressive theology, including feminist theology, has also argued for a reconsideration of the body and sex in Christian thought. Some of these practices have relied on discourses of "naturalness," others on discourses of revolution, liberation, desire or pleasure. One of the contexts of these theoretical, practical and political developments is the development of consumer culture over the twentieth century. The history of consumerism is intertwined with those of a range of liberalizing formations – secularization, globalization and feminism, to name just three.

Consumer culture both fuels and reflects moral change. As Mike Featherstone (1991: 173) puts it, the "progressive expansion of the market" helps to "discredit traditional norms and unhinge long-held meanings which were firmly grounded in social relationships and cultural objects." Featherstone claims that "consumer culture permits the unashamed display of the human body" (p. 177). Although it is tempting to replace "permits" with "promotes," the understatement is more accurate, since consumer culture is currently characterized less by an unequivocal incitement to permissiveness than by an intricate dialectic of display and concealment. The mix of positive and negative meanings surveyed above means that nudity can function as a metaphor for the liberation (often "naughty" or "bold") that consumer culture repeatedly promises us. Since nudity is *partially and differentially* permitted – encouraged in some contexts, prohibited in others – it is an ideal vehicle to capture both the vestigial puritanism of early capitalism and the emergent hedonism of late-modern capitalism (see Turner 1994: 3–4). Thus, the increasing though uneven acceptance of representations of nudity in the public sphere is a moral shift that is best understood in its larger context: that of the increasing naturalization of the logic of commodity exchange.

Organizations like the Eros Foundation are a clear example of the role of commodity exchange in moral liberalization. This foundation is an adult-industry body devoted to the political challenge of undoing the religious inheritance of largely negative meanings of sex. Its objective is to "seek logical perspectives on sex and rational law reform of the sex industry" (www.eros. com.au). Among other activities, the organization lobbies politicians on censorship issues, fights for the rights of workers in all facets of the adult and sex industries, runs personal development workshops on sexual issues, and holds trade meetings. Political goals, personal development, industrial relations and trade are different and overlapping facets of their work.

Consumerism is, however, a complex and often contradictory set of formations, and so the relation between the spread of consumerism and moral change is not simple. Some pathways of commodity exchange are as reliant on self-disgust, sexual repression and somatophobia as others are on the celebration and promotion of sexual liberation.

Nudity and Death

> Man is a little soul carrying around a corpse
>
> Epictetus, Fragment 26

Naked death is a common iconographic motif, found, for example, in some depictions of the corpse, and in some *memento mori*. In one strand of the Christian tradition, nudity, sex, death and sin are connected. Flesh does have positive meanings in Christian thought, notably as the temple of God, the housing of spirit. Indeed, the Incarnation makes theological sense only if human embodiment is seen as worthy and meaningful.[16] Nonetheless, there has also been a somatophobic strain of Christian thought, in which flesh is seen as both the source of sin (likely to lead one astray) and the dwelling place of sin:

> For I know that in me (that is, in my flesh,) dwelleth no good thing . . . (Romans 7:18)

> Let not sin therefore reign in your mortal body, that ye should obey it in the lusts thereof. (Romans 6:12)

The mortality of flesh and its sinfulness are connected, death having been the punishment for sin:

> Wherefore, as by one man sin entered into the world, and death by sin; and so death passed upon all men, for that all have sinned. (Romans 5:12)

Similar elements are found in Platonic philosophy, despite the Greek tradition of ideal nudity and the Platonic metaphysics in which truth is understood as an unveiling. In Plato, flesh is seen as prone to sin, and liable to divert attention from the higher and truer life of the spirit: "According to Plato, the body, with its deceptive senses, keeps us from real knowledge; it rivets us in a world of material things which is far removed from the world of reality; and it tempts us away from the virtuous life" (Spelman 1982: 111). Elizabeth Spelman notes how in Plato this applies equally to the bodies of both sexes, but when Plato wants to exemplify the degraded aspects of body, he often chooses the lives of women, children, slaves, animals or effeminate men to do so.[17]

Neither the Bible nor Christian commentary consistently blames either Adam or Eve for the fact of human mortality. Sometimes, Adam's role is emphasized: "As by one man sin entered the world, and death by sin" or "For as in Adam all die." But in the apocryphal book of Sirach,[18] sin and its punishment, mortality, are linked not to Adam but to Eve: "From a woman sin had its beginning, and because of her we all die" (25:24). Although the Bible sees both Adam and Eve as sinning, many biblical commentaries and visual images focused on Eve's role (Miles 1989: xi). Eve's fall was understood to have wrought not only the legacy of painful childbirth (a punishment for women), but also the corruptibility and mortality of the flesh more generally.

The association between sex, death, nakedness and sin was spurred along by literal events, such as the rise of virulent forms of syphilis in Europe in the sixteenth century, which led people to associate sex with death (Mumford 1944: 213). Indeed, Stanislav Andreski has argued that the syphilis epidemics were responsible for "a wave of virulent misogyny" (Miles 1989: 218), as men blamed women, and especially prostitutes, for illness and death. Andreski argues that this was a fundamental motive in the sixteenth-century persecution of witches. The nineteenth-century European figure of the prostitute again brought together sin, disease, pollution and death. Some believed the prostitute to have specifically marked genitalia, through either vocation or heredity (Gilman 1986: 242–5).

Despite the Christian understanding of flesh as feminine, weak and mortal, the negative meanings of nakedness were slower to evolve. Female nakedness came to be "a cipher for sin, sex, and death" quite late in Christian thought – only in the sixteenth century, according to Miles (1989: xiv). There has developed, however, a more general gendered dimension to the association between nakedness, sex, sin and death. To the extent that "Woman" is aligned with (vulnerable, weak, ultimately uncontrollable) flesh, then death (the epitome of the vulnerability and uncontrollability of flesh) can be understood as a "feminine" state (and, perhaps, femininity itself as a form of death or non-being). Hélène Cixous (1981), for example, in her enunciation of the hierarchical binaries that sustain phallogocentrism (discussed in Chapter 1), aligns death with the "negative" side of these oppositions: nature, night, passivity, matter, woman, mother. Death is the ultimate example of passive matter, the opposite of culture, activity, form. Woman plays the role of non-being, the "unthinkable, unthought of" (Cixous 1981: 92) Other to thought, culture, form. Elisabeth Bronfen (1992) understands death as the "limit of cultural representation," associated with "that other enigma, the multiply coded feminine body" (Goodwin and Bronfen 1993: 13). Certainly, the Freudian tradition figures femininity and death as the ultimate (and connected) enigmas. Goodwin and Bronfen (1993: 15) claim that femininity, in effect, "intersects with death by way of enigma," and that therefore, death inevitably calls a gendered problematic into play: "Probably without exception, at least in Western culture, representations of death bring into play the binary tensions of gender constructs, as life/death engages permutations with masculinity/femininity and with fantasies of power" (p. 20).

This fact is reflected in some of the representational traditions of modernity. Bronfen's study of death and the aesthetic takes as its starting point the prevalence of "the conjunction of beautiful woman and death" (Bronfen 1992: x). Representations of feminine death are, she argues, "so excessively obvious that they escape observation" (p. 3). One of their functions is to allow us to experience death vicariously. Bronfen's detailed studies of examples from fine art and literature are used to argue not only that "western culture dream[s] of beautiful women to repress its knowledge of death," but that death and femininity serve "as ciphers for other values," signalling moments or sites of instability and disruption (Bronfen 1992: xi–xii). Representations of death function like a symptom, a failed or incomplete repression of that which makes us anxious. But death, as that which is most alien, almost unconscionable, can also be alluring. Death and the erotic are not poles apart. In fact, the affinity between the sexual drive and the death drive, Eros and Thanatos, is a staple tenet of psychoanalysis.

The conjunction of eroticism and death is also a commonplace of literature, and of pornography. The corpse can be seen as the ultra-naked body, stripped not only of its clothes, but also, potentially, of its skin. The exposed, flayed or decaying corpse can be imagined as the ultimate peeling back of layers. Such stripping away constitutes a transgressive, destructive and horrifying undoing of the subject – one that is for some, however, exhilarating for precisely those reasons. In Georges Bataille's erotic novel, *Story of the Eye* (1928), the corpse is disgusting but also strangely beautiful, and is connected to the (sexual) drive toward disorder:

> The horror and despair at so much bloody flesh, nauseating in parts, and in part very beautiful, was fairly equivalent to our usual impression upon seeing one another. Simone was tall and lovely. She was usually very natural; there was nothing heartbreaking in her eyes or her voice. But on a sensual level, she so bluntly craved any upheaval that the faintest call from the senses gave her a look directly suggestive of all things linked to deep sexuality, such as blood, suffocation, sudden terror, crime; things indefinitely destroying human bliss and honesty. (Bataille 1982: 11)

Though it may not immediately be recognizable as such, Perniola (1989: 245) sees this pornographic fantasy as the descendant of that side of the Christian tradition that "assigns great spiritual value to undressing." He conceives of Bataille's thought in relation to the post-Reformation understanding of Christ's suffering as "the pinnacle, the ultimate point, of Christian experience" (Perniola 1989: 245). From this theological point, he argues, "it follows that perdition, torture, annihilation, the abyss, confusion, disorder, fear, trembling and death present themselves as models of erotic experience" (p. 245). Many commentators have pointed to the eroticism of images of the suffering or dead Christ. Although Perniola considers Bataille to be "the most acute contemporary interpreter of the erotics of undressing" (p. 245), he nonetheless agues that Bataille pushed the erotics of undressing to its very limits. Bataille's erotics of exposure – exemplified at its limits in the utter exposure of the opened body

– is so extreme as to constitute a new absolute. Allowing no possibility of a return to clothing, it makes an absolute of nudity, an orgiastic one, certainly, but a metaphysical unity nonetheless. Movement, return, or transit (the *sine qua non* of eroticism) are evacuated from this corpse.

But Perniola's account is of a dual erotics, of undressing and dressing, and oddly enough, the corpse can figure in the latter as well as the former. The corpse can be imagined bi-directionally, as it were. From the "outside-in," it can be imagined as stripped, exposed, ultra-naked; from the "inside-out," as an enwrapped, encased, incarnated, "clothed" soul. Even the naked body of the corpse can thus be depicted as itself a form of clothing, rather than the most extreme example of the lack of clothing. Perniola sees the anatomical drawings of Vesalius, among others, as rendering the entire body, even its internal organs, as fabric-like: richly textured flesh, folded back to reveal yet more luxuriant movements of sinew and muscle (cf. an example from John Browne: Figure 2.3). Such corpses are full of life, still imaginable as en-souled nature, unlike the much more abstract and mechanical anatomy reproduced in Figure 2.4.

So far, then, I have alluded to three different ways in which death has been theorized as connected to sex and the erotic: first, deconstructively, as the feminized Other to masculine order; second, psychoanalytically, as one half of the two fundamental drives of Eros and Thanatos; third, metaphysically, in that the corpse has been represented within an erotics of both dressing and undressing. By and large, though, these connections between nakedness, sex and death are unwelcome in everyday life. They are especially unwelcome to the modern scientific imagination, which has aimed to exorcise such disorderly connections. Of course, the chilling and thrilling possibility of their intersection haunts medical science, at least in the popular imagination, where urban myths abound about the treatment of corpses in morgues and laboratories. And they are not totally fictional.[19] Most institutions, of course, aim to keep death and the erotic separate. When women were first admitted as medical students to Melbourne University in the late nineteenth century, the question of the propriety of mixed anatomy classes arose. This question was solved by having separate laboratories for men and women. Today, first-year anatomy students at one university I know of are given the so-called "Fear of God" lecture, where the Anatomy Act is read and explained to them, and the responsibility of working with donated bodies is reinforced.

Moral and especially sexual sensibilities are unwanted intruders into the putative objectivity of medical science. And yet, the corpse is arguably central to modern science. Drew Leder (1992: 19) argues that modern medicine's Cartesian foundations mean that it paradoxically reposes not upon the lived body but upon the dead or inanimate body. Leder argues that the corpse played

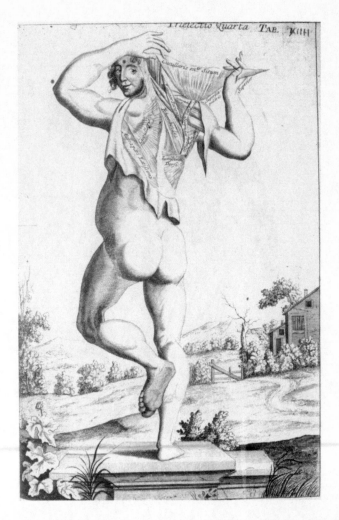

Figure 2.3 An example of a life-like corpse. John Browne (1698) *Myographia Nova*, London, p. 48, Table XIIII. Reproduced by kind permission of the President and Council of the Royal College of Surgeons of England.

a threefold role in Descartes' project: it motivated it, and provided it with a method and a metaphysics (p. 19). Descartes' philosophical inquiries were motivated by perturbation about his own mortality and by a corresponding need for a *rational* belief that the body's decay does not mean the end of the soul. Death was therefore at the core of his endeavour. Leder (1992) argues that death is at the metaphysical core of Cartesian thought as well, and hence of modern Western medicine, which stereotypically understands the body mechanistically as a set of interacting parts. Although Descartes was modern

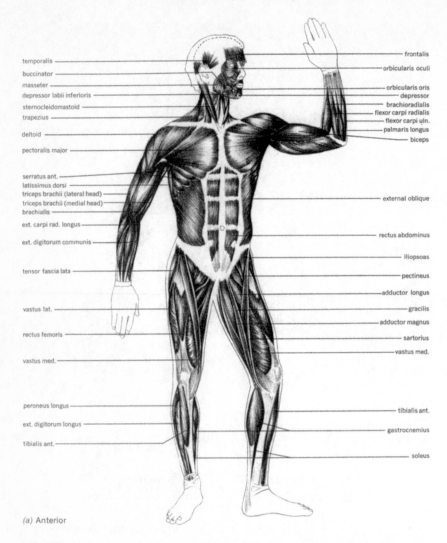

temporalis
buccinator
masseter
depressor labii inferioris
sternocleidomastoid
trapezius

deltoid

pectoralis major

serratus ant.
latissimus dorsi
triceps brachii (lateral head)
triceps brachii (medial head)
brachialis

ext. carpi rad. longus

ext. digitorum communis

tensor fascia lata

vastus lat.

rectus femoris

vastus med.

peroneus longus

ext. digitorum longus

tibialis ant.

frontalis
orbicularis oculi

orbicularis oris
depressor
brachioradialis
flexor carpi radialis
flexor carpi uln.
palmaris longus
biceps

external oblique

rectus abdominus

iliopsoas

pectineus
adductor longus
gracilis
adductor magnus
sartorius
vastus med.

tibialis ant.
gastrocnemius

soleus

(a) Anterior

Figure 2.4 A typical modern anatomy illustration. "Views of the Skeletal Muscles of the Human." © 1997 James E. Crouch and J. Robert McClintic (1976) *Human Anatomy and Physiology*, 2nd edn. New York: John Wiley & Sons, p. 253. This material is used by permission of John Wiley & Sons, Inc.

in ascribing vitality to the body (unlike the Stoic thinker Epictetus, quoted at the start of this section),[20] he nonetheless saw it as machine-like; in Leder's (1992: 20) words, "The living body is not fundamentally different from the lifeless; it is a kind of animated corpse, a functioning mechanism." The human body is understood as *res extensa*, a-subjective matter, like the rest of nature, no longer understood as agentic or intentional. Modern diagnostic and therapeutic techniques reflected this shift. From the eighteenth century, the corpse rather than the lived body came increasingly to be seen as "the scene of revelation" (p. 22). Leder claims that archetypal modern medicine can in fact treat the patient "in a cadaverous or machine-like fashion," most especially in the traditional physical examination:

> The patient is asked to assume a corpse-like pose, flat, passive, naked, mute. The entire ritual and context serves to reduce the living body to something almost dead. Personal identity is stripped away as the patient is removed from his or her habitual surroundings, activities, even clothes. Then too, the patient's voice is, for long stretches, silenced . . . While the doctor performing a physical examination is an active and engaged explorer, the patient is placed in a position of corpse-like passivity. (Leder 1992: 22)

The literal stripping that is the basis of the physical examination is technologically mirrored in diagnostic techniques like the X-ray, ultrasound or dissection, which involve getting closer and closer in to the truth of the body, a kind of metaphorical stripping.

Leder cites Foucault's description in *The Birth of the Clinic* (1973) of the shift towards the inanimate body as the scene of truth: "That which hides and envelops, the curtain of night over truth, is, paradoxically, life; and death, on the contrary, opens up to the light of day the black coffer of the body" (quoted in Leder 1992: 21). For our purposes, Foucault's description is noteworthy because his metaphors draw on that of the naked truth – revealed, paradoxically, in death rather than life. His description makes use of the recurring binaries of openness and closure, visibility and invisibility, revelation and concealment. In terms of Perniola's categories, the corpse in modern medicine is not the older en-souled nature, but the empty box. If we accept Leder's argument, the patient, imagined as the (stereotypical) object of modern medicine, is also structurally the object of the exposing gaze and the penetrating touch, rather than an embodied ideal and eternal spirit.

In a predominantly clothed society, there is a shared, if tacit, recognition that clothes carry something not only of personality but also of humanness itself. In our societies, clothing records and symbolizes both an individual life history and sociality (and therefore humanness) itself. Thus, the stripping away of clothes has the potential to symbolize the stripping away of sociality and even of humanness. This was evident in an interview with a funeral director, who saw clothing as a very important part of how his staff continue to treat the corpse as a human person. He told us that in contemporary Australia, bodies are always buried clothed. If no clothes are provided, bodies are wrapped in a shroud-like cloth. Those who work intimately with the dead are committed to maintaining elements of the dead person's humanity and even, where possible, their individuality. Relatives are often encouraged, for example, to dress the body in such as way as to remain true to the life of the deceased person: "If somebody wore jeans all their life, we ask [the relatives] to bring jeans. If somebody wore a suit . . ." Where individuality cannot be maintained, death workers still pay careful heed to the maintenance of humanness itself. In circumstances in which the body *needs* to be de-humanized, as in the preparation of bodies for medical research, those involved in the process may well still work with a layered conception of the human body rather than a single one. For example, I interviewed a technician who cuts up bodies donated for use in the medical faculty of a university. For her, clothing is a marker of the dead person's humanness – their personality, their individual life and their place in society. Her job involves embalming the bodies, turning them from human person into medical specimen. The removal of clothes is an important marker in this ontological change, a removal of both individuality (a particular history, an identifiable social position) and humanness (part of the transition from person to specimen). Psychologically, she said, it is an easier process to strip the bodies of their clothes when the person arrives from a hospital rather than from a home or nursing home; the hospital gown has already helped to de-particularize the body, and the transition from individual to human to specimen has already begun. For psychological, ethical and ultimately social reasons, however, the process of evacuating subjectivity from the body is not always final, and the ascription of humanness must needs always be a suspension rather than a finality:

> From that point [where their clothes are removed, their hair shaved and their bodies embalmed], they've really become a specimen. [But] there's a few that no matter what, you will still remember their name personally. There's just something about them that you remember, and right through to the time you actually put them in a coffin you know exactly who they are and can identify their specimens as well. From then on you still treat them with respect – but you don't treat them like you do a living human, I suppose.

Clearly, any statement of the metaphysical premises of the scientific-rational worldview needs to recognize not only that many individuals dissent from such premises but, more complexly, that people can hold contradictory views about the human body simultaneously. For example, one might expect that those who work in the industries that resulted from the increasing rationalization, industrialization and secularization of death might look on the body simply as a soulless machine. But this may not necessarily be the case at all. Indeed, all the nurses, medical practitioners and death workers with whom I spoke shared an implicitly or explicitly religious sense of the human body, believing that one could detect the moment at which the person's spirit left and at which the body remained a mere empty shell. The two anatomy workers, for example, agreed on this:

> *Angela:* You can sit there and say this could be silly, but when people say that the soul leaves, it does.
>
> *Ivan:* It's not a physical thing you can see but you just know that the person's dead and it becomes a specimen to us.

When I asked these workers what their profession had led them to believe about the human body, their responses included both classic scientific precepts and humanist axioms (as well as the spiritual beliefs quoted above):

> *Interviewer:* I want to ask you whether your profession's led you to conceive of your own body in any particular way?
>
> *Angela:* It's the best machine made to cope with what we do to it.
>
> *Ivan:* As a general overview we're exactly the same from one person to the next regardless of race, colour or creed, but on closer inspection everyone has slightly different anatomical variations.

Angela's profession has led her to have, at least in part, a rational approach towards death. She believes it should be demystified:

> I think the way that culture brings everyone up to fear death when you really don't have to. I've got a young daughter who has grown up coming in to work with me and she has absolutely no problem whatsoever because it hasn't been a culture that she's grown up with. But other people grow up with this culture where you don't ever get to know what death is except everyone's really sad so therefore it's bad.

This is a modern scientific viewpoint, one that ostensibly robs the corpse of its power to terrify or unsettle. No doubt in practice few can adhere completely to this viewpoint; presumably working closely with the dead requires some disavowal or repression in order to allow the scientific approach its sway. Outside of the scientific viewpoint (and perhaps a religious one), the corpse is potentially a thing of horror, since it shows us what we must become and what we "permanently thrust aside in order to live" (Kristeva 1982: 3). Julia Kristeva names the corpse as the ultimate example of bodily waste; it is, in fact, the body *as* waste. The corpse reminds us that the body is, in the final instance, matter that can't be controlled. In all cultures, it is treated within strenuously defended rituals, which aim, according to Kristeva, to prevent it from "contaminating" the living: "The corpse, seen without God and out-side of science, is the utmost of abjection. It is death infecting life" (Kristeva 1982: 4).

If this is so, then we might expect that attitudes to our living body are always subtly working to expel the shadow of the corpse – that which our body will ultimately become. Certainly, this is how Mikhail Bakhtin (1984: 317) characterizes the moderns' preference for the idealized, smooth and impenetr-able surfaces of the classic bodily canon over the excrescences and orifices of the grotesque body of the medieval schema. The most obvious championing of this classical bodily schema comes in the sculptural legacy. In Kenneth Clark's (1956) discussion of nudity versus nakedness, for example, we can clearly hear an echo of the fear of mortality. Clark's conceptual opposition denigrates the real, lived nakedness of the human body in favour of the idealized classical nudes of representation:

> It is widely supposed that the naked human body is in itself an object upon which the eye dwells with pleasure and which we are glad to see depicted. But anyone who has frequented art schools and seen the shapeless, pitiful model which the students are industriously drawing will know that this is an illusion . . . A mass of naked figures does not move us to empathy, but to disillusion and dismay . . . We are immediately disturbed by wrinkles, pouches and other small imperfections which, in the classical scheme, are eliminated. (Clark 1956: 3–4)

The nude/naked distinction privileges nudity (the illusion of a preserved perfec-tion) over nakedness, the state of change, decay, vulnerability and ultimately mortality. Clark's evocation of the pitifulness of the naked body is no doubt bolstered by the early Christian association of nakedness with vulnerability and weakness (Miles 1989: xi–xii). Is our fear of nakedness, our ability to be shocked by it, related to the fear of death?

There are many, however, who would sneer at the taste for preservation, seeing in the sculptor's skill, the beautician's touch, the embalmer's art and the hygienist's fetish, a fear of process, indeed, of life itself. Eric Michaels (1990), an academic whose path towards death is recorded in his diary *Unbecoming: An AIDS Diary*, denounced this as a form of "tidiness," a postmodern obsession with gleaming surfaces:

> Tidiness is a process which, while avowedly in the service of cleanliness and health, in fact is only interested in obscuring all traces of history, of process, of past users, of the conditions of manufacture (the high high-gloss). Tidiness inhabits and defines a "moment," but one outside time, ahistorical, perhaps the ancestral dreamtime home of all "Lifestyles." It is a perfect bourgeois metaphor. The tidy moment does not recognise process, and so resists deterioration, disease, aging, putrefaction. (Michaels 1990: 42)

Michaels' critique accords with accounts of modern and postmodern corporeality as increasingly characterized by preservationism (see Featherstone
1991: 170–1).

Such preservationism is quite modern, sitting at odds with more traditional
earthy relations to the grotesque elements of the body and its processes. Women
(especially working-class women) have had a special relation to such processes,
through their traditional role of carers for infants, the sick, the elderly and the
dying. They have become associated with "the quintessentially grotesque
events of birth, sexual intercourse, and death" (Miles 1989: 147): "As the
mother, 'woman' is the original prenatal dwelling place; as the beloved, she
draws fantasies of desire and otherness; and as Mother Earth, she is the
anticipated final resting place" (Goodwin and Bronfen 1993: 13). Thus, the
conjunction of femininity and death need not always evoke a forbidden, morbid
or repressed erotics; in pre-modern contexts it has been ritually celebrated,
via the imagery of the grotesque body. The grotesque played an important
psychological, social and ritual role in pre-modern societies. Mikhail Bakhtin's
study of medieval carnival argues that grotesque body imagery was at the heart
of a pre-modern conception of time, life and death. The grotesque body of
carnival doesn't die with death, because it is not an individual body, but a social,
indeed cosmic, one. It is a body that is continually becoming – never completed,
never sealed off, always outgrowing itself (Bakhtin 1984: 317). It is thus
fundamentally ambiguous; it "swallows and generates, gives and takes"
(p. 339). In the cosmic cycles of traditional societies, ends and beginnings are
not as radically separated as in modern societies. The temporalities, rituals
and myths of pre-modern societies brought the nakedness of birth and death
together, since death was understood as being in cyclical as well as linear
relation to birth. In some societies, these two fundamental states of nakedness
could be literally connected. Funeral rites and mourning practices, for example,
sometimes involve nudity. So too, naked burial is known to some cultures (e.g.
in traditional Aboriginal practice (Watson 1998: 1), or ancient Roman practice).
In such systems, death has a (re)productive quality, and neither the grotesque
elements of the body, nor even death itself, can thus be understood as simply
or only "negative." Death might mark the end of an individual life, but it was
also associated with fertility and renewal. Thus, in the Christian tradition, even
though death is understood as a punishment for sin, it is also imagined as
something to be welcomed, because it is the moment when one rejoins God:

> A good name is better than precious ointment; and the day of death than the day
> of one's birth. (Ecclesiastes 7:1)

> Better is the end of a thing than the beginning thereof: and the patient in spirit is
> better than the proud in spirit. (Ecclesiastes 7:8)

Ecclesiastes contains strong, oft-quoted evocations of the patterned rightness and properness of life's rhythms ("To every thing there is a season" 3:1) and of the stability at the heart of the comings and goings of individual lives: "One generation passeth away, and another generation cometh: but the earth abideth for ever" (1:4). Likewise, the book of Romans understands faith in Christ as a sharing of both life and death:

> Know ye not, that so many of us as were baptized into Jesus Christ were baptized into his death? Therefore we are buried with him by baptism into death: that like as Christ was raised up from the dead by the glory of the Father, even so we also should walk in newness of life. For if we have been planted together in the likeness of his death, we shall be also in the likeness of his resurrection . . . Now if we be dead with Christ, we believe that we shall also live with him: Knowing that Christ being raised from the dead dieth no more; death hath no more dominion over him . . . Likewise reckon ye also yourselves to be dead indeed unto sin, but alive unto God through Jesus Christ our Lord. (Romans 6:3–11)

In this sense, the nakedness of birth and that of death are connected: "Naked came I out of my mother's womb and naked shall I return thither; the Lord gave, and the Lord hath taken away; blessed be the name of the Lord" (Job 1:21).

Nudity and Shame

> Thy nakedness shall be uncovered, yea, thy shame shall be seen
>
> Isaiah 47:3

In a number of biblical usages, "nakedness" is more or less synonymous with shame. In the Adam and Eve story, at least in its modern interpretations,[21] shame emerges as a grand human theme – the legacy of primal sin and thenceforth part of the condition of humanness. In the Bible, the fig leaf, the first piece of clothing, becomes the symbol of this legacy. In *Penguin Island* (France 1909), clothing is part of the cultural apparati that alienate human beings from nature and from each other. Freud read the Adam and Eve story as a parable about the paradisiacal period of childhood innocence before the awakening of shame and anxiety (Freud 1953: 245). The moral problem of shame can be detected in another paradigmatic story, that of Lady Godiva. For John Langdon-Davies (1928: 7), the moral of the Lady Godiva story is that the husband, who kept his clothes on, was the one who felt shame. To read the tale that way is to see it as based on an inversion: the naked woman is innocent, the clothed man ashamed.

Of course, even if shame is a universal human experience, it is certainly not caused by the same conditions nor experienced in the same way by all people.

Norbert Elias' (1994) classic study *The Civilizing Process* traces the rise of a particularly modern experience of shame, one of whose effects has been to make modern people more detached from their bodies and from the bodies of others. Feminist work on shame (e.g. Bartky 1990) emphasizes the relationship of shame and gender. Women in the modern West have a special relationship with shame, the legacy not just of theological misogyny, but also of male violence, practices of oppression and protection, discourses of modesty, and centuries of image-making over which women had relatively little influence.

Gender is, however, only one of the factors at work in experiences of shame. Despite the persistence of a gendered equation between sex and immorality, discomfort with nudity needs also to be understood as part of the broader question of our relations to our body in postmodern culture. While Elias' (1994) work is limited in that it doesn't consider the specificity of different forms of embodiment (such as gender or race), its historical focus alerts us helpfully to what might be specifically *modern* about certain bodily experiences. His history of the advancing "embarrassment threshold" provides a broader context for understanding modern experiences of shame as not simply or necessarily involving the exposure of sexual parts. My interviews with physical education teachers, for example, found that young people are as ashamed by the exposure of size or "flab" as by sexualized parts of the body. For girls, the twin "problems" of sexualization and "floppiness" often coincide in the breasts. A PE teacher we interviewed told us that adolescent girls tend particularly to be embarrassed about their breasts; having breasts that are large or that bounce during movement, or not wearing a bra when most of your peers do, are all sources of self-consciousness. This is not really a surprise. Susan Bordo has convincingly argued for many years that canons of "acceptable" body types now focus not just on weight or thinness, but on the tautness and tightness of flesh, which should not be allowed to bulge, wobble or become flabby (Bordo 1993b: 187ff.). Girls are acutely aware of this. Several teachers we interviewed felt that actual teasing of others was relatively rare, and that most of the self-consciousness (which ranged from slight to acute) came from students' own internalized ideas about their body. This accords with Elias' contention (developed later by Foucault in his theory of "discipline") that the hallmark of modern relations with the body is an increasingly potent and effective *internalized* surveillance. Elias describes

> how constraints through others from a variety of angles are converted into self-restraints, how the more animalic human activities are progressively thrust behind the scenes of men's communal social life and invested with feelings of shame, how the regulation of the whole instinctual and affective life by steady self-control becomes more and more stable, more even and more all-embracing. (Elias 1994: 443)

While these pressures may be particularly intense for women, they are increasingly being applied to (and felt by) men.

Viewed in this light, the increasingly liberal use of nudity in advertising can be as symptomatic of a *narrowing* of tolerance for the body as of an increased acceptance. The day after drafting this section, I was getting changed in the dressing room of my university's swimming pool, a facility that is shared with local high school students. I was alone in the room, and was drying myself with a towel. A group of high school students entered suddenly. On seeing me, the first girl shrieked in embarrassed horror, and retreated immediately, accompanied by her peers. "Oh no! Oh no! There's a lady getting changed in there!" she hooted. She made two more attempts at coming into the room, each time backing out in embarrassment. When she finally came in, accompanied by a dozen or so others, each of them queued for the toilet and shower cubicles in order to get changed. Not one of them changed in the open dressing room.

Such attitudes appear to be common to modern urban societies. In the US, for example, students have been known to use civil liberties legislation to resist showering after gym classes at school. A newspaper report quoted students saying that they preferred to cake on deodorant rather than to shower and change at school (Johnson 1996). Some even reported that their parents would drive them home to shower rather than let them shower at school.[22] In Australia, anecdotal evidence from teachers supports this. Secondary school teachers taking children away on camps or to sporting fixtures report that adolescents are becoming less and less likely to undress or shower in front of each other. One explanation is that consumer culture has made young people increasingly aware of body image and increasingly unhappy with their bodies, and that contemporary urban society is becoming more and more obsessed with privacy and individualism. Moreover, young people are also highly aware of questions of sexual orientation, and some commentators believe that anxiety about homosexuality has led students to become more modest about showering in public.[23]

Contemporary public architecture is beginning to reflect such changes. A new swimming centre near my suburban home first opened with communal showers. Within weeks, these had been individualized into separate shower cubicles. Such matters are not straightforward, however. One interviewee told me that a council-run pre-school at which he worked had communal toilets for girls and boys. This was, he believed, in response to public fears about paedophilia. In this clash between different kinds of anxiety, surveillance was considered desirable. Domestic architecture also reflects attitudes towards privacy; I have had many tertiary students express amazement that some people have bathrooms without locks on them.

But despite the cultural focus on shame (found not only in the paradigmatic biblical account, but also in assumptions of deviance in psychological and criminological literature), the bodily experience of nakedness and even of self-consciousness need not necessarily be shame at all. In different contexts – the bedroom, the nudist beach, the life class – there may well be other forms of corporeal self-consciousness: erotic, delighted, or technical, to give just three examples. Nakedness might be an experience of erotic awareness of the body's surface, a feeling of sexiness, or a feeling of liberation or relaxation. Nor need nakedness always bring self-consciousness at all. Many nudists, even women, claim that one of the pleasures of nudism is the loss of awareness of the naked body (see Barcan 2001).

Nudity and Anxiety

Fears with pedigrees, are the worst fears, and nakedness has a distinguished pedigree . . .

John Langdon-Davies, *Lady Godiva: The Future of Nakedness*

In the domain of psychology, the classic association between nudity and anxiety is evidenced in the dream of feeling embarrassed at being fully or partially naked. Freud (1953: 37) considered the dream of being naked in front of strangers, feeling anxious about it, yet unable to move away, as "typical" – that is, occurring "in large numbers of people and with very similar content." Freud (1953) devoted a small section of *The Interpretation of Dreams* specifically to this dream, using, indeed, one of his own dreams as an exemplum. He interpreted such dreams as a species of anxiety dream, one related to the enforced renunciation of infantile exhibitionism.

Typically, the nakedness dream involves the dreamer being naked in public, with no one paying him or her any notice (Myers 1989: 118). In his analysis of three case histories, psychoanalyst Wayne A. Myers interprets the dream of being naked in public as a traumatic repetition of the patient's feelings of being unnoticed or overlooked (often by parents). The dream appears thus to be spurred on not only by infantile exhibitionist wishes (as the early Freud would have claimed), but also by the attempt to master "chronic strain traumata" (Myers 1989: 129). This, claims Myers, is in accordance with the views of the later Freud, who revised his view that infantile wishes were the only cause of dreams, and argued that repeated dreams were an attempt to belatedly master earlier traumatic events. In Myers' case histories, the dream appears to have been associated with actual childhood incidents (a little boy exposing his genitals to his mother, who didn't react; a teenage girl walking about the house in her bra unsuccessfully trying to attract her father's attention).

Regardless of whether or not this is "true," the currency of this dream and the importance of it to psychoanalysis signal nakedness's role within modern European cultures as symbol for and provoker of unease. This assumption is so deep-seated as to have allowed it some valency in academic psychology. For example, an odd little study about "distancing behaviour in relation to statues" carried out in the late 1970s tried to find a correlation between subjects' rating on the Taylor Manifest Anxiety Scale and the physical distance that they placed between themselves and photographs of nude statues in a mock museum setting (Breuer and Lindauer 1977). They found none, though they did find strongly gendered differences. Men placed the photos of male and female nude statues markedly further away from themselves than they did the photos of dressed statues. Women did not. The researchers concluded from this that men "were affected by nudity" while women were "indifferent" to it. Wisely, the researchers chose not to infer too much from what is to us now a methodologically crude experiment, finishing by saying that "we need to know more about the sexes' attitudes toward nudity as such, *in vivo*, about which very little is known" (Breuer and Lindauer 1977: 378). (Of course, this study itself relies on another deeply embedded cluster of assumptions, spatial metaphors and experiences, namely the use of physical proximity as a sign for psychological security.)

The symbolic and potentially experiential connection between nudity and anxiety allows nakedness to become a weapon or a form of power. Simon, a masseur I interviewed, described how some clients who are, he believes, nervous about their first encounter with him will begin to strip as soon as he enters the room. Sometimes this is an overtly erotic proposal, but it is also as likely to be a means of signalling that they are not to be disempowered in the massage experience. Their anxiety may well have nothing to do with nudity itself (it may be related instead to issues of trust or intimacy or touch), and nudity can thus provide them with a weapon of defence and/or aggression. This happens less with his regular clientele than when he works for a large luxury hotel, where his clients are more likely to be one-offs:

> So there are these power sort of things that do occur like that, where I've had both males and females – part of it is the challenge to try and unnerve me; there is attempts of power play like that. They're trying to protect themselves and keep themselves empowered and they've only just met me.

The masseur understands such gestures as implicit challenges to his professionalism, and as attempts to ensure that the encounter begins on the client's terms. In effect, such clients are playing off the ever-present potential for nudity to signify eroticism against the healthcare profession's attempts to repress such meanings:

In dealing with the nudity of the person, to maintain a professionalism is to maintain the eye contact. And what they're looking for in that is just the eyes to drop down a little bit, to give a body scan – that's exactly what they're looking for, and that can really change the power play and it can change the nature of the massage. So it's something that I have to be very conscious of and very aware of in dealing with people that are comfortable with their own nudity like that.

In response to my question as to whether such tactics are in fact likely to be quite conscious exercises of power, Simon replied:

I think they are using it. They know it is a . . . means of gaining or maintaining power. I suppose it's a game that's played in the same way as the male/female courting role that's sort of played – you know, the woman wears a sexy dress to attract the man, to appeal to that aspect of him. In the same way that she empowers herself by wearing a sexy dress that she knows she has that control, in the same way that being naked unexpectedly like that also gives them, potentially, the upper hand.

(Note, incidentally, another occurrence of the idea that nudity can be the equivalent of a form of clothing.) The idea of nudity's potential as a weapon, which arises from its associations with anxiety, will be explored more fully in Chapter 3, in relation to criminal or deviant behaviours like flashing and in the use of nudity as a vehicle for political protest.

Even a highly professional masseur is not immune from interference from his *own* unconscious anxiety, if not about nudity *per se* then about ensuring that his clients are comfortable with the situation. Simon told a funny story that he uses as an example when teaching massage to students, since it shows the difficulties of keeping one's own ego involvement and anxiety at bay during a massage. He was massaging a woman who had announced that she was a nudist. When he had told her to leave her underpants on, she had replied that she was proud of her body and was happy to take all of her clothes off. While he was massaging her front, he put the towel over her as normal. She said: "If it's all right with you, I'd prefer not to have the towel." He thought about it and then agreed, and began folding the towel up. He wound it up from the feet upwards until her genitals were exposed, at which point she said, "No. I didn't mean *that* towel, I meant the towel behind my head" (he had put a cushion there as a pillow). So he rapidly replaced the towel and apologized, explaining that it was a cushion and that he had misunderstood her: "So I well and truly embarrassed myself from having judged that lady. So it was a very important lesson to me about getting clarification." The moral he tells his students is: "Be aware. Even when you think you've got it all together." It also serves as a useful reminder for himself: "The other thing is that I was hooking into my own ego there too, thinking, 'Well, if you're cool with it, then I'm cool with it too.' So I was really playing a power game there."

Nudity as Punishment, Humiliation or Degradation

Because of its association with shame, nakedness can readily be used both metaphorically and in practice as a form of punishment, humiliation or degradation. The metaphor of nakedness as powerlessness, degradation and humility is the underside of nakedness as docility and obedience. In the Bible, it can appear as a metaphor for divine punishment. For example, in the Old Testament book of Nahum, which tells the story of the fall of Nineveh, God damns the capital city of Israel's enemy Assyria, personified as a woman: "Behold, I am against thee, saith the Lord of hosts; and I will discover thy skirts upon thy face, and I will shew the nations thy nakedness, and the kingdoms thy shame" (Nahum 3:5).

In modern times, the humiliating power of nakedness is still put to use, as in the stripping of victims in torture, or the importance of stripping in initiation rites or bastardization practices. It is also used as a rite of passage, especially in all-male assemblies like sporting teams or university colleges. It can form part of sexual practices involving humiliation. In fetishistic practice, clothing is usually associated with power, nakedness with the lack of power (Steele 1996: 171). Mostly, the master/dominatrix is clothed and the slave/bottom/masochist is stripped naked or wearing clothing that exposes the breasts, buttocks or genitals. In her study of fetishism, Valerie Steele (1996: 171) describes a master–slave heterosexual couple who reported to her that they spend entire weekends with the slave totally naked.

Written in to the laws of many Western countries are protections from the humiliation and violation of bodily integrity associated with involuntary nakedness. Police strip searches, for example, are in theory subject to stringent controls.

Nakedness as Poverty, Wretchedness, Vulnerability

The downside of nakedness as openness is nakedness as physical, psychological and even spiritual vulnerability. "Naked" could mean unprotected from the wind, as in a naked light or flame. Take King Lear's lament in the storm:

> Poor naked wretches, wheresoe'er you are,
> That bide the pelting of this pitiless storm,
> How shall your houseless heads and unfed sides,
> Your looped and windowed [*i.e. full of holes*] raggedness, defend you
> From seasons such as these? (III.iv.28–32)

In this as in countless other uses of the term "naked," the term implies wretchedness and poverty. It need not have anything to do with the literal state of one's clothing. "I am a poor man, naked," says the eponymous Lieutenant in John Fletcher's *Humorous Lieutenant* (1625), as he writes his will (III.v.77).

In the sixteenth century, "naked" could also mean "unarmed" – without weapons or means of defence. Shakespeare uses it thus in *Henry VIII*, when Cardinal Wolsey laments to Cromwell:

> O Cromwell, Cromwell,
> Had I but serv'd my God with half the zeal
> I serv'd my king, he would not in mine age
> Have left me naked to mine enemies. (III.ii.454–7)

The equation of nakedness with lack of weapons and hence with vulnerability to attack arguably underpins Christopher Columbus' repeated comments on the nakedness of the American Indians. Peter Mason (1990: 170) sees in Columbus' comments the bringing together of erotic and economic components. The Indians' nakedness thus has political consequences, as Columbus saw in it not only an invitation to sexual conquest but also a sign that their military defeat would be easy.

In the modern world, nakedness is often used as a *visual* image of wretchedness. In Victorian times, documentary photos of nude children were used by well-meaning Victorian charities as evidence of deprivation (Townsend 1996). During the Vietnam War, the naked image of a napalmed girl, Kim Phuc, circulated globally as an icon of devastation, both individual and national, when Nick Ut's photograph, "Napalm Bomb Attack" (Vietnam, 1972), won the World Press photo award.

Bare Humanity

In the book of Revelation, John sends messages of hope to the Christian churches facing persecution. In his message to the church of Laodicea, nakedness serves as a metaphor for the spiritual condition of the apathetic faithful, who, rich in worldly goods, do not perceive their own abjection:

> Because thou sayest, I am rich, and increased with goods, and have need of nothing; and knowest not that thou art wretched, and miserable, and poor, and blind, and naked: I counsel thee to buy of me gold tried in the fire, that thou mayest be rich; and white raiment, that thou mayest be clothed, and that the shame of thy nakedness do not appear; and anoint thine eyes with eyesalve, that thou mayest see. (Revelation 3:17–18)

Here, nakedness is the raw spiritual condition of the lukewarm faithful, who need to be clothed in true spiritual raiment. Nakedness, then, is not always

close to truth or self-understanding; it can be a sign of self-deception, symbolizing both distance from and proximity to the Godhead.

This is a pessimistic image of the human being as at base a vulnerable wretch,
an image in which total exposure can symbolize the human condition itself.
If one strips away all cultural trappings – the protections of clothing, shelter,
rank, ornament – one is left with the raw human being, the essence of humanity.
This is how Shakespeare in his tragic mode imagines raw humanness. Lear,
stripped of his royalty, his connection with his daughters, even of his sanity,
merely completes the picture of his nakedness when he tears off his clothes:

> Thou art the thing itself; unaccommodated man is no more but such a poor, bare,
> forked animal as thou art. Off, off you lendings! Come, unbutton here. [*Tearing off
> his clothes*] (III.iv.108–11)

This "existential" stripping also has a historically definable dimension.
Marshall McLuhan (1997) reads *Lear* as a drama about the transition from
feudal to modern (i.e. Renaissance) modes of personhood. Fundamentally, this
is a shift away from the person-as-role towards a new individualism. Lear calls
this a "divestment" of the responsibilities of kingship, retaining however "the
name, and all th'additions to a king." McLuhan repeatedly characterizes Lear's
attempt to "de-role" himself as a denudation or stripping away. Lear's later
literal "unbuttoning" is, perhaps, a dramatization of both forms of stripping
– the descent from king to person and from person to wretched "unaccom-
modated man."[24]

Nakedness as an Index of Savagery

One of the most telling uses of nakedness to symbolize raw, almost bestial,
humanity is in racist thought. In the nineteenth-century European imagination
– a product of the interaction between global exploration, colonialism,
industrialization, religion and Darwinism – the fear that it is not a big step
from "bare humanness" to savagery took on a specific, racist form. To the
European explorers, the (supposed) nakedness of non-Europeans was a marker
of their "savagery." In the loaded binary categories of Western modernity,
"primitives" were understood "positively" as childlike and closer to nature;
in the negative, these same qualities were seen as savage, barbaric, primitive,
irrational. Indigenous peoples' supposed closeness to nature was a cause both
for romanticization and denigration. Nowadays, in the nostalgia characteristic
of late modernity (see MacCannell 1989), indigenous peoples are increasingly
being characterized as being more "authentic" (whatever that might mean)
than Westerners. By holding up a mirror to whiteness, indigenous cultures pose
moral problems for a modernity unsure of its achievements and its direction.

The valuation of "native" nakedness took a number of forms, including: the romanticization of native nakedness (the noble savage); the eroticization of female nakedness (the "nubile savage": Sturma 1995); the ascription of physiological primitivism to indigenous nakedness or naked body parts (e.g. the belief that the genitals of Hottentot women were primitive versions of European labia: Gilman 1986: 232); "scientific" scales of measurable female beauty (e.g. Ellis 1923); the colonial and/or religious imperative to clothe nakedness; the subjection of nakedness to the medical, anthropological or popular gaze (e.g. the display of images and even body parts (buttocks and genitals) in medical texts, exhibitions and museums: Gilman 1986: 232ff.); and the ascription of uncleanliness, degeneracy or lasciviousness to "primitive" nakedness, especially to women (Gilman 1986).

Darwin's work makes use of both of the two extremes – nakedness as noble and wretched. In the *Voyage of the Beagle* (1906), he describes a Gaucho man: "A naked man on a naked horse is a fine spectacle" (Darwin 1959: 135). The descriptions of the Tahitians in Chapter 18 draw on the figure of the noble savage:

> There is a mildness in the expression of their countenances which at once banishes the idea of a savage; and an intelligence which shows that they are advancing in civilization. The common people, when working, keep the upper part of their bodies quite naked; and it is then that the Tahitians are seen to advantage. They are very tall, broad-shouldered, athletic, and well-proportioned. It has been remarked, that it requires little habit to make a dark skin more pleasing and natural to the eye of an European than his own colour. A white man bathing by the side of a Tahitian, was like a plant bleached by the gardener's art compared with a fine dark green one growing vigorously in the open fields. Most of the men are tattooed, and the ornaments follow the curvature of the body so gracefully, that they have a very elegant effect . . . The simile may be a fanciful one, but I thought the body of a man thus ornamented was like the trunk of a noble tree embraced by a delicate creeper. (Darwin 1959: 388)

But Darwin does not always use nakedness as a sign of nobility: "The black children, completely naked, and looking very wretched, were carrying bundles of firewood half as big as their own bodies" (p. 3). In a section subtitled "The Miserable Condition of the Savages," Darwin describes a group of Fuegins:

> These were the most abject and miserable creatures I anywhere beheld . . . [T]hese Fuegians in the canoe were quite naked, and even one full-grown woman was absolutely so. It was raining heavily, and the fresh water, together with the spray, trickled down her body. In another harbour not far distant, a woman, who was suckling a recently-born child, came one day alongside the vessel, and remained

there out of mere curiosity, whilst the sleet fell and thawed on her naked bosom, and on the skin of her naked baby! These poor wretches were stunted in their growth, their hideous faces bedaubed with white paint, their skins filthy and greasy, their hair entangled, their voices discordant, and their gestures violent. Viewing such men, one can hardly make oneself believe that they are fellow-creatures, and inhabitants of the same world. It is a common subject of conjecture what pleasure in life some of the lower animals can enjoy: how much more reasonably the same question may be asked with respect to these barbarians! At night, five or six human beings, naked and scarcely protected from the wind and rain of this tempestuous climate, sleep on the wet ground coiled up like animals. (Darwin 1959: 202–3)

Returning to the first extract, we see that even the "noble" nakedness is animal in nature: "A naked man on a naked horse is a fine spectacle; I had no idea how well the two animals suited each other" (p. 135).

As a final point, it is worth also noting the taxonomic question mentioned in Chapter 1. In European eyes, only certain forms of dress counted as "clothing." It was Europeans who defined whether body paint, feathers, ornaments, skins and so on constituted nakedness or dress, before ever they went on to determine that nakedness noble or wretched.

All or Nothing: Nudity as Plenitude and Lack

Clearly, nudity can mean many things, as this survey of Judeo-Christian-influenced meanings makes evident. Today, religion no longer provides "the primary interpretative framework for depictions of nakedness" in the West; Miles (1989: xv) argues that this ceased from around the seventeenth century onwards. Families, the media, the entertainment industries and schools are today's sites of intense ideological work. Nonetheless, this ideological work takes place in a cultural field in which Judeo-Christian influences are still tangible, despite the diversity of religious thought and practice in modern societies and enormous changes to the place and importance of religious traditions. Although in some modern societies there is very little theological debate in the cultural mainstream, the early Christian meanings of nudity have permeated the Europeanized West to such an extent that they persist in contemporary discursive forms and occasionally resurface in their quite specific forms, despite the secularizing forces of modernity, the diversifying forces of multiculturalism and globalization, and the moral changes encouraged by consumerism. In Australia, the Aboriginal experience of nakedness is largely visible in the public sphere only in colonial terms, either as devalued primitivism or as romanticized naturalness. This does not mean, however, that Aboriginal *experiences* of nakedness are completely contained by the colonial legacy.

It is clear that a fundamental paradox underlies this infinitude of possibilities: the "natural incompleteness" of the human body. Put starkly, nudity can be imagined as a lack in need of supplementation or a plenitude in itself. Clothing in all its forms (including body decoration, scarification, ornamentation and so on) marks the subject's entry into a symbolic order. But clothing is not a layer around a non-social, biological body; it is part of the processes by which that body becomes not only a socially functioning but also a physiologically functioning subject. Both nudity and clothing are paradoxical. Clothing is superfluous yet necessary; nudity is natural but also potentially always a state of lack. Nakedness is a natural insufficiency, a "natural" state we rarely see. It is, if you like, the deviant natural. Clothing on the other hand is a necessary excess, the protective layer we "don't need" but must have.

Perniola's (1989) study gives a sharply outlined history of how this paradox has come to function in the modern West. What his work doesn't articulate, however, is something of the politics of this, either past or present, since he doesn't ask the question of *which kinds* of bodies have been held most fully to embody either ideal or abject meanings of nudity. His discussion of athletic nudity in Ancient Greece, for example, mentions neither the subordinate position of women (Bonfante 1989: 558) nor the political point implicit in the historical observation that the Greeks used their valorization of nudity to "distinguis[h] themselves from all other peoples" (Perniola 1989: 238). In the contemporary examples that follow this chapter, I am interested in exploring the contexts in which, and the degree to which, a particular meaning of nudity can adhere, and what particular experiences of nudity might actually *feel* like. Which nude bodies can be innocent, ideal, shameful, corrupt, or vulnerable, and why? When is nudity elevated, when shameful, and when can it simply masquerade as nothing at all? For the seeming literalness of the nude body means that it can sometimes masquerade as a nothing – the degree-zero of humanity, the asignifying blank slate on which culture writes its message. But as Raymond Williams (1976) points out in the quotation that forms the epigraph to this chapter, the unrecognized metaphor is the most powerful one of all.

Notes

1. Interestingly, Fadwa El Guindi (1999: 10) notes a similar phenomenon with regard to one of nudity's "opposites," the veil, which, while frequently used either as a title keyword or a metaphor, is little studied.

2. "Full frontal" was first used, incidentally, in relation to Ken Tynan's play *Oh! Calcutta!* (1969) (Safire 1996: 30).

3. For example, Holder (1995) suggests that even an expression like "in the altogether" has Christian origins, involving a linkage between nudity, origin and sin: "Thou wast altogether born in sins" (John 9:39). Neaman and Silver (1983: 16–17) have a very different interpretation, though, tracing its earliest usage to the lounging poses of drunks and nude models.

4. On the level of idiom, the association between nakedness and the world of children is evident in a number of childlike expressions for nakedness, like "rudey-nudey," "in the nuddy" or, in French, "*cul-nu*" ("bare-bottomed") whose rhyme makes it an acceptable phrase for children, despite the etymology ("*cul*" = "arse").

5. In a number of US states (e.g. Arizona, Virginia, Washington, New Jersey) criminal nudity becomes a felony if performed in front of a child, and penalties for indecent exposure reflect this (see Posner and Silbaugh 1996). In Australia, indecent exposure is dealt with under the Summary Offences Act rather than the Crimes Act, unless it is performed in front of children, in which case it is considered a more serious offence – Active Indecency Toward A Child Under 16.

6. For an account of an early scandal involving an Australian naturist photographer arrested and prosecuted for paedophilia see Clarke's (1982) account of "Uncle" Lawford White.

7. I have explored this issue in depth in Barcan (2001).

8. The earliest example of the "real blonde" nudist joke I have found dates from the 1920s.

9. Most of the examples discussed in this section are canvassed by Blumenberg (1998). My thanks to Stuart Ferguson for his expert assistance in translating this and other German texts.

10. This too is a difficult-to-translate metaphor of clothing being ripped to shreds. Marx describes the feudally organized farmers as *buntscheckigen Feudalbande*, which translates as "feudal groups dressed in their *Buntscheck*," i.e. traditional farmer's outfits. These traditional clothes, emblems of the farmers' place in feudal society, have been torn to shreds by the bourgeoisie.

11. I am grateful to Jane Goodall for recounting this anecdote.

12. Derrida (1987) notes the etymological proximity of "text" and "textile."

13. This is the relevant passage from Augustine (1998). Whether or not Ellis (1937) is justified in his interpretation is open to doubt:

[Adam and Eve were not attentive enough] to recognize what a blessing they had received in the garment of grace, inasmuch as their members did not know how to oppose their will. When this grace was removed and a punishment commensurate with their disobedience inflicted on them, there appeared in the movements of their body a certain shameless novelty, as a consequence of which their nakedness was made shameful; and, when they noticed this, they were dismayed. (Bk. 14, ch. 17: 615)

This seems to my non-specialist eye to be much more about the loss of blissful unselfconsciousness than about the origin of erections.

14. For a discussion of this, see Miles (1989: 176ff).

15. This is not to say that female exposure is impossible as a means of shock, protest or power. It is to say, however, that the almost inevitable and often primary erotic

140

meanings of female nakedness are likely to interfere with or complicate any such meanings. This is discussed at greater length in Chapter 3 and in Barcan (2002a). See also Kirby (1996), and a brief discussion in Wolff (1990: 120–1).

16. "Know ye not that ye are the temple of God, and that the Spirit of God dwelleth in you? If any man defile the temple of God, him shall God destroy; for the temple of God is holy, which temple ye are" (1 Corinthians 3:16–17). Christ's body is itself the model for this: "Jesus . . . said unto them, 'Destroy this temple, and in three days I will raise it up.' . . . But he spake of the temple of his body" (John 2:19, 20).

17. Plato sometimes speaks of the soul too as internally divided between higher and lower parts (e.g. *Gorgias* 505B). Spelman (1982: 113) sees this as replaying at another level the tug-of-war between soul and body.

18. Also known as Ecclesiasticus, recognized in Catholic but not Protestant or Jewish teaching.

19. Two examples: in 2001, public scandal erupted surrounding goings-on at Glebe Morgue, Sydney, including rumours about the stealing of body parts. A technician I interviewed who works in a university anatomy lab told me that body parts do occasionally go missing. She said that the stealing of penises and so on was the kind of prank that would go on in the 1970s and 1980s, but that nowadays, thefts were just as likely to result from competitiveness, especially as institutional exigencies mean that students have less access to anatomy labs: "If I've got [a brain] at home under my bed, I can study at any time."

20. Epictetus was influential on the early Christians. Leder ascribes to Augustine a similar belief to the one used as an epigraph to this section – in the body as "something corpselike unless infused with soul" (Leder 1992: 19).

21. Berger (1972: 48–9) tells us that medieval representations of the Adam and Eve story were often a series of illustrations that followed the narrative scene by scene. In the Renaissance, this ceased to be the case; the single moment represented was the moment of shame.

22. See also a discussion by Rotello (1996) and by the alt.nudism.moderated newsgroup ("Them Modest Highschoolers").

23. Rotello (1996) points out that many gay men experience shower anxiety as well, particularly about the "hostile macho atmosphere and the mortal danger of an unscheduled erection." For gay males, the suppressed homeoerotics of the locker room can be both exciting and dangerous: "We were placed in close proximity to the naked forbidden, then made to understand that even an errant peek would bring utter social death."

24. For a study of nakedness and *King Lear* specifically, see Kronenfeld (1998).

3

Unnatural Nature: Mess, Savagery, Perversion, Crime

> In a "clothed" society, where garments are a social obligation, nakedness is an exception, and as such a monstrosity.
>
> E.J. Bickerman quoted in Bonfante, "Nudity as a Costume in Classical Art"

In his 1928 book *The Future of Nakedness*, John Langdon-Davies tells the story of a Californian couple who encouraged their sickly 6-year-old son to take regular sun-baths in their backyard. They were taken to court by their neighbour, who testified that the sight of the lad's nakedness "had completely undermined his wife's health" (p. 16). This little story neatly encapsulates two opposite conceptions of nakedness – as therapeutic or as dangerous to morals and even to physical health.

This chapter is a study of nakedness in some of its perverted, monstrous or criminal guises. It examines, by turn, the "messiness" of hairy nakedness, the uncultivated nakedness of the "savage," the "deviant" undress of the nudist and the criminal nakedness of the "pervert." We will see that in each case, nakedness is understood as both a symptom and a problem to be fixed. When it comes to body hair, the rawness of nakedness needs to be cleaned up into nudity; the nakedness of the "savage" needs to be "civilized" by clothing (though it is also subject to nostalgic romanticization); that of the social deviant needs to be contained, often by ridicule; and that of the criminal pervert needs to be treated, corrected or punished. Finally, I suggest that the ambivalence about nakedness is related to an ambivalence about nature itself.

Cleaning up the Body: Hair and Mess

In Chapter 1, I discussed the classic distinction between nakedness and nudity, and I argued that body hair and pubic hair are currently acting as a kind of raw and unpleasant nakedness increasingly understood as in need of "cleaning up." Contemporary depilation practices aim to transform "nakedness" (nature) into "nudity" (culture).

Hair can arouse strong feelings. This is in part because it is a boundary marker, whose cultural work includes signifying individual attributes as well as marking out social divisions. At the most fundamental level, body hair is used as a sign of the border between animal and human. Overlaying this fundamental division are many others, including those between civilized and savage; child and adult; male and female; and heterosexual and homosexual.

All cultures invest hair with a great deal of social and ritual significance. Although the meanings of hair vary across cultures, the cutting, shaving, plucking, waxing and styling of body and head hair always carries religious, economic, sexual or social meaning. By reason of its ceaseless growth, hair has often signified fertility and renewal.[1] It has served as a marker of sexual difference and sexual availability (e.g. "putting your hair up" as a sign of marriageability). For women, flowing uncut hair has signified either virginity or promiscuity and wantonness (Cooper 1971: 67, 77). Cutting and/or concealing the hair have often been a marker of chastity, and are commonly used as a device in religious orders for both men and women. Shaving the head can also be a sign of penitence or used as a punishment.

The meanings of pubic hair are, obviously, mostly erotic. In Ancient Egypt, pubic hair was considered ugly and unhygienic; depilation was practised by both men and women. In Ancient Greece women were completely depilated; young boys depilated their legs but kept their pubic hair, which was considered highly erotic (Cooper 1971: 84). In Europe in the Middle Ages, aristocratic women adopted depilation after the Crusaders brought the practice back from the Middle East. (The practice was, apparently, terminated by Catherine de Medici: Cooper 1971: 114). For most of European history, however, the shaving of pubic hair seems to have been a minority practice (p. 115). In art, however, it has been a different story.[2] The absence of body hair is an important part of the classical aesthetic. The statues of Ancient Greece presented women without pubic hair and men with highly stylized pubic hair. The Romans omitted the latter. The ideal of the hairless nude was picked up in the European art tradition, where for the most part, nudes were painted without pubic hair (although there are exceptions).

A hairy male body has signified virility, power and sometimes nobility. As the Roman satirist Juvenal put it: "A hairy body, and arms stiff with bristles, gives promise of a manly soul" (Ramsey 1982: 19). Even today, "too much" body hair "masculinizes" women, especially if it is in the "wrong" places: armpits, face or legs. The refusal of depilation was thus an important tactic for second-wave feminists.[3] It was, in essence, a refusal of domestication. "Correct" management of one's gender requires attention to hair, and, for a supposedly liberal culture, we remain surprisingly (or perhaps not) unforgiving of breaches. In the 1980s, a Seattle woman was fired for refusing to remove "excessive hair growth" from her chin (Synnott 1993: 119). In the mid-1990s, I remember the flurry of publicity (and heated opinion among my students) when a magazine published a photograph of film star Julia Roberts in an evening gown with a little bit of hair showing under her arms. Similarly, an art teacher at a Catholic boys' school told me the story of taking some students to an exhibition of nudes, and organizing a life class at a major state gallery in conjunction with this visit. The female model was young and beautiful, and when she came out from behind the screen, the young men responded approvingly. When she put her arms behind her head, they saw that she had underarm hair. At this the boys began to get agitated; "It was almost as if they were *angry*!" recalled the teacher. What is the cultural significance of this almost compulsory female depilation of underarms, bikini line, legs, face and now (increasingly) arms? It is certainly an extension of the aesthetic of idealism into the everyday, a continuation of the classical requirement for women to be less hairy than men. Depilation can (in part) be read as a form of enforced "domestication" that makes woman more "nude" than "naked" – bringing her into culture.

Compulsory depilation can also serve as a ritual device facilitating entry into and subordination to a particular institution. In such cases, obligatory shaving acts in the same manner as the forced adoption of a uniform. For example, the heads of US marines are shaved (ostensibly against lice) and so too, sometimes, is the pubic hair of women in labour (ostensibly against infection). Anthropologist Robbie Davis-Floyd, in an analysis of the rituals of modern birthing, sees such forms of shaving as more ritual than rational. Shaving is a strange-making device, whose purpose is to mark a ritual separation from the everyday world. In the case of the labouring woman, Davis-Floyd determined that shaving has a largely ritual purpose, since the obstruction of vision and, arguably, the question of infection, could be solved by clipping rather than shaving:

> The ritual shaving of her pubic hair further intensifies the institutional marking of the laboring woman as hospital property. States Hallpike, "Cutting hair equals social control." . . . [P]ubic shaving separates the laboring woman from her former conceptions of her body, and, like the gown, further marks her as being in a liminal state and as belonging to the hospital. It also (1) ritually establishes a boundary separation between the upper and lower portions of a woman's body; and (2) strips the lower portion of her body of its sexuality, returning the woman to a conceptual state of childishness and its accompanying characteristics of dependency and lack of personal responsibility (it is significant here to note that the hospital gown, while exposing the woman's genitals, thoroughly covers her breasts, which retain their sexual connotations); and (3) continues the powerful process of symbolic inversion begun with the hospital gown. (www.birthpsychology.com/messages)

The rationalization of such symbolic work as "hygienic" is, according to Norbert Elias, absolutely typical of the modernization of attitudes to the body.

As that which needs to be "treated" in order firmly to locate a social subject one side or other of any of these borders, hair can be considered a form of "dirt" in Mary Douglas' (1984) anthropological sense. Douglas sees purity and dirt as oppositions that help structure and stabilise any given social order. Nothing is intrinsically "dirty." Impurity exists at the margins of any structure – at the edge of a body, a society or even an idea. The body is a ritual site on which ambivalence and equivocation can be played out. At the heart of Douglas' study of pollution is the claim that the body is a prime site for the ordering of social hierarchies:

> The body is a model which can stand in for any bounded system. Its boundaries can represent any boundaries which are threatened or precarious. The body is a complex structure. The functions of its different parts and their relation afford a source of symbols for other complex structures. (Douglas 1984: 115)

Dirt is anything that threatens such boundaries.

Contemporary beauticians take the idea of dirt quite literally. In our interviews, the idea that waxing "cleans up" the body was unconditionally accepted, and phrases and terms like "tidy it up," "clean it up," "hygienic" and "dirty" were used unhesitatingly by all. For example, when asked whether a lot of people hate pubic hair, one beautician replied: "Yes, they do. I don't know why. I mean, it's a natural thing but people can't stand it. When it's all gone they feel a lot cleaner." Another, when asked whether hair was dirty, said that it depended whether there was an "excess" of it, where it was, and what people did with their hair. Nonetheless, this didn't prevent her from replying moments later that removing hair "definitely" made the body cleaner: "It's a lot more hygienic."

Body hair appears to be currently playing a role in the shifting idea of what constitutes a "clean" (i.e. properly disciplined) body. This process inevitably has a lot to do with categories such as gender, race and class, but it is also part and parcel of a current shift in the embarrassment threshold, and one that seems to support Elias' (1994) theoretical reflections about the processes by which such shifts occur. Elias (1994: 95) insists that rational explanations about hygiene always antedate the "undefined fears and anxieties" that they claim to explain. In other words, changes in the structure of society help to produce changes in the structure of the psyche (new distastes, new taboos). New forms of behaviour are only later sealed over as "hygienically correct" (p. 94).

Body hair is certainly beating a fast retreat. As beautician Elizabeth puts it: "Hair's just not acceptable . . . in this day and age." Even the bikini line is retreating, as more and more people opt for "the whole lot" (i.e. full genital waxing). Currently, this is mostly a female practice, but full genital waxing for men is not unknown, especially in homosexual men. True to Elias' theory of "hygienic correctness," Elizabeth explains women's adoption of full genital waxing as a form of cleanliness: "People feel cleaner if there's no hair. They feel dirty if there's hair all over them." Both the women and their boyfriends like it, she claims. Elizabeth returned several times during the interview to the term "clean:" "It's cleaner. I think a lot of guys like it cleaner. It [i.e. the penis?] doesn't get caught up and things like that."

The strangest instance that I have seen of this discourse of cleanliness came from the head of a modelling agency, who was quoted as saying:

> We're very conscious of our environment now. We want a cleaner society and clients require a cleaner look. And, without hair, you can see the muscle better. (quoted in Norman 1995: 26)

Why this environmental analogy? I'd like to return to Eric Michaels' salutary sniping at what he calls the discourse of tidiness:

> Tidiness . . . does not assure the cleanliness it promises. Instead, it merely obscures dirt; indeed, all natural (and finally, historical) processes. Tidiness is a process which, while avowedly in the service of cleanliness and health, in fact is only interested in obscuring all traces of history, of process, of past users, of the conditions of manufacture (the high high-gloss) . . . The tidy moment does not recognise process, and so resists deterioration, disease, aging, putrefaction. (Michaels 1990: 42, 40)

I think we can understand the modelling agent's otherwise bizarre use of an environmental discourse as a consumerist idea of "cleaning up" messy nature. Late-modern consumer culture is marked by an ambivalence about nature. On the one hand, it is easy to romanticize nature, to *forget* that it is "dirty," "messy" or dangerous. On the other hand, there is also a strong acknowledge-ment of the "dirtiness" of nature and a desire to "clean it up." Seeping, smelling, decaying, fecund nature – a nature in which life and death are closely connected – is not the kind of nature that we late-modern subjects are very keen on at all. (As a *system*, though, consumer culture needs this kind of nature, in order to sell products to combat it.) Contemporary ideals discourage bodies that overspill their boundaries – that flow, leak, seep or intermingle. As many writers have noted,[4] the visual ideals of postmodern consumer culture increas-ingly favour the hard, taut, youthful, autonomous bodies of disciplined subjects. As Mikhail Bakhtin's (1984) study of medieval carnival made clear by contrast, the modern bodily canon is classical; it favours the sealed off, idealized, smooth-surfaced, individual over the oozing, procreative, coarse, inter-connected social/cosmological body.[5] This is a gendered ideal to the extent that the procreative, oozing body has been largely construed as feminine.[6] Thus, it is interesting that one of the effects of waxing, according to Smith (1996) at least, is that it tightens up the body's boundaries (thus "masculiniz-ing" it) and, in the same process, renders visible those most masculine of signifiers, muscles.

In a convergence typical of our age, hairlessness is coming to signify not only cleanliness but also physical fitness, owing to the increasing overlap between the discourses of beauty, health and fitness. Hence, despite the dominant association of bodily hairlessness with femininity, hairlessness can also increasingly signify (male) sportiness and physical fitness. Elizabeth the beautician told us that heterosexual male bodybuilders, athletes and bicycle riders are now increasingly having their arms, legs and chests waxed. They usually begin with just the legs, but "Every time they come in they get more taken off." For hairlessness to be acceptable within the codes of hegemonic masculinity, it must disavow its association with femininity and with the hairless aesthetic of gay male gym culture. Sport can sometimes be a powerful enough vehicle to carry this disavowal. The beginnings of a new aesthetic of male hairlessness in mainstream consumer culture are evident (see Figure 3.1).

The demise of body hair has been a very rapid shift. As we saw in Chapter 1, mainstream porn fashions changed fast and absolutely. The rapidity of the shift is further corroborated by the differences between current attitudes and those found by Wendy Cooper, whose book on hair was published in 1971. Cooper organized a survey of around two hundred women and men at a British university. She found that 65 per cent of men claimed that they were aroused by female pubic hair (Cooper 1971: 88) and that 80 per cent of women believed their pubic hair to be "a powerful weapon in their sexual armory" (p. 89). Only a very few women in her survey shaved or shaped their pubic hair – but if they did, it was always at the request of their male partners (p. 89). Almost all (98 per cent) shaved their armpits (p. 116). Some women believed, as Mary Quant did, that women would soon be required to pay attention to their pubic hair (presumably on the assumption that fashions were getting more and more revealing). The following caption to two of the photos in Cooper's book (one showing naked body-painted males and the other a female hippy dancing naked among clothed men at a festival) shows just how unpredictable changes in body fashion can be, and how fast they can alter:

> As well as rejecting conventional hair styles, rebellious youth today rejects also conventional ideas of modesty and nudity. They see no reason to be ashamed of the nude body, which they may decorate . . . or display . . . Against this background we

To find out more about Permanent Hair Reduction, call Australasia's Largest Laser Clinic on
1300 365 273 Toll Free or click onto www.laserclinic.com.au

THE AUSTRALIAN
L A S E R   C L I N I C

*Clinics located at: Bankstown, Burwood, Castle Hill, Hurstville, Liverpool, North Sydney, Parramatta, Penrith
Randwick, Sydney CBD, Top Ryde • Bowral, Canberra, Central Coast, Newcastle, Wollongong.*

Figure 3.1 "Before and After Laser Hair Removal." Advertisement for the Australian
Laser Clinic. Reproduced with permission.

may expect rising interest in body hair as a sexual and decorative feature – an interest
that is becoming apparent in the refusal of many girls to shave their body hair as
their mothers did. (Cooper 1971: 137)

Nowadays, it is more likely that daughters will be pleading with their mothers
to be *allowed* to shave their body hair!

Shaving and depilation have served in many cultures as a puberty rite. In the West, "the first shave" is one of the markers of a transition from boyhood to manhood. For young girls, initiation into womanhood involves participating in feminine beauty rites. There is much pleasure and bonding in this, just as men and women have taken pleasure from fashion and body modification throughout history. There is also, however, compulsion: witness the misery of those young girls *not* allowed to shave their legs, or the embarrassment of any woman who has ever gone to the beach with her bikini line unshaved.[7] Currently, the shift from primary to high school is one obvious point of transition. Girls in their last year of primary school (Year 6) come to salons, preparing themselves for entry into high school. According to Elizabeth, their mothers often try to refuse them, claiming that they are too young at age 12 to start shaving or waxing. Elizabeth reads this as a form of maternal denial of the fact that their daughters are growing up. Be this as it may, among 12 year olds, the start of high school is a clear marker of a shift towards womanhood and obligatory "cleanliness:" "As soon as they hit Year 7, they're all doing it."

"Civilizing" the "Savage" Body

[I]f hairy strength and a certain nobility sometimes go together, so also does hairy strength and bestiality.

Wendy Cooper, *Hair*

While Darwinian Man, though well-behaved,
At best is only a monkey shaved!

W.S. Gilbert, *Princess Ida*

The modern nude emerged in European art at around the same time as a period of intense European colonial activity. Clark (1956), in fact, draws this link in the very first paragraph of his book, but he never again returns to this glaring political fact:

[T]he word ["nude"] was forced into our vocabulary by critics of the early 18th century in order to persuade the artless islanders that in countries where painting and sculpture were practised and valued as they should be, the naked human body was the central subject of art. (Clark 1956: 1)[8]

Although Clark's aesthetics is ostensibly apolitical, this conjunction of colonial politics and the modern nude is compelling, and his belief in nudity as the "civilizing" of nakedness must inevitably imply, at some level, some theory about primitiveness. Certainly, Clark's history of the nude is evolutionary, as is made clear in his passing comment that the nude represents a "far wider and more civilising experience" (Clark 1956: 6).

One way to begin thinking about nakedness and colonialism is to return to Elias' (1994) theories of "civilization," and introduce the question of race into them, even though it is not something foregrounded by Elias himself. Elias maintains that changes to social mores begin as social habits in the upper classes, and trickle slowly down to the middle and working classes, finally to install themselves as psychological mechanisms – new thresholds of disgust and aversion with their corresponding taboos. These taboos are retrospectively given rational explanations. The final step in this process is a kind of amnesia and projection, whereby cultures forget that things have ever been different, and project this repression onto other cultures, whom they characterize as "barbaric" (Elias 1994: 77). Thus it was that nakedness, one of those bodily practices brought increasingly under "control" in modernity, could be used by modern peoples as a sign of savagery.[9]

As a bodily sign, nakedness was particularly important to colonial thinking, since, as William Ewing (1994) has argued, the rise in the nineteenth century of theories of social evolution and of race meant, in practice, "the close scrutiny of the human body, since an understanding of the body was considered to be the key to an understanding of race and culture" (p. 15). From the 1860s onwards, anthropological photography furnished data by which humans could be measured, analysed and classified into types, using naked human bodies as "specimens." John Lamprey devised a system of grids in front of which naked figures could be photographed to enable the comparison of people from different races. The method was widely adopted and adapted, and was used to provide data for research in medicine as well as anthropology.[10] As Emmanuel Cooper (1995: 55) puts it in his chapter on ethnographic photography, nakedness and race together form a "potentially explosive mixture."

The "Naked Savage"

One of the key arguments of this book is that nakedness has operated as a corporeal sign that allows human beings to be divided into types or kinds. In the modern era, one such type was "the savage," a category developed within colonial discourse and validated by evolutionary and racial theories. The idea of the savage presupposes a progressivist conception of humanity – that is, one that imagines human societies along a continuum from base to noble.

The concept of the savage dates from some time between the sixteenth and seventeenth centuries.[11] Ashcroft et al. (1998) consider it a specifically colonial form of the much older concept of the barbarian, although other writers see the two terms as a little more distinct than this. The term "barbarian" was used by the Ancient Greeks to designate a foreigner, and did not *necessarily* connote inferiority, although it usually did (Thomas 1994: 72). From the fourth century BC, it mostly implied *lack* – the absence of civilization, which was, for the Greeks, epitomized in the *polis* (Thomas 1994: 72). This association of the city with civilization is found too in the popular medieval figure of the wild man/woman, a hairy, bestial creature who lived in the forests. Some Enlightenment thinkers made a distinction between the savage and the barbarian. Anthony Pagden (1993) argues that Montesquieu made the classic modern articulation of this distinction in 1748, when he considered savages as a primal form of human. For Montesquieu, savages were those peoples who "have not been able to unite," whereas barbarians were those who had learnt to come together in simple social groups (Pagden 1993: 14). The savage was thus understood as a "wholly pre-social being" (p. 14). The savage was a universal type – what all men had once been before they became civilized – whereas the barbarian was a more simple figure of lack and threat (p. 14). Audrey Smedley (1998) has made a well-cited argument that English conceptions of the savage were formed out of the isolation of English people from other Europeans. In the seventeenth century, the English used an idea of the savage, derived from Spanish discourses about the indigenous peoples of the New World (Baker 1998: 12), to deride the "wild," "barbarous" Irish. Ter Ellingson (2001) agrees with Smedley's theory, but stresses that European views of savagery were formed within the much wider multinational experiences of exploration and trade, in which numerous European countries partook, although not in identical ways (Ellingson 2001: 389).

In Darwinian thought, the savage was a step up from animals. This was an assumption of scientific, ethnographic and philosophical thought (Ellingson 2001: 126). The contiguity was also a popular one, as evidenced in the nineteenth-century penchant for theatrical displays, such as the one recorded by Ewing (1994: 14) in which a group of Zulus were put on display in the Brussels Zoo. Similarly, Alexander Wilson (1992: 27) records that in the early days of North American national parks, the native peoples were presented to tourists as part of the landscape.

The two epigraphs to this section suggest that hair has served as a marker in the Darwinian gradation of animal–savage–man. In this context, attitudes to body hair can be seen to operate in colonial and evolutionary thought alongside those towards clothing and nakedness, as ways of separating the "subhuman" from the "fully human." Following on from the discussion of hair in the previous section, I would like to explore the conjunction of hair and savagery as cultural ideas.

Human hairiness or lack thereof is no mere biological fact, but a profound cultural idea. On the one hand, there is the characterization of humans as *lacking* in hair. The human being, the "naked ape," is a "biological oddity" (Ableman 1994: 2), whose mysterious lack of body hair requires an evolutionary explanation: did it arise from our descent from the trees, or our discovery of fire (Cooper 1971: 8), or was it a cooling device, a way of minimizing parasites or a form of sexual signalling (Ableman 1984: 4)? This lack sets humans apart from the rest of nature.[12] To the medieval theologians, *nuditas naturalis*, "the human condition of animal nakedness," should "inspire humility" (Warner 1985: 295). For Carlyle (1987: 44–5) too, humans were even more naked than animals, pitifully exposed in comparison to the "self-tailoring" animals.

Humans' biological "nakedness," though, has also been seen as a *positive* attribute, something that lifts humans "above" the animals. It has therefore been able to be used as a cultural instrument for separating humans into "grades." The association between hairiness and bestiality has meant that lack of hair has been able to signify greater humanness, in one of those processes of "adjusting the boundaries of the human species" (Montag 1997: 287) that have often worked to privilege whiteness. Hairiness has often been associated with "barbarity." Julius Caesar (bald himself) spoke of his foes as "the hairy Gaul," and imposed the shaving of moustaches and head as humiliating punishment on the defeated Gauls and Britons (Cooper 1971: 44). The Britons defied Caesar by wearing long drooping moustaches dyed green and blue (p. 41). The figure of the "hairy Scot" survives as a remnant association between hairiness and wildness. In the Middle Ages, the wild man and woman figure was imagined as a hirsute denizen of the woods, in marked contrast to "civilized" people: "For much of the Middle Ages, hairy, cannibalistic, sexually omnivorous wild men and women . . . represented the antithesis of the civilized Christian" (1996: Schama 97). Such figures were precursors of the savages imagined by European colonists as hairy creatures, barely a step up from the animal world. Explorers' journals frequently compared indigenous peoples to monkeys and other animals, even while in their more scientific moments they noted quite carefully the differences between the hair of the indigenous peoples of different lands.[13] This contradiction is possible because the ideological cluster linking native, savage, animal and hair is so strong as a cultural *idea*.

In my interviews with beauticians, I was keen to find out whether a residual unconscious association between hairiness and "foreignness" (if not savagery) might still exist for Australians of Anglo-Celtic origin. In other words, is there an ethnic dimension to the pressure towards hairlessness exerted by the norms of contemporary body culture? And if so, can such body ideals be seen as in any way continuous or congruent with the nudes of the fine art tradition? Do these latter exhibit not only their cleaned-up status, but also their whiteness? This question is obviously a research topic all its own, and one too far-reaching to broach here. However, I have been led to think, cautiously, that ethnicity is certainly at least one factor in the depilation question, and to be made more aware of the *whiteness* of both those cleaned-up paintings and statues in the classical tradition and their arguable descendants, the doctored images in magazines.[14]

The figure of the hairy savage could also be found in the reverse, in the figure of a poor naked wretch appallingly or piteously naked.[15] We saw in Chapter 1 that the Christian tradition has made clothes the mythical exemplum of "civilization" and indeed of humanness, via the story of Adam and Eve. This helps explain why to the Christian colonists, nakedness became the exemplary sign of "savagery." Christopher Columbus' very first comment on the native Americans was on their nakedness (Todorov 1984: 34–5). Clothes, as we have seen, function as a symbol of culture, and nakedness as a sign of all the other supposed lacks of indigenous peoples:

> The nakedness of "savage" peoples, dwelt on by virtually every ethnographic account, had [by the seventeenth century] assumed an emblematic status for framing the problem of every kind of perceived negativity, from a European comparative standpoint, of features lacking in their cultures. They were said to have "no laws," "no property," "no religion," no analogue of almost any feature that Europeans assumed to be an indispensable characteristic not only of civilization but even of human society. (Ellingson 2001: 25)

Nicholas Thomas (1994: 72) points out that again and again, colonisers characterized native peoples via lists of what they lacked rather than by positive attributes.[16] Anthony Pagden (1993) claims that this idea of lack took its force from an implicit theory of humans' relation to nature. He argues that the distinctive feature of European thought was *not* the fact that Europeans considered themselves superior to other cultures (for many cultures encounter difference in this way) but that it based this belief on a theory of nature. Christianity inherited and developed the Graeco-Judaic view that nature was a potentiality waiting for the action of humans to complete it. According to Pagden (1993: 6), it is an unusual and particular part of European thought that it be based on the belief that "to transform nature . . . is a crucial part of what it is to be a man."

The association between nakedness, savagery and lack persists today. In a cross-national survey of children's attitudes to nakedness, Ronald and Juliette Goldman (1981) asked children between the ages of 5 and 15 why they thought humans needed to wear clothes. They then judged the responses according to Kohlberg's scale of moral reasoning and compared them cross-nation-ally. There were many interesting findings, but the one of relevance here is the persistence of an equation between clothing and "civilization," and a corresponding one between nakedness, savagery and rudeness. To the question, "Do we need to wear clothes in a warm climate?" a 9-year-old Australian boy replied, with unhappy logic:

> Yes, because you'd get badly sunburnt. You need to wear T shirts. You'd go black after two or three years. Then you'd be mistaken for an aborigine and you couldn't get a job then. (Goldman and Goldman 1981: 171)

When asked why we should wear clothes, a 13-year-old North American boy replied:

> It's self-respect, when you see natives running around with no clothes on, they don't know any better. We do. (Goldman and Goldman 1981: 173, original punctuation)

In a response that connected clothes with "civilization," a 13-year-old Swedish boy said: "Yes, you can't simply be all naked. This is not educated" (p. 173).

To a post-structuralist critic, the question as to whether indigenous peoples were "naked" depends very much on one's definition of clothing – one that excludes the myriad forms of body ornamentation and modification practised by all indigenous peoples.[17] British writer Paul Ableman (1984), for example, prefers to refigure the question of indigenous nakedness as a contrast between unconcealed and concealed cultures. This is not, however, an argument that all indigenous people would necessarily see as helpful. In a culture in which the naked body is a source of discomfort or disdain, the relativizing of nakedness might seem to reinforce the perception that nakedness carries with it some stigma. In contrast, Aboriginal scholar Irene Watson (1998), in an extended meditation on nakedness, unequivocally characterizes the land, Aboriginal people and traditional Aboriginal law as naked:

> My ancestors were naked peoples, and at some point in the history of humanity we were all naked, our beginnings in Kaldowinyeri [the creation time or dreamtime] were as naked as the law and the land. (Watson 1998: 1)

Watson evokes the process of colonization as a form of enforced *covering*:

> The coloniser – the bringer of cloth to Australia – through the use of force, rape, and violence dragged us into their world of dress and the covering of the naked body ... As we were forced out of nakedness we moved away from living raw in the law. (Watson 1998: 2)

While many modern white commentators might be more used to thinking of colonization as a process of *stripping away* – the taking away of land and rights, the removal of children – it can clearly also be imagined as an imposition, a covering over. Watson in fact uses both metaphors:

> By forcing the ancestors to be other than they were, the colonisers did not apply law; instead they imposed theft and tyranny upon the indigenous law, its lands and peoples . . . The dominant colonising culture has covered our being with its rules and regulations. It imposed a system that violated the law, and its peoples and lands. This was more than an act of dispossession of land; it was a dispossession of law, and the disposal of nakedness. (Watson 1998: 2)

The idea of colonization as a form of enforced clothing is crucial, conceptually and politically. The idea of covering rather than stripping allows one to envisage – indeed, Watson would say to *recognize* – that underneath the colonial imposition, Aboriginal authenticity is *still there,* waiting to be uncovered again:

> The carriers of law await the time that is still coming where the covering layers will be peeled away, to be naked again . . . A cycle destined to begin again: when the *muldarbi* [the demon spirit] is dismantled, we will again be naked. (Watson 1998: 3)

Clothing the Naked

In Australia, the early explorers were often shocked by the nakedness of the "savages." For example, in a section of his journal entitled "Wretchedness of the Natives," English explorer William Dampier wrote:

> The inhabitants of this country are the miserablest people in the world . . . [They] have no houses and skin garments, sheep, poultry, and fruits of the earth, ostrich eggs, &c., as the Hodmadods have; and setting aside their human shape, they differ but little from brutes . . . They have no sort of clothes, but a piece of the rind of a tree, tied like a girdle about their waists, and a handful of long grass, or three or four small green boughs, full of leaves, thrust under their girdle to cover their nakedness. They have no houses, but lie in the open air, without any covering, the earth being their bed, and the heaven their canopy. (Dampier n.d.:254)

Again, this is a picture of *lack*: the Aborigines are understood as having no clothes, no religion, no houses, no agriculture, and "no one graceful feature in their faces" (p. 254). Dampier describes his attempts to trade clothes for service, hoping to persuade the Aborigines to carry barrels of water from the springs on shore back to his canoes. His journal records his surprise that the Aborigines seemed not particularly to admire the proffered "old pair of breeches," the "ragged shirt" and the jacket that was "scarce worth owning"

(p. 256), which he had thought would have been "very acceptable" to them and enough to encourage them to "work heartily for us." As it turned out, the people stood grinning, and the explorers were forced to carry the water themselves. Dampier notes, though, that the Aborigines "very fairly" took the clothes off again, and laid them down "as if clothes were only to work in" (p. 256).

Botanist Joseph Banks (1998), too, found that the Aborigines were uninterested in the clothes and other gifts the white men brought. In his *Endeavour* journal, he recounts stumbling across a pile of clothes they had given to the Aborigines, which had been abandoned – "doubtless as lumber not worth carriage" (p. 69). Banks makes a number of references to the nakedness of the Aborigines, but his comments are both more careful and more sympathetic than Dampier's (in fact, he is explicitly critical of Dampier's account).

The attempt to "civilize" the "natives" was an explicit part of the colonial project, framed unhesitatingly in those terms. The civilizing imperative was inseparable from religious conversion. The British monarch and parliament sent explicit instructions to the early administrators of the colony that the Aborigines were to be imparted "that degree of civilization, and that religion, with which Providence has blessed this nation" (*Report from the Select Committee on Aborigines (British Settlements)* 1837, quoted in Woolmington 1988: 9). The "peaceful and voluntary reception of the Christian religion" was likewise explicitly specified by kings and parliament (ibid., quoted in Woolmington 1988: 10). "Peaceful and voluntary," however, this process was not, whatever the intentions of those in Britain: "A degree of force we find to be absolutely necessary to urge man towards civilisation, in his primitive debased state, and cause him to break up those habits he had acquired" (Peter Cunningham 1828, quoted in Woolmington 1988: 20).

The symbolic importance of clothing to Christianity cannot be underestimated. As we saw in Chapter 1, the story of Adam and Eve made clothing a metonym for all human culture, and for proper positioning in the social order. "Clothed and in their right minds" was a biblical quotation that seemed to confirm the rightness of this order.[18] According to Lee Baker, the very category of the savage is embedded in religion. He claims that it initially took its meaning and authority from a religious discourse and later from a scientific one (Baker 1998: 12). Whatever their differences, evolutionary and religious thought do rely on the shared assumption of an essential humanity. For evolutionary thinking, the primitive is "a necessary stage of development through which every race has passed," as Freud put it in *Totem and Taboo* (quoted in Torgovnick 1990: 8). Likewise, two "basic tenets of Christian theology – the unity of creation and the prospect of a Second Coming" encourage an idea of humanity as a single population (Thomas 1994: 73). Nicholas Thomas claims that in the case of the Spanish in America, the Christian conception of the unity of creation provided the overriding justification for the project of conquest, which can thus more properly be seen as arising from a religious imperative rather than a racial or national one (Thomas 1994: 72–73).

By the time the missionaries arrived in Australia in the early decades of the nineteenth century, many of the Aborigines they encountered were those living on the margins of the large cities, often likely to be clad in "the cast-off rags of European clothes" (Harris 1994: 528). John Harris claims that this may help explain why the early missionaries found the Aborigines to be in a state of wretchedness. Harris' book *One Blood: 200 Years of Aboriginal Encounter with Christianity*, cites many first-hand accounts by missionaries, whose shock and horror at the nakedness of the Aboriginal people is evident:

> Could they see from fifty to one hundred of these poor creatures half or entirely naked, lying on the ground, pulling to pieces an oppossum [a small mammal] with their hands and teeth, and covered with filth and dirt, they would indeed with a heavy heart enquire, "Can these bones live?" (William Watson, quoted in Harris 1994: 530)

Harris claims, nonetheless, that most missionaries were also compassionate; this same Watson, like many other missionaries, "found his compassion much stronger than his revulsion, not hesitating to dress infected wounds and wash diseased bodies" (Harris 1994: 530).

To the medieval Christians who invented the term *nuditas naturalis*, humans' proximity to animals was a cause of humility, if not shame. Many of their European descendants still shared this view. In many biblical uses, nakedness was the state of the damned and the dispossessed. Clothing the naked was a biblical injunction, and missionaries went to "extreme lengths" (Harris 1994: 530) to ensure that Aboriginal people were clothed. His citation from Bishop Augustus Short, for example, makes it evident that to many Christian missionaries, clothing represented a form of salvation:

> Many young adult natives, who would have belonged to the most degraded portion of the human family, are now clothed and in their right minds, sitting at the feet of Jesus . . . (quoted in Harris 1994: 531)

Clothing, here, is equated with both sanity and sanctity. This is in stark contrast with an Aboriginal perspective, in which the shared nakedness of the law, the land and the people is an index not of human depravity but of "the inter-relationship of all things and of humanity's responsibility to act as custodians of the natural world" (Watson 1998: 1).

If clothing was theologically and ideologically central to the colonizing project, it was also of economic importance to Britain, as can be seen in the following stunningly blatant example of how the Christian imperative to "clothe the naked" could be bound up with the profit motive. It is found in a speech made in 1884 to the Manchester Chamber of Commerce by the explorer Henry Morton Stanley, in which the relations between colonialism, clothing and profit are laid shamelessly bare.

The speech in question concerns the economics of clothing the inhabitants of the Congo Basin, a colonized territory over which there was an ongoing sovereignty dispute between Portugal and England. The English cotton industry was in decline, suffering from the imposition of tariffs by other nations trying to develop their own cotton industries. Stanley's speech is a combination of exhortation and chastisement. He castigates the Chamber of Commerce for complaining but failing to take action to develop new markets.

Stanley's suggestion comes in the form of a "curious calculation" (Stanley 1884: 12), beginning with the claim that if all the inhabitants of the Congo Basin could be persuaded to buy one Sunday dress each then this would necessitate the sale of 320,000,000 yards of cotton material. He continues: two Sunday dresses and four everyday dresses would amount to 3,840,000,000 yards annually, which at two pennies per yard would be £16,000,000:

> The more I pondered upon these things I discovered that I could not limit these stores of cotton cloth to day dresses. I would have to provide for night dresses also, and these would consume 160,000,000 yards. Then the grave cloths came into mind. (pp. 12–13)

About 2 million people die every year, he claimed, and

> to bury these decently, and according to the custom of those who possess cloth, 16,000,000 yards will be required, while the 40,000 chiefs will require an average of 100 yards each, or 4,000,000 yards. I regarded these figures with great satisfaction, and I was about to close my remarks upon the millions of yards that Manchester would perhaps be required to produce when I discovered that I had neglected to provide for the family wardrobe – or currency chest. (p. 13)

Stanley continues to do his calculations, stretching his mind to specialty cloths and handkerchiefs (p. 14). Africa was, he claimed, the place to begin, because India was starting to develop its own industry: "It is the easiest matter to teach Africans to wear cotton dresses, but centuries must elapse before they can make their own cottons" (p. 30).[19]

The final equation is simple: "I have proved to you that if every inhabitant of the Congo Basin had only six dresses of cheap cottons each every year, your trade would be worth £25,000,000 per annum" (p. 30). Here, one can see with unusual clarity the coincidence of moral and economic imperatives. The "immeasurable and incalculable millions" (p. 14) that could accrue to the Manchester cotton-makers prove that "civility" has its economics. Today, transnational corporations continue to use the same tactic.[20]

Romanticization: The Noble Savage

As we have seen, the nakedness of indigenous people was understood as an emblem of all their other supposed lacks. But if non-Western societies were understood as lacking in comparison to the developed civilizations of modernity, they were also sometimes understood as repositories of all those values and freedoms that these same societies were imagined to have squandered or lost – an authentic relation to nature, a simple untroubled life, a primordial innocence. Within this discourse, indigenous nakedness could be understood as "natural" in a positive sense. In fact, euphemistic expressions for nakedness as "natural" (e.g. "in a state of nature") date from the second half of the eighteenth century – a period of intense European colonial activity and the corresponding cults of primitivism and the noble savage (Ayto 1993: 154).

It is commonly believed that the myth of the noble savage had its origins with Rousseau. This is quite unequivocally a misattribution, whose persistence is itself a phenomenon worthy of study, as Ter Ellingson's (2001) thorough and sceptical history of the myth attests. Ellingson argues that a literal European belief in noble savages has been overstated, and that the noble savage is a piece of "anthropological folklore" (p. 3). Neither the label "noble savage" nor its content should be accepted at face value (p. 7), he argues, but should be examined for the role they have played in the racist history of anthropology itself. Ellingson warns that the myth helps feed a broader analytical knee-jerk, by which any European critique of civilization and any idealization of primitive life are labelled "romantic naturalism" and are attributed to the "noble savage" myth (p. 6).[21]

Accepting this caution, it is nonetheless important to note that European responses to Australian Aborigines, from explorers' journals down to the present day, have included idealization, exoticization and romanticization as well as denunciation. To Christian explorers, the nakedness of the savage could be understood as the primordial and innocent unselfconsciousness of Adam and Eve in paradise. This idealization required a corresponding view of nature as benevolent (Edenic); "natural man" needs no clothing because nature is all-providing. Joseph Banks made use of the comparison with Adam and Eve on several occasions:

In the morn 3 or 4 women appeard upon the beach gathering shellfish: we lookd with our glasses and to us they appeared as they always did more naked than our mother Eve. (Banks 1998: 82)

The comparison was not always made approvingly. Judge Barron Field of the Supreme Court of NSW, for example, made the following dismissal in 1825:

Without faculties of reflection, judgement or foresight, they are incapable of civilization. They are the only natives in the world who cannot feel or know that they are naked and they are not ashamed. (quoted in Watson 1998: 9).

In a system in which clothing was enforced and nakedness could be punished by fine or imprisonment, there was often nothing positive to be gained from this Christian analogy.

Often, though, the trope took its place among the genre of nostalgic self-reflection that Dean MacCannell (1989: 3) has characterized as intrinsic to modern societies and central to their expansionist spirit. The journals of both James Cook and Joseph Banks, for example, include extended philosophical reflections on the gains and losses attendant on "civilization." In both, there is a reprise of the traditional Christian use of clothes as a metonym for civilization, social division and distance from true need:

Thus live these I had almost said happy people, content with little nay almost nothing, Far enough removd from the anxieties attending upon riches, or even the possession of what we Europeans call common necessaries: anxieties intended maybe by Providence to counterbalance the pleasure arising from the Posession of wishd for attainments, consequently increasing with increasing wealth, and in some measure keeping up the balance of hapiness between the rich and the poor. From them appear how small are the real wants of human nature, which we Europeans have increased to an excess which would certainly appear incredible to these people could they be told it. Nor shall we cease to increase them as long as Luxuries can be invented and riches found for the purchase of them; and how soon these Luxuries degenerate into necessaries. (Banks 1998: 104–5, original spelling and punctuation)

From Cook:

From what I have said of the Natives of New-Holland they may appear to some to be the most wretched people upon Earth, but in reality they are far more happier than we Europeans; being wholy unacquainted not only with the superfluous but the necessary Conveniences so much sought after in Europe, they are happy in not knowing the use of them. They live in a Tranquillity which is not disturb'd by the Inequality of Condition: The Earth and sea of their own accord furnishes them with all things necessary for life, they covet not Magnificent Houses, Houshold-stuff &cᵃ, they live in a warm and fine Climate and enjoy a very wholsome Air, so that they have very little need of Clothing and this they seem to be fully sencible of, for many to whome we gave Cloth &cᵃ to, left it carlessly upon the Sea beach and in the woods as a thing they had no manner of use for. In short they seem'd to set no Value upon any thing we gave them. (Beaglehole 1955: 399)

This eloquent elegy repeats the fundamental Christian rejection of clothing as a form of vanity and the related paradox of clothing as an unnecessary necessity – a "Convenienc[e]" both "superfluous" and "necessary."[22]

We can note, once again, the importance of sex and gender in this treatment of nakedness. First, primitivism itself is arguably a gendered discourse. According to Marianna Torgovnick, gender issues are *always* a part of Western ideas of the primitive, a fact that has been underestimated or ignored by many eminent theorists of Western primitivism:

Sooner or later those familiar tropes for primitives become the tropes conventionally used for women. Global politics, the dance of colonizer and colonized, becomes sexual politics, the dance of male and female. (Torgovnick 1990: 17)

This politics of this dance are, of course, enormously complex. On the one hand, the category of the primitive was identified with all the feminized ideas feared and denigrated in the name of rationality and civilization – body, nature, irrationality. Western thought tended to "identify the 'lower,' the 'irrational,' the 'instinctual,' the 'swarming' with the primitive" (Torgovnick 1990: 80). On the other hand, the logic of binary definition means that the denigrated term is pivotal to the self-definition of the primary term. Primitivist discourse can thus be understood as a yearning for the dissolution of these boundaries (Torgovnick 1990: 253), and the feminization of the category of the primitive could be a sign of positivity as well. Nicholas Thomas (1994), for example, has noted the interplay of gender with evolutionary thinking, arguing that in some instances, sexualization and feminization implied progression towards civilization, an evolutionary "advancement." The seductive and/or noble primitive was a feminized image, in contrast to the masculine image of the "repugnant and threatening" savage (Thomas 1994: 35).

In addition to this feminization of the primitive on the level of discourse, there was also a flourishing fascination with indigenous sexuality. Torgovnick (1990: 3–8) cites the importance of studies of the sexual practices of indigenous peoples to anthropology and ethnography, noting the repressed lasciviousness of many anthropological texts, such as Bronislaw Malinowski's *The Sexual Life of Savages* (1929). Attitudes to the sexuality of indigenous peoples were not consistent and could range from disgust to exploitation to idealization. Sexualized tropes and images enjoyed wide currency, and not just within popular discourses. Michael Sturma (1995) coins the phrase "the nubile savage" to describe the sexualization of indigenous people, especially the women of the South Pacific (and sometimes Australia). He claims that this typified many accounts of the late eighteenth century, which idealized the nakedness of South Pacific women as "innocent" and "modest," while also eroticizing it. He points to the significance of the fact that male writers were insisting on the natural modesty of islander women at the same time as in Europe Enlightenment philosophy was starting to erode the faith in these same qualities as traditional bases of male dominance.

There was, then, a voyeuristic element to the colonial encounters. Peter Mason (1990: 170ff.) has commented on this aspect of the accounts and images produced by many explorers of America, and has noted the interpenetration of erotic and economic preoccupations. Such preoccupations continued over the centuries after Columbus. The invention of photography provided a new vehicle for this voyeurism, and photographic images of naked "primitives" circulated in scientific, anthropological, artistic and popular realms. The role of photography, including scientific and anthropological photography, in the eroticization of indigenous women has been well documented (see, for example, Cooper 1995; Ewing 1994). William Ewing records that in Britain in the late nineteenth century there was a trade in images of naked peoples, especially Zulus and especially nubile young women. Anthropology was one way in which the early pornographers hoped to avoid charges of obscenity.

Indigeneity continued to provide a semiotic avenue and a legal pretext for white prurience into the late twentieth century. The use of *National Geographic* magazines as a tool of fantasy or a form of pseudo-pornography is a common-place of popular anecdote. The anthropological gaze could also provide a legal alibi. Magnus Clarke (1982: 202) claims that the first Australian popular magazine to show naked breasts was *People*, in 1964, as part of a current flutter about the fashion for topless bathing that had recently hit Europe. Australian tabloid magazines began to speculate about whether it would ever be permitted in Australia. Images of the "monokini" were shown, but only from behind. *People* skirted the censor by showing a picture of topless Malaysian women and accompanying it with an article written by a progressive Christian minister about the possibility of moral toplessness (Bond 1964). It is not that either the article or the photo was prurient, rather that anthropology provided an avenue of legal and moral legitimation for depictions of toplessness in that era.

The following year, the African Ballet Company's tour of Australia provoked a dilemma for the censors. Should the women be permitted to dance topless?

The *Sydney Morning Herald* argued that "any attempt by local prudery to compel immemorial Africa to forsake its innocence and to clap brassieres on the Stone Age" would be not only prudish but also hypocritical:

> There is surely more offence to modesty in the three-penny-sized sequin which is the symbolic breast adornment of a Kings Cross "stripper" at the climax of her performance than in the absence of any covering on the breasts of these brilliant dancers. (Anon. 1965)

Against the natural nobility and skill of timeless Africa is contrasted the hypocritical false modesty of the modern degenerate dancer. When the company performed in New York the following year, prudery and hypocrisy were again denounced, as another Australian newspaper noted that the ballet's performance was received without complaint in the same week as two topless waitresses in Manhattan stood trial for indecent exposure (Anon. 1966). "Timeless Africa" forced Australians to look to their *own* value systems, clearly the object of some ambivalence.

Modern Ambivalence

So far, we have pointed to the repeated characterization of indigenous people as in *lack*, and of nakedness as a powerful metaphor for that supposed absence. But we have also seen that the savage's lack and the plenitude of the primitive were two sides of the same coin. Indigenous nakedness could be construed as both absence and presence – *too much* covered (in hair or paint or ornaments) or *too little* covered (by clothes), *having* harmony with nature or *lacking* civilization. They could fill the metaphysical position of both lack or plenitude, as could the "nature" for which their nakedness was so often made an emblem. For example, when Captain Cook remarks of an Aboriginal woman that "even those parts which I allways before now thought nature would have taught a woman to conceal were uncover'd" (Beaglehole 1955: 359), he sees the woman as not only *of* nature but in some sense *beyond* nature.

Ken Gelder's and Jane Jacobs' (1998) book on sacredness in contemporary Australia includes a helpful discussion of such paradoxes. They begin their study of the place of Aboriginal spirituality in contemporary Australian nationhood with a discussion of Emile Durkheim's book on Aboriginal religion, *The Elementary Forms of the Religious Life* (1915). They note a seeming inconsistency in Durkheim's characterization in his opening pages of "the lower religions" as both "rudimentary" and "gross" (Gelder and Jacobs 1998: 5). Moreover, they note that Durkheim fleetingly uses the metaphor of nudity, when he imagines primitive societies as revealing, in all their "nudity," the foundational truths of all societies, modern ones included

(Durkheim 1976: 6).[23] Durkheim wants it both ways: he argues that all religions are "true in their own fashion" yet that it is "undeniably possible to arrange them in a hierarchy" (Durkheim 1976: 3). For Gelder and Jacobs, such contradictions suggest that for Durkheim, modernity is no simple "development" of a lack. Instead, Durkheim imagines "primitive" cultures as both plenitude and lack: lacking in civilization but having the authentic fullness that an ambivalent and nostalgic modernity considers itself to have lost. For our purposes, this would help explain why the nakedness of the primitive person seesaws between being a sign of savagery and hence of lack (the absence of civilization) and one of innocence (reminding Christian modernity of its *own* lack – the innocence it supposedly lost in the Garden of Eden). This paradoxical conception of primitive cultures as being both "full" and "empty" is, Gelder and Jacobs (1998: 1) contend, part of the attempt to make "modernity reconcilable with itself."

This nostalgia and sense of loss are still evident today. Paul Ableman's (1984) book on nakedness, for example, contains a powerful evocation of that which has been lost – that is, of "primitive" nakedness:

> And if primitives lost their culture, they also lost their environment. They lost the sun, the rain, the grass underfoot, the foliage which brushed their skin as they moved through forest or jungle, the water of lake, river or sea slipping past their bodies, above all the ceaseless communion with the wind. Anyone who has ever spent any time naked outdoors knows that the play of the elements over the body produces an ever-changing response that may reach almost erotic intensity. The skin becomes alive and responsive and a whole new spectrum of sensation is generated. Clothe the body and this rich communion is replaced by mere fortuitous, and often irritating, contact with inert fabric. It is a huge impoverishment. (Ableman 1984: 16)

While this is powerfully written, and while it does speak to modern people's very real distancing from nature, it is also in the grip of the myth of nakedness as a non-cultural authenticity. It ignores the complexities of both clothing and nakedness: how, on the one hand, the skin may become alive to *fabric* and, on the other, how it may become desensitized to its natural surroundings. Any modern nudist can testify to the wealth of bodily sensations described so poetically by Ableman; what they can't tell you is whether all indigenous people would have felt these (all the time). Ableman's lament cannot help but be part of a *myth* of modernity, part of that paradoxical and very modern idea of civilization as impoverishment.

The European ambivalence about "natural man" reflects modern societies' unresolved ambivalence about nature (is it a lack or a fullness?) and hence about humanness (is it the absence of nature or true alignment with nature?). We will see the same questions at play in contemporary nudism.

Nudism as Deviant Naturalness

Every society constructs a system of taboos and proscriptions that regulates norms of behaviour. Adult public nudity is a prime example of this proscription. Most socially regulated practices, however, have sites of ritual exception; in the case of the modern proscription of public nudity, the nudist camp or beach is an obvious example of such a ritual site.

The key foundations of nudism are the "naturalness" and "innocence" of the human body and the socially and psychologically therapeutic effects of non-sexually segregated social nudity. But the naked body's ambiguity makes it a highly unstable foundation on which to build a movement. In fact, the general proscription of adult nudity in public space produces nudism as a deviant practice in the sociological sense; public nudity is, to recall E.J. Bickerman's term, a "monstrosity."[24] Nudism is, then, a paradoxical practice of "deviant naturalism," a form of sanctioned but circumscribed public nudity. Nudists enjoy a form of naked embodiment that they idealize as authentic and natural and yet which is widely conceived of by others as perverse. Nudism is inherently paradoxical – the natural, authentic practice that needs to argue constantly for its own normalcy. Wholesome perversion, uncommon naturalness, nudism is a practice both banal and extraordinary.

The degree of social deviancy of nudism differs from country to country. In many European countries, tolerance of public nudity (e.g. in parks, pools or bathhouses) is much greater than in Australia, the UK and the US, and nudism (or naturism, as it is also known) is a widely accepted, if statistically minor, family practice. In Australia, nudism is a minority practice popularly understood as anything from comic to strange to downright perverse. Despite this, nudists continue to stress the therapeutic effects of nudity in the face of their detractors' mystification, ridicule or moral condemnation. The positive meanings of nudity – its cultural association with honesty, innocence, beauty, nature, truth and freedom – can help render the experience of nudity affirming and pleasurable. But so too can the "negatives," which themselves accord people the self-affirming pleasures of resisting and rupturing social taboos. In other words, at least some of the pleasure and benefit of nudism is in fact the *result* of the taboo that renders it a marginal practice.

Historical Nudism

Nudism arose in the early twentieth century in Europe. Early names included the German *Freikörperkultur* (or *Nacktkultur*), French *libre-culture* and English Gymnosophy. There were differences and occasionally rivalry between these national cultures (for example, German nudism is usually characterized as somewhat more stolid and austere than its cousins),[25] but there was also significant interaction between them. Nudism spawned a range of proselytizing books and studies. Many were of a testimonial nature – openly evangelical first-person accounts, often written in the face of incomprehension, social stigma, or overt hostility. Many take the form of narratives in which the ostensibly objective writer goes to observe this little-known phenomenon and reports back on its healthfulness. Christian accounts are quite common – as for example, the Reverend Norwood's (1933) brave study, *Nudism in England*.

By and large, nudism was a movement endorsed and organized by educated people – physicians, scientists, lawyers, clergy, and, in France especially, occasionally by members of the aristocracy. In many countries, though, its constituency was the unemployed and the working poor.[26] In Germany, Russia and Greece it was an especially proletarian movement. In England, however, it was *not* a working-class movement (contemporary observer Jan Gay (1933: 121) claimed that the English working class was likely to be offended by nudity). In all its forms, however, it was a critique of modernity, which nudists understood as having alienated its subjects from nature, from each other, from the body and from natural sexuality. It was no simple critique of modernity, however. Nudism also understood itself as very modern – having a scientific basis and pointing the way to a new, rational, future.[27] In both its nostalgic and rationalist forms, nudism was a utopian movement. It was seen by many European writers in the late 1920s and the 1930s as a sign of the inevitable, healthy, scientific, liberal, democratic future to come. The early exponents of naturism saw it as a recipe for a healthy individual, for healthy relations between the sexes, and for a healthy society. In the words of French journalist Roger Salardenne, the shared goal of naturism throughout Europe was:

> The complete development on all levels of the human personality and the obtaining of a harmonious balance of the individual and society based on the worship of Honour, Beauty, Truth and Health. (Salardenne 1931: 61)

As this example illustrates, early nudism made use of moral, aesthetic and medical arguments. The medical emphasis was particularly strong in France, where many of the early public advocates were doctors, for example Pierre Vachet, Henri Nadel, Robert Sorel, Jean Poucel, the brothers Gaston and André Durville, and Fougerat de David de Lastours. Many of these doctors wrote influential books espousing a link between nudism and physical, mental and psychological health, such as Henri Nadel's (1929) *La Nudité et la santé* (*Nudity and Health*). Even as late as 1953, Jean Poucel wrote a book titled *Naturisme, ou la santé sans drogues* (*Naturism, or Health without Drugs*).

Early European naturist clubs enforced a range of health measures, especially physical culture lessons. One of the most famous exponents of physical culture was the German Adolf Koch, the socialist founder of the *Körperkulturschule* in Berlin. Koch was a school gymnastics teacher who, with parental consent, got the pupils to exercise nude. Other teachers were critical and Koch was expelled, although, following a court case, the school offered to reinstate him. But his working-class constituency were loyal and by this stage his night classes were so popular that instead he founded the *Körperkulturschule*. This exercise school was organized along socialist lines and had several thousand students, over half of them unemployed (Gay 1933: 64). Students gave a small percentage of their income. Koch organized nude swim nights at the local pool once a week for his pupils. These were enormously popular, with queues of two hundred people, for many of whom the swim nights provided the sole weekly opportunity to bathe, since most had no washing facilities at home (Gay 1933: 66). Formal exercises, conducted by Koch from his piano, were followed by a free-for-all in the pool.

German naturism was relentlessly communitarian, practised only in clubs, whose membership was strictly regulated. It was a particularly ascetic brand of health practice, accompanied, as in many other countries, not only by physical culture exercises, but also by compulsory vegetarianism, and bans on alcohol and tobacco, though Jan Gay (1933: 46) reports spying some older men hiding behind a hedge enjoying beer, sausages and a pipe! *Freikörperkultur* is in general characterized as more austere, earnest and unsmiling than, for example, French *libre-culture*. Even its free pleasures sound somewhat constrained; Salardenne (1931) describes one colony who, at the blow of a whistle, would all go down to the sea to bathe, alerted to the presence of passers-by by another whistle.

Physical health was only one part of the goal of naturism. Social nudity was seen as the solution to all kinds of ills, both personal and social. It was understood to bring moral, psychological, sexual and social benefits. Nudism was an antidote to shyness (Salardenne 1931: 33) and to sexual obsession, a pathway towards better understanding between men and women, a boon to physical health, and a reliever of social burdens like alcoholism, tuberculosis, syphilis and cancer (p. 91). Physical, mental and social benefits were seen as interlinked: "Now, a healthy strong being is, inevitably, a free being whom one cannot subjugate, who brooks no tyranny and who is quick to rid himself of prejudices" (Ennemond Boniface, quoted in Salardenne 1931: 90).

Nudism was anti-materialistic and sometimes, though by no means always, explicitly socialist. For a fervent believer like Ennemond Boniface, for example, (whom Salardenne (1931: 85) calls the "apostle of total nudity"), the workers have only two options for escaping from their misery: bloody revolution or naturism, which he conceived of as a form of peaceful revolution (Salardenne 1931: 92). The corollary of naturism was, he believed,

> the renunciation of this madness of production and the endless possession of material goods that poisons the life of modern societies and that is one of the most certain and direct causes of war. Then, there will be an exodus, imperceptible at first, but ceaseless, from the cities, and the willing return, methodical and organized, to the good nourishing earth. Little by little, men will desert the monstrous, nauseating agglomerations that are our big and even our small towns, in order to found, in the regions and in spots judiciously chosen, new and increasingly numerous naturist towns. Then, especially, the factories, those places of hard labour where decent folk are imprisoned, will progressively become empty. The ferocious reign of the industrialist and his accomplice the banker will be over. (Boniface, quoted in Salardenne 1931: 93)

There were many Christian advocates, whose writings were also unabashedly utopian. Nudism was understood as a reinstatement of the previous glory of humankind, a return to Eden. Naturism "tends to bring man back to his original [*primitives*] form and perfection" (Boniface, quoted in Salardenne 1931: 90). It was also, though, seen as part of the evolution of a new human-kind. Its more fervent advocates imagined a Naturist Era that would function as the starting point of a new civilization: "This path will soon become a road, a magnificent concourse, dazzling with light, leading straight to a new Eden of which Man, this time, will have been the sole Creator!" (Salardenne 1931: 20).

Modern Nudism

Today, almost without exception, nudists are more inclined to describe their practice as a source of personal relaxation, freedom or esteem than to see it as a fully fledged health practice. The closest thing to a discourse on physical health comes in the form of beliefs about the relaxing properties of nudity. In the early 1980s, Magnus Clarke (1982: 329) reported as a novelty the comment by the proprietor of one nudist resort who considered nudism to be useful in counteracting "stress." Nowadays, though, most nudists speak of the relaxa-tion encouraged by nudism. I asked an elderly English female nudist whether the freedom enjoyed by nudists is the freedom from clothes or some other kind of freedom:

> I think it's a mixture, really. I think when you shed your clothes you shed your worries and when you're free of clothes you enjoy the environment where you are so much more, and the space and everything around you. It's not just a physical feeling; it's a sort of mental relaxation.

Nudists are likewise highly unlikely to see nudism as a recipe for social reform. The most common term that people I interviewed used to describe nudism was a "lifestyle:"

> *Interviewer:* Do you think of yourselves as nudists?
> *Margaret and Bill*: Yes.
> (simultaneously)
> *Interviewer:* Would you use the label "nudist" to describe yourself?
> *Bill:* Well, I don't know about a label as such. It's just a lifestyle. We do it as a matter of course at home.

The early naturists debated whether nudism was, in fact, an "ism." Very few contemporary nudists are happy with the idea that it might be a "philosophy." After we discussed the early naturists, I asked Bill and Margaret whether they thought of nudism as a philosophy. Does it have a set of values that goes with it?

> *Margaret:* I'd like to think so. But I think the modern naturist . . .
> *Bill:* Not consciously. It's not something that I think of. I mean, it's just a way of life. It's just integrated into the way that we live.

A 69-year-old nudist and I had the following interchange:

> *Interviewer:* A lot of early nudists in Europe were very much part of other big movements and philosophies and they were very anti-materialist . . .
> *Bert:* Oh, yeah, in them days . . .
> *Interviewer:* . . . and thinking that nudism was like vegetarianism and non-smoking and not drinking and not acquiring goods and so on. Is it part of that philosophy for you? Is it part of a philosophy of simple living?
> *Bert:* No. It's something I like doing. That's the main thing. It's something I like doing, and that's it.

The critical discourse most likely to be adopted by nudists concerns body image and self-esteem. This is a resistive discourse about which nudists have no qualms. The slogan of the post-1980s naturist journal *Clothed with the Sun*, for example, is "The Issue is Body Acceptance." Nudists are critical of the cult of the body beautiful, and see self-acceptance and the acceptance of others as going hand in hand, and at the core of nudist freedom. When I asked a large woman, Michelle, whether being a nudist has flowed through as confidence to other areas of her life, she replied, "about three hundred fold."

Self-acceptance, the acceptance of others, and a critique of image culture and the hypocrisies of fashion are the main ideologies that bind contemporary nudists together. Other than this, nudists are largely unwilling to see their practice as "radical," "political" or connected to other types of social reform, as I have discovered by asking this question in interviews. Contemporary nudists are bound as much if not more so by their pursuit of a "relaxed lifestyle" as by any programme for social reform beyond a liberal and often laissez-faire critique of image culture and body ideals. When I asked Bill and Margaret whether they thought nudism was radical or political they answered:

Bill: No. Neither.
Margaret: I certainly don't. I feel that now I'm not part of the paid workforce any more, I feel like I don't have to hide it any longer.

Nudism belongs to a long, if minor, tradition of therapeutic nudity.[28] The therapeutic effect is attributable to the combined effects of liberal and progressive ideologies, the positive cultural meanings of nudity and the physically relaxing properties of sun and fresh air. These benefits are not, however, gained without effort. In a society in which nudity has many contradictory meanings and in which public nudity is both socially and legally proscribed, nakedness is always going to be a tricky basis for a social movement. So too is nature itself. Since modern societies see the human as both a part of and separate from the rest of nature, nature can be shifting ground on which to build a movement. In short, both the nakedness and the nature at the heart of naturism are culturally unstable.[29]

Nature Trouble

As we have seen, nudism's foundational paradox reposes on what might be an almost inevitable human ambivalence – that concerning nature. Although this ambivalence must play out very differently in different societies, which each have their own relations to nature and which conceive of nature in vastly different ways, I still wonder whether there can be a society without some form of double relation to nature. After all, humans are aware that they are *of* the natural, but all human societies have some also distance from it. Certainly, *modern* relations to the idea of the human in nature are complex, and therefore nudism must inevitably be caught up in of some kind of nature trouble. The following are just two examples of the "nature trouble" that nudism, as philosophy and practice, has to contend with.

Sex and Nature

The first concerns the place of sex. Nudism has always had a troubled relation with the erotic. The popular equation of nudity with sex must inevitably cross paths at some point with nudism's core claim about the naturalness of nakedness, obliging nudist thought to grapple with the problem of conceptualizing the "natural" place of sex in the human world. This is a theoretical problem in conceptualizing sexuality in relation to ideologies of nature, a practical problem in regulating sexual behaviour at nudist sites, and a promotional problem, in repudiating accusations of sexual depravity.

As a minority practice, nudism has always felt the need to protect its image from popular stories of sexual libertarianism or perversion. Historically, nudism has been the frequent target of assumptions, jokes, attacks and law suits, all taking the link between nudity and immoral or debauched sexuality for granted. In response, the official discourses of nudism have often been quite puritanical. Popular accusations of orgies and spouse-swapping have obliged nudists to repeat, for an entire century, that nudism and sex have little to do with each other. This position is understood by many commentators as an "ideological posture" (Bryant 1982: 137) or a bit disingenuous, to say the least. Nor is it helped when some naturist magazines adopt a "cheesecake" aesthetic in order to compete with girlie magazines, as occasionally happens (Clarke 1982: 154–5).

Gender issues are clearly at the fore when it comes to the problem of formulating an acceptable nudist conceptualization of sex. Nudist philosophy has always insisted that the participation of both sexes is intrinsic to nudism. But women have good reason to be sceptical of the invitation to undress in public. In a kind of circular logic, nudism had to seem non-sexual in order to attract women and it needed women in order to prove that it had nothing to do with sex. Nudism needed women as guarantors that the nature championed by naturism was wholesome and complete rather than raw. Early nudist magazines contained plenty of images of "maidens," mothers and children. A 1947 issue of the *Australian Sunbather*, for example, includes a photo of a mother and her five children looking at their reflection in a pool. The young women who even today still adorn the covers of nudist magazines help(ed) to sanctify nudism via the legitimizing balm of fine art. They also provided a naturalized discourse of womanly beauty through which nudism could interrogate its relation to the question of aesthetic ideals:

[Woman's] creation was a masterpiece of physical perfection. From the beginning she has been there to bring beauty into the life of her man . . . Attributed to her beauty is her most important factor, a lovely bust, which is woman's proudest outward proclamation of her sex. (Ashworth, 1948: 6–7)

So, even while Freud could imagine the repressive forces that ban adult nudity as a maternal figure (the mother who says "Ugh! Shocking! You mustn't ever do that!"), it is clear that nudism needs the "other" mother – emblem of a gentle, nurturing nature – to guarantee its normality.

Women were also needed to help men solve "problems" of their own. Even today, they act not only as the bearers of nudism's claim to naturalness but also as tacit guarantors of male nudists' heterosexuality. Most nudist clubs had policies excluding single males (and some still do). (This is one of the divisions between older style and modern nudist venues.) Nudism's traditional "woman problem" and its "single male problem" are thus subtly interrelated.

All this has historically put nudism in a double bind with regard to sex and has made many nudists wary of discussing the place of sex in nudism. For the purposes of analysis, I have isolated four nudist discourses around sexuality, though there are of course others. These discourses fulfil a variety of functions – scientific, educative, moral and promotional. The puritanical or platonic ones had the added advantage of being palatable to women and were used to encourage women into the movement, their reluctance having until recent times been a perennial problem for nudist clubs, continuing to be one for some styles of nudist activity (e.g. indoor swim clubs).

The first discourse to be considered is a highly puritanical one, characteristic of the early days of nudism in the 1930s and 1940s. Denunciations of the immorality of non-marital sexual activity were to be found not only in the censure of anti-nudists, who saw nudism as an attack on Christian morality, but also, sometimes, from *within* the movement itself. In the late 1940s, for example, the Australian nudist Ron Ashworth, who was the founder and editor of *The Australian Sunbather*, warned of the evils of seduction and prostitution:

"Irresponsible Sex relations destroying Mankind"
Could seduction be made a criminal act, and I know of no felony more atrocious, and punished by severe imprisonment, a considerable check would be imposed on the cowards who look on a girl as fair game, and a prime object on which to exercise their unbridled and ungovernable animal propensities. (Ashworth 1946)

[M]any [women] feel disinclined to a life of patient, humble industry, and listen to the voice of temptation, falsely, and fatally, believing it to be the signal for their emancipation, while not a few fall victim to the perfidy of men. (Ashworth 1946)

Repudiations of the link between nudism and sex are usually more mildly couched: "Mother nature usually knows when you should be aroused sexually and it is not at a nudist club" (Mary, quoted in Clarke 1982: 233). Or, to take a rather lofty example from the 1960s: "To watch the wholly unadorned female form raises the admiration of the male naturist to platonic heights at which it would be unthinkable for him to tarnish the object of his esteem" (quoted in Clarke 1982: 239).[30]

Nowadays, a very common nudist response to the question of sex in nudism would be that sex is a private matter, unrelated to nudism, or else enhanced only indirectly, via the relaxation, enhanced body-esteem or friendly social relations developed by nudist life. The following example comes from an interview with Bert, a 69-year-old nudist:

Interviewer: Do you think of nudism as a movement?

Bert: Well it is a movement, really, isn't it? It's a gathering of happy people, I reckon! A gathering of happy people enjoying life! [laughs] What else?! You know, the sex bit, that don't come into it. Who's worried about all that? I mean, privately, that's OK. We're here to enjoy our health. I mean, we're healthy aren't we? I'm healthy and I've got no worries. It's a healthy life.

A second discourse is an ascetic one in which nudism is understood as a moderating influence. The practice of social nudity encourages discipline – the control and mastery of wayward sexual urges. The founder of French nudism, Marcel Kienné de Mongeot, claimed that

> Nudity . . . is a shield against unhealthy desires. It doesn't so much suppress desire – which would be a shame and abnormal – so much as balance it, destroying sexual turmoil and according man an undeniable sensual mastery. Nudism isn't the school of chastity, even less that of continence, but the school of will, of self-control and of sexual calm [*sang-froid*]. (paraphrased by Salardenne 1931: 41)

William Welby (1934: 14) considered nudism to be "a very useful sexual lightning conductor," a helpful counter to sexual obsession. Salardenne (1931: 51–2) used this argument to score a few points for the French in their traditional rivalry with Germany, claiming that the popularity of nudism in Germany could be explained by the fact that they needed it most in order to counter their sexual obsession!

A self-consciously modern approach to these questions comes in a third discourse, that of early sexology. Sexology was a progressive medical discourse, whose most famous champion was Havelock Ellis. Ellis wrote the Introduction to Maurice Parmelee's (1929) influential book *Nudism in Modern Life*, and his work was used as the epigraph in another important text, John Langdon-Davies' (1928) *The Future of Nakedness*. Parmelee, himself a medical doctor, claimed that the concealment of the body "hampers the rearing of the young, gives rise to unhealthy mental complexes, and creates abnormal relations between the sexes" (Parmelee 1929: 5–6). In France, Dr Pierre Vachet wrote pro-nudist sexological manuals such as *Connaissance de la vie sexuelle* (1949). Most nudist writers considered sexual curiosity to be totally normal. Parmelee (1929: 12), for example, considered the desire to see the opposite sex as it really is to be a "normal and sane desire." Likewise, the Reverend Norwood was surprisingly liberal in this area; he considered the ban on sex instruction to be "dangerous" (Norwood 1933: 22), and he believed that the ban on seeing members of the opposite sex naked was perverse, dangerous and needlessly tormenting (p. 21). Curiosity is, he argued, a perfectly natural thing. Nudism was understood to have an educative function:

> As I became increasingly more conscious of the appalling ignorance about sexual matters which exists in the vast majority of the inhabitants of this country [i.e. England], and of the frightful frequency and degree both of sexual repression and of the accompanying sexual obsession which is the consequence of that repression, I began to realise that . . . nudist groups might be useful in teaching people about the anatomy of the opposite sex. (Welby 1934: 11–12)

The medical discourse could have a political edge. There was, in Germanic body culture especially, an explicitly feminist nudism that urged women to strengthen, discipline and beautify their bodies through naked exercise, and that fought for the right for nude gymnastics and sunbathing in public schools (Toepfer 1997: 39). In English nudism too, women's issues featured, often via the influence of sexology rather than dance or gym culture. Havelock Ellis for example, saw nudism as an extension of the dress reform in women's garments of the first decade of the twentieth century:

> It is women who are the natural pioneers in these matters, and always have been, as is indicated by the symbolical though prejudiced story of the Garden of Eden in the Book of Genesis. Women have, quite wholesomely, a larger dash of Narcissism in their temperaments, as Milton made clear in his picture of Eve in Paradise. Men, moreover, in these matters are extremely conservative, and only change their habits of clothing, however ugly and unhygienic, with extreme deliberation. (Ellis 1929: 3).

For Maurice Parmelee, nudism, like equality between the sexes, was *rational*:

> A very little consideration should indicate that gymnosophy [nudism] is a powerful aid to feminism, because it abolishes the artificial and unnecessary sex barrier and distinction of dress. The gymnosophy movement is indeed the logical continuation and consummation of the women's movement, for it at last brings woman into the man's world and man into the woman's world, so that they can see each other as

they really are. This is one of the most significant and valuable results from gymnosophy. (Parmelee 1929: 75)

Women had more to gain from gymnosophy than men did, he claimed (Parmelee 1929: 84). He specified that gymnosophy aids and supplements feminism by rendering visible natural differences, thus ending deception about bodies; by destroying the idea that sex – especially women's sex – is mysterious and inexplicable; by weakening sex solidarity and strengthening human solidarity;[31] and by encouraging comradeship between the sexes (pp. 75–7). All this, he argued, promotes intimacy and understanding between the sexes and makes men and women more alike (p. 79). Parmelee was really quite radical in all this. He saw modesty as having been *imposed* on women rather than being a natural female attribute;[32] he even argued that it was debatable whether one sex was more highly sexed than the other (p. 81). He was thoughtful enough to see the complexities and the material base of women's subordination, claiming that it remained to be seen whether women's increasing freedom would result in "economic, political and social equality between the sexes" (p. 80). Many decades were to pass before more radically pleasure-centred approaches to sex would come into being, but these early progressive debates lay the distant foundations for the fourth nudist discourse on sex, an actively pro-sexual discourse.

For many contemporary people, the idea of nudism is imaginatively linked not only with the mysterious space of the "nudist camp," but also with the hippy counter-culture – the joyful nakedness of Woodstock or the beaches of California. Nudity certainly was important to the counter-culture; Jack Douglas, for example, speaks of the 1970s nude beach as an important part of the "nude revolution" in the US, claiming that in this, as in many things, California set the pattern for other states to follow (Douglas and Rasmussen 1977: 29). For the hippies, nudity served as both a symbol of and a pathway to sexual and social liberation. However, the radical nudity of the hippies is really best understood as a moment when the nudist movement enjoyed a period of convergence with the 1960s counter-culture, rather than as central to the longer history of twentieth-century nudism, which has, by and large, been characterized more by caution and even puritanism in matters sexual than by a commitment to a radical idea of pleasure-centred sexual freedom, although there were currents in Germanic body culture in which eroticism was an unashamed component (Toepfer 1997: 42). A radical pro-sexual nudist discourse is still a rarity, believed in, perhaps, in private, surfacing occasionally in conversation, but rarely articulated in "official" nudist discourse.

Nudist discourse has, instead, tended to underemphasize pleasures of the flesh, unless it be the pleasures of sun, sea and air on skin. Critics (both nudist and non-nudist) of this coyness argue that perhaps the nudists protest too much. For one thing, there are occasions where popular accusations have some truth to them, or at least circulate as suspiciously persistent rumours. Clarke (1982) reports that many club nudists in the 1980s believed swinging to be a feature of some clubs. A former editor of the English magazine *Health and Efficiency* also reported that some English nudists were involved in the production of pornographic movies (Clarke 1982: 274). The overlaps between liberal sexual subcultures of various kinds and nudism are no doubt substantive, but how substantial they are is a question I cannot answer. (There is perhaps, but I am surmising here, a covert overlap between cultures of club nudism and those of swinging. Certainly, in terms of *visible* overlaps between sexual cultures, the most significant question for beach nudism is male homosexuality, a relationship that would need a chapter of its own.) By and large – and with the single and significant exception of male homosexuality and beach nudism – such overlaps are discreet and covert, and hence resistant to the researches of an ethnographer.

There are of course exceptions to the rule that nudists take care with sensual discourse. A 1968 essay in the US naturist journal *Modern Sunbathing Quarterly*, for example, argued that nudists have more sexual energy than non-nudists (Mayrand 1986). By and large though, nudists don't want to privilege sexual pleasures over all the other freedoms offered by nudism – the feel of water and sun on skin, or body on sand, air on body, an unbounded experience of space, and participation in the pleasures of the natural world. Touch and smell, many would argue, are as much a part of the pleasures of nudism as any pleasures of looking. On the other hand, there are also those who fear that *any* such discourse of bodily pleasure will reflect badly on a practice already widely understood as deviant – an understanding that can have very practical consequences, such as the banning of nude bathing in response to lobbying by nervous locals. Such hesitancy is palpable within nudist communities, especially when the tape recorder is running. The following exchange between a late-middle-aged couple who own a cabin in a nudist resort is carefully balanced, focusing on relationships rather than bodily pleasures:

Bill: I think it broadens the way you relate to people, because of the socialising you do. There's no TV and you're forced to – well, not forced to – come here and talk to people. And you talk to people each weekend.

Margaret: We actually talk to each other across a table when we're having a meal! We don't do that at home . . . The marriage didn't need any help, but it's certainly given it a bit of a boost! And after twenty-two years, that's a pretty nice thing to have!

Of course, I am not in a position to know what male respondents would say to a male interviewer. It may well be different. Magnus Clarke's interviews with club nudists, for example, revealed a disparity between the replies of men on women on this score, as these two examples illustrate:

> When you go to a nudist club, you have the children running around, it is a very family oriented thing, it is the titillation of various clothes that makes something sexually attractive. Mother nature usually knows when you should be aroused sexually and it is not at a nudist club. (Mary, quoted in Clarke 1982: 233, original punctuation)

> I think it is a source of sexual satisfaction to all people, I'll say yes, definitely, goodness me, why not! (Brian, quoted in Clarke 1982: 233)

Clarke found that when men and women were interviewed *together as couples*, men tended to say that nudism wasn't sexually exciting. This is a fascinating finding, but Clarke's corollary is over-simple: "It appears to follow that the sexual denial norm of social nudism has been a female creation" (p. 234). "Whatever the truth," he claims, "most denials of a sexual element in nudism come from female nudists and are views primarily advanced for consumption by women" (p. 234).

I am unsure whether this claim can be substantiated.[33] Plenty of men I have interviewed have seemed genuinely distressed at the "mis"reading of nudism as inherently sexual. John, for example, initially believed that private socializing in the home with other nudists would be a less intimidating introduction to nudism for his shy wife than the open spaces of a nudist resort or club. This idea backfired rather spectacularly when his advertisement in a naturist magazine produced only people interested in group sex:

> That kind of frightened me, because Jane is very . . . comes from a very sheltered background where any sort of nudism isn't condoned, is frowned upon, and I was too, but I probably broke away because I always had that interest. It was very confronting. You know, you'd ring up to talk to these people later and they're kind of having sex on the phone. "Do you want to join in?" It's kind of a bit weird – from people which [sic] you would say would be pillars of the community as well. Not sleazy people. No – far from it! So we kind of backed away for a while. (John)

Nudist literature contains a long-running debate as to whether exhibitionism is necessarily a part of nudism. Most nudists you talk to, however, are not very comfortable with such discussions. This doesn't stop as eminent a researcher in the field as Clarke from contending that nudism is fundamentally about visual pleasure. Assuming a rather simple link between voyeurism and sexual desire, he says that he has never met or heard of a single blind nudist: "Nudism is not a tactile experience in its essence; it is not about wind, sun, water or naked skin. It is a purely visual experience and the rewards are visual" (Clarke 1982: 246). He is unequivocal on this point: "Most nudists are . . . voyeurs" (p. 259).

Underneath all these discourses is a mostly implicit debate about where sex fits into a concept of "naturalness." We can expect that sexual liberalization will continue to produce new discursive avenues in which pro-sex attitudes can be more comfortably articulated. The popular link between nudity and sex is, however, hundreds of years old, as is the profound ambivalence around nature itself. Given this, awkwardness about the nudity/sex/nature cluster can be expected to persist.

Social Deviance

Maurice Parmelee (1929: 6) described nudism as a return to "the natural and normal life." But of course, it's not normal – in the sense that most of the society acts differently. Nude may be natural, as the slogan goes, but in a clothed society it's not "normal," a paradox that leads to confusion:

> *Interviewer:* Do you think of yourselves as nudists?
> *Dean:* No. Not really. Normal. Not normal as in nudist normal; not normal as in clothed normal. Just average people who you'd meet in the workplace or on the streets. We're not ra-ra-ra nudists or ra-ra-ra anything. We're just average, across the board people.

There are some nudists who speak of having instantly felt comfortable. Their body, they claim, instantly recognized that it had rejoined its natural condition. A retired woman, Margaret, described to me her first visit to a clothes-optional resort. Despite having been a beach nudist for a while, she was "very hesitant" as they drove down the long steep road to the resort. To her surprise, she instantly felt comfortable:

> Before we started unloading [the car], the gear was off. It just felt right to be like that. I felt so comfortable, straight away. There was no warm up, or peek out the windows to see what everybody else was doing. It was just the right thing to do.

By the end of the weekend, she had to be "dragged away kicking and screaming."

But for most nudists, learning to be "natural" is a slow and often confronting business, achieved incrementally. Almost all nudists recall particular markers: getting used to having a shower in the open, or getting in the spa, or playing tennis nude. For women especially, nudism involves getting over the sense that everyone is looking at you, as well as getting used to the idea of seeing naked men:

> *John:* It took me a long time to convince Jane to come up [to the club]. We stayed at the motel. I don't think we saw one nude person all day. It was a cold day.
>
> *Jane:* We saw one. And I freaked out at first! I thought, "Oh my God! Look at that!" I was really shocked. [laughs] "Oh no!"

John describes a female friend who is interested in joining them at their nudist camp, but who is afraid about how she might react to the sight of naked men:

> *John:* She said, "I'll laugh at seeing guys nude – all different shapes and sizes and their bellies and stuff like that." She said, "I'll embarrass you. I'll come up here and I'll laugh." She's worried about *her* size too. She's not big, but she's really self-conscious. And I said she didn't have to be nude. She seems to be interested in coming out, but . . .

Nor is the achievement of comfort and/or unselfconsciousness necessarily final. Having heard so many accounts of eventual comfort and ease with nakedness, I expected (naively) that such comfort would function like a kind of attainment. I was surprised to find that nudist women of long standing might feel uncomfortable in a different *kind* of nudist site. Many nudist women are comfortable on the beach but not indoors, another reason that nudist swim clubs have trouble with membership. (Margaret's tale of having felt uncomfortable on the beach but instantly comfortable at a resort is an unusual one.)

In sum, nudism has been constantly placed in the paradoxical position of having to argue for its own taken-for-grantedness. Nudists may understand their practice as simple, healthful and "natural," but as members of a wider community they are inevitably aware that this is not how public nudity is generally understood, and so they frequently find themselves condemned to secrecy, or to fending off accusations of social and sexual deviance. Little wonder, then, that historically and even today many nudists have been quite private and occasionally defensive about their practice.

As a postscript, it is worth noting that sometimes nudism's "naturalness" is secured by transferring the deviancy onto other groups. Most nudists have encountered Peeping Toms who hide behind the nudist beach armed with their binoculars and cameras. So too, people in yachts regularly come in close to the nudist beaches on Sydney's harbour, likewise provisioned. Some heterosexual beach nudists may also make veiled grumpy comments about the homosexual men whose sexual activity in the dunes helps fuel attempts by locals to ban nude beaches, though in general the liberal tolerance that runs deep through nudism tends to promote a live-and-let-live philosophy. In a process of pure comic inversion, though, it is in fact, the "textiles" who frequent "normal" beaches who are likely to be joked about as strange. This joke is always done in the mildest of fashions. Nudists are far too liberal – and far too relaxed – to waste their opprobrium.

Danger, Crime, Perversion

Very few sane people are comfortable in public with no clothes at all.

US newsreader Hugh Downs

In 1928, John Langdon-Davies summed up what he saw as the paradoxical place of nakedness in modern societies:

The Present of nakedness can be stated in a brief sentence: nakedness to-day is a crime in all civilised countries and a sin in all Christian congregations; it is an unnatural and vicious condition of the human body; it is the fruit of that forbidden tree the eating of which men have no intention of risking again. (Langdon-Davies 1928: 12)

Sin, vice, perversion, crime – this was what Christianity and modernity had made of "natural" nakedness. The medieval theologians' category of *nuditas criminalis* had, it seemed, triumphed over the other possibilities of nakedness. Langdon-Davies could easily have added "insanity" to his list, for inappropriate management of one's own nakedness can serve as a sign of mental illness, or psychological perversion. The biblical snippet "Clothed and in their right minds" is still occasionally heard today, as though the former state proves the latter. In modern secular understanding, the idea of sin has by and large become dispersed across psychological categories of illness, sociological categories of deviance, legal categories of criminality, and moral categories of right and wrong. Within these various discourses, certain forms of naked behaviour can be understood as signs of psychological disturbance, social rebellion, or criminal activity, and can be seen as in need of correction, control or punishment.

The taboo on adult public nudity arose out of a process of slow proscription that eventually came to have social, psychological, moral and legal force. The sight of a naked adult on the street is both unusual and shocking. Jack Douglas, indeed, considers it to be one of the biggest taboos of all:

What social rules are more important, more iron-clad and rigid? The rules against incest and murder are two, of course. But what else? Treason? I doubt it. I've known plenty of people who would shamelessly commit treason, if they knew anything worth giving to an enemy. Violence? I've seen a good bit of violence in our society. Theft? I've known lots of thieves. Though public nude displays occur in our society, they are quite rare. Before [visiting] the nude beach, I do not remember seeing anyone nude in a public situation. Until recently, intentional public nudity has been seen in our society as an act of madness, extreme immorality, and criminality. That is a severe combination. (Douglas and Rasmussen 1977: 9)

That "severe combination" does not, however, operate in the same way for men and women. Their public nudity is interpreted and treated quite differently.

Male Exposure, Power and Criminality

Male exposure is a paradoxical phenomenon. On the one hand, the West inherited from Classical Greece a tradition in which male nudity could signify virtue. The Classical Greek openness around male nudity is, historically, an exception, but its legacy of idealized male nudity was highly important to art, and hence some of the noble meanings of male nudity lived on. The male body was "studied . . . lovingly" and "taken as the norm and the ideal" in the two most formative periods of Western art (classical Greece and the Italian Renaissance) (Walters 1978: 7). Today, however, a naked male body on the real-life street is a shocking anomaly, cause for suspicion, alarm or merriment. Indeed, except in strictly circumscribed circumstances like art or theatre, such a body is, in fact, breaking the law.

Many cultures have made ritual or magic use of male nudity, often according particular mystery or reverence to the penis. Phallus worship is ancient and widespread. Benjamin Walker describes a number of ancient religious rituals that involved the kissing of the penis of a priest or chief. Reverence often entailed prohibition; Walker (1977: 194) says of ceremonial nudity, "it is generally held that men should in no circumstances show themselves nude, especially to the opposite sex, as this reduces the power of the male organ." Walker cites three reasons for the reverence and ceremonial importance traditionally accorded the penis: the penis is a source of intense pleasure, an organ of generation, and able to be understood as being endowed with a life of its own (p. 210). Margaret Walters considers that over the course of Western development, emphasis shifted away from the earliest symbols of fertility and generation, which were female, towards the phallus. In the Greek and Hellenistic worlds, the phallus and not the vulva was the most sacred fertility symbol:

It was the phallus, and not any image derived from the female body, which came to represent human fertility, and the creative and renewing powers of nature. At the same time, the phallus was associated with tools and weapons, the means by which man asserts his control over nature and other men. (Walters 1978: 9)

The phallus could thus symbolize both "nature" and "culture." Women, however, could make use of phallic imagery. The "chaste and pious matrons of antiquity" (Knight 1957: 50) wore bracelets adorned with erect penises as a sign of devotion to the god of procreation and generation. Richard Payne Knight, author of an eighteenth-century study of phallus worship, argued that, though it seems "monstrous and indecent" to the Christian worldview, priapic worship was neither "ludicrous [n]or licentious" (Knight 1957: 28), but solemn and secret.[34] In some cases, it was open only to the initiated, who had to purify themselves beforehand (p. 29). Knight describes priapic statues, amulets, bracelets and sacraments, the use of which has sometimes survived into modern times, either directly or in transmuted form. The magical powers of the phallus were often protective in function, as in the use of images of the god Priapus to warn off intruders (Dover 1978: 105). Its powers were also commonly believed to protect against the evil eye (Bonfante 1989: 544–5). For example, the Roman god of luck, Fascinus (from whose name we derive the word "fascinate"), was a personified phallus who warded off evil (Walters 1978: 9).

In Greece, male nudity gradually shifted from being a religious phenomenon to a civic one (Bonfante 1989: 556). This represented a transition away from the ritual or magic powers of nudity and the taboos that kept these powers in check towards civic (military, athletic) uses of nudity (p. 546). The shift towards civic nudity constituted "an unprecedented departure from a norm accepted in every other time and tribe" (pp. 546–7). Larissa Bonfante stresses that it was a *gradual* development – incipient in Homer and in Athenian Geometric art (approx. 900 BC), developing in sculpture by the seventh century BC, but not fully developed until Classical Greece, when nudity was redefined – "as heroic, divine, athletic, and youthful for men; and something to be avoided for women" (p. 549). It was part of everyday modern life, a marker of power, prosperity and democracy, in contrast with the luxurious dress of barbarian rulers (p. 557). By the time of Plato and Thucydides, athletic nudity was "the dress, one might almost say the uniform, of the citizen who exercised in order to maintain himself in readiness for military service" (p. 557). This male nude was a *civic* figure; statues represented public virtues and were often situated in public space. This is in contrast to the female nude which, even in its allegorical mode, usually carried private connotations (after all, Greek women were not citizens):

The male nude is typically public: he strides through city squares, guards public buildings, is worshipped in Church. He personifies communal pride or aspiration.

> The female nude, on the other hand, comes into her own only when art is geared to the tastes and erotic fantasies of private consumers. (Walters 1978: 8)

The male nude was also a figure for the glorious striving of humanity to touch the divine, "a symbol of order and harmony between human and divine," the embodiment of "man's supreme cultural values" (Walters 1978: 13).

The classical ideal did not focus specifically on the penis (indeed, a large penis was considered ugly). But some remnant forms of magical or ritual nudity using exaggerated phallic imagery continued to exist in Greece.[35] Moreover, even within the dominant civic strain of Greek male nudity, some of the magical and ceremonial meanings of male exposure persisted. While Greek statuary diminished the importance of the literal penis compared with magical phallic imagery (a *small* penis was the mark of a beautiful young man; Bonfante 1978: 552), it still glorified the authority of the phallic principle of paternal power. The whole body, rather than just the penis, stood in for the phallus. Thus, even though the male nude has nothing of the unashamedly literal virility of the priapic satyrs or the herms and phallic ornaments that survived even into the late Hellenistic world, it can still be considered a phallic figure par excellence, whose "physical integrity and . . . phallic potency are superstitiously protected" (Walters 1978: 55).

The phallic principle survived even in regimes overtly hostile to the body's sexual attributes. While Christian art underwent periods of prudery (e.g. thirty-eight loincloths were painted over the nudes in Michelangelo's Last Judgement fresco in the Sistine Chapel between the sixteenth and eighteenth centuries: Shulman 1994), it sometimes also compensated for the hidden penis by making use of phallic postures and props (Walters 1978: 9–10). Even today, reverence for the male nude derives in large part, according to Margaret Walters, from reverence of the phallus. Although contemporary cultures have almost entirely outlawed public male nudity, phallic power is still their central organizing principle and the power of the phallus depends precisely on the invisibility of the penis, which remains "private and protected territory" (Bordo 1993a: 698). As Susan Bordo (1993a: 699) points out, it is still possible for a little girl to "grow up in this culture with an acute sense of what phallic power and danger is all about without having any idea of what a penis looks like." In this resides the power of the phallus as a "symbolic construc[t]" (p. 696); it is a symbol that works only when it is veiled (Lacan 1982: 82). But Bordo claims that the symbol is both threatened and maintained by the "insufficiency" of its anatomical analogue: "the phallus is haunted by the penis" (Bordo 1993a: 697). Men live in the shadow of the all-powerful (though historically and culturally variable) ideal of masculinity. The penis – "perhaps the most visibly mutable of bodily parts" (p. 697) – cannot possibly live up to the aura of "the singular, constant, transcendent rule of the phallus" (p. 696). Lee Edelman (1996: 155) calls the man's penis "the part of his body least his own," presumably because it is the most visibly subject to unconscious desires, the least easily controllable by willpower, and also, perhaps, because it is that part of the male anatomy over which cultural imperatives have most say. Our culture deems that the penis must scarcely if ever be seen, especially in public, yet its symbolic counterpart, the phallus, is overwhelmingly evident.

What, then, of the flasher, he who chooses to expose his most private part in public? Given the importance of invisibility to phallic power, it could be expected that the exposure of the penis would almost inevitably represent a moment of vulnerability rather than of power. The risk for the flasher is that his penis might provoke not alarm but disappointment or comedy. After all, what actual penis can match the power of the phallus? Many women have stories about seeing a flasher and having responded with laughter. But the flasher does have surprise and taboo on his side, as well as the powerful heritage of magical meanings of the penis, and the widespread fear of male violence.

Flashing draws its power from the universal modern taboo on the penis in public space. It can also be seen as evidence of the persistence of the ancient attribution of secret or magical powers to the penis. It also draws on the prevailing cultural homology between the penis and a weapon and on women's fear of the actualization of this homology in rape. In the words of a police-woman we interviewed, flashing is frightening because the penis "poses a lot of sexual threat." Flashing's effect is psychological, its mechanism visual. It is a crime based on *showing* something to someone, without their permission. Its efficacy reminds us of the importance of vision in establishing a secure sense of self, in drawing the boundary between self and other (see Kirby 124–5). Vision is important to the flasher himself, since it is the sight of his victim's reaction that provokes his erotic pleasure. The exhibitionist "must be seen and must feel that he is seen" (MacDonald 1973: 7). Unlike rapists, who often wear masks, few exhibitionists try to disguise themselves (p. 50).

Flashing is an often silent assertion of male power, whose intent is to shock and distress, and sometimes to reassure the exposer of his own virility. Flashers always choose female victims.[36] According to a study by Gittleson et al., (1978: 62), the greatest proportion of victims are young women (21 years or under). MacDonald (1973: 50–2), by contrast, found that most victims were adult (over 16), though he too found that children, especially in groups, were frequent victims. A large proportion of the victims interviewed for Gittleson's et al.'s (1978) study were sexually immature at the time of their first incident, in that 40 per cent had not begun to menstruate, 31 per cent did not know "the facts of life," and 36 per cent had not heard of indecent exposure (p. 62). Gittleson et al. (1978: 61) note the "striking" clarity of recall of their female subjects, even though an average of almost fifteen years had elapsed between the time of the incident(s) and the interview. Despite their clear recall of the incident, the vast majority of those interviewed believed that flashing left few or no lasting effects on its victims, although their responses show that such incidents clearly did shock and frighten in the short-term. Women reported having felt a number of emotions at once, with fear being the most widely shared one, followed by, in descending order, disgust, curiosity, amusement, anger, pity and embarrassment (p. 63).

Indecent exposure (known in Australian law as "wilful and obscene exposure") is the most common form of sexual crime, accounting for between 30 and 50 per cent of sexual offences. It is, however, hard to ascertain the number of incidents of indecent exposure because many of them go unreported to either family or police. Of the hundred women interviewed in the study by Gittleson et al. (1978), 44 per cent had experienced indecent exposure on at least one occasion, and multiple occurrences were common. A psychologist with whom we spoke ("Richard") believed it is not only the most common offence but also the most recalcitrant, a claim backed up by statistics indicating that flashing has the highest rate of recidivism (Slovenko 1965: 75). "The flasher" is understood to have a particular psychological profile, fitting one of two very distinct types. This is the psychologist Richard's description of the first category:

> There are those that we regard as impulsive regressive so that they, under stress and tension . . . They're usually inadequate sort of people who regress back to that almost childlike exposure of their penis as a sort of a flouting convention and they get some vicarious pleasure out of this. Usually they will do it when their anxiety rises and they feel inadequate or fairly impotent or their esteem is very low and they will have this drive to go out – and it's a real impulse. Then they go out and expose themselves. It's usually planned. They will plan to do this and where they will go. Usually to younger females. The idea is to create shock, to demonstrate how powerful they are.

Such people often choose public places. They do not always have an erection. For this group, exposure is an addiction, a "real driving impulse" that is compulsive in nature:

> *Richard:* They will just expose themselves in all sorts of places – buses, bus stops, trains, public transport, or they will be on beaches, but they certainly know that they're doing it and they're certainly looking for a response. The exposure without the response is really not terribly gratifying.

Interviewer: Are they wanting fear or just shock?
Richard: They tend to have a bit of the fantasy that people are amazed
at their proportions. It's the full fantasy thing.

MacDonald's (1973) research supports this. He says that flashers sometimes accompany the exposure with remarks – often questions – about the size of their penis ("I have the biggest peter you ever saw," "Have you ever seen one so big?" and so on). Not all flashers, however, are proud of their penis. Spitz quotes one offender who justified his choice of child victims on the grounds of the smallness of his penis (quoted in MacDonald 1973: 50). The flasher often welcomes not only the woman's shock, but also the punishment of the law, both of which reassure him that he has something to show (Slovenko 1965: 75). Given the prevalence of "the full fantasy thing," Richard suggests, partly in jest, that "perhaps we [should] train women to say, 'That is pathetic!'" In the light of this, the immediate responses of the women interviewed by Gittleson et al. (1978) are interesting. The biggest response was to run away (52 per cent), with many women also reporting feeling "stunned." About 10 per cent verbally rebuked the man; 7 per cent screamed; the same number "did nothing." Only one woman laughed. The talent for symbolism of one quick-thinking woman must not go uncelebrated. In an act of truly Freudian magnificence, she stubbed out her cigarette on the exposed penis.

The second group of exposers is quite different from the first. Their exposure is part of a bigger picture of crime, including not only violent acts such as assaults, but also other crimes, such as robberies. Their other sexual crimes will involve physical contact, as opposed to the non-contact sexual crimes (such as frotterism) of the former group. The first group will never carry through with any form of sexual assault (in fact, Richard claimed that if their victim displayed any interest they "would run a mile"). For the second group, though, exposure *is* associated with further sexual crime. Unfortunately, there is no way of telling whether a given person is of one type or the other until he has, in fact, gone on to commit an attack.[37]

It is the specific focus on the penis that helps give flashing some of its power to shock or distress. By contrast, the exposure of the *entire* male body in public is much more prone to have comic effects. Although streaking is technically a minor offence under the same section of the Summary Offences Act that governs flashing (in Australia), it functions differently culturally. Nowadays, it is quite likely to be considered a joke, or at least a form of insolence rather than mastery. Streaking is a very public act, mostly performed in front of crowds. It is usually carried out by young men, sometimes in groups. It involves the exposure of the entire body and not just the penis, and that body is, literally, on the run. The streaker usually aims to shock, surprise or entertain (and occasionally to self-publicize for commercial reasons). Many streakers are intoxicated, or accepting a dare. Nowadays, sociologists, police, psychologists and a fair proportion of the public are likely to consider streaking and other practices such as mooning as neither particularly perverse nor dangerous and only marginally criminal. Instead, these acts are mostly understood as a joke, a fad or perhaps a nuisance. Streaking at large events has to some extent been curtailed by large fines at major sporting venues and by the agreement of television crews to turn their cameras away from the streaker.

It is usually accepted that streaking and mooning are not sexual behaviours, although some have seen them as a "spring ritual" or a "spontaneous out-pouring of youthful sexual energy" (Toolan 1974: 157). Miller (1974: 158) views such practices as an adolescent struggle for authority. This struggle has been taken with different degrees of gravity. In the 1970s, a medical doctor, while conceding that streaking was not "in itself a sex act," condemned it unequivocally as an unwanted form of social deviance:

> Streaking is a recent dramatic example of the thumb-to-nose hurray-for-me-and-to-hell-with-everybody-else syndrome in modern society. It is the latest attempt to erode and destroy convention, decency, and decorum and is primarily an act of teenage and young adult defiance rather than an isolated, innocuous student prank. Its precursors are long unkempt hair, dirty jeans, dirty feet, hippyism, "ups," "downs," LSD, heroin, and so-called total female liberation. (Elkins 1974: 157)

Though Elkins would not agree, streaking is for many people, both observers and participants, good fun. To the extent that we define streaking as something performed for an audience (as opposed, say, to running naked along a remote beach), then its pleasures actively rely on the prevailing taboo on public naked-ness. The strength and universality of this taboo mean that any rupture is likely to be both physically and psychologically exhilarating. In the case of streaking, there are also new bodily sensations to enjoy – the whistle of wind on skin, the flapping of body parts – as well as the approbation of spectators, who may take vicarious as well as visual pleasure from the new social space that briefly opens up.

Unlike flashing, male streaking often occurs in front of other males. This suggests another, more serious, context in which streaking and/or other ritualized forms of male group nudity occur. Naked rituals are an important part of all-male institutions such as university colleges, sporting teams, board-ing schools and military barracks – especially at the time when new recruits are taken in. In these contexts, ritualized nudity plays an important role in establishing the patterns of both bonding and hierarchy that constitute what Eve Kosofsky Sedgwick (1985) calls male homosocial relations. By this, she means the full (and troubled) spectrum of male–male relations. Her analysis of the gender order, which usefully focuses attention on the centrality of relations between men, starts from a definition of patriarchy suggested by Heidi Hartmann:

> relations between men, which have a material base, and which, though hierarchical, establish or create interdependence and solidarity among men that enable them to dominate women. (quoted in Sedgwick 1985: 3)

This definition and Sedgwick's subsequent discussion make it clear that a patriarchy relies on the division of men from each other via the organization of hierarchies, and via the denigration of non-dominant versions of masculinity. The often pleasurable experiences of male bonding may thus be bought at the price of the exclusion of certain men, or certain forms of masculinity. And they are often directly or indirectly oppressive to women.

Homosocial rituals can range from the brutal (as in bastardization practices) to the joyful. What they have in common, though, is that they create community by defining and testing masculinity itself. One long-time member of a university rugby club ("Patrick") described the features shared by a number of sporting rituals: they were held at night, they were mostly competitive, women were strictly excluded, alcohol was always involved, and they were vividly remembered, mostly fondly, by members for decades afterwards, the champions attaining a kind of legendary status. Naked races held at night in public streets, obstacle courses to be negotiated while holding a penny clenched between the buttock cheeks, and races run in public streets with flaming newspapers held between the buttocks – such events are joyous expressions of sexual freedom that serve also to bond the team and to define and test approved forms of masculinity. The sexuality both expressed and repressed (or displaced) in such events is complex, simultaneously a ritualized expression of homoerotic feeling and a tacit repudiation of homosexuality. Occasionally, the sexual content was unusually prominent, as in an initiation ritual (the "Elephant Walk") practised at one prestigious university in which the new college residents walked around the main quadrangle holding the penis of the man in front of him. Patrick likewise described a rugby club competition in which naked men were tickled on the testicles by other men and eliminated one by one by judges standing behind them monitoring their buttocks for signs of quivering.

Within the logic of homosociality, certain forms of nudity can be temporarily normalized in order that other sexual behaviours be more radically excluded. To walk through a university quadrangle holding the penis of the man in front can, under the liminal conditions pertaining to ritual, be temporarily deemed "normal;" taking any homoerotic interest in the procedure can not. The ritual can in fact be understood as a form of tacit challenge to the new recruits to prove, in the most visible fashion, their heterosexuality. The naked body, after all, supposedly has no secrets to hide.

Such events were common in all-male sporting and college clubs in Australia in the 1960s and 1970s – a time when the sexual liberation movement was encouraging freedoms that sat at odds with dominant mores and with the previous educational backgrounds of most of the young students, and when there was less public awareness and visibility of homosexuality than today. Many college residents and rugby club members came from the country; many had been educated in repressive Catholic boarding schools and had had little contact with women. Such events still exist, but in the case of the rugby club in question, they have been transformed into much "safer" expressions of heterosexual masculinity, as in the hiring of female strippers. Perhaps the greater public awareness of homosexuality has rendered the more homoerotic forms of male bonding too "dangerous" and a third term – the woman – is needed to mediate the relations between men.[38]

Not all sporting nudity is of this ritual kind, and the male nudity displayed at the rugby club was capable of subtle differences in meaning. Patrick contrasts, for example, the clearly competitive naked strutting of dominant players in the changing-rooms pre-match (while others around them modestly got changed) with the joyous, egalitarian and, in Patrick's words, "magic" communal nakedness in the showers *after* the game. Everyone participated in the latter, since prowess had already been demonstrated on the field, and the changing-room was now a site in which bonding could displace hierarchy. Clearly, as Sedgwick's model of homosociality makes clear, male–male relations (and hence male nudity) needs to be understood as complex, especially where sexuality is concerned.[39]

To sum up, nudity has always played an important role in ritual, ceremonial or magic contexts, and the penis in particular has often been the privileged and protected centre of these ceremonial meanings. Classical Greece was exceptional in its normalization and idealization of male nudity in both art and everyday life. The lofty meanings of male nudity have suffered a gradual erosion, but they have persisted in art longer than in everyday life. The ideal nude body was revived as an artistic symbol during the Renaissance, a time when, ironically, naked bodies were beginning to disappear from the streets. From this modern exclusion springs the possibility of the rebellious and often joyous activity of male streaking, which can function as an expression of exuberance and exultation, reminding us of the uncontainability of the energetic body. It may also, however, remind us of a subtle form of gender violence, the intra-male violence that is at the heart of a patriarchy and that helps secure the hierarchical relations between men that arguably enable the oppression of women.

Flashing represents an obvious, if complex, form of this gender inequity, in that it is so clearly a form of symbolic violence against women, occasionally associated with actual physical violence. It draws on the more sinister meanings of male nudity, in particular, the symbolic and sometimes literal association between the penis and danger. The flasher assumes and tries to reaffirm the symbolic dominance of the phallus as well as the equation of the penis with a weapon. Flashing makes visible the interweaving of sex and power. It shows up the difference between Lacan's (1982) theoretical proposition that the penis is not the same thing as the phallus and the realistic feminist rejoinder that there are many circumstances where, as Kathleen Kirby (1996: 123) puts it, "it might as well be." In the moments where flashing *fails*, however – when women are indifferent, or laugh derisively, or make inventive use of their cigarette – we are reminded of the gap between the potent abstract principle of the phallus and the potentially vulnerable actuality of the penis. Here I agree with Susan Bordo's (1993a: 697) claim, at once compassionate and astute, that we can learn more from reading the male body "through the window of its vulnerabilities rather than the dense armor of its power – from the 'point of view' of the mutable, plural penis rather than the majestic, unitary phallus." That the flasher needs to be *seen* suggests the possibility that his own identity is not secure, as do the guilt and shame he inevitably feels afterwards. The psychological profile of the two types of flashers is interesting in this regard. The violent type reaffirms the traditional association between the penis, violence and fear. The other type, despite his own intentions, unwittingly affirms not his own phallic mastery but, in fact, the gap between the phallus and the penis, and the pressures that the phallic ideal puts on men as well as women. One does not need to be Freud to read the bravado about penis size as a sign of anxiety. The flasher "suppresses great unconscious fears" (Slovenko 1965: 75). This second, anxious, flasher unconsciously knows all too well the harshness of the phallic ideal, for he experiences it in his own sense of powerlessness. Unfortunately, he tries to compensate using the same old tool.

Female Exposure, Power and Danger

In ancient times, female nudity had magic power, like the phallus, and there exists a long history of wild, powerful, sinister or sacred meanings of female nakedness. The process of modernization involved the curbing and limiting of some of the archaic meanings of female nakedness and the domestication of many of its wilder meanings. Nonetheless, the conjunction of danger, evil, sex and magic, as well as the tension between asceticism and eroticism, means that even today, when the female body so often signals an ornamental eroticism, there is still a richness of potential other meanings. Four currents of historical meanings are relevant: first, the archaic powerful associations of female nudity with fertility and power (i.e. a "positive" tradition); second, sinister meanings of female nakedness or sexuality (i.e. a "negative" tradition); third, an ascetic religious tradition, in which female nakedness can strive to attain the exalted meanings of masculine spirituality (i.e. a tradition in which women strove to neutralize the "limitations" of femininity); and fourth, the ornamental meanings of female nakedness (in which female sexuality takes on a largely passive tenor, functioning as the object of the gaze). These currents are not historically or culturally distinct; the point is, of course, that the naked female body may mean many things simultaneously.

The earliest images of the human body were not male but female, the fertility icons of Palaeolithic art (Walters 1978: 8). Cave art seems to have focused attention on the vulva as a sacred symbol rather than on the phallus. Later, the divine nudity of goddesses like Ishtar, Aphrodite and Venus symbolized "fertility, fecundity, and power" (Bonfante 1989: 545). Female nudity has had a range of auspicious meanings, especially in rituals for rain-making, crop success and human fertility (Sharma 1987: 8–9), and has had apotropaic (protective) and magic functions:

> Female exposure . . . has a special significance. The sight of female breasts is believed to be a wonderful charm, and the female sexual organs have immense talismanic virtue, are charged with occult power, and promise the blessings of bountiful fertility and good luck. Female figures with vulva exposed were widely used as amulets in ancient times in Egypt, Greece, Rome, Christian Europe and various other parts of the world. It was believed that bad weather could be mitigated, storm [*sic*] quelled, lightning averted, rain brought down and fertility to the land ensured, by women baring their private organs to the sky and fields, or to the sea. (Walker 1977: 194)

The ancient story of Baubo, who cheered up the grieving goddess Demeter by shaving off her own pubic hair and exposing her genitals to her, is another frequently cited myth about the therapeutic properties of female exposure.

The power of female nudity has sometimes been expressed negatively. The myth of the naked-breasted Amazons, for example, can be interpreted as testifying to a male fear about women "out of place" – independent, aggressive and sexually dominant. The myth arose, interestingly, at a time when fertility goddesses were being replaced by phallic gods (Yalom 1997: 24). Witches too were associated with nudity (Sharma 1987: 7–8). Sinister meanings for female genitals have also endured. The image of the *vagina dentata* ("toothed vagina"), for example, figures in many mythological systems "and is one of the characteristic fantasies of misogyny" (Walker 1977: 305). In this wide-spread image, the vagina is a destructive orifice and a devirilizing element in the feminine structure, and sexual intercourse results in a kind of castration. Woman then becomes the devouring female, the vulva incarnate. (Walker 1977: 305)

Centuries later, Freud would draw on this misogynist heritage and universalize it: "Probably no male human being is spared the fright of castration at the sight of a female genital" (Freud 1966: 154).

Perhaps the most common ancient form of female ritual exposure involved the breasts. Marilyn Yalom (1997: 32) argues that breasts were one of the "dominant features of the sacred" in the ancient world. Images of suckling, for example, survive in Etruscan and Italian art as descendants of fertility symbols. And yet, in Classical Greek art, such images are remarkably absent, entering only in the Hellenistic period. Bonfante (1989: 568) interprets this taboo as an indication of the power of female nudity; any kind of female exposure was, she claims, "felt to be too private, special, shameful and danger-ous, all at the same time." In this sense, she sees the bared maternal breast as sharing many of the apotropaic powers of the phallus and the Gorgon (pp. 568–9). Other forms of naked breast did, however, appear in classical art. Beth Cohen (1997: 68–72) identifies four categories of breast exposure in classical art: women wearing garments designed to expose the breast, women purpose-fully exposing their own breast, accidental breast exposure due to an action or pose of the wearer, and breasts exposed through violent struggle. Cohen's examples make it clear that divestment had different meanings according to context. It could be a sign of victory in war or athletics, of physical activity, such as dancing, or of sexual or military defeat.

The breast was gradually eroticized and/or domesticated, with the result that it often became a sign either of male desire or of sanctioned femininity, losing its potentially wilder meanings as a sign of female power. Some of the sacred meanings of breast exposure continued in an arguably more docile form into the Christian tradition, via the figure of the Virgin Mary.[40] Although medieval Christian art either flattened women's breasts or associated them with something negative (e.g. hell or the devil), breast milk was nonetheless an important symbol in the Middle Ages (Yalom 1997: 32). The sudden and start-ling emergence of images of the suckling Virgin (the *Maria lactans*) in the early fourteenth century testified to the ongoing importance of the sacred breast. In the subsequent European fine art tradition, the single exposed breast (more than the double breast) continued to carry exalted or sacred overtones (Hollander 1993: 202).

Much of the history of female nakedness in the West is, however, a story of *restriction* – the curbing of its powers and the limiting of its meanings to erotic or domestic ones. Even in Classical Greece, "female nudity, even when erotic, carries with it [a] sense of weakness and vulnerability" (Bonfante 1989: 560). In Greek art, naked women are defenceless (p. 561). Margaret Walters (1978: 39) sees the Greek goddesses as a dilution of the power of the archaic mother goddesses, yet even they are separated by an "impassable gulf" from the lives and conditions of actual Greek women. There is, she claims, no female equivalent to the glorious nudity of either Apollo or Christ (p. 13). The only naked Greek goddess is Aphrodite, and she rarely appears naked before the fourth century BC. According to Walters, she becomes unveiled only once her "earlier, more disturbing associations with fertility and childbirth had been suppressed or transferred to other figures; when she had been reduced to an object of sexual desire" (pp. 39–40). Yalom likewise sees the later Aphrodite as "something akin to a pin-up figure, an object of male desire as well as awesome worship." Greek goddesses have less complexity and richness of meaning than male gods; unlike the gods, each represented only one quality (Walters 1978: 39). Their power was both fragmented and limited (Yalom 1997: 17). The goddesses could inspire only a less complex religious awe than the gods, an awe "always on the point of dwindling into a connoisseur's pleasure in a beautiful object, into voyeurism, or into simple lust" (Walters 1978: 40). The female nude cannot stand in for the universal or the timeless, and female bodily ideals have been more subject to fashion and change than male ones (p. 13). The female nude signified in the private rather than the civic domain. By the time of the Renaissance, the female nude had been reduced solely to sexual meanings, which themselves become linked less to active sexual agency than to passive ornamentation.

Of course, as with the phallus, older, earthier, meanings continued to exist in certain contexts. The apotropaic meanings of female genital exposure occur, for example, in Rabelais' *Gargantua* (*c.* 1535), in an incident where the resourceful Panurge suggests fortifying Paris with a wall built of vulvas, arranged according to size, and interlaced with stiff penises procured from the codpieces of the clergy. In this carnivalesque world, both female and male genitals are still associated with protection against evil:

> What devil could possibly overthrow these walls; what metal on earth could stand up as well against punishment . . . God help anyone who touches them, by all the devils! What is more, no lightning could strike them. Why? Because they are consecrated. (Bk 2, ch. 15: 221)

Rabelais' bawdiness is evidence that a celebration of the fertile female grotesque was not completely expunged from medieval Christianity (Rabelais was for a time a Franciscan monk). Moreover, even at the opposite end of the scale from Rabelais' earthiness, there remained in medieval Christianity other possibilities for a religious expression of nudity – in the form of an active, ascetic, spiritual nakedness (Miles 1989: 81). But within the mainstream of the Christian tradition, female nudity by and large lost its magic or ritual powers. Its secular meanings became largely negative, as the female body became increasingly a spectacle. So too did the religious meanings mostly become negative, with female nakedness functioning as a symbol of "sin, sexual lust, and dangerous evil" (p. 81). Only in that negative sense did female nakedness retain some of its dangerous power within Christianity – in its theological and iconological association with disobedience and sin, especially the sin of lust (Warner 1985: 295). Woman was dangerous to herself and to others; her nakedness could put her own soul in danger, as well as that of the hapless men ensnared by it.

An extended example is found in the 1678 text by Jacques Boileau, *A Just and Seasonable Reprehension of Breasts and Naked Shoulders Written by a Grave and Learned Papist*. The *Reprehension* is an extract, published separately, from Boileau's earlier and even longer (110 pages) work, *De l'abus des nudités de gorge* (1675) (*On the Abuse of the Naked Bosom*). The chief argument of both these texts is that "nakedness of the bosom and the shoulders is culpable and harmful" (Boileau 1675: 1). Boileau's wrath is reserved specifically for the breast because of the current fashion of décolletage. He saw in this fashion a re-enactment of Eve's primordial sin: "by the nudity of their bodies [women] become reflections of guilty Eve" (p. 37). A naked bosom corrupts both women and men:

> For it is with Reason that the Prophet Ezechiel hath told us that a naked and discovered Breast was a Bed whereon Impurity repos'd and became fruitful in corrupting her who laid it open, and him that beheld it. (Boileau 1678: 24)

Worse still, both women and men were *aware* of the dangers: "MEN do very well know how dangerous it is to look upon a naked bosome; and your vain and light Women are sensible how advantagious [*sic*] it is to them to shew it" (p. 83). Women, then, were consciously using their nakedness as a weapon. Boileau is mystified as to why it is that women, knowing, just as Eve did, that they sin, do not follow Eve in making amends:

> Why then will [women] judge otherwise of themselves than of their common Mother? and why will they not infer that from their own nakedness which they conclude from hers? that it is a mark of the deprivation of their Souls: Why do they not conclude that they displease God since they see themselves naked? (Boileau 1678: 24–5)

The idea of the dangerously seductive potential of the (naked) female body persists even in modern times, though the discourse of sin is no longer widely used. A nudist of the 1930s describes how she was accused of indecent exposure by her elderly female neighbour when she walked naked around her house in suburban New York during the heat wave of 1929 (Gay 1933: 22–3). Nudist literature still abounds with such tales. The most infamous persistence of the idea of seductive femininity is in rape judgements, where women may all too often be assumed to be partly responsible for the attack perpetrated upon them. Even contemporary sexual harassment legislation has made it possible for female nakedness to be construed as "dangerous." This has especially been the case in the US, where sexual harassment legislation has been used on numerous occasions to ban the display of artworks. For example, in 1993 artist Carmen Trujillo was invited to exhibit some of her paintings at the Central Intelligence Agency (CIA) headquarters. Among them were a number of works depicting female nudity, mostly in abstract form. Following complaints, Trujillo was forced to take the installation down. A CIA spokesperson explained that the CIA's annual family day was coming up and they did not want small children to be exposed to artworks containing nudity. According to Trujillo, "One female [CIA] employee escorting her through the building . . . sternly told her that even an abstract representation of women's breasts constitutes sexual harassment and could lead to rape" (Cash 1994). This despite the fact that the paintings contained no depictions of sexual acts or genitalia, "merely abstractions of the women's forms." This formulation neatly positions the female body as at the same time dangerous and vulnerable.

This contemporary example shows how the idea of the moral and psychological danger of nudity can have legal force. On the whole, though, female nudity in public space, while it may be deemed offensive, is unlikely to be understood or experienced as *dangerous* or *criminal* by the vast majority of the modern public. The significant exception to this is nudity in the sex industry, where moral and criminal categories blur and overlap. In most other cases, though, the proliferation of images of naked women has rendered female criminal exposure something of a logical impossibility. Kathleen Kirby (1996: 131) considers female flashing, for example, to be invisible in law. Of course, there is no reason, in law, why female exposure should not constitute wilful and obscene exposure. Indeed, exposure of the breast (in the form of both toplessness and breastfeeding) is currently proving a fascinating legal test case in many countries (see Barcan 2002a, Bartlett 2002), and one that proves that certain forms of female exposure can still be both offensive and criminal just as male nudity can. In practice, however, instances of criminal female exposure are less likely to occur than male exposure, less likely to be reported, and less likely to be taken seriously. They are also, it seems, potentially treated more casually or even pruriently by police themselves:

Policewoman: I think that generally people become very complacent looking at breasts. Men especially – they probably enjoy it more than looking at another man's penis. A lady doing her thing, she can do that if she wants to . . . I don't think I've ever heard on the [police] radio of a job where people go, "A woman's exposing her breasts!" . . . I have to say, when I was in Sydney, there have been two or three maybe where there have been a couple of females. It's usually been in the middle of the night. There have been ladies walking around with no clothes on and there's a very big response by police. And that's because they're men. And that's the only reason – because they're males. You'll normally get two or three cars going to do it.

Interviewer: To have a look?

Policewoman: Yeah, that's exactly it.

This story encapsulates some of the paradoxes surrounding public female nudity in consumer culture. Exposure of the female body is often tolerated, or indeed actively encouraged. Female nudes adorn billboards, canvasses and screens. Female exposure is, as the psychologist Richard pointed out, less likely than male exposure to be punished, and more likely to be rewarded, including financially. The naked female body is "common cultural property" (Bordo 1993a: 698) and female exposure is more readily justifiable within aesthetic discourses that see female nudity as more "beautiful" (and hence more acceptable) than male nudity. Female nudity is paradoxically both more "natural" and more "artistic" than male nudity. Female display is, likewise, able to be considered both more "normal" and more "pathological" than male display. Even contemporary psychoanalysis can sometimes read the cultural fact of widespread female exposure as a psychological one – having no penis, the young girl is forced to displace the infantile desire to expose her genitals onto a desire to expose all her body *except* her genitals (Rhoads and Boekelheide 1984–5: 1).

Clearly, this public approval of female nudity is a mixed blessing. For one thing, the meanings and potential of female nudity are highly circumscribed. The almost total incorporation of female nudity within the erotic means that female nakedness is not all that available as a weapon of resistance, subversion and scarcely at all as one of aggression. While a naked female protestor does have a powerful repertoire of historical meanings of female nudity on which to draw, she may also have to struggle to keep unwanted meanings at bay. A young woman baring her breast or genitals at a man in an act of defiance is more likely to be leered at than feared, though perhaps she might have more luck with her buttocks.[41] An older women, on the other hand, is likely to be considered mad, as in this story from Richard:

> Richard: I actually saw a lady years ago, an elderly lady. She was scheduled [i.e. hospitalized], and then there was a question mark about whether she was cognitively intact sufficiently to write a will and I had to go down and test her. The way in which she'd come under notice was she'd exposed her breasts in a hospital. And when she explained it all to me, she said the young intern that was there kept calling her "dear" and "love," almost like she was a little girl. And she'd actually said, "Look, I'm a woman and . . ."
>
> Interviewer: So that was a rebellious thing!
>
> Richard: It was a protest, yeah, and she was a very, very clever lady. But that's a rare . . .
>
> Interviewer: You don't expect an older woman to do that. If it had been a young person . . .
>
> Richard: She was a real protester, this lady. And very intact and a joy to talk to.

This woman's reappropriation of her own breasts as symbol of her mature womanhood (as opposed to the flat chest of a little girl) was a powerful symbolic action, but one that was misunderstood. The misreading of the woman's action is testimony to the ease with which public nudity can be interpreted as a sign of insanity, especially if the body being exposed is not youthful. An aged *woman*, in particular, may also be a cipher for the sexist and ageist fantasms of our heritage – figures like witches, hags and crones, who were often associated with nudity. The nudity of elderly people is rarely prized or publicized.[42] There have been some (isolated) efforts to address this over recent years. Plays like Nell Dunn's *Steaming* (1981), which features six naked mature women in a bath-house, or public exhibitions of photographs of naked elderly women are attempts to bring the nakedness of elderly women into visibility. During the writing of this book, I have heard of a number of fundraising calendars featuring elderly women with names like Beryl and Dot "tastefully" naked in domestic settings. These calendars are invariably popular. One produced by the Rylstone Women's Institute in the north of England was celebrated in Nigel Cole's film *Calendar Girls* (2003).

In psychology too, the normalization of youthful female nakedness can result in a kind of invisibility of female nakedness, as it does in criminology. We asked Richard about the debate on female flashing within the psychological literature, and his reply says much about the precariousness of the category itself:

> *Interviewer:* And in those textbook cases, when a woman flashes – I assume it's baring breasts or is it also the genitals?
>
> *Richard:* I've only ever read of one in – whose book is it? I forget now – that's actually exposing their genitals. But these days it would be terribly difficult to discern who was exposing their breasts for pathological reasons as against acceptable behaviour.

We might briefly recall the study cited in Chapter 1 that aimed to find a correlation between psychological openness and bodily display. As a "clarification," the authors wrote:

> We would like to clarify that the phrases "display their bodies" and "fond of their nudity" do not refer to the behavior of the so-called sexually deviant exhibitionists, but rather the normal tendency of many people to enjoy nudity or at least showing their legs in miniskirts or their breast form in tightly fitted sweaters. (Ehrentheil et al. 1973: 363)

We noted in Chapter 1 that this general discussion of "people" and "bodies" slips, without the authors seeming to notice it, into the description of an everyday exhibitionism that is, by implication, *feminine*. (I am assuming that the authors do not intend us to understand that enjoying showing one's legs in a miniskirt is a "normal tendency" in men!) This slippage is made possible by the assumed normalcy of female display.

The same predicament surfaces in psychiatric literature, in the form of a debate as to whether female exhibitionism is even possible in the first place, then as to whether it is perverse. (For a summary of this debate see Rhoads and Boekelheide (1984–5: 2), who argue, among other things, that female participation in pornography, despite being to some extent socially sanctioned, is a psychopathology, since it is carried out in the knowledge that it violates cultural norms). The tendency to individualize and pathologize non-mainstream responses to the double-bind placed on women with regard to bodily display is evident also in sociology, in the form of a literature studying strippers, parade dancers, porn models and others to see if they are more exhibitionistic than the general population. In a sense this represents an unacknowledged test of our whole culture's asymmetry regarding naked display. What constitutes "normal," proper or decent display in a world that insists on female "morality" and yet runs on the commodification of female display? In a culture in which the nakedness of women is not only permitted, but encouraged and systematically commodified, the idea that there might be circumstances in which female exhibitionism is "perverse" is uncertain. In a culture in which the display of female nakedness is encouraged in representation and erotic performance, but in which other forms of public nakedness are outlawed, female erotic display is both "normal" and "abnormal."

The contradictions described above really all arise from the strange potential of nakedness to be both normal and abnormal. A clothed society will always breed this contradiction. In this chapter, the contradiction has surfaced in difference guises. In fine art, we encountered it in the belief that the naked body is the most perfect subject for art but yet that nakedness needs to be aesthetically treated in order to be beautiful. This paradox resurfaces today when people want their bodies "cleaned up" and will pay money to be made to look "natural." In colonial thought it underlay the belief that indigenous nakedness needed to be covered up and yet also represented the innocent origins of humankind. Our third instance was the paradox that makes nudism a strange social practice even though it is based on an idea of benign nature. Finally, we have seen examples of the potential for nakedness to work as a weapon or as a sign of criminality or of mental disturbance. In the final chapter, we will look specifically at *images*, and at the slippery meanings that images of nakedness can have in a modern consumer culture.

Notes

1. Psychoanalysis has tended to see head hair as a symbol of the genitals, a reading not always supported within anthropology. For a sample anthropological discussion of the sexual and other significance of hair, see Derrett (1973), Hershman (1974) and Leach (1958).

2. Representation is not always an accurate guide to actual bodily practice with regard to pubic hair, though it is to eyebrows and head hair (Cooper 1971: 118).

3. Note that for a large part of the twentieth century "too much" hair on the head could feminize men, as with the hippies. Before this, the flowing locks of Romantic poets or of dandies could do the same.

4. See, for example, Bordo (1993b), Elias (1994), Featherstone (1991), Giblett (1996) and Willis (1991).

5. Presumably this ideal will be modified in a world of global networking.

6. Although Bakhtin (1984) doesn't address the issue of gender conceptually, it is notable that the "universal" body of carnival that he idealizes has all the properties normally associated with the female body. The body idealized by Bakhtin is "the body of generation, and the swellings that indicate this are its breasts and pregnant belly; it is the metaphoric equivalent of mother earth, to which the degradation of grotesque realism returns" (Dentith 1995: 83). Bakhtin is unusual among theorists in taking a feminized body as a model for "the" body, especially for a highly valued body.

7. This is certainly true in Australia, but not in all European countries. In Germany, for example, few women depilate the bikini line.

8. What a strange sentence this is! I have never been able to decide whether or not there is any irony in the words "as they should be," although I assume that "artless" must be a deliberate pun.

9. The Ancient Greeks did this in reverse, seeing their custom of athletic nudity as a marker of their own civilization – one that distinguished them from their own ancestors and from the "barbarians."

10. The scientist T.H. Huxley, for example, was a follower of Darwin who systematically used a version of John Lamprey's system to investigate racial types. See Cooper (1995: 60ff.) and Ewing (1994: 12–21).

11. Ashcroft et al. (1998: 209) date the concept to the end of the sixteenth century. Anthony Pagden (1993) claims that "savage" was first used of human beings (and not plants) in the seventeenth century. He sees the "modern definition" of the term as having originated with Montesquieu in 1748.

12. In fact, humans do not lack body hair. According to Wendy Cooper (1971: 16), adult humans have more hairs than the chimpanzee. It is simply that the hairs are nearly invisible because of their fineness.

13. Well into the twentieth century, popular stereotypes ("Sambo" in the US, the golliwog in Britain) made use of "frizzy" hair as "an essential aspect of the iconography of 'inferiority'" (Mercer 1990: 250).

14. It is not so much that the hairiness–savagery equation persists (though it is not impossible that it does as a hidden subtext), as that current ideals of the "clean" hairless body will have different impacts on different ethnic groups, insofar as body hair has a racial component. To the extent that different ethnic groups have different patterns of body hair, then the question of the "properly cleaned-up" body will involve a tacit racial norm. In Australia, for example, the subtle equation between hairiness and "barbarousness" will probably have most impact on those of Mediterranean or Middle Eastern origin. It seems indubitable that pressure is put on non-Anglo bodies to Anglicize themselves. One beautician told us, for example, that young Indian girls with facial hair "want it off, 'cos they're getting teased by the boys." On the other hand, the beautician was careful to point out that Australia is so diverse and changing so rapidly that it is hard to make generalizations. For example, generational issues come into play, with some young women of non-English-speaking background asking beauticians not to confirm waxing appointments at home because their mothers wouldn't approve. So, while it may be true that in *some* contexts, hair can function as a marker of the border between Anglo (looking) and non-Anglo (looking) Australians, any such assertion would need to be made with caution, especially given the fact that depilation has been a part of many ethnic traditions for far longer than it has been practised by Anglo-Celtic people. For example, female depilation was a part not only of Ancient Greek culture but also of many Muslim and Middle Eastern countries. The pressure to depilate cannot be seen as springing only from Anglo-Celtic norms, nor can the practice be seen as having only a single meaning or import. It's also a hard practice to track socially. A senior figure in waxing in Australia told us that depilation is an important part of a Muslim feminine aesthetic, but that Muslim women do not in general go to public salons, but practise waxing at home. Different cultures have

different depilation techniques, including running a ball made of sugar and water over the skin, or a Middle Eastern technique called "threading," in which the hair is tweaked out by means of an arrangement of cotton threads.

15. There is also a third possibility apart from those of being "over" or "under" clothed, that of being "inappropriately" or "incorrectly" dressed, as when indigenous people dressed in European clothing. The sight of Aboriginal people dressed (often "incorrectly") in European clothing sometimes discomforted European observers. Thanks to Simon Ryan for alerting me to this. For a discussion of the somewhat analogous question of the asymmetry of cross-dressing (whereby men dressing as women is a form of dressing down and hence often understood as comic, whereas women dressing as men is a form of "dressing up" and hence less amenable to comedy), see Bonner (1998).

16. Nicholas Thomas (1994) cites a sixteenth-century French writer (H.L.-V. de la Popelinière) who considered savages to be *sans roi, sans loi et sans foi* ("without king, without law and without faith") as a particularly succinct example of this point. Thomas also points out that this "vacancy" tends gradually to become filled in as the administrative and governmental projects of colonization go on to constitute native people as a (frequently problematic) population.

17. A somewhat analogous point still holds today with regard to "fashion." As Jennifer Craik (1994: 3–4) notes, it has been usual, following Georg Simmel, to think of fashion as a product of capitalism and hence as belonging to the West, a view that excludes the clothing of pre-modern and non-Western people from the category.

18. This phrase is used in Mark 5:15 and Luke 8:35, both of which describe an incident where Jesus exorcises the demons from a possessed man known as "Legion" (because of the many devils in him) who lived naked in the tombs. The phrase still has a certain popular currency. I have seen it used in the preface to a very ladylike volume from the turn of the twentieth century on changes in ladies' fashions, and a cursory web search reveals that it still holds good in evangelical sites. The King James Bible includes a comma, conveniently omitted in most transcriptions.

19. For an early twentieth-century critique of Stanley, see Langdon-Davies (1928), who satirically suggested a Swiftian Modest Proposal to *un*clothe the world. Using the same kind of economic arguments advanced by Stanley, he proposed an elaborate system of easing the shock by slowly introducing the mandatory wearing of suits made of brown paper.

20. A contemporary example of the economics of civility is the French lingerie firm currently engaged in persuading women in rural India that they "need" to wear underwear. This project is enhanced by "educational" seminars at universities and beauty salons (Anon. 2003).

21. Simon Schama (1996: 97) describes the process whereby the mythical hairy wild men figures began to be made over in the later part of the fifteenth century into "exemplars of the virtuous and natural life." This process of sentimentalization and "cleaning up" prepared the way for the later emergence of the fully fledged noble savage figure.

22. It is interesting to note that similar arguments could be made of the poor. In Charles Lamb's "A Complaint of the Decay of Beggars in the Metropolis" (1822), for example, we find the following evocation of the freedoms of penury:

> Rags, which are the reproach of poverty, are the Beggar's robes, and graceful *insignia* of his profession, his tenure, his full dress, the suit in which he is expected to show himself in public. He is never out of the fashion, or limpeth awkwardly behind it. He is not required to put on court mourning. He weareth all colours, fearing none. His costume hath undergone less change than the Quaker's. He is the only man in the universe who is not obliged to study appearances. The ups and downs of the world concern him no longer. He alone continueth in one stay... He is the only free man in the universe. (Lamb 1903: 116)

The trope occasionally survives today (e.g. in George Gershwin's "I've got Plenty O' Nuttin").

23. Cf. Torgovnick (1990: 7) on Freud, Ellis and Malinowski: They "sought the universal truth about human nature and conceived of primitive societies as the testing ground, the laboratory, the key to that universal truth."

24. My use of the term "deviance" is not intended to be derogatory. I am keeping this very loaded term from sociology precisely because it is itself symptomatic of the moral values that overlay judgements about social norms.

25. An American visitor to the Klingberg community, Jan Gay (1933: 53), describes enduring the "tiresome" long eulogies of Nietzsche and "the endless recitations of romantic German poetry" performed by the founder Paul Zimmerman.

26. Maurice Parmelee (1929) lists the occupations of his nudist friends as: actor, architect, army officer, author, banker, barber, bookseller, chemist, clergyman, clerk, commercial traveller, electrician, engineer, furrier, factory worker (in Gay 1933: 129).

27. For a detailed study of such contradictions, see Toepfer (1997) and Barcan (2004).

28. The therapeutic potential of nudity can be accounted for in part as a corollary of the general proscription of public nudity. This proscription means that it is possible to feel pride and self-confidence from overcoming or confronting such an intimate bodily taboo. Therapeutic uses of nudity can perhaps be seen as descendants of the magical, religious or ritual uses of nudity. For a detailed study of the therapeutic possibilities of nudity see Goodson (1991). See also Sussman (1977).

29. Paul Ableman (1984) points out the instability in the names for nudism even within any one language: *Nacktkultur; Freikörperkultur; Lichtkultur; Lichtfreunde* ('naked culture'; 'free bodies culture'; light culture'; 'friends of the light'); Gymnosophy; *amis de vivre* ('friends of life'); naturism; nudism. "When the name of a thing keeps changing, the thing itself is usually unstable," notes Ableman (1984: 98).

30. Clarke (1982) notes, though, that the nudist "doubt[s] his own rhetoric," when he goes on to say that in any case a female nudist would have plenty of visible warning if a male nudist had evil intentions.

31. To clarify: Parmelee describes how, when he was a university teacher, he saw sex segregation hindering women's progress. Women "herded together in a dull and inexpressive mass" (Parmelee 1929: 77). He would mix up the seating and the women would participate more.

32. Unlike Havelock Ellis, who wrote the introduction to Parmelee's book.

33. Clarke (1982) also found that women were less likely to self-disclose as nudist than men, a fact that may suggest not only a differential in modesty training but also a gender differential in the symbolic meanings and social consequences of female and male nudity (see Chapter 4).

34. No doubt one of the reasons his book shocked his contemporaries (though the scholarly Knight had apparently not expected it) is that he continually compared phallic worship to Christian practices, including seeing the Christian cross as a descendant of phallic symbols of creation and generation (Knight 1957: 53). Knight was forced, in fact, to withdraw his book and to suppress as many copies as he could find. Ashley Montagu, author of a modern introduction to Knight's study, sees it as still useful today, since prudery has meant that phallic religious practices have been little studied. Indeed, Knight's *Discourse* is still hard to obtain. My own discussion is deeply indebted to the work of Larissa Bonfante, where I found the reference to Knight's study, and which has been the source of much of my reading on this topic. Many of the references I cite in this section can be found in Bonfante's (1989) essay "Nudity as a Costume in Classical Art."

35. While the classical nude depicted an unobtrusive penis, phallic figures making use of the magical powers of nudity continued to exist, even in Classical Greece. Satyrs, herms and the theatre are three sites where phallic imagery remained (Bonfante 1989: 549–50). These two types of Greek male nudity were "quite distinct" by classical times (p. 550). (Herm = "a squared pillar surmounted by a head or bust (usually of Hermes) used as a boundary-maker, signpost etc": *OED*). For a discussion of the ongoing importance of phallic imagery even through to Roman times, see Bonfante (1989), and Walters (1978: 55–8).

36. I have some hesitancy in using the term "victim," given the assumptions about the effects of flashing that accompany it. In the late 1970s, Gittleson et al. (1978) used it repeatedly, even though their own study concluded that in the vast majority of cases, flashing left no long-term effects. The term does not encompass the full spectrum of female responses to flashing. On the other hand, flashing *is* an event that the woman has not chosen and that a significant proportion of women find shocking or distressing.

37. MacDonald (1973) characterizes this slightly differently. His statement, for example, that some child molesters and rapists are also exhibitionists repeats Richard's two psychological categories, but notes the possibility of their coexistence.

38. Note too that a limited number of these previously all-male rituals have been adopted by women in all-women sporting clubs.

39. Sedgwick's (1985) discussion of homosociality starts with the Ancient Greeks. It is clear that these contemporary rituals share something in common with their Classical forebears, especially the emphasis on physical prowess and the validation of male–male relations over male–female ones. The place of homosexuality within the spectrum of male–male relations is, of course, a key difference. Perhaps more similar is the Roman context, where both homosexuality and public nudity were frowned upon, but released in ritual contexts. Indeed, Patrick, a Classics scholar, used to entertain his rugby club fellows with comparison between their own "bollocky race"

and the Roman *lupercalia*, an annual purification and fertility ritual in which naked men sacrificed a goat and ran around the boundaries of the city of Rome, and women vied to be touched by the goat skin as a fertility blessing.

40. Jane Caputi (2001: 19), for example, claims that "despite her dogmatic whitewashing," the Virgin Mary "still ineluctably suggests the presence of the ancient Great Mother Goddesses."

41. The slightly greater subversive potential of female buttocks results no doubt from the fact that they are not a sign of sexual difference as the breasts or genitals are. Women can thus, to an extent, share in the long carnivalesque tradition in which the bared buttocks signify scorn or derision. The question of the subversive possibilities of female nakedness is fascinating and complex. I do not, unfortunately, have space to treat it thoroughly here. It is discussed in passing in the opening of Wolff's (1990) *Feminine Sentences*, and in depth in Barcan (2002a).

42. This is so even for deviant nudity; exhibitionism among elderly people is less likely to be reported, no doubt because it is considered less threatening (Kenyon 1989: 95).

4

The Nude Republic: Celebrity, "Ordinariness" and Identity

Introduction: All or Nothing

This chapter deals with nudity in consumer culture. In Chapter 2, I argued that nudity can signify both plenitude and lack – "all" or "nothing." This duality, combined with the popular link between nudity and sex, makes nudity a valuable tool in the marketing of commodities. In advertising culture, the body in general is made to operate according to what Derrida would term a logic of the supplement; it is that zestful thing that needs vitamin pills to pep it up; that sexual thing that needs lipstick to make it sexy, and so on. John Frow (1995: 97) characterizes this as a kind of prosthetic logic – the "paradox of an originary state which comes into being only retrospectively and by virtue of a prosthetic addition." Commodities are needed to make the body whole, while the body's potential symbolic weight as repository of the whole and the natural serves to disavow the assumption of lack upon which the system relies. The body is posited as at the same time complete (natural, authentic) and lacking (needing a commodity). The paradox at the heart of conceptions of the natural body is particularly strong when it comes to the *naked* body, for our largely unconscious oscillation between thinking of the naked body as deprived of something (i.e. as in lack) or as full and complete in itself (i.e. as the naked truth) allows it to signal the naturalness of the body's need for a commodity.

The naked body is both sufficient to itself and in need of supplement. Naked, your body's lack is exposed. An advertisement for an aloe vera cream shows a naked woman sitting legs outstretched on the floor, her hands modestly covering her breasts, and one leg bent to cover her groin. The naked body, here invoked precisely for its "naturalness," is still needy. "The less you wear the more you need new Palmer's Aloe Vera Formula," runs the caption. In other words, the more "natural" your body, the more it needs a commodity. Nakedness, the emblem of the body's naturalness, not only is unable to be represented fully (for censorship reasons) but also serves to expose the naked

Figure 4.1 "Cover Your Body Needs." NIB advertisement. Professional talent supplied by Models and Actors and Paradox Model Management – Newcastle, NSW. Photograph by Karl Hofman. Agency: Peach Advertising.

body's vulnerability or lack, which then needs to be supplemented by an equally "natural" "new therapy." The ad for health insurance (Figure 4.1) works on the same logic.

The naked body works particularly well as part of what the French post-modernist Jean Baudrillard (1987) calls "the system of objects." Just as one object needs another, so the "empty" body begs us, not only to undress it, as the moralist and the sensualist alike might expect, but also metaphorically to dress it – to adorn it with commodities. In consumer culture, then, commodities play the same structural role as clothing does in the philosophical dialectic explored in Chapter 1. They are paradoxically unnecessary *and* necessary, superfluity and essential supplement.

Nudity, on the other hand, functions as that which cannot be freely repres-ented. Nudity is a good device to sell commodities, because in late modernity nude images work as dynamic and unstable frontiers – pointing always to the limits of what can be lived, shown or accepted. A naked image can point towards that which was previously unrepresentable, thus highlighting itself as naughty, liberated, or "modern." By contrast, it can gesture towards the past in order to sanctify itself, cushioning itself within the protective bosom of history or the fine arts. An image can signal its own limits: what we'd like to be able to show, but can't; what we don't think you'd accept yet; what lies just outside the frame; what you'd *like* to see; what you *don't* want to see, and so on. These types of naked images thus point towards their own conditions of (im)possibility. As that which cannot be freely represented (whether it be for legal, moral or customary reasons) in an era that likes to think of itself as one of unrestrained representability, nudity is thus often a device of the edge – teasing, playing, shocking or simply pointing out the limits and boundaries of representability (see Figure 4.2). It's a site of pressure. Naked images are thus images with a high degree of self-consciousness; they gesture to what must lie outside the frame or, in the case of porn, they point to the remarkable nature of what lies within the frame, and hence to their own transgressive quality.

Figure 4.2 "And The Rest Is All In Your Mind." *International H&E Monthly* 90(5) (1990): 4. Photographs by Leif Heilberg/*International H&E Monthly*.

The paradoxical qualities of the Western apprehension of the body in general and the naked body in particular are thus of special use to consumer culture. The naked body's naughty naturalness and its brimming lack, along with the intertwining of moral liberalism and consumerism, can lead us to expect an increased role for nudity in advertising culture. This certainly seems to be the case at present. Images of nudity are beginning to proliferate, selling not just obviously contiguous products like lingerie and swimwear, but everything from housing loans to electric kettles, watches and telecommunications companies. Nudity has, in a sense, become the latest fashion. This is not surprising. Advertising and fashion need a constant stream of novelty and there's nothing so new as nudity, the oldest fashion of all.

Naked Images

> Images invite comparison; they are constant reminders of what we are and might with effort yet become.

> Mike Featherstone, "The Body in Consumer Culture"

> We want to *be* pictures, not just to be in them, and so when I look at a picture I am also looking at myself, at a way that I might be.

> James Elkins, *The Object Stares Back*

This chapter focuses on naked *images*. Overall, this book is concerned less with representations of nudity than with nudity as an embodied experience. But of course images and experiences are not separable, not least because images form such a large part of our everyday life. Our experiences of the naked body occur in relation to images, and representations play an active role in producing bodily experience. Images are also part of the way a society sets up and polices norms. They are one form of what feminist philosopher Judith Butler (1990: 16) calls "regulatory practices," and they have a *performative* as well as a *constative* function. That is, while they may seem simply to report, reflect or describe the world as it is, they also help to constitute it. Images help persuade us as to who or what we might desire or hate, and who or what we might want to *be*.

Naked images are particularly interesting in this regard, since they can so often signify "naturalness." It is scarcely possible to imagine a more ideological device than a claim to the bedrock of humanness. Moreover, nudity can signify not only nature or normality but also, at one end of the scale, heroism, and at the other, degradation. Add to this the sexual meanings that almost invariably attach to the naked body in consumer culture and it is not hard to see why nudity is such a useful tool for marketing and for individual identity work.

This chapter explores some of the different modes in which naked images circulate in consumer culture, and how people use such images as a form of social engagement and/or as a tool in their own identity work. In particular, it focuses on a particular opposition important to late-modern identity – that between celebrity and "ordinariness."

The age of mechanical reproduction of images has brought about what is arguably a substantial new ordering of images, a "modern revolution in the order of production (of reality, or meaning)" (Baudrillard 1987: 13). As the epigraphs to this section suggest, identities are formed in circuits of imitation, desire and fantasy (as well as revulsion, aversion or rejection, which neither epigraph mentions). This identity work is particularly intense and particularly visual in the image-saturated environment of modern consumer cultures, where forms of image and image-making multiply and hybridize. Baudrillard described a world in which images multiply exponentially, bombarding us so totally that any original "reality" gets lost in the welter. Trapped in the hyperreal, we can no longer distinguish artifice from reality. Although Baudrillard's foundational opposition – that between an absolute reality and artifice – cannot be sustained philosophically, his work is nonetheless important for the sense it gives of the speed with which artificially produced images or simulacra hybridize,[1] and of the importance of images to both economics and identity. We, who are both consumers and participants in the image economy, inevitably form our own identities in relation to the pantheon of glamorous or not-so-glamorous others who circulate through our universe in photographic, cinematic and digital form. We are, in a sense, "mixed up with images," and naked images play an interesting part in this circuit.

The fascination with images described by Baudrillard needs to be situated within a larger social shift – the rise of a new, distinctively modern, form of selfhood in the West. Michel Foucault argued that modernity gave rise to a new form of "subjectification" (or identity formation) – one based on the internalization of invisible disciplinary power rather than subjection to external, spectacular power. Foucault pointed out that new forms of identity work have been made possible (indeed mandated) by the dominance of such disciplinary modes of power as well as by the new forms of knowledge (such as psychology) they have enabled. Identity work takes place via "technologies of the self" equivalent, according to Foucault, to a modern version of the confessional. He argued that modern subjects come into being via new forms of self-making, a specifically modern form of "work of the self on the self" (Veyne, quoted in Gutting 1994: 119). Social control has come to take place less by visible external force than via internalized self-surveillance: "the government of the self by the self" (Foucault, quoted in Gutting 1994: 119).

Foucault's analysis is more careful than Baudrillard's. Put together, though, Foucault's analysis of new forms of self-making and Baudrillard's fascination with the workings of images in postmodern society allow us to see how important images are as a means by which people in late-modern societies create and negotiate their identities. For late-modern subjects, images constitute a major technology of the self.

This chapter is organized around a number of intersecting categories of nakedness. I have made up a mini-taxonomy of what I call satirical, heroic, celebrity, glamour and homemade nudity.[2] Two of these modes – the satirical and the heroic – have long and venerable histories that I will not trace here. But I have included some snatches from history in order to make it clear that old traditions persist subtly in contemporary Western consumer cultures. Throughout, I am interested in the polarity between an idea of the "ordinary person" and the famous, glamorous or powerful person. As new forms of image-making develop, categories of person (star, politician, ordinary person) and of image (glamour, snapshot, porn) multiply, fracture and blur into each other in what Baudrillard (1987: 20) called "relations of contagion and unspoken analogy." We will see, for example, that boudoir photography is an imitation of chic celebrity nudity; Home Girls are both a rejection and an imitation of classic porn; homemade sex videos are both home movies and porn; stolen sex videos of celebrities are both celebrity images and homemade ones. This chapter examines the role of nude images in the increasing failure of these categories (ordinariness and celebrity) to contain themselves. It examines nudity as, by turn, a mode of bringing down the famous (satire); a mode of elevation and celebration (heroicization); of becoming famous or capitalizing financially on one's fame (celebrity nudity); of imitating celebrity (glamour nudity); and finally of rejecting glamour ("homemade" nudity).

Satirical Nudity: Stripping Authority Bare

[N]ot much is really sacred.
But even the President of the United States sometimes must have to stand naked.

Bob Dylan, "It's Alright Ma (I'm Only Bleeding)"

There is a long tradition of the use of nudity for critical or satirical purposes. Imagining authority figures naked or dressed only in their underwear used to be a classic piece of advice to those nervous about speaking in public, or being interviewed for a job. This personal anti-anxiety tactic fits into a longer, more explicitly political, tradition of social critique in which nakedness has been a useful metaphor.

One of the most sustained uses of nakedness as a critical metaphor is in Thomas Carlyle's (1987) *Sartor Resartus*, which I discussed at some length in Chapter 1. In this work, nudity is a symbol for radical egalitarianism, and clothes function as both examples and symbols of fallible and changeable human institutions. Although Carlyle was a quite ambivalent revolutionary, he was very happy to use nakedness as a way of debunking pomposity, self-importance or vanity:

> [W]hen I read of pompous ceremonials, Frankfort coronations, Royal Drawing-rooms, Levees, Couchees; ... how Duke this is presented by Archduke that, and Colonel A by General B, and innumerable Bishops, Admirals, and miscellaneous Functionaries, are advancing gallantly to the Anointed Presence; and I strive, in my remote privacy, to form a clear picture of that solemnity, – on a sudden, as by some enchanter's wand, the – shall I speak it? – the Clothes fly-off the whole dramatic corps; and Dukes, Grandees, Bishops, Generals, Anointed Presence itself, every mother's son of them, stand straddling there, not a shirt on them; and I know not whether to laugh or weep. (Carlyle 1987: 48)

Despite Carlyle's ultimate uncertainty about radical egalitarianism (or "sansculottism"),[3] he makes forceful use of nudity as a metaphor for the fundamental equality of all humans and clothes as the makers and markers of class and power:

> Lives the man that can figure a naked Duke of Windlestraw addressing a naked House of Lords? Imagination ... will not forward with the picture ... And yet why is the thing impossible? Was not every soul, or rather every body, of these Guardians of our Liberties, naked, or nearly so, last night; "a forked Radish with a head fantastically carved?" And why might he not, did our stern Fate so order it, walk out to St. Stephen's, as well as into bed, in that no-fashion; and there, with other similar Radishes, hold a Bed of Justice? (Carlyle 1987: 49)

The trope, though expressed idiosyncratically, is very familiar, as is the utopian sentiment it so easily and frequently inspires. Take, for example, Harold Bloom's championing of Carlyle's vision:

> A little application of Carlyle to current American society would do wonders. Envision a House of Representatives and a Senate required to deliberate absolutely naked (presumably in a sufficiently heated Capitol). Clearly the quality of legislation would rise, and the quantity of rhetoric would fall. Envision professors, quite naked, instructing equally naked classes. The intellectual level might not be elevated, but the issue of authority would be clarified. Envision our president, naked on television, smilingly charming us with his customary amiable incoherence. We might be no less moved, but reality would have a way of breaking in upon him, and even upon us. (Bloom 1986: 12)

This is the egalitarianism, and its key metaphor, of which nudists so frequently speak. "We're all the same. We're all the bloody same," was how one elderly nudist put it to me. As I discovered in my interviews, people who work frequently with naked people repeatedly speak in terms of the superficial diversity but deep equality of human beings. A manager of a nudist resort said simply:

> People are people. All kind[s] of people – some fat, some skinny, some tall, some shorter. We're all different . . . Everybody's beautiful in their own way. We're all beautiful people.

In her philosophy, clothes figure as a metonym of social class and human division. For example, she referred to the world outside her resort as "label world," by which she meant not only the discriminations and distinctions epitomized by designer label clothing, but also those embodied in clothes *per se* (she told the story of trying on a dress in an ordinary small-town clothes shop and walking out naked to get another one, having forgotten that she was in "label world").

For some reason (perhaps because their role intertwines the legal and the moral), judges frequently turn up as an example of social respectability neutralized by nudity. For example, the masseur Simon used the judge as the quintessential example:

> I might be massaging someone . . . and they might say "Yes, well, I'm a QC" or "a High Court judge" and . . . I wouldn't have known that from the body lying here. But if I were to walk that evening past them on their way to dinner I would certainly think, now that looks like a High Court judge, because they then have the costume on and they have the mask on.

Likewise, when Sydney's Waverley Council was deciding the fate of the famous Bondi Icebergs' clubhouse, up for demolition, long-serving member of the Icebergs' swimming club, 85-year-old George Caddy, defended it thus:

> It's a place where judges and wharfies, the rich and the poor, the unemployed and retired can get together on equal footing. After all, we're all the same standing around in the sun in the nuddy. (Anon. 1994)

This egalitarian vision is often a masculine one, since women's nudity is, as we have seen, less able to signify simple humanness.

Nudity, then, has a levelling effect. When a woman wrote a letter of complaint to the *Sydney Morning Herald* about its coverage of the Gay and Lesbian Mardi Gras (specifically, about its inclusion of a photograph of two men whose bare buttocks were enclosed in a garland of flowers), her letter received the following response from another reader:

> What is it exactly that she finds so offensive? Surely not the bottom, for we all have one of those . . . And surely not the flowers . . . [T]he bum is one of society's great levellers. For all his loads of dosh, Rupert's bum is as effective and useful as mine. Hooray for bums! (Crowley 1998)

The Rupert is, presumably, media magnate Rupert Murdoch, who in no way figures in this story except, it seems, as an allegorical figure. As we will see, he is not alone.

Nude Leaders

In 1999, the glossy women's magazine *marie claire* organized a blind dinner-date for twelve singles, who afterwards had to assess each other in print. Among the welter of mostly dismissive comments, one caught my eye:

> [H]e did make the most entertaining comment of the evening. We were talking about disturbing dreams and he said he'd dreamt about patting a naked John Howard [the Australian Prime Minister] on the head. (Walker and Renkert 1997: 106)

In researching this book, I have stumbled across many such references to naked notables, especially politicians and royalty; so much so that one could almost detect a minor genre! Naked premiers, prime ministers, presidents, senators, party leaders and royals have, it seems, flourished in the imaginations or unconscious of artists, activists and writers, as well as blind-date hopefuls. Whether it be former Australian Prime Minister Malcolm Fraser losing his trousers in a Memphis hotel room, nude photos of Prince Charles being circulated globally, discussions of US President Bill Clinton's penis, Internet sites with fabricated images of the Queen Mother naked, or a naked effigy of morals campaigner Reverend Fred Nile, complete with oversized genitals, the Naked Politician or Monarch thrives. In the following sections, I will explore some of these examples.

Naked Politicians: The Calendars of Larry Pickering

Perhaps the most famous and consistent Australian example of nudity as a symbolic weapon against the potential self-importance of politicians were the calendars drawn by cartoonist Larry Pickering, produced annually over about a twenty-year period from 1974 onwards. These calendars, which became an Australian institution, were cartoons of the nation's leaders naked, in mocking imitation of "girlie" calendars. Known as *Pickering's Playmates*, they depicted politicians of all political persuasions, completely naked, front-on. The vast majority of the figures were men (since most politicians were men), although the number of women included did increase over the years. By the mid-1980s Pickering had thrown in an assortment of pop stars, TV personalities, royal personages and sporting figures to add to the mix. The first calendars were labelled "a politically candid calendar," but the less subtle warning "Careful! They're starkers" became the ritual tag-line.

The calendars arose from Pickering's weekly comic strip in *The Australian* newspaper called "The Jungle," which featured the antics of politicians living naked in the jungle, who did things like holding reverse-striptease nights in which they gradually put on more and more layers of clothing. The calendars were enormously popular. The first edition sold out within days, fed in part by the excellent TV publicity generated by Pickering's brave but astute choice of an all-nude launch. Surprisingly, the calendars had a large international market. They were, for reasons unknown, particularly popular in India and Pakistan, where they were sold on the underground market.

In Pickering's story of the origin of the calendars, the psychological and the satirical converge:

> Australia in particular has this atavistic background where a lot of us were convicts at one time and we hated the people that were supposedly above us. That's why we have this egalitarian attitude towards all people. So basically when I was a kid at school and I used to get in trouble with the teachers, or the headmaster or whatever – and I always was – I used to imagine them with nothing on and I wasn't scared of them any more. So it has a levelling thing which Australians love. They hate tall poppies.[4]

For Pickering, the calendars were "a way of bringing the politicians back to the people. It makes them like you and me." His favourite targets were "people that set themselves up. People that had themselves on a different echelon than the norm. They were more of a target than others." He was not above self-exposure (having himself been one of the earliest *Cleo* centrefolds) or self-mockery (he always included himself on the cover and his own penis makes a microscopic appearance in 1986).

So how potent a weapon can satirical nudity be? Were the politicians genuinely afraid of being represented, and was Pickering in danger of being sued? In mid-1970s Australia, the use of nudity in this way was quite daring. In fact, the publisher pulled out of the project shortly before the first calendar was to appear. Pickering, however, was always confident that he wouldn't be sued, and went ahead, organizing his own distribution. Only two newsagents in Sydney were willing to stock it. But the calendars were an instant hit and from then on there were no problems.

Over the years, several politicians did threaten to sue Pickering, but only one ever began the attempt. Pickering did lose a lucrative television advertising contract over his depiction of the Pope naked in prayer (with a mitred penis peeping out from under his robe at a group of nuns). Mostly, though, the levelling effects of nudity were themselves his best defence:

> I mean, what are they going to do? Get up in court and say, "Exhibit A, it's not really like that?!" I mean, it's ridiculous to even think about it! You'd look like you had no sense of humour, you couldn't take a joke, you weren't one of the people. Everyone would laugh at you.

The more famous the target, the greater the protection:

> If you attack someone that wasn't up there it's dangerous, but if you attack someone that's a Prime Minister or someone that needs electoral support or someone on a pedestal somewhere then you'll never ever have a problem because it's a blatant.... It'd be a joke for them to do anything about it.

In fact, inclusion in the calendar also perversely became a form of flattery. Pickering recalls that politicians' minders would not infrequently sidle up to him at parties and drop none too subtle hints: "To be a politician you've basically gotta have an overload of vanity anyway, so to them, to be on the calendar was something good . . . They all wanted the original." Even Prince Charles wrote to Pickering asking for the cartoon that depicted him with a blue ribbon around his penis (Figure 4.3).

According to Pickering, to be effective in the popular marketplace, satire must steer clear of a certain kind of moral offence. It may be daring – rude even – but not banally offensive. This is, clearly, a difficult thing to judge. Unnecessary anatomical detail is out, he claims. Pickering was shocked at what he perceived as the failure of judgement displayed by his imitators:

> I was appalled at the other people that tried to do it. When I saw it, I thought "You don't know what it's about." . . . Established guys got it wrong. They just got the formula wrong; they didn't even think correctly about it. It was dirty. You can't sell dirty things. The market shrinks to nothing when you try and sell something dirty.

This fine line is medium-specific:

> A cartoon is something you can get away with murder with . . . You see, there's a fine line between a cartoon and a physical representation of someone; it's different. Trust me, I don't know where the line is, I don't know where to draw it [in the abstract], but I just know where it is when I sit down to draw. I can't explain it but

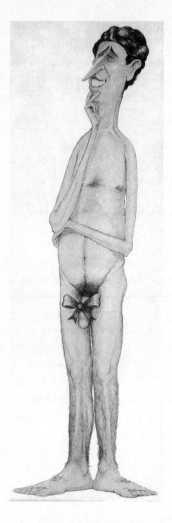

Figure 4.3 Larry Pickering. "Pr. Nocember." *Pickering's Playmates of '79.* © 1979 Pickering Enterprises Pty Ltd. The ribbon is in blue.

there is a red line you just don't go over and a lot of people have tried to duplicate my calendars. Plenty of people brought out the same sort of thing but they all went broke in the first year because they didn't know where that line was. They didn't know that you couldn't put holes in the ends of dicks.

Pickering's claim about medium and context rings true, as the following case study makes clear. For in a particular historical moment, a life-sized naked sculpture of the Queen and Prince Philip caused more controversy than twenty years' worth of Pickering's pollies cavorting naked on a calendar.

A "Divisive Monstrosity:" *Down by the Lake with Liz and Phil*

> I think the King is but a man, as I am . . .
>
> His ceremonies laid by, in his nakedness he appears but a man . . .
>
> *Henry V* (IV.i 101–2, 104–6)

In 1995, two naked sculptures caused a brief but intense furore in ways that highlight nudity's ongoing potential to mean very different things and its availability in battles over both individual and group identity. The sculpture in question, *Down by the Lake with Liz and Phil*, was created by Gregory Taylor as part of the 1995 National Sculpture Forum. Positioned on the shores of Lake Burley Griffin in front of the former Parliament House in Australia's capital, Canberra, it depicted the Queen and Prince Philip sitting on a park bench stark naked – except, as the joke soon had it, for the crown jewels. Liz and Phil didn't stay down by the lake for very long. After a few days, the sculpture of the Queen was beheaded; shortly afterwards, that of the Prince was attacked with a sledgehammer. The statues were progressively damaged until, less than a week after their installation, the organizers and the sculptor had them removed, leaving only the park bench "as a sort of ghostly reminder" (Fuller 1995), along with a written message to explain their absence to the crowds who were by now coming to see them (Figures 4.4 and 4.5).

The purpose of the attacks on *Liz and Phil* was never clear. It seemed such a symbolic action, and yet it could have symbolized very different things, from republican critique of the monarchy to monarchist critique of republican satire. Regardless of the iconoclasts' intent, the incident rapidly took on a violent life of its own. Four interlinked characteristics of this life are of interest. First, the sheer passion the statue and its destruction aroused is worthy of note, since it suggests that something deep, something at once intimate and public, was at stake. Second, every part of the affair – the statues themselves, the iconoclasm, the protests and the blustery letters to the editor – was strikingly *bodily* in nature. Third, discussion of the statues was repeatedly characterized by a slippage between treating them as art, as symbols of the monarchy and as real people. And fourth, the debate rapidly moved from the statues themselves to an outpouring about everything that was wrong with Australia. These two naked statues and their creator became symbols, not of creation, but of loss, and an alienated populace took the chance to lament everything from republicanism to multiculturalism, globalization, political correctness, feminism and even the loss of manners.

Let's start with the passion. Although the sculptor intended the statues as an allegory of *The Emperor's New Clothes*, few people interpreted them that way. Certainly, there were one or two abstract interpretations ("a sensitive

Figure 4.4

Figures 4.4, 4.5 Gregory Taylor. *Down by the Lake with Liz and Phil*, 1995. With permission of the Committee of the Canberra National Sculpture Forum Inc., from the Canberra National Sculpture Forum 95.

study of a couple, three-quarters of their way through life, together yet apart, stripped of all accoutrements, staring pensively and with resignation in different directions across a melancholy space": Mainsbridge 1995), but these were a distinct minority. The uproar was particularly intense, taking over most of the local newspaper (especially the letters pages) and attracting plenty of publicity in other Australian newspapers, and even overseas. The newspapers were filled with emotional responses, ranging from sarcasm to despair and anger. The sculpture was seen as "a vulgar attack on a democratic symbol" (Farouque 1995), but so too was its destruction, which was compared to fascist book burning. The artist reported having received death threats (Fuller 1995) including, allegedly, one from the head of the Returned Services League, Bruce Ruxton (Roberts 1995). Letters to the editor were also ferocious:

> The artist, those who supported this disgusting project, together with the Prime Minister of Australia ought to be stripped naked and put in a cage next to the Royal couple. These people belong in the trees with the apes, or in cages in the zoo. (Kramilius 1995)

> In past years heads have rolled for much less acts of sick humour. (Muir and Muir 1995).

> How things have changed since the first Elizabethan Age. In those high and far off times the Royal Headsman would have severed the right heads – those of the artist who had the gall to produce this divisive monstrosity, the approving bureaucrats [and other administrative bodies] . . . But then, Sixteenth Century gentlefolk had better taste than us and such a statue is unlikely to have been conceived, let alone displayed in a public place! (Exon 1995)

The climax of the affair was when a Carey McQuillan, reported variously as an off-duty policeman and a Vietnam veteran, was so incensed by the statues that he leapt into his car and drove the four hours from Sydney, brandishing a tube of glue and a T-shirt, and vowing to defend his sovereign lady, the Queen. A ruckus erupted as he attempted to glue the T-shirt onto the sculpture and drape the figures with a quilt, spraying the organizer of the Sculpture Forum with glue during the altercation.

As this example indicates, responses to the statues were very bodily: from the original sledgehammer attacks, to McQuillan's scuffle, to the imagery used by letter writers (who called for the sculptor's head, or for the prime minister to be stripped), or to the active political response of the thousand or so people who joined Australians for Constitutional Monarchy in the week following the event. The horrified letter writers of Australia countered the insult to royalty by vengefully imagining a horror-show of nude politicians; for a week or so the newspapers were alive with naked Howards, Clintons, Mahatirs, Suhartos and Keatings. In somewhat self-negating fashion, most writers commented on the *impossibility* of producing such figures:

> They wouldn't do it to President Suharto of Indonesia or any other head of state from a South-East Asian country. They wouldn't put Paul and Annita Keating [the Australian Prime Minister and his wife] naked on a park bench down here. They just wouldn't be game. (quoted in Contractor 1995)

Despite the intensity of the repeated calls (not) to imagine other world leaders naked, actual genitals got surprisingly scant mention in the whole affair. One would have imagined that the sight of the princely penis would have aroused the most ire of all, given the cultural imperative that the penis "remai[n] private and protected territory" (Bordo 1993a: 698). But neither the prince nor his penis was given much press attention. Indeed, his penis scarcely rated a mention, though the sculptor did report that a woman had been "totally disgusted" with him for giving Phil "what she perceived as too small a willy" (Delvecchio 1995). There was one letter-writer who quite ingeniously imagined a matching set of monstrous genitals: "Are we now going to have a 12-metre high penis called the 'Prime Minister' or a giant walk-through vagina called [health minister] 'Carmen Lawrence' mounted in Martin Place?" (Nelson 1995).

Such notable and inventive suggestions aside, however, it was scatalogical imagery that prevailed. Critics denigrated the sculptures as the two "concrete blocks" (Savage 1995), or the "pathetic bit of baked clay" (Ewin 1995). Detractors repeatedly saw them as infantile: "[M]ost would expect better 'art' to be cobbled together by an average kindergarten" (Benyon 1995). Many letters made reference to Prime Minister Paul Keating's infamous description of Australia as the "arse-end of the world:"

> I used to take exception to our Prime Minister's reported description of Australia. Now, after seeing the statues on the bench in Canberra, I think it rather apt. That's the sort of stuff one would expect to see emerge from that end. What bravado to display that work in our capital city for the whole world to see. Are our trading neighbours laughing with us or at us? (Greaves 1995)

> [P]erhaps there should be a series of such "sculptures." One could imagine Mahathir dangling his genitals at Parliament House or perhaps Suharto giving the Department of Foreign Affairs a "brown eye" – the ideas are endless. (Senior 1995)

> My own instinctive reaction to that offensive sculpture (sic) was to ignore it. After all, isn't that how we are told to treat a spoilt brat of a child who deliberately makes a disgusting mess on the living room carpet, when the natural reaction might be to turn it over and spank its bottom? (Sir David Smith 1995, original disclaimer)

This barely submerged scatological imagery can be accounted for, perhaps, when we remember how inescapable has been the motif of Australia as an infant or child trying to grow up. The trope of the maturing nation is a perennial characteristic of discussions of Australian nationhood. In recent years, it has been used by the Australian Republican Movement. For example, novelist and republican Thomas Keneally said on the occasion of the Queen's 1992 visit to Australia:

> [T]he Australian Republican Movement still has to persuade the bulk of Australians that this is an act of maturity, not an act of denial, that this will not involve denying Australia's historical connection with Britain or the House of Windsor, but that there has to be a time when, out of self-respect, you leave home. (Cameron 1992)

This imagery is, according to Castles et al. (1992: 195), typical of republican discourse in Australia, which often images republicanism as involving "no more than asking Mum to go and live in the national granny flat." But the trope recurs in anti-republican discourse as well, as when republicanism is seen as the tantrums of a disobedient child. The image of Australia as infant, boy or adolescent dates back to the nineteenth century, and it has modernized along the way; from the 1960s onwards, the development of the Australian nation has been explicitly conceived of as an "identity problem" (Inglis, quoted in Stratton 1998: 116). Thus, one letter writer considered that the *Liz and Phil* affair represented a failure to deal with nudity in an adult fashion, and diagnosed that familiar teenage identity problem: for her, the incident was "indicative of the nation's general lack of self-esteem" (Taylor 1995).

Graeme Turner (1994: 174) is highly critical of this trope and of the psychologizing of the nation on which it implicitly relies. He argues that any attempt to rethink nationalism and to create an inclusive, hybrid republic must part company with the tradition of analysis that treats the nation as a psychic entity and not a socio-political institution. While this may be so, this way of thinking about Australia is so entrenched that it is not at all far-fetched to imagine that it has penetrated the unconscious of many Australians. Certainly, this is the assumption underlying a reading of the event made at the time by academic Kurt Brereton, who read the upset as an Oedipal drama: "It's something to do with the mother figure, seeing mother without her clothes on," he said. "Infant Australia is growing up and is shocked at seeing Mum and Dad without anything on" (Cosic 1995).[5]

Whether or not this Freudian reading is valid (I personally prefer a Kleinian reading),[6] it is certainly the case that a vast proportion of the written responses treated the statue as though it were alive and/or imbued with something of the essence of the Queen herself. One letter writer considered it to be an act of sexual harassment (Wright 1995), an increasingly common accusation against artworks depicting nakedness, as we saw in Chapter 3. It was frequently condemned as cowardly, on the grounds that the Queen wasn't able to defend herself. Some saw it as a form of discourtesy: an attack on the dignity of a lady (Wheeler 1995), or an offence against "common decency" (Wright 1995). Monarchists were more likely to defend the Queen in this mode, not only as a sign (of a political system or a set of values) but also as a human being. The Queen deserved better because she had endured hard times and preserved her dignity throughout, wrote one elderly man (Wheeler 1995).[7]

McQuillan's attempt with glue and quilt was perhaps the most striking example of "the sign . . . becom[ing] the living embodiment of what it signifies" (Freedberg 1989: 28), and for this reason, it was derided by many:

> McQuillan confused the abstract with the flesh and bone subject, Elizabeth Windsor, and then compounded his delusion by displacing the same feelings and emotions onto a couple of rather badly rendered lumps of stuff. (Cockburn 1995: 44)

This is the "fusion between image and prototype . . . against which all [modern Western] image theory has always raged" (Freedberg 1989: 30), and hence Cockburn (1995) calls it a "delusion." But this denunciation is too easy. Even in consumer societies, where the dominant form of exchanged material object is the commodity form, we still have occasion to treat some objects (gifts, relics, texts, clothing) as though they had something of the human in them, and this is especially the case with privileged objects like artworks. In any case, though modern image theory may rage against this slippage, the standard processes of unconscious identity work may well subliminally support it. Certainly, psychoanalysts like Melanie Klein (1988) would say that reality and phantasy are in constant cooperation and interaction and that "there is never a moment in which we are not unconsciously phantasizing, never a moment in which this phantasizing is not influencing our perception of reality" (Alford 1989: 45). If so, then the perception of humanness in body replicas is not really an aberration but a standard though disavowed part of modern aesthetic responses. But the "tacit belief that the bodies represented on or in them somehow have the status of living bodies" (Freedberg 1989: 12) is not accorded much cultural capital. Westerners tend to deride such responses as unsophisticated or "primitive," and our tradition of art appreciation prizes a more rational and distanced apprehension of the artwork. Approaches that "over"-emphasize the work's effect on the spectator tend to be derided.[8] Western art appreciation and art history call for the active repression of responses (or discussion of responses) that are "too embarrassing, too blatant, too rude, and too uncultured; because they make us aware of our kinship with the unlettered, the coarse, the primitive, the undeveloped; and because they have psychological roots that we prefer not to acknowledge" (Freedberg 1989: 1).

Freedberg's reference to the "unlettered" is apposite, since in the *Liz and Phil* incident the nature of a person's response to these statues functioned quite explicitly as a marker of their class and/or politics, especially since the responses had an overtly political tenor. Anger at the statues flowed into despair or rage at a whole range of contemporary issues: multiculturalism, political correctness, freedom of speech, Australia's relations with Asia, and republicanism. Those more likely to be offended were older people, the politically conservative, and monarchists. Republicans, younger people and the left-leaning were more likely to see the statues as humorous and/or to be highly critical of the monarchy itself. From what one can tell, ethnicity was not an unequivocal predictor of response; people of both Anglo and non-Anglo heritage were horrified, like the Lithuanian man who claimed that "[e]ven the Communists after overrunning [his] country of birth, Lithuania, hesitated in resorting to such vulgarity" (Kramilius 1995). Most judged the Royal Family as human beings with a right to dignity, and most implicated Prime Minister Paul Keating in the offence.

This then was another slippage – one concerning not the statue itself, but its symbolic maker. Who was the author of this atrocity? The statue's location in Canberra enabled it to be read as representing an official Australian view, as did its precise location, aligned with Old Parliament House and placed "only metres" from the High Court and opposite the War Memorial (Contractor 1995). Although Keating had nothing to do with its commissioning, the statue was read as an emblem of Keatingism, in part because it was Keating who had pushed the republican movement, hitherto a relatively quiet force in Australian politics, into the political spotlight. One letter writer was particularly savage on this score:

> No doubt our Prime Minister, who has sworn an oath of allegiance to our Queen, is having a sordid little snigger to himself about the attack on her dignity by the pathetic bits of baked clay (not to be dignified by the noble name of sculpture) on the shore of the Canberra lake. (Ewin 1995)

There is something about nudity that in the right contexts can stir up the most fundamental questions – of identity, home, naturalness and even humanness itself. The public understood *Liz and Phil* as a sign of the times, an emblem of everything that was wrong with a too-rapidly postmodernizing Australia. The ferocity of the responses indicates just how deeply Australia was becoming divided by the time of the *Liz and Phil* incident, which occurred just three weeks after an unprecedented swing away from the Keating government in a Canberra by-election. The *Liz and Phil* incident, occurring in the same city, can likewise be read as a kind of revolt – confused and emotional perhaps, but emanating from similar discontents and yearnings.

The event provoked a series of opposing accusations: the vandals were an example of the ugly Aussie; the sculptor himself was an ugly Aussie; the sculpture was vandalized; the sculptor himself was a vandal. Art as vandalism? Clearly people felt that an image close to home, perhaps an image *of* home, was being destroyed. Australians for Constitutional Monarchy even spoke of a "threat to the stability of our country" (*Seccombe* 1995: 36). The naked figures came to symbolize the social body under attack. They came to symbolize for many people an idea of Australia (home, normalcy, stability) that was being threatened and that needed urgently to be repaired. The naked body, that metaphor for the lack of metaphor, that symbol of the unadorned natural state, can be a particularly intense carrier of such fundamental meanings. The strength of feeling that these statues sparked makes it clear that deeply personal fears and longings were triggered for some people. The image of McQuillan rushing towards his sovereign lady with a tube of glue and spraying it on all and sundry seems an almost achingly appropriate symbol (especially in Melanie Klein's terms). It powerfully suggests a yearning for the whole body and its social correlate, the unified, centred society, a desire for both a personal and a national identity that feels whole and unified.

We see here again, then, how nakedness can function as an emblem of loss and destitution, in this case, doubly. The sculptor, participating enthusiastically in a long satirical tradition in which nakedness symbolizes the powerful losing their privilege, could scarcely have been aware how that same nakedness could make a varied constituency of "ordinary Australians" fear and lament the loss of their own known world and make them feel, at least for a while, vulnerable, unprotected and unsheltered.

Nakedness, though, is not always about loss and destitution, and I turn now to an entirely different mode of representing leaders naked.

Heroic Nudity

Eroticism and Heroism

Classical Athenian art is full of homages to both male and female beauty. Physical perfection symbolized moral and ethical virtues; ethics and aesthetics went hand in hand:

[T]o a Greek of the 5th century [the naked male body] stood for a set of values of which restraint, balance, modesty, proportion and many others would be applied equally in the ethical and the aesthetic sphere. (Clark 1956: 36)

Even though the body in art could carry such exalted meanings, in Platonic thought it still had to take its place in a hierarchy of mind, body and spirit.[9] Classical Greece left the West a complex philosophical legacy with regard to the body.

The West has inherited the memory of the Greek association of naked male athleticism with virtue, beauty and heroic manliness. Athletic nudity for males probably began in Greece in the late eighth century BC, though both Thucydides and Plato record that the practice began only shortly before their time (McDonnell 1991: 182–3).[10] Whatever the case, the Greeks came to understand the practice as a "civilized" one. Herodotus, for example, recounts that among "most barbarian races," being seen naked causes great shame, "even for a man" (Bk 1, sec. 10: 17). In Book Five of Plato's *Republic*, in the section on the status of women, Socrates argues that women should be trained like men, and hence should exercise naked in the gymnasium. He acknowledges that this will at first be a source of humour, but experience will prove what reason knows: "that it [is] better to strip than wrap [oneself] up" (Plato 1955: 205):

> We will ask the critics to be serious for once, and remind them that it was not so long ago that the Greeks thought – as most of the barbarians still think – that it was shocking and ridiculous for men to be seen naked. When the Cretans, and later the Spartans, first began to take exercise naked, wasn't there plenty of material for the wit of the comedians of the day? (Plato 1955: 205)

While the Romans were more circumspect than the Greeks about nudity, and disapproved of the custom of nude athleticism, the association between nudity and virtue or heroism did pass into some representational practice in Rome. The elite would commemorate themselves in statuary that was naked or draped according to quite precise codes (Christ 1997). Such nudity was emblematic of both civic status (i.e. full citizenry) and the personal virtue believed to accompany it,[11] unlike the nudity of slaves or the dispossessed, which signalled exactly the contrary.

The Greek ideal informed the early Christian tradition, in the form of an association between male nakedness and both physical and spiritual strength: "Male nakedness represented spiritual discipline and physical control and order – the body as perfect vehicle and expression of the difficult and committed work of the creation and cultivation of religious subjectivity" (Miles 1989: 143). Of course, Christian thought also inherited some of the Platonic suspicion of the body, but Christian artists of the Renaissance nonetheless made use of the iconographical traditions of Classical Greece when representing the naked body of Christ and the saints. But Christ's nudity also involves feminization and vulnerability, especially in contrast to the idealized nudity of Greek and Roman heroes. Christ's nakedness may be heroic, but the nature of his heroism is very different from that of the naked male warriors of Greek art. As we saw in Chapter 1, in Renaissance art Christ's nakedness served as a vehicle for depicting his "humanity, vulnerability and strength in weakness" (Miles 1989: 143, drawing on Steinberg 1996). It was a complex piece of iconography, in which "strength and weakness, triumph and vulnerability [were] resolved" (Miles 1989: 143).

Other male figures partook of this ambiguity. Angela Carter stresses the importance of depictions of the naked male body in pain, noting the abundance and significance of crucifixions, pietas, saints in anguish, "martyrdoms, executions, dissections" (Carter 1982: 105). While some may argue that such depictions feminize the male body, Carter sees this tradition of suffering as the often unthought-of underside of the heroic nude, one that made of "the formalised body of the 'perfect' man'" a "superior icon of sado-masochism" (p. 104). Religious art thus constituted one exception to the more general cultural rule that male heroic nudity "inspired no anxiety comparable to that of female nakedness" (Warner 1985: 313).

But heroic nudity has not always been restricted to men, and traditions exist of exalted and even heroic female nudity. The allegorical mode in particular has allowed for this. Many of the virtues – Justice, Charity, Liberty – have been allegorized as naked or lightly draped women. Marina Warner (1985: 285) records that after the seventeenth century "it becomes almost routine [in France] for noblewomen to be depicted as aspects of Charity by baring their breast," though of course the allegory could be a thinly veiled erotic pretext. In France especially, representations of bare-breasted women were used to represent Friendship. A famous example is the eighteenth-century sculptor Pigalle's bust of Madame de Pompadour, which exposes her right breast (Warner 1985: 285). Apparently, daring nineteenth-century aristocrats also sometimes themselves appeared undraped at public events, their nudity supposedly transfigured by the power of allegory (p. 285). This last example reminds us that various devices – historicity, allegory, religious sentiment and so on – can function as pretexts, and that the heroic meanings of nudity can often commingle with some of its other meanings, especially, though not only, erotic ones.

In religious art, a figure like the Virgin Mary tempers the "dangerousness" of the erotic. She is traditionally depicted suckling the infant Christ and her bare breast is a sanctified and exalted form of female exposure. Warner argues that Mary "transforms the erotic dangerousness of the breast in Christian imagery to a symbol of comfort, of candour, of good" (p. 284).

Even in a secular context, women's nakedness could be idealized. It could not often be as straightforwardly heroic as youthful male beauty, but it could still be understood as a powerful tool. One classical tale of female perfection – the story of the trial of the courtesan Phryne – circulated so widely that it became a rhetorical topos. Phryne was a female model used by the sculptor Praxiteles. A nude statue of her was erected in her honour at Delphi, and she shared the credit with Praxiteles for his statues (Clark 1956: 74). She was put on trial for impiety, and defended by the orator Hyperides. Hyperides, prone to dramatic courtroom displays, dolefully bewailed his client's fate, then disrobed her before the jury, thus ensuring her acquittal. In Athenaeus' account, Hyperides accompanies the disrobing tactic with a "piteous lamentation," which caused the jury to feel not only compassion but also "superstitious fear of this handmaid and ministrant of Aphrodite" (quoted in C. Cooper 1995: 304). Afterwards, though, a decree was passed that no trial lawyer should ever again "indulge in lamentation, nor should the accused man or woman on trial be bared for all to see" (quoted in C. Cooper 1995: 305). The tale of Phryne's disrobing is probably an invention, or at least an embellishment, but it circulated as a parable about the powers of female physical perfection.[12]

Since nudity can signify so many things – eroticism, ideal beauty, vulnerability, destitution – even heroic nudity can often be quite ambiguous or precarious. But the erotic need not cancel out heroic possibilities, even though it may complicate them. Indeed, for women, it can often be the very condition of possibility *of* heroism. Lady Godiva is a case in point. On the one hand, she is a secular example of the ascetic tradition in which chastity is figured as a form of heroism (as with Joan of Arc and the Virgin Mary). But Godiva's heroic nudity is complex. Her hair-clothing reminds us of woman's "natural" modesty and vulnerability, a condition that is confirmed rather than ruptured by her exposure. And yet, the erotic meanings of nudity can also be understood as the *source* of Godiva's heroism, since her heroism resides precisely in the courageous act of exposing her vulnerable female body to prurient interest. The shuttering of the town's windows metaphorically symbolizes the act of exclusion needed to defend Godiva from both her own erotic nature and the unwanted attentions of others, while the presence of the Peeping Tom figure reminds us of the impossibility of this banishment. He may be blinded as punishment for his impudence but this symbolic punishment speaks less of the unequivocal triumph of the heroic meanings of female nudity than of their "inevitable" fettering to a sexuality conceived of as vulnerable.

The varying interpretations of the Godiva legend are made possible by both the ambiguity of nakedness as a metaphor and by the different versions of the story that have prevailed historically. Daniel Donoghue (2002) reports that in thirteenth-century versions, Godiva *tricked* her husband into lifting the taxes; her ride was a triumph of her volition and her cleverness. Two centuries later, it is Godiva's husband who is coercing Lady Godiva into the ride. Later still, the Victorians read the story as that of a sacrificial woman, who did her duty then returned to the domestic sphere. Clearly, the tale has acted as a mirror to other values.

There is, though, an unequivocally wilder kind of female nakedness. Anne Hollander (1993: 205–6) gives examples in European fine art of breasts that look threatening, almost weapon-like, as does Marilyn Yalom (1997).[13] Nineteenth-century Romanticism added violence and eroticism to the other sanctified meanings of the single breast (Hollander 1993: 199). Two famous examples are the allegorical figures of Liberty and Marianne, icons of the French Revolution who hark back to the virgin goddesses (e.g. Artemis) and warrior Amazons of classical mythology. Delacroix's famous allegorical painting of *Liberty Leading the People* (1831) is in the Romantic tradition of exposure, and shows bare-footed, bare-breasted Liberty fearlessly storming the barricades, trampling over the fallen heroes of the July 1830 revolution. As Anne Hollander points out, Liberty's dress is deliberately cut to expose one breast. The breast has not accidentally fallen out, and thus it signifies not vulnerability but power; her exposure is "at once holy, desirable, and fierce" (p. 202). Marina Warner (1985) reads Liberty's bared breast as a kind of visual pun, as capable as any male "bosom" of signifying the seat of heart and courage. Wild or heroic meanings of the breast can thus sit alongside the breast's other meaning as fount of charity and nurturance. But of course, the breast both is and isn't the chest, and while the conventionally recognized erotic connotations of women's nakedness do not necessarily work against heroic meanings, there are many occasions where they certainly complicate them, both producing and tempering female heroism.

Appropriately, Liberty signifies an unfettered heroism that Godiva, parading before shuttered windows and a hidden voyeur, cannot achieve. Not that Liberty's heroism has nothing to do with eroticism. On the contrary, Warner's argument is, in fact, that erotic meanings are indeed the *condition of possibility* of female heroic meanings:

> As eroticism is a condition of the depicted female body, a semi-naked figure, who is no longer constrained by it, becomes free. The slipped chiton is a most frequent sign that we are being pressed to accept an ulterior significance, not being introduced to the body as person. (Warner 1985: 277)

In other words, it is precisely because the female body unavoidably signifies eroticism that nakedness (or semi-nakedness) can signify transcendence and freedom. The meanings of nakedness, though, are never stable or fixed. Liberty, for example, did not remain a figure of lawlessness. Even by the 1870s, when France was sending the gift of the Statue of Liberty to the US, the wildness had already been taken out of her; her revolutionary Phrygian cap has disappeared, she is fully dressed, "static and matronly," and her hair is tidy (Warner 1985: 277).

In modern times, the maternal meanings of the bared breast are not always sufficient to carry even the discreet "exposure" of a breast in public space. The acceptability of public breastfeeding continues to be quite precarious. During the writing of this book, there were numerous incidents in which Australian women were ejected from cafés and even a cinema for breastfeeding. In 1999, one member of the Queensland Young Liberals (a junior adjunct to the Liberal political party) even prepared a motion for the state convention proposing on-the-spot fines for women caught breastfeeding in public areas other than designated parenting rooms (Bartlett 2002: 116)! Equally strange was the story that circulated about the role of breastfeeding in a scandal that engulfed the British prime minister, Tony Blair, and his wife Cherie in late 2002. Mrs Blair's financial dealings with an alleged Australian conman were trumpeted to devastating effect, especially in the UK's *Daily Mail*. Why? The story (front-page news at a time when Britain was on the brink of war with Iraq) went that the *Daily Mail* editor had been "appalled and incensed" when the prime minister's wife had breastfed her new son Leo in front of him at a dinner party (Leigh et al. 2002: 2). True or not, this story of the "scandal" of a prominent woman breastfeeding threatening the stability of her husband's government is both alarming and telling – bizarre, yet all too familiar.

A few months later, scandal erupted when a young Australian Member of Parliament (MP) was (genteelly) shepherded from the parliamentary chamber after she began breastfeeding her 10-day old baby. The justification used was the so-called "no strangers in the house" rules, whereby non-members are not allowed in Parliament House during Question Time (to prevent strangers from voting on parliamentary business). But why was she ejected only when she began breastfeeding and not as soon as her baby was brought in? Perhaps, as a colleague of mine astutely pointed out, it was not so much the baby as the breast that was the stranger in the house.[14]

Heroic Nudity in Modern Times

In the contemporary West, the possibilities for heroic or exalted nudity are rather limited, except, perhaps, in fine art. Still, the Classical legacy has some resonance. Nudism, for example, has traditionally made a partial and strategic uptake of ideas about classicism in order to justify and dignify itself. The following comment in 1958 from a female proponent of nudism makes it clear that Roman nudity was often seen as an inferior descendant of the "pure" Greek ideal, which was often (incorrectly) understood as asexual:

> The same nudity of the Golden Age of Greece . . . was debased in Imperial Rome into the exhibitionism of drunken and sex-mad men and women at Imperial . . . revels. A horde of naked girls rowed Nero's gilded raft on an artificial lake, to become the prey of drunken nobles. Bevies of "nymphs" and groups of "satyrs" disported shamelessly at garden fetes, and it is best to draw a veil over the antics of Tiberius on the Island of Capri. (quoted in Clarke: 1982: 232)

Nudism initially relied on the Greek "model" quite strenuously, but this association became less habitual as the years went by. It persists only in remnant form (in club names or in the statues that often adorn the gardens of nudist resorts).

The heroic meaning of nudity did survive into the early twentieth century as a viable iconographic possibility, but only precariously, as is illustrated by the case of the sculptures planned as part of the Anzac Memorial, a war memorial in Hyde Park, Sydney, which opened in 1934. They were designed by G. Rayner Hoff, an English sculptor who emigrated to Australia in the early 1920s. Hoff intended to downplay the glory of war and to represent women's as well as men's participation and suffering, both abroad and at home. Three of the proposed sculptures, however, caused an outcry, and two of them were never installed. The first, *Sacrifice*, is a bronze that can be viewed from below and above. It depicts three women bearing aloft a shield on which lies the naked body of a male soldier, face-up, arms outstretched on a sword, head back. The man's penis is quite visible from above (the only example of this in an Australian war memorial). From above, the naked body stretched out on shield and sword resembles the crucified Christ. The three women bearing him aloft represent a mother, a sister, and a young widow with a baby, and the latter is topless. Two other group statues were cast in plaster, but were prevented by public controversy from being completed and installed. *The Crucifixion of Civilization* allegorized civilization as a naked young woman crucified on a cross. She stands on a pile of dead soldiers. The Catholic community of Sydney was outraged at this blasphemy and at the fact that "a nude woman should be selected as the symbol of civilization" (quoted in Jeans 1981: 57). The third controversial design, *Victory after Sacrifice*, depicted a young nude woman, representing Australia, again in quasi-crucificial pose, placed in front of a helmet representing Britannia. There was certainly much to offend in these statues – the depiction of suffering rather than glory, the suggestion of something sacrificial in Australia's relation to Britain, the possibility that a woman could represent either the nation or civilization itself, the perceived blasphemy of the crucifixion references – and, of course, the incendiary effect of nudity. Hoff's remonstrances, that there were nude statues in the Vatican and that he wanted to depict women's role in war, were supported by some, but two of the three groups were abandoned, allegedly because of lack of funds to cast them in bronze. It says a lot about the different meanings of male and female nudity that the male statue was the only of the three nudes to be acceptable, but it is also the case that by the 1930s, the inclusion of a realistic penis on a prone figure was stretching the capacity of nakedness to bear heroic allegorical meanings.[15]

By now, of course, heroic nudity has become largely inconceivable as a vehicle for expressing either abstract ideals or the virtues of particular leaders. It is impossible to imagine contemporary prime ministers choosing to have themselves represented in what Anne Hollander (1993: 65–6) describes as the "Statesman Emerging from the Bath" genre, as did both Napoleon and George Washington. As with all social changes, the possibilities for heroic, statesman-like nudity must have faded out unevenly. Winston Churchill, for example, had no qualms about walking about naked when Franklin D. Roosevelt visited his bedroom (pointing out that the prime minister of Britain had nothing to hide from the president of the US) (MacDonald 1973: 3–4); and yet, as we have seen, the British prime minister W.E. Gladstone had earlier revised history to conclude that it was impossible that Homer's heroes could have been nude (Langdon-Davies 1928: 70–1).

Is there a version of heroic nudity in contemporary consumer culture? After all, consumer culture is permeated by its own brand of heroism, in the form of the routine use in advertising of the grandiose, the majestic and the enormous. Moreover, pop culture requires the ceaseless creation and celebration of heroes. Although sexuality may well be a key ingredient of their allure and power, actual nakedness is rarely a component of popular heroism. This may well change as time goes by. For the moment, though, the puritanical heritage of modern consumer cultures means that the most ready use of nakedness is in a banal equation between nakedness and sex, the latter constructed as titillating, naughty or subversive. For that reason, it is very rare for nakedness to signify heroism in pop culture (though some exceptions will be described later). Moreover, as we have seen, consumer cultures structurally require the human body to be in lack; for only then can it be in need of a commodity-supplement. Thus, they are less interested in picking up the Greek tradition of the unadorned (i.e. uncommodified) body as complete and ideal unless the heroic qualities can be transferred onto the commodity in question. Even so, one does find attempts to revive or utilize heroic nudity – sometimes parodically. But since the meaning of public nudity is so circumscribed in consumer culture, such attempts are often prone to misinterpretation by an offended portion of the public.

Figure 4.6 Garry Shead. *Bare Queen*, 1995. 66 × 51 cm. Oil on board.

The following are two attempts to use the tradition of the exalted female breast. The first example, from Australian painter Garry Shead's "Royal Suite" series, involves a deliberate play on the ambiguity of images of female top-lessness. These paintings depict the Queen and other royal figures in Australian settings, especially outback ones. The paintings are both reverent and satirical, a gently absurdist fantasia inspired by the Queen's 1954 visit to Australia, which made a strong impression on the young Shead. In many of these paintings, the Queen appears naked or semi-naked. Her naked body still carries some heroic associations, a residual association with divinity and virtue.

Bare Queen (1995), for example, draws semi-ironically on the tradition of the slipped chiton,[16] which helps accord the Queen a form of majesty, while also making her quaintly ridiculous (Figure 4.6). Although the Queen appears fully naked in a number of these paintings, it is mostly a single breast that is exposed or accentuated by the composition. For those familiar with the tradition of the single bared breast as an emblem of sanctity, self-sacrifice and devotion (Hollander 1993: 199), Shead's paintings clearly situate the Queen in the tradition of both the Madonna and the Amazons, as well, ironically, as putting her in the company of the republican figures of Marianne and Liberty. She is a very static and self-contained Amazon, though, her bare breast signifying nothing of the violence, distress, disarray and "complex passion" (Hollander 1993: 199) characteristic of the exposed breasts of nineteenth-century Romantic painting. Rather, the heroic, indeed divine, associations of nudity are brought into play in a deliberately naïve and nostalgic way in order to capture a young boy's (and an era's) naïve faith in the "white goddess" from afar (Grishin 1998: 14). Surrounded by the icons of majesty and garbed in her nakedness, the Queen is remembered as "a celestial apparition" (Grishin 1998: 27), who is nonetheless absurd, out of place, anachronistic. In these paintings, nakedness is thus richly ambiguous, suggesting the Queen's virtue, devotion and godliness as well as her ordinariness and distance from the Australian world around her. These opposites are subtly and gently combined. As Sasha Grishin (1998: 27) puts it, these paintings are not "the cruel mockery of a republican, but the confessions of a gullible, adoring subject." Nonetheless, the bright pink sticker on the cover of Shead's collection *Encounters with Royalty* ("Warning! This book may offend monarchists") makes it clear that the profound ambiguity of nakedness, along with the decline in modern Australia of the convention of heroic nudity, will leave the paintings open to variable interpretations, which indeed was the case when they were exhibited in Sydney in 1995.

Occasionally, some brave woman attempts to appropriate heroic meanings of nakedness. In 1997, the actor Rachel Griffiths protested topless outside Melbourne's Crown Casino on the night of its gala opening. "I was dressed as Christ," she said. On the night in question, Griffiths stepped out of a stretch limousine wearing only a loincloth and a crown of thorns. Her torso was painted white and covered by a banner reading "Need not greed," which she dropped to reveal her bare breasts, while a friend's daughter threw coins upon the ground. According to Margaret Miles (1989: xii), the idea of nudity as a symbolic imitation of Christ was popularized by St Bernard of Clairvaux in the thirteenth century. The complexities of Christ's nakedness become even more pronounced when female Christians strove to emulate Christ. For while the body could serve for female Christian martyrs in late Rome as "the site and symbol of resistance to a society they saw as wicked and lawless" (Miles 1989: 57), the naked female body was *itself* also prone to meanings of wickedness and lawlessness: "In Western Christian representations of women, the unambiguously good woman is a clothed woman, a fully socialized woman" (p. 144). Miles argues that in many accounts of naked female martyrdom, there is a tension between respect for them, interest in their bodies, and the concern to establish the inferiority of their sex. She reads this tension as emblematic of "male confusion and conflict over heroic Christian women" (p. 57).

But such ambiguity can also give female nakedness strategic value, especially in modern media cultures.[17] When Griffiths was asked by a journalist whether she had had to appear topless in order to protest against a society bent increasingly on economic values, she replied: "Absolutely . . . [F]lash your tits and get on television" (Button 1997). In choosing to use her (semi)naked body as a site of protest, Griffiths was entering a difficult terrain for women: striving to draw on centuries-old religious connotations of the naked body (in its "neutral" or masculine guise as purity, innocence, strength) while both utilizing for strategic purposes and striving to keep at bay its secular connotations (the female body as object of male desire). No wonder she was "very scared of making a fool of [her]self" (Anon. 1997a).

The crowd's reaction outside the casino (it cheered) is also ambiguous. Was this a cheer for Griffiths' political values or a cheer of the "show us your tits" variety? Crowd reactions to early female martyrs varied but certainly did include "voyeuristic glee" (Miles 1989: 57). In the case of the contemporary protesting woman, it is hard to make one's body the emblem of heroic resistance since the naked female body is, structurally and inevitably, always already overdetermined by its ancient historical function as spectacle. It is harder for the naked female body to represent purely spiritual qualities (see Barcan 2002a).

So, while nakedness can still be made to function heroically in the modern world, it must work particularly hard to repel its other, secular or satirical, associations and it is still likely to work more troublesomely for women than for men. But old traditions often persist in some form or another in new contexts and in that light it is interesting to observe one context in which heroic nudity appears to be unironically emerging, at least in contemporary Australia: that of sport. If heroic nudity is to re-emerge at all, it should not surprise us that it be in this domain, since in sport we are very aware of the symbolic content of bodily performance, and we take for granted the metonymic operation whereby individual struggle and achievement can be made to stand in for an imagined national heroism. Sport is also one of the few Australian contexts in which an ideal of heroism does not have to be tempered by traditional Australian scepticism or anti-authoritarianism. It is, for example, possibly the only context in Australian discourse in which the word "elite" is not derogatory, and is, indeed, a highly prized adjective. Sport, seemingly untainted by that most anti-Australian offence – intellectualism – has come to be one of the few domains in which nudity can retain (or regain) its heroic aura and meaning. Since the early 1990s, the cult of celebrity and the Australian obsession with sport, especially sports played by males, have begun to overlap, and the imagery of the ancient Greek gymnasium has come to have at least a minor currency in popular representations of sportspeople, a currency aided, of course, by Sydney's hosting of the Olympic Games in 2000.

The acceptability of nakedness in this context is both recent and limited. The heroic nude is an old genre making a comeback, and has to fight off not only satirical meanings but also nudity's associations with femininity, narcissism and (homo)eroticism, as well as the laconic Australian tendency to knock what it perceives as pretension. The heroic (near) nudity of sportspeople is most popularly acceptable when it is associated less with ("feminine") spectacle than ("masculine") action, when it is aestheticized away from the realms of the everyday and into the hallowed domain of "art," or when it is yoked to popular nationalism.

Modern Olympians

The most deliberate and comprehensive attempt that I have seen to unironically revive heroic nakedness was a 1996 special edition of the glossy magazine *black+white*, a much advertised and discussed collection of images of Australia's Atlanta Olympians naked, advertised as "the publishing event of the year." This beautiful 200-page volume was very popular, running into a second edition.

The issue began with an exultant epigraph from Milton's *Paradise Lost*: "Sage he stood. With Atlantean shoulders fit to bear the weight of mightiest monarchies." Readers were thus quite explicitly guided into interpreting the naked Olympians within the tradition of heroic nudity and the epic genre. The routinely voyeuristic and objectifying functions of popular magazine photography were explicitly countermanded by the issue's subtitle, "A Photographic Tribute," which functioned as an implicit instruction on the correct way to understand the collection. The photos made use of all the classic idealizing devices – the eschewing of contemporaneity, the absence of backdrop, the inclusion of classical props (laurel wreaths, swords, ropes, drapery, columns and plinths) – to imitate the "perfect" bodies of the Greek gymnasium (Figure 4.7). Cyclist Tracey Watson was depicted as a semi-naked Joan of Arc, with full heroic iconography. The overarching idealizing frame was, of course, the

Figure 4.7 Photograph of champion triple-jumper Andrew Murphy, as an example of the neo-classical style. *The Atlanta Dream* (1996), a special issue of *black+white*, 2nd edn. Sydney: Studio Magazines, p. 143. Photograph by James Houston.

Olympics themselves, figured as a quest for personal and national glory. Nakedness was thus sanctified by the appeal to history, a tactic as old as history itself:

> The ancient Olympics . . . came to celebrate physical excellence and sportsmanship while recognising that sport had a crucial part to play in promoting a moral and ethical education . . . The ancient Olympics were also a celebration of the inherent aesthetic beauty of the human form . . . Athletes initially competed wearing

loincloths, but according to legend, one day a youth lost his during competition. Unashamed, he carried on, beating all his rivals, and from then on all participants competed naked. (Anon. 1996: 7)

Since the 1980s, competitive sport has become a major metaphor and metonym for the transnational corporation itself, and this collection drew a link between the supposed values of the magazine and those of Ancient Greece. The introduction claims that the spur to producing this collection was "the recognition that *black+white* shares Olympian ideals," that *black+white* is also committed to celebrating "the beauty of the human body and the quest for both physical and aesthetic perfection." The athletes, it is said, were happy to accept the invitation because they realized that the magazine's "commitment to aesthetics paralleled the ideals of the Games" (p. 9).

Elite athletes are highly aware of the need to protect their star image. Although it may be true that most of the athletes "were quick to accept the invitation to be photographed while in peak condition by Australia's best photographers" (p. 9), it is also evident that, given the usual meanings of nakedness in consumerism, the collection would need to work hard to persuade not just the audience but also the athletes themselves that their nudity would be heroic rather than "cheap." The accompanying text is important in this regard. The athletes' initial reluctance becomes part of the story itself, and their ambivalence has a pedagogical function – to guide the reading public into an awareness of the newly reviving genre of the naked heroic. By themselves articulating the potential ambiguity of naked imagery, the athletes limit the scope for "improper" readings, even while some of the close-up images of wet-haired, sultry-eyed, oiled-up stars borrow from visual repertoires other than the heroic:

> I'd always said I wouldn't be photographed nude, because I'd been approached by *Playboy* in the past and turned it down flat. But my reaction to the idea of this shoot was to immediately say yes because I realised the emphasis would be entirely different. (Basketballer Trish Fallon, Anon. 1996: 40)

> When I was asked to pose my initial reaction was, "Why?" I don't have what you'd normally consider an athlete's body, just a normal, well-toned one. But then I realised I'd never be offered an opportunity like this again and how great it would be when I'm 70 to have these photos of me at my physical peak. (Yachtswoman Jeni Lidgett, Anon. 1996: 193)

Attempts to revive a heroic athletic nakedness are gradually increasing, often using humour to cushion the impact. Given the strong sexualization of nudity in the media, the most likely effect of such attempts is less a wholesale re-emergence of heroic nudity so much as the rise of celebrity nudity, with "sporting nudity" a minor subgenre. Two more instances should suffice to indicate the current hybridization of nude genres and the struggles over the meanings and tactical value of heroic, athletic female nudity.

The first was in December 1999, when the Australian women's soccer team, known as the Matildas, dismayed by the ongoing lack of publicity, funding and sponsorship for women's soccer, launched a nude calendar aimed at generating both funds and publicity. It was not the first such calendar in Australia, but it was large in scale and launched to great media éclat. The print run increased ninefold after one day's media coverage.

The Matildas' nudity was widely construed as heroic – courageous, assertive and bold. Their decision not to hide their genitals or pubic hair coyly behind the usual props was widely supported, with one of the players laughing sarcastically at the latest edition of a popular women's magazine in which twenty-three naked male athletes had posed with a variety of such modesty props, presumably for censorship reasons. Nonetheless, female nudity was inevitably the occasion for sniggering voyeurism: "Every media jock in town who didn't have to be somewhere else was there with pen and lens posed for the 11am kick-off. It wasn't so much a launch as an invasion" (Evans 1999). But the discourses of pride and courage overwhelmingly won the day:

> Flanked by blow-ups of their own nudity and confronted by more cameras than have ever been focused on them in their sporting careers, the Matildas did not dissolve into blushing models but stood tall and proud to face the enemy accused of ignoring their skill and sporting success in the past. (Evans 1999)

The Australian veneration of sport clearly has much to do with this possibility. Although the team's heroism was constructed in opposition to more conventional modes of female bodily display (they "did not dissolve into blushing models"), much of the praise and defence of them did seem to mention the fact that their bodies were athletic, taut, healthy, trim and firm – as though this somehow lessened the photos' potential to be sleazy or immoral:

> Sydney forward Katrina Boyd . . . said she had enjoyed pushing the boundaries . . . "The photos show we are great athletes with great bodies. I think it's art. If people want to call it porn, that's their problem. No-one could make me feel low or sleazy about this. I feel strong and confident with what I have done with my body." . . . Sandra Bartlett, mother of Matilda defender Traci, said: "The first time I saw it I thought, 'Shock, horror!' But posing nude, it's art; they are all so trim and firm . . . good on them." (Evans 1999)

Both these speakers seek to defend nudity via the aesthetic and athletic properties of the bodies depicted.

One male commentator, though, was more cynical:

> The fact that a squillion men in suits were suddenly interested in women's soccer shouldn't necessarily be seen as a great, saucy leap forward for the sport . . . Will it have the bonus of squeezing more people through the turnstiles at Matildas' games or put women's soccer on newspaper back pages? Maybe not. Women's soccer and nude women's soccer players are probably two very different stories. (Squires 1999)

The second example, also from 1999, occurred when the Ohio State University women's rugby team hit the headlines when about half their members briefly took off their shirts and posed for a photo at the Lincoln Memorial in Washington. A reporter and photographer from the *Washington Post* were passing by at the time, and the story became a scandal, attracting media attention as well as discussion on nudist Internet lists. Although according to park police the women had broken no laws, the university suspended the team for having attracted bad publicity. As many nudist commentators pointed out, the Pagan ritual at the Memorial (the reason the photographer was there in the first place) attracted little or no publicity. Some nudists on the alt.nudism.moderated Internet list condemned the hypocrisy of some of the Ohio State University executives, who censured the women but who nonetheless were allegedly board members of Victoria's Secret, an Ohio-based chain of lingerie and clothing stores whose marketing relies on scantily clad models. Debate was divided as to whether the women were advocates of freedom or simply engaged in an adolescent prank, and therefore whether the incident was worthy of nudist discussion. One contributor considered that, either way, the women were heroic – "accidental heroes" caught up in the ongoing fight for a freer and more just society (Fake Name website). In one little corner of public opinion, their nudity achieved heroic status.

From Phyrne to Godiva to the Matildas, women's heroic nudity has never been able to be disentangled from erotic meanings of nudity. And while the erotic was an important component of Greek male heroic beauty, it has always worked a little more equivocally for women.

Celebrity Nudity

> In a world where everyone seems to be going public, it's inevitable we're obsessed with what's left of the private.
>
> Catharine Lumby, "The Naked Truth"

Fame is one of the obsessions of contemporary consumer cultures. The structural linchpin of any celebrity system is, though, the "ordinary" person, since fame exists in dialectic relation with an idea of "ordinariness." There are contexts in which ordinariness can be, paradoxically, a sought-after subject position. "Ordinariness" is a powerful regulatory fiction, a bid for the unmarked term, a claim about normality or reality. And since the naked body can sometimes signify naturalness or normality, images of naked bodies have a particularly interesting role to play in the construction of ordinariness.

The public's interest in illicit photographs of famous people is not new. What is new, according to David Marshall (1997), is the intensity of that desire and the efficacy of new technologies in procuring and reproducing such images. There are two faces of celebrity nudity – the willing and the unwilling. In this opposition between the voluntary revelation and stolen or fabricated images, we again see nudity in its positive and negative guises. The meaning of celebrity nudity depends very much on whether or not it is freely chosen.

The Good Career Move: Celebrity Nudity in its Positive Guise

"Suddenly, nudity is a good career move," writes Terry Smyth (1996); indeed, it does seem that over recent years, artful nakedness has become almost *de rigueur* for film stars, models and elite sportsmen and women. The star's body is their prime commodity, and their nakedness becomes an asset to be managed with care. This is especially tricky for women, who have to take their chances with the perennial possibility of moral disapproval.

Female celebrity nudity increasingly puts a glamorized spin on a familiar phenomenon – the revelation of women's nakedness for commercial reasons. In a postfeminist twist, female celebrity nudity has come to be seen by some as a sign of liberation. What was once imagined as the exploitation of women can now be repackaged as a victory for feminism, with economic freedom seen to coincide with both sexual liberation and freedom of choice. Indeed, there are circumstances in which female nudity can be a form of economic power; celebrity nudity in particular, can be extremely well paid. But of course, it still positions women's power as emanating from their beautiful bodies and it is in any case subject to social privilege – applied less unreservedly to the youthful, the beautiful and the famous.

The beautiful body is an asset in a commodity culture, and for those of the right race and class there is potentially a deal of both chic and cash attached to a savvy use of one's most intimate asset.[18] But the idea of treating one's nakedness as an asset can easily still bear the trace of the bourgeois mother's injunction to her daughter that her virginity is her greatest asset – once lost, lost forever. In other words, where female nudity is concerned, there exists an all too familiar residue of moral disapproval. This emerges most strongly when the subjects are working class and/or using their naked body as an asset either in waged labour (stripping, topless waitressing, nude modelling) or in culturally denigrated forms of image like porn.

The nakedness of ordinary people has less cachet and often less economic value than that of the rich or famous. An acceptable asset of the famous or the rich, it is less acceptable as a means of *becoming* famous or rich. Those who display their naked bodies for cash in an everyday context are less likely to be accorded widespread acceptance or admiration. In 1995, the magazine *New Woman* interviewed two women who worked as topless waitresses at restaurants and clubs catering for businessmen's lunches. The interviewees saw the economic benefits as the major advantage (along with meeting famous people like politicians and businessmen), answering unequivocally that it was money that prompted them to enter the field. Both were keen to differentiate their work from the sex industry, and each stated that they were just doing "what thousands of women are doing on the beach," only carrying plates. For "ordinary women," nudity commodified as waged labour carries little cachet, plus the risk of moral disapproval. In the case of female nudity, even economic self-interest, so often championed in hegemonic discourses, is morally tainted (in contrast, for example, to the nakedness of those celebrities (usually men) who strip for charity fund-raisers). This is partly because the celebrity is a privileged category of person; it is also partly because the nudity of the waitresses is commodified as labour and not as fetishized images. For this reason, the exchange value of their nudity is not very high. Thus, the two topless waitresses must argue for their own banality either as familiarity ("we're just doing what thousands of other women do on the beach") or through the acceptable rationale of economic necessity ("we get paid much more than for waitressing"). They must therefore paradoxically disavow themselves as objects of prurient interest, even while accepting to be interviewed (anonymously) by a women's magazine. Clearly, economic and moral discourses still do battle. Even while liberal discourses congratulate women on ensuring their economic self-interest, congratulatory discourses are usually unevenly applied. It is more acceptable for the beautiful and the famous to treat their bodies as assets than for ordinary people (or children).

Moral disapproval and economic approval came together most interestingly in the defence used by a 16-year-old girl who posed naked for *Hustler*, her photos advertised on the cover with the invitation: "Meet Jessica. She's 16. She's a virgin and she is naked inside." This incident provoked a moral furore that prompted the Film Censorship Board chief to admit that he may have erred in judgement in permitting publication of the photos. If it is true that women find themselves in a tussle between moral and economic discourses which may accord a differing value to their nudity, then Jessica's defence is extremely interesting: "On the positive side, people should know I'm still a virgin and I made a good business contract to pose nude" (Abbott 1996). I find the word "and" fascinating. With a similar grammatical logic, Jessica conjoined the discourses of legality and pleasure, an unlikely combination if ever there were one: "There is no law against what I did and I did it for fun."

Most often, such contradictions find their supposed resolution in some notion of free choice, a discourse favoured by liberalism and consumerism alike. Consumerism, and its whole host of attendant ideologies like economic rationalism, postfeminism, new traditionalism and so on, often reduce the complex structural dilemmas of late modernity to a matter of individual "choice." As Elspeth Probyn (1990) points out, the discourse of choice is rehearsed persistently within consumer culture, where "choice" (understood as an individual matter) functions as an absolute value, an unquestionable good. Thus, in a harsh paradox, the nudity of those who can be perceived to have chosen it freely is less likely to be disdained than that of those who have less choice in the matter.

Stolen Pleasures: Celebrity Nudity in its Negative Guise

It used to be axiomatic that we, the ordinary public, didn't resent or even envy stars, since although they are an elite group they may in principle be joined by anyone (Francesco Alberoni, in Dyer 1979: 7). I'm not sure how true this axiom ever was (surely it was always more a question of a *tension between* envy, admiration and indifference), but regardless, popular admiration of stars can nowadays sometimes be precarious. The enormous interest in stars and stardom persists, as does the economic value of star images, but the fundamental dialectic of difference and similarity on which stardom reposes has become complicated by the technological changes that have made star images of the most intimate kind readily available, and also able to be fabricated. These changes have also allowed us, the ordinary people, to participate in the image-work that used to help separate star from schmuck. For this reason, as well as by dint of the sheer superabundance of stars, personalities, celebrities, heroes, legends and leaders, the public's response to stars and stardom can oscillate with remarkable rapidity from devotion to weariness and even ill will. While some commentators emphasize the forgiving nature of the general public (Kleinhans 2001), others see the spirit of *ressentiment* as coming to predominate (J. Marx 1997).

The stealing or fabrication of images of naked celebrities is motivated, obviously enough, by economic interest. It relies, though, on a fundamental curiosity that is intensified by the teasing logic of stardom, which constantly promises insights into stars' private worlds. Such insights serve, of course, ultimately not to quench our appetite but to fuel it. These robberies mobilize

nudity in the negative tradition, for the star experiences the robbery as deprivation, violation and humiliation.

Intense consumer interest in stolen star images reflects both a systemic logic
– the endless and impossible quest for authenticity that is a structural feature
of the working of the star system (see Dyer 1979) – and a psychological one
– the voyeuristic thrill of the forbidden and the stolen. The one intensifies the
other. The star's ontological ambiguity (stars are both images and "real people,"
familiar and otherworldly) allows the public to indulge in voyeuristic pleasures
in a way that is safer than with people of our acquaintance. The celebrity
industry allows us the pleasures of gossip without the moral responsibility that
is inevitably attached to the act of gossiping in one's immediate community.

Stolen and unauthorized images are interesting because they bring together
the aesthetics and meanings of celebrity nudity and a kind of amateur,
homemade nudity (which I will discuss in detail later). Stolen images repackage
for a broad market something that was produced for intimate use. Paparazzi
shots are another example of the intrusion of the public gaze into the home.
In both cases, the aesthetic produced (e.g. graininess, blurriness, indistin-
guishability of faces, long shots rather than close-ups, poor lighting, shadows,
unretouched faces) contrasts markedly with the glamour aesthetic in which
stars are more habitually represented, with its highly controlled, usually
retouched product. Graininess becomes a virtue, a sign of the authenticity and
the brazenness of the image. Moreover, since stars themselves appear in so
many different media, there is an inevitable blurring of images, meanings and
contexts, sometimes with legal consequences (e.g. Pamela Anderson's earlier
appearances on *Playboy* videos contribute in some way to the meaning of her
private stolen sex video). Genres blur. Thus, a five-hour TV special titled "The
100 Most Shocking Moments in Rock and Roll" could list the Anderson video
at number 20, between "Michael Jackson's Pepsi commercial disaster" at
number 19 and the death of Elvis Presley at number 21 (Anon. 2001).

As with any commodity, privacy is subject to the laws of supply and demand,
subject both to careful preservation and to eager violation. Magazines exist
devoted solely to capturing (and/or fabricating) images of naked stars.
Paparazzi photos, long-lost nude scenes or porn films, nude look-alikes, close-
ups of inadvertently bared nipples, all are the fodder of magazines like *Celebrity
Skin*. Such is the intensity of the desire to enter the most private world of the
star, that even the very *idea* of celebrity nakedness has a high exchange value.
The names of famous people are widely used on the Internet as false search
terms, leading almost always to images of "ordinary" people.

A taste for what MacCannell (1989, following Erving Goffman) characterized as the "backstage" of representation is built into the fundamental logic
of the star system, but nowadays it's open to a bit of *Schadenfreude*. Women's

magazines take delight in publishing photographs of stars having bad hair days, or caught without make-up or displaying their cellulite. Sold daily the images of perfection, we naturally relish the revelation of imperfection. "The Photos the Stars Don't Want you to See," smirks the subtitle of *Celebrity Skin*. This resentful one-upmanship is more easily waged against women than men, since ageing, cellulite, hairiness, flab and so on are outlawed with especial vigour for women. Thus, *Celebrity Skin*'s two hundred or so photos are all of women, despite the cover's repeated use of the gender-neutral term "stars."

The market in stolen photographs and sex videos of stars is vigorous. Both the reach and the rapidity of circulation of pirated images are enormous. One newspaper estimated that 50 per cent of Americans saw a bootleg copy of a video of actor Rob Lowe having sex with two young women (S. Williams 1997), though this must surely be an exaggeration. Sometimes, the market is surreptitious, but increasingly less so. Video footage purporting to be of Mimi Macpherson (sister of supermodel Elle) and her boyfriend was quite openly being sold by a hawker in a Sydney tourist precinct in 1997. It's also big criminal business. In 1997, Elle herself was blackmailed for US$ 60,000 after eight graphic nude photos of her were allegedly stolen from her boyfriend's wallet, the blackmailers threatening to post them on the Internet. Stolen celebrity images are also big business in the mainstream. Apart from the commodities they themselves engender (such as mainstream news discussions of the scandals), their on-sale is by no means always discreet. In the US, mainstream porn magazines have advertised and sold copies of some of the more famous celebrity sex videos (J. Marx 1997: 47), and enthusiastic reviews of various celebrity sex sites can be found in publications such as *Business World*. In 2000 even the *Wall Street Journal* allegedly suggested that the Internet porn company Internet Entertainment Group (IEG) was one of the few dot-com successes, and that Internet porn might prove to be the sole Internet enterprise that makes a profit (Moskowitz and Li 2002).[19]

Of course, stars have a quite ambiguous interest in protecting their privacy, since the name of the celebrity game is, after all, optimizing public exposure. Moreover, in the US, celebrity brings with it a slight diminution of legal protection, since the public's right to know is also legally recognized to some degree, under the rubric of "newsworthiness" (Kleinhans 2001: 291). Such complexities may well leave aggrieved stars caught between different modes of defence. Unable to physically stop the image from circulating, the celebrity may try to deny the connection, to affect the economic value of the image or to grab a share of it. So, a star might claim that the images are fakes, they might fight for them to be banned as an invasion of privacy, or they might try to claim copyright ownership. Often, a celebrity starts with one logic and moves on to another. US talk-show psychologist Dr Laura Schlessinger, for example, when confronted by the posting of a dozen naked photos of herself on the Web in 1998 by a former lover, initially claimed that the photos were fakes, then that she owned the copyright to them (Maurstad 1998). She lost her action to keep them off the Net; copyright apparently belonged to the photographer rather than to the subject of a photo. In this case, the former lover had sold the copyright to IEG. Ultimately, any attempt at retribution or self-defence is caught up in the logic of the very same system it seeks to refute. Australian singer Debra Byrne, for example, whose stolen sex video did the rounds of detectives, football clubs, media outlets and fire brigades, was eventually forced to try to blast away the shock value (and hence the exchange value) of her own violated privacy by flooding the market with her "secret." Having initially refused A$20,000 from a women's magazine to go public, she discovered that her former lover had already sold his story to the magazine. There was little option but to engage in a kind of arms war in privacy: "Byrne said she had gone public to expose the invasion of privacy and to stop a magazine profiting by touting an 'exclusive' story on her private life" (Silvester 1998).

The infamous case of the honeymoon video of *Baywatch* star Pamela Anderson Lee and her husband Tommy Lee makes clear both the economic importance of celebrity sex videos and the star's odd predicament as a victim torn between moral distress and economic gain. The story began with the alleged theft of the video from their Malibu home in 1996. The footage began circulating underground shortly thereafter, and Anderson and Lee's first action was to go on prime-time TV to discuss the theft, a decision that was later to have legal ramifications. In May 1996, *Penthouse* published stills from the video. After a court case and subsequent appeal (both of which Anderson and Lee lost), *Penthouse* sold the tape to IEG, who posted it on their Seattle-based website in November 1997. Anderson and Lee threatened to sue and the parties negotiated an agreement. Shortly afterwards, IEG put the tape back on its site and also began selling VHS video copies. By 1998 Anderson and Lee were in court arguing with IEG for their share of the copyright, arguing that they had never given permission for distribution beyond the website. By this stage hundreds of thousands of copies of the video had been sold globally by IEG for US$40 each, making it perhaps the most widely seen stolen sex video ever. Anderson and Lee lost the case. They appealed, and in December 2002, they were awarded US$741,000.[20] This represented a moral victory only, for by this time IEG had gone the way of many dot-com companies and was out of business, its owner allegedly in Thailand setting up business there. Anderson and Lee's case demonstrates the difficulty of physically controlling the spread of images in the digital age; their legal losses demonstrate not only certain legal niceties but also the star's ambiguous relation to publicity. Anderson and Lee's case was weakened not only by legal oddities (such as the decision that the tape was not private because it had been filmed in part in "public" places, such as in their car and on a boat), but also by the nature of modern celebrity itself. They were deemed to have compromised their invasion of privacy case by discussing intimate details in public forums before.[21]

Sexual images do not have to be real to cause pain and to generate money. Mimi Macpherson, for example, strenuously denied that the video was of her, but since even the *idea* of celebrity nudity has an exchange value, denials are of little use. Indeed, they serve only to fuel the speculation. As McKenzie Wark (1999: 59) says, in his discussion of the Mimi Macpherson incident, "The denial cannot countermand the will to suspend disbelief." It doesn't actually matter whether the blurry image is of the star or not; provided enough people believe it to be the case, the images are invested with the requisite aura of stolen authenticity. Indeed, a wonderfully Baudrillardian logic can come into play, whereby fakes can be much better than originals. In the words of one owner of a nude celebrity website: "Frankly, there's less hassle that way, there's no copyright problems . . . [I]t's fun. That's what it's all about, fun. People just need to lighten up" (Maurstad 1998). In any case, even if they're *not* widely believed to be authentic, the images still resonate with an aura – that of their *own* celebrity. Daniel Boorstin's (1971) caustic definition of stars as famous for being famous looks well and truly outdated. One can, it seems, also be famous for being not-or-only-possibly-famous, as Wark recognizes when he calls the woman in the "Macpherson" video "Not-Mimi." This woman is, according to Wark, "twice removed from celebrity:"

> She is not supermodel celebrity Elle Macpherson. She is not Elle's celebutante sister Mimi. She is just a Not-Mimi, Nonpherson . . . It's a shock when she looks straight into the camera and we recognize who it isn't. (Wark 1999: 59–60)

In the phenomenon of stolen or fabricated star images, the age-old belief in nudity as authenticity gives such images their aura and their exchange value, and all the while a savvy public is nonetheless fully aware that in postmodern visual culture the naked body can be a lie. Moreover, the very possibility of this lie escalates the arms race in images still further, as authenticity is countered with counter-authenticity, successful fabrications, and even fabrications never intended to be successful. There is a place in the "public fable" (Wark 1999: 59) for them all.

Glamour Nudity

> Positive images of women . . . play a very important role, even, or especially, in the most misogynist societies.

> Margaret Miles, *Carnal Knowing*

In the twenty-first century, images of perfection are part of the air we breathe. Responses to the onslaught of perfection come in many forms, but we can usefully, if simplistically, isolate two ends of a continuum: imitation and rejection. Glamour photography is one example of the former, in which the ordinary person responds to the perpetual gauntlet thrown down by celebrity culture by proving his/her potential fitness to enter it. The opposite tactic – rejection and/or proffering up an alternative aesthetic – will be discussed later under the rubric of the homemade.

The culture of stylized imagery of which the celebrity system is so key a part has provided ordinary people with a set of body ideals against which we inevitably measure ourselves, and a set of visual codes that can be utilized in acts of self-making and self-confirmation. These images can be sources of both anxiety and pleasure. As Miles argued in a discussion of "positive images" of women, images of "good women" are prescriptive. They instruct women on how they are meant to be, and thus can help feed misogyny: "Praise for the 'superiority' of women . . . can operate to justify vilification of women" (Miles 1989: 139). Pressure is now increasingly exerted on men too, as they are targeted more and more by glamour culture.

We interviewed a studio photographer (Michael) who specializes in glamour photography, including naked photography, and who has recently begun aiming his services specifically at the gay market. He was insightful about the reasons that people have glamour photos taken. Such practices are a form of identity work. For many clients, even the decision itself to be photographed nude (regardless of the actual photos) helps build self-esteem, since it represents a triumph over fear: "[For most clients] it's almost like a baptism of fire, [something] they've *got* to do; they've always wanted to do it." Most people have nude photos made at symbolic moments like anniversaries or after key moments of identity transformation, such as post-divorce or post-childbirth. As Michael says: "It's almost like a watershed in their life and they want to basically celebrate it, or show it or capture it." Mostly, this occurs when identity and/or body image have become self-conscious or precarious in some way.

Michael's experience has suggested to him that the function of these photographs, whether of individuals or couples, is, broadly speaking, more often about confirmation than escapism. For example, couples are less likely to get glamour nude photos done at the beginning of their relationship than when they have successfully passed through obstacles, or when they're well established, or on the verge of losing their looks. In other words, such photos are often a gesture of stabilization, confirmation or preservation rather than of inauguration. Michael identified three broad groupings among his inner-city clientele: gay people using it as a form of post-coming-out identity confirmation, couples (often with mundane or respectable jobs wanting to record and/or prove that they have exciting private lives) and good-looking young people who are just simply proud to show off their well-toned bodies. There are also a number of men showing off their beautiful wives, a theme that will recur in our discussion of the Home Girls phenomenon. Identity stabilization, self-memorialization and awareness of future deterioration are all important components. Of his gay clientele, Michael says:

> These are people in their late 20s to early 30s who've gone through a rather difficult time, and they've got to a point now where they're comfortable with themselves. Their body is kind of on the verge of – let's be really ugly about it – falling apart; it's not what it used to be, but internally, mentally, they're feeling much more comfortable with themselves. And so they've got to a point now where they're comfortable with themselves and they want to capture this youthfulness before it dissipates and this is a way of doing it.

These individual acts of self-making also have a collective and political dimension. In a world in which individual and collective identities are made in relation to visual images, and in which the ability to self-represent is connected to political power, glamorizing a marginalized group has political effects.

We interviewed a lesbian in her mid-30s who had decided to have some nude glamour images made as a gift for her partner. She chose Michael's studio, since he had advertised himself in a lesbian magazine as gay-friendly. Barbara conceived of her decision as an act of agency and individuality: "I thought I'd really be pushing boundaries here. I've never done anything like that before and none of my friends have." The photographs were meant to express her own sense of self. When the results came back, though, Barbara was disappointed. Not only did she not like the photos, but also she couldn't work out why the whole experience had discomforted her. Months later, she decided that for her, the photos were not expressions of her most intimate individuality, but hackneyed imitations of other images:

> It took me ages to work this out too. I got the photos back and I thought, there's something – not only did I not like the photos, I just thought there's something not right about this. Not right in the sense that it just doesn't make any sense to me. It doesn't make any sense to me as to why I was doing that. I just remember doing it because he thought it was a good idea, and I look at the poses and I think, it's like cheesecake photography.

Barbara analyzed this in terms of a relation between aesthetic codes and fantasy structures: "He had the ordinary – ordinary being the operative word – fantasies of a straight male. You know, everything that you see in the mainstream media of what a sexy female is." She experienced this mimetic structure as tautological, a simulacrum; the images were not of her but were "pictures of some woman posing." The net result was that Barbara felt disappointed and compromised at having been caught up in a web of images and image-making that did nothing to express her sense of self or to enhance her self-image but that made her, on the contrary, lose some faith in her ability to discriminate: "I thought it was different, but thinking about it now I just think that it was so *not* different."

In this case, nudity did not function for the subject as experience or emblem of an authentic self, nor even as a valuable practice in self-constitution. On the contrary, Barbara's efforts at asserting herself (i.e. at using nudity as the kind of personal asset in the way permitted to film stars) ultimately made her question the strength of her own agency:

> I actually feel quite stupid about how I related to this guy initially . . . I felt stupid in the sense that when I went there, I was so like, "Oh yeah, I'm really going to do something different" and I was so in that mindset, and I tend not to be a good judge of personality.

Barbara nonetheless bought three photos. Rather than seeing this as a Foucauldian moment of self-making or self-confirmation, or as a Baudrillardian purchase of a fake identity, it was, in fact, a moment of half-hearted disavowal; Barbara says she bought the photos so as to try to convince herself that the whole thing hadn't been a waste of time. Of course, Barbara's story is no simple tale of "failure." After all, she may not have got what she wanted, but the incident clearly gave her insight, which may itself feed back into an enhanced sense of self.

The incident sounded quite different from the photographer Michael's point of view. It was clear he prided himself both on how well he makes women feel comfortable in the studio and how original, artistic and tailored to the person he considers his glamour photography to be. He prides himself on his gender sensitivity, structuring the shot around a slow process of increasing revelation, a structure which, sadly, Barbara experienced as a form of enforced striptease. Clearly, it is a difficult task to invent "new," gender-sensitive practices of image-making when our selves have already been constituted within asymmetrically structured regimes. Lisa Tickner's (1978) phrase seems apt again; female corporeality is "occupied territory."

In the Raw: "Homemade" Nudity and Reality Genres

I am tangled in a web of seeing.

James Elkins, *The Object Stares Back*

The "Homemade"

In his well-known reading of striptease, semiotician Roland Barthes claimed that striptease is, ultimately, a chaste affair, since the stripper's nudity is so ritualized as to negate its erotic value.[22] Professional performance turns the stripper's nakedness into something "unreal, smooth and enclosed like a beautiful slippery object" (Barthes 1973: 92). Barthes argued that there was far more eroticism in the "weakness and timorousness" of the amateur than in the "miraculous ease" of the professional (p. 93). In rejecting the idea that a naked body is necessarily "natural," Barthes prefigured the core claims of later forms of feminism (notably postmodern and post-structuralist feminisms), which conceive of gender not as a natural essence but as a series of mundane, repeated, often unconscious actions or performances that become second nature. Like Barthes, postmodern feminists see striptease not as a performance that reveals the truth of gender, but as a performance *about* truth and authenticity.

Barthes's *preference* for the rawness of the timorous amateur over the slickness of the professional has, however, been viewed with some suspicion. Jennifer Blessing (1977), for example, suggests it might amount to a sexist preference for a woman evidently "in lack." Be that as it may, it's interesting to note that Barthes, writing in 1957, anticipated a wave of popular taste that was to come several decades later. His implied preference for raw beginners anticipates the development of an erotics/aesthetics that gained momentum in the 1990s – that is, a growing interest in watching "real people" rather than the glamorous bodies and stilted scripts of traditional commercial porn.

This section examines that erotic preference for "ordinary" people, using different kinds of "homemade" porn as examples. Before turning to these examples, though, it is important to set the scene a little more broadly, since the growing market for "authentic" porn needs to be seen within the context of an exponential growth in "reality" genres more generally.[23]

The 1980s and 1990s saw an exponential rise in reality genres of many kinds. Since the 1990s, mainstream television has become saturated with these genres, from the recycled footage genres (à la *Greatest Car Crashes*), to lifestyle programmes (cooking and gardening shows, including those with a game element, like *Changing Rooms* or *Backyard Blitz*), to the more dramatic games such as *Big Brother* and *Survivor*. New televisual forms have rapidly evolved and they will no doubt continue to do so in order to keep pace with viewer sophistication. Jon Dovey (2000: 58) has identified four categories within televisual camcorder genres alone: happenstance amateur video, surveillance-derived programmes, covert investigative films, and self-made diary projects. TV networks have been keen on such genres because they are cheap (minimizing the costs of scriptwriters and actors), and because they tap into voyeuristic impulses that prove popular with audiences. The 1990s were not the birth of a desire for authentic. It was, however, the decade of its institutionalization as a major televisual form (Dovey 2000: 55).

Reality genres will undoubtedly impact on both the experience and the conceptualization of personal identity. Digital technologies both extend and transform the kinds of late-modern identity work described by Foucault, by making possible new forms of images and new circuits of exchange. In postmodern times, practices of self-depiction and self-making have become increasingly public, in two senses: first, we rely on public images to a large extent in determining who we are; and second, there is an increasing encouragement to describe our personal identity in public. In the words of Jon Dovey (2000: 1), intimate revelation has become "a key part of the public performance of identity."

We saw in the previous section that glamorizing practices are enjoying a deal of popularity. But so too is the opposite tactic – the rejection of glamour culture via a taste for "rawness." A democratic (and occasionally rambunctious) celebration of "ordinary people" has been given new weight by the technological changes that have democratized access to image-making technologies and to circuits of both amateur and commercial exchange of images. Celebrating the ordinary can be not only a rejection of celebrity culture but also a paradoxical expansion of it – to include us all! And homemade genres can form part of both of these moves – democratizing celebrity by allowing everyone to participate in highly prized image-making practices, or rejecting celebrity culture altogether, and bypassing the controls of commercial producers.

The late-modern taste for the ordinary can thus be seen as a reaction to the glut of glamour media images with which we are all constantly bombarded. Familiarity with these images has produced a public that, though it still plays the game, is savvier and more rapidly sated than its forebears. Sophisticated consumers, we have learnt to be alert to and rapidly wearied by the tricks of the TV trade. Reality genres, though they certainly emerge from current economics of production, also meet sated consumers' desire for something new.

"Reality Porn" and Staged Authenticity

There has always been some sort of parallel system between public and private sexual images. Before the advent of video, there existed a minor home practice of erotic still photography and Super-8 film. While this latter format has been superseded, homemade erotic photography still exists, using both Polaroid cameras and commercially developed photographs.[24] It is likely that the popularity of homemade images may have receded a little during the high era of commercially produced pornography on a mass scale (with the exception of images catering to minority and criminal sexual tastes). Regardless, the dominance of the mainstream industry has in any case now produced its own saturation effect, which has helped give rise to the current twin system, in which commercially produced porn vies with the increasing popularity of "real" porn made both by amateurs and professionals. According to a director of home-made porn, "Keith," (whose views will be canvassed in detail later), around 70 per cent of Internet porn is amateur. Whether or not this is so, the figure for video rather than Internet porn is significantly lower, though not insubstantial; Jon Dovey (2000: 67) cites one assertion that amateur porn might constitute 25 per cent of all the hard-core videotapes in circulation.

There are many phenomena that could be grouped under the heading of "reality porn" – from older forms like amateur erotic photographs and snapshots, to the Home Girls and Blokes pages of soft-porn magazines (where readers send in photos of themselves naked for cash), to exhibitionistic Internet sites like JenniCam (discussed later), to sexy reality TV shows. The trend towards "rawness" is evident in a range of erotic forms, from explicit snap-shots, to the Home Girls pages of tabloid magazines, to "live" phone sex lines and chat rooms.[25]

The 1990s was the decade in which reality genres boomed within porno-graphy, after the "early murmurings" of the amateur phenomenon in the mid-1980s (O'Toole 1999: 181). Technological changes have been rapid over the last few decades, and have impacted on both the economics of porn production and the cultures of porn viewing. The invention of the video cassette recorder (VCR), for example, was responsible for the downturn in the so-called "golden age" of porn, when pornography was shot on film, watched in cinemas, and often had high production values (O'Toole 1999: 75–6). The VCR helped fuel the advent of commercially made video porn as a major mass industry, by making porn cheaper, more widely available and more easily consumed at home than either cinematic porn or early domestic forms like homemade photographs or Super-8 movies. O'Toole names 1986–90 as the peak era for low-grade pornographic videos (p. 180). The recent explosion of "real" porn corresponds to the Internet and other digital technologies (like scanners and digital cameras), which allow people to post images of themselves to the world rapidly and anonymously. Homemade porn did exist well before the Internet. Three things, however, seem to me to be distinctive about the kind of techno-logical explosion made possible by digital technologies and the Internet: first, the sheer scale, reach and quantity of pornographic images it makes available; second, the increased visibility of pornographic practices (in the sense that many different kinds of porn become available, or known about, to any home in which there is a computer connected to the Internet); and third, changes to the experience of privacy itself, owing to the ambiguously public/private nature of the Internet.[26] As a technology, the Internet helps fuel moral change, since it encourages both anonymity (and hence experimentation) and community (which encourages both the sharing of interests and a consequent push towards moral normalization).

I want to consider this phenomenon by returning to the work of sociologist Dean MacCannell (1989), in this case, to his concept of "staged authenticity." MacCannell coined this term as part of his analysis of the experiences of Western tourists visiting "exotic" locations. He argued that these visits were structured by a discontent with Western modernity and a longing to temporarily reclaim the perceived authenticity and naturalness of non-Western cultures. Modernity is characterized by elegies about progress and development, but these are always underpinned by ambivalence, if not downright discontent, at that which modernity has destroyed along the way. In other words, MacCannell diagnosed modernity as a state of lament, loss and fantasy.

Many years have passed since MacCannell's book *The Tourist* first appeared in 1976, and some would say that the tourist, desperately seeking the real, has been well and truly replaced by the post-tourist, happily (or at least resignedly) enjoying the fakery (Feifer 1985: see Urry 1990: 110). And yet, I believe that MacCannell's core insight – the strength of our *desire* for authenticity – still holds good – more than ever, in fact. In a world in which we are all encouraged to perform our subjectivity in public, "the private" becomes even more strongly fetishized as it disappears. We long for a glimpse of private things, knowing full well that we help change or destroy the realm of privacy the more we consume it. Of course, this desire for the ever-receding real is matched by an awareness of, and often a joy in, performance itself. Postmodern culture is thus characterized less by a simple desire for and romanticization of authenticity (although this still very much exists) as by a complex mixture of attitudes – desire for the real, fetishization of the real, resignation to the fact that the real is always elusive, fun in fakery, and celebration of the delights of role-play and performance. For one example, see Figure 4.8, in which identity is conceived of as both revelation and play, and in which (semi) nakedness figures as both a revealed authenticity and a tool in identity play. In the case of reality porn, both these impulses are evident; it is popular because of its "truthfulness," and yet no participant could be unaware of the performative dimensions (indeed, for some, this is the pleasurable part of the process). Nakedness, that metaphor for the lack of metaphor, that unnatural natural state, thus remains an ideal vehicle for the playing out of this cultural tension.

Amateurism is now so prized that it has become a genre unto itself, and one that can be fabricated professionally! I turn now to two different kinds of sex video, each of which can be considered a form of "professional authentica."

Show Him The Real You!!!
and have fun at the same time

Glamour Photo Shoots from $50

Figure 4.8 "Show Him the Real You!" Reproduced with permission.

The first is where a couple has a video made of themselves for their own use; the second is where a professional hires "real people" to "star" in videos that are scripted and staged to varying degree depending on the filmmaker, and which are sold to the public. They are both of interest since, according to Jon Dovey (2000: 55), video is that form "that represents better than any other the shifting perimeters of the public and the private."

Commercially Made Sex Videos, for Home Use

Apart from the cameraman it's a private and personal business.

Advertisement for a video service, quoted in Hepworth and Featherstone,
Surviving Middle Age

Professionally made sex videos for personal use arose before the widespread introduction of the camcorder. Mike Hepworth and Mike Featherstone cite an advertisement for such a service in the early 1980s in Britain:

> Many folk like to see themselves making love, but until now the only way has been to produce a home movie. Often the results aren't very good. We think it best to shoot the action in video. Customers get an instant replay and mistakes can be put right. To try to make things really interesting we work out some sort of script for the couple beforehand – give the thing a storyline like TV. Apart from the cameraman it's a private and personal business. And the customer has the only copy of the film. We're sure it will give a lot of happy memories. Who knows, couples might want to look at themselves in later years when all the passion has gone. (Hepworth and Featherstone 1982: 153)

The ad is a little dated now, and you can see the discursive work that was going on at the time – particularly the redefining of boundaries between the public and private, the authentic and the fabricated. But this text nonetheless bears witness to many of the ongoing late-modern circumstances (the cult of youth, the redefinition of the public and the private, the narcissism encouraged by consumer culture, the commodification of sex and intimacy). It also voices a number of the preoccupations of late-modern subjects (the desire for glamour, the fear of ageing, and the desire to preserve aspects of one's life on film). Because of the intimacy of the professional encounter, the status of the filmmakers is uneasy: they are both insiders and outsiders. Potential clients are described as "folk" and "couples" as well as "customers." Throughout, there is a conjunction of a cosy, homey lexicon ("folk," "home movie," "making love," "happy memories") with a gentle paternalism ("we think it best"). The idea of giving over one's privacy to an external authority raises its own spectres, which are evoked and dispelled in one discreet sentence: "And the customer has the only copy of the film."

This aesthetic is the very opposite of the grainy, unscripted style prized in stolen tapes. It is based on an idealization of the real, where mistakes can be corrected, real life can be just like TV, and "the thing," at last, can get the storyline it deserves. But it appears that the phenomenon of professionals filming couples to produce a video for their own private use is relatively minor. We might imagine that the cheapness and availability of camcorders will keep it so or indeed will render it obsolete. This form does, however, do something slightly different from either commercially made porn or a self-made video. First, it allows the subjects to participate in the glamour aesthetic, and to combine glamour and intimacy. Glamorizing practices have an important role in a world where intense pressure is put on us to look good and where ongoing sexual fulfilment and novelty are widely shared ideals. Imitation is one way of gaining (or celebrating) a sense of sexual agency.

For some people, such tapes may also form part of the battery of memorializing practices in which most of us engage. This is certainly how the service quoted above advertised itself. Was that just a coy alibi, or can glamorous erotic photography be used as an anti-ageing strategy? Hepworth and Featherstone (1982) thought so; they discuss this ad as part of their study of ageing in modernity, in which they examine the rise of preservationist attitudes towards the body. O'Toole (1999: 282) also hints at this when he says that video has impacted on people's sense of time, record and memory. As we saw with the glamour photographer Michael, preserving the memory of one's youthful body is often a motivation behind many forms of personal image-making. The photographic editor of a major magazine company, whose job involves recruiting women off the streets as photographic models, likewise thought that self-memorialization motivated many women to work as naked models for erotic reality genres:

> Frankly, what we find with photography, is that most women like a very good image of themselves and if they can be shown as a very sexy, alluring type of person, it has a real appeal to them as they feel like they're getting older. After children, this is what I can still look like! It's a very good ego boost.

The director Keith, on the other hand, disagrees that the professionally made home-sex video results from a preservationist relation to the body, for he believes that contemporary Westerners tend to disavow the thought of their own eventual ageing. When I showed him the above ad, he disagreed that recording oneself while in one's prime is much of a motivation in the home-sex video game. Rather, he believes that self-confirmation is the principal source of pleasure: "I think it's the fact that we're told that we have to have the perfect body and we have to have the perfect look and you need confirmation that you have it." But he does not see this as a glamorizing function, or about gaining access to a mode of being that until recently belonged only in the domain of the commercial:

> As a society we're a lot more body conscious now than we ever have been and it's a reasonably new phenomenon. I think if you are working on your body and you have a certain pride in the fact that you have achieved a certain body look, I think it's important that you see yourself and say, "mmm, that's working." . . . [P]eople want to be looked at and people want to look at themselves and the body form that they create.

For Keith, the professionally made home-sex video is principally neither a preservationist nor a mimetic phenomenon, but one resulting from a dynamic that he considers absolutely fundamental to humans: that between exhibitionism and voyeurism. He is one of those people who believe that there are two types of people in the world. In his case, it is voyeurs and exhibitionists. In keeping with this theory, Keith believes that many couples who have a film made would show it to others, or post it on the Internet. To my question as to whether watching oneself is a form of voyeurism, Keith replied, "I don't know. I can play you some tapes."

This, then, may be the second function of the professionally made video. The presence of external people and indeed of the camera itself would serve for some people as an erotic stimulus; making the act of recording as much about role-play and performance as about privacy and authenticity. While for some people, the presence of a camera and crew in the home would be an embarrassing intrusion, for others it would constitute an erotic moment in itself. It is possible then that this minor industry will not die out despite the ascendancy of the camcorder, for it caters to a taste for a public performance of intimacy.

Commercially Made Sex Videos, for Sale on the Open Market

Keith's own work is different from the service advertised above. It involves using "ordinary" people recruited via advertisements. The tapes are sold not to the participants but to customers over the Internet. Keith calls his brand of porn "real" porn, a term he preferred to my "homemade." He calls it real because it is unscripted, undirected, unglamorized and only very rarely involves any fakery. Unlike the British example cited earlier, there is no script, and "mistakes" *are* left in: "'I've got a cramp.' 'Get off my hair' – it's all in there." Noises, farts, squelches – the sounds of sex – are recorded.

From the point of view of a critique of the cult of the body beautiful, this is really quite subversive. Keith is, in fact, quite explicit about his political agenda: "I have huge agendas that I'm not secretive about and I tell the people that are auditioning what my agendas are." His videos are made for both men and women, and they are not about turning subjects into glamorous objects. In fact, he explicitly tells participants not to glamorize themselves:

It's actually a charter of mine . . . that I want to produce pornography for men and women. So I will give equal air time to men's faces, arses, backs, legs, toes, chests as I will the woman's bottom, chest, legs, back . . . It's very important to me and personally I find the human face *the* most erotic thing in the human body, as opposed to a dick going into a cunt which is essentially what commercially available pornography focuses on . . . I give as much time for women as men.

Keith is interested in combining commercial incentives with social interest ones. For example, he strenuously promotes safe sex and non-drug-use, and he wants to make pornography using, for example, lesbians, disabled people and people over 40. In all of those cases, he explains, he is wanting to provide opportunities for under-represented groups to see themselves as sexual subjects, and he is most insistent that he will sell such tapes only to the relevant groups and not to a wider market.

Keith is, clearly, an unusually progressive maker of porn. He occasionally wonders whether his social agendas will be to his commercial detriment. I was interested in finding out the *limits* of Keith's inclusiveness, not in order to catch him out, as it were, but to try and get a hint of the limits of what a commercial market will accept. Surely he must have to concede *some* ground to the glamour market? Well, perhaps:

Keith:	Basically, what I cast is personality. It's not so much about body image and shape and size and dick size and tit size. What it's about is vitality and vivaciousness. . . . Most of the women that I've cast are Rubenesque in their appearance. It's not about waif-like bimbettes.
Interviewer:	Would there be forms of body that you wouldn't use, or that you know just wouldn't sell?
Keith:	It's a commercial venture. So if you're 120 kilograms with a one-and-a-half inch dick, then odds-on you ain't going to sell.

I was also interested in putting to Keith the post-structuralist argument that the "reality" he captures must necessarily be produced in relation to the norms of visual culture, especially commercially available porn. Keith admits that the authentic is never extra-discursive, in that his participants' erotic ideas have had to come from somewhere, and he realizes that this "somewhere" is by and large commercially available porn. Thus the paradox is that in seeking to make something different from mainstream porn, he has to rely on participants whose ideas are in fact formed in relation precisely to pre-existing ideas of the erotic. Nonetheless, the sheer number of participants in any given tape – scenes range from two participants to large groups – means that his tapes are inevitably marked by at least some measure of diversity and spontaneity: "We kind of get over that formulaic approach because we each have a different view of what it's all about." In the classic problem known as the "be spontaneous" paradox, Keith also instructs his participants at the moment of audition not to imitate porn!

Keith recognizes that it doesn't take much to turn ordinariness into mimetic performance. This dilemma is reflected in his own uncertainty as to what the most appropriate terminology for his participants should be: "I'm stuck between model, actor or talent." He runs a constant race against the staginess that always threatens to contaminate the authenticity he and his clients desire:

> I have a rule, which is essentially [that] after a model, an actor, a piece of talent has made three or four scenes or tapes for me then I'm not going to use them again because they're going to assume the bravado of being a porn star.

Authenticity (itself always already discursively produced) becomes staged authenticity with remarkable rapidity. Keith describes the transformation of one of his participants in just three weeks (and four shoots):

> In the three weeks, his bravado, his persona, has dramatically changed . . . You could actually produce a graph to plot his . . . He had body hair. He's progressively got rid of body hair, he has shaved pubic hair, he now has the most enormous rash – shaving rash – on his arse which I can't shoot . . . He [has] gained a significant amount of confidence.

Given the inevitability of this phenomenon whereby the desirable ordinariness of real people gets contaminated by performance so rapidly, Keith plans to start up another branch of his company where he'll produce more traditional porn and make use of "the people that think they're porn stars."

It is evident that Keith is not a typical maker of pornography. He is tertiary trained (indeed, a graduate of feminist subjects on gender and sexuality), and his aesthetics of porn is bound up very explicitly in an ethics and a politics. He considers himself a feminist (and a "masculinist"), and his ideology is liberal:

> I find it really objectionable that women object to women expressing and wanting to share in sexuality. I find that so offensive. I just want to slap a woman that says "No, you can't watch pornography!" How dare she? I find it inconceivable.

For me, brought up on a feminist distaste for porn and a deep suspicion of the economics that underlie it, it is a strange thing to contemplate the idea that raw porn might be progressive. But put beside the worked-over, un-blemished, white-bread perfection of glamour porn (and indeed, of standard women's fashion magazines) the imperfect, blemished bodies of Keith's participants were something of a relief. The process clearly has the potential to be liberating for the participants too, given the importance of image-making practices to identity, including sexual identity. Avedon Carol has suggested that amateur porn was "a woman-led development," an extension of the (sup-posedly) feminine desire to record events (quoted in O'Toole 1999: 180). Whether or not this is so, the development of a female and couples market in pornography is a major trend. But in a consumerist society in which dislike of one's body is increasingly being imposed on men as well as on women, it is not only women who will celebrate any moments outside of this regime. Keith described, for example, the response of one of his male participants:

> I had one guy who literally had a tear in his eye auditioning for me . . . I actually cried after he left. [He said,] "Thank you so much for giving me the time. Thank you so much for allowing me to get over my phobia about doing this, allowing me to feel valid and non-dirty. I know you're not going to use me in these films but I just so appreciate the opportunity to get over this barrier and express myself." A lot of people use the opportunity to do this – to get over those phobias.

Whatever else it taps into, perhaps the "home" porn phenomenon also opens up possibilities for valuing the body as the home of feeling, memory, subjectivity, experience, over the emptied, perfected, universalized body of the glamorous pin-up nude.

Having said that, it must be made clear that one cannot *a priori* idealize the homemade as a progressive genre in itself. Anti-objectification is not intrinsic to this mode. Rather, it is a function of the beliefs and ideologies of the maker, which are reflected in recruitment and filming strategies:

> I think a lot of commercial producers perhaps have the mindset of objectifying women. [They] package and market and produce stuff from perhaps the home-made and amateur point of view but still follow the mindset and mode of operating of traditional porn. I think there's a difference between the true home made and the commercial, the professional home made.

There are plenty of other porn-makers working within the homemade aesthetic who in no way share Keith's values or ideals, and there are many truly nasty aspects to the interest in "reality" – from snuff videos to Internet sites frequented by adolescents in which one scores a photo of a real person (male or female) on a scale from one to ten and then compares one's selections with the "norm" (www.hotornot.com). This is a reality-fantasy based entirely on objectification – not a rejection of glamour logic but an invidious extension of it. "Reality" is not neutral ethical, political or emotional territory. On the contrary, whenever things are done in the name of "reality," we can be assured that something important is at stake.

Home Girls and Blokes

Home Girls are, in the words of *Picture* magazine, girls who "flash for cash."[27] Their pictures appear each week in the back of a number of tabloid magazines, just after the pages of phone sex ads. The phenomenon began some time around 1994, apparently arising organically from male readers' practice of sending in unsolicited photos of their wives and girlfriends naked.[28]

The segment has become extremely popular; in fact, readers' surveys show it to be the most popular feature of *Picture*. It is not short of participants either; the Sydney office alone of Australian Consolidated Press (which publishes *People*, *The Picture*, *Dingo* and formerly *Australian Women's Forum*) receives between 30 and 50 entries per week. Home Girl videos are now also available for purchase via the magazine. The Home Girl pages were a successful experiment, and they have been taken up by other magazines. *Picture* has extended the phenomenon to men, with the introduction in 1997 of Home Blokes. Only one Home Blokes Annual has ever been allowed by management, despite the enormous popularity of those "80 Pages of Daks-Down Dudes." The "Home" game is thus still a predominantly female affair by both policy and proclivity, with Girls outnumbering Blokes two to three times in the one magazine that does include Blokes.

Most "Home" photos depict the person fully naked, though some women are dressed in lingerie (and until the relaxation of Australian censorship laws in 1997, men were required to wear underwear). "Homies" are always photographed alone, and their photo is accompanied by a number, their first name, the town they come from and a short biography, staged as a dialogue with the anonymous editor. Most Home Girls are Caucasian, and few are aged above about 40. Home Blokes (where they exist) are more diverse in age but not ethnicity.[29] In the *1997 Picture Home Blokes Annual*, the oldest man is 83, the youngest, presumably 18. Most look about 30–40.

Homies are paid.[30] The Home pages include instructions, a consent form, and a strong warning about fraud. Men are not given the option of having their heads covered for privacy as women ("Bag Girls") are, and are paid less than women. The rules for Home Blokes are spelled out quite clearly: both face and penis must be visible, but no erections are permitted (defining an erection can be quite tricky!).[31] These conditions ensure compliance with the current regulations for the "unrestricted" category.[32]

Any forum that depicts and indeed celebrates ordinary bodies, with all their flabbiness, jutting bones, stretch marks and shaving shadows, is a welcome relief from the depressingly narrow range of body types approved by magazine culture at large, including those images purveyed elsewhere in *People* and *Picture* themselves. *People* makes this non-judgementalism explicit: "We don't care if you're 18 or 80, fat or thin, tall or short. Send in a photo of yourself NAKED and we'll proudly publish it in Oz Girls." All the editors we interviewed stated that there was no body type that they would *a priori* reject; in practice, most (though not all) participants are white, and most women are young. Reader feedback and surveys make it clear that male readers find the "warts-and-all" images highly appealing. The variety of body types satisfies their curiosity about what everyday people (their next-door neighbour, the woman in the shop) might look like, and it satisfies those whose taste lies outside the bodily ideals purveyed repetitively by consumer culture. Readers' feedback makes it clear that many men appreciate the softness, fleshiness or curves of non-models. They also like to see how well they've done in the partnership stakes, comparing their partner not only with models, but with other "real" women: "Neville loves reading *The Picture* and comparing our Home Girls with his wife, who's 'taut and terrific.'" The editors claim that men enjoy the opportunity to compare themselves with other men in the Home Blokes section but are too scared to admit it in readers' surveys, which regularly position it last. The segment was nearly abandoned as a result until the editors realized that the vote of unpopularity was unlikely to be a true reflection of readers' behaviour.

That ordinary people should have a public forum in which to represent themselves, that ordinary nakedness should be given free rein, ought to be a cause for celebration, and to some extent it is. But since the "ordinary" bodies are published after scores of glamour images of thin, white, young women and are situated directly after the pages of phone-sex ads, there is an inevitable blurring of meaning across genres. There are simply too many lurking contiguities between the Home Girl space and other female nude genres for it to be much of a new space for women. While the Home phenomenon certainly does affirm many individual women, according them sexual agency (see Albury 1997), proving to them that they matter, that they are beautiful, that they are worth representing, the wider context of the magazine nonetheless preserves a sexually asymmetrical "culture of representations" (Bordo 1993a: 706), in spite of the superficial symmetry between the Home Girls and Blokes pages.

However, in the face of the thousands of images of perfection we are all fed every day, "ordinariness" is no bad thing. Of course, the Home pages do not simply reproduce ordinariness; they *produce* "the ordinary" as a category. Many photos are in fact taken in the home, and thus the floral curtains and textured carpet of the living room, the cotton-print sheets, the rock posters on the bedroom wall and so on are important features of the genre. These are real-life backgrounds, but they also construct an *aesthetic* of the ordinary, of which the clearest signal is *Picture*'s inclusion of a white border around each shot, a typical gesture of staged authenticity in which the photo emulates the snapshot.

The Home pages are fascinating in that they do not discriminate between porn imitation and holiday snapshots, thus implying that there are a variety of modes of female sexuality. Home images can also be both imitations and rejections of glamour imagery. As one employee put it: "The biggest appeal of the Home Pages is its rawness and the fact that it's not stylized, it's not directed at all in any way. It's just 'here I am!'" And yet, many women clearly do want to be seen as contenders in the glamour stakes, understandably enough, and the Home pages offer women and men the chance to be a star for a while. All the editors we interviewed agreed that for most participants it is a "15 minutes of fame" thing. This appears to be a motive for both men and women, though one editor believed that this glamour function is particularly important for young working-class women in the suburbs, who may well have married and had children young and possibly feel disappointed that they missed out on the chance to feel young and sexy. The Home Blokes editor, Samantha, put it more bluntly: "You feel sorry for a lot of them. They're just stuck at home and they don't have any independent thoughts for themselves and you try and give them a bit of encouragement."[33] While this might sound harsh, Samantha's underlying point is that photographic practices can have a compensatory function.

The Home phenomenon is not merely an imitation of celebrity, though, for some Home Girls do in fact go on to become stars and generate their own fan culture among the readership. A possible career trajectory within *Picture* magazine is from Home Girl, to "Me and My Boobs," to pin-up to so-called "tits-out reporter." Although only about two girls have made this full ascent, Home Girls do quite often go on to model elsewhere in the magazine and use it as the start of a modelling career. The upward mobility of Home Girls is driven by economics. A shoot in *Picture* using an ex-Homie takes three to four hours and costs the magazine A$500, compared with a three to four day shoot costing up to A$2,500 with a professional model for a shoot for *Penthouse*. Home Girls are mainly working class and, according to a senior publishing official, are attracted to the genre because it is a source of good money. The result of this is yet more blurring of the boundaries between ordinary people and stars, professional and amateurs, readers and participants, even anonymous model versus "personality:" "Some of our ladies [i.e. Home Girls] have gone on to become characters in the magazine themselves, and have become consistent stars, so they become a theme."

Very few men try to use the forum as a career move. For most, it is a question of some fun, perhaps some easy money, and some good-humoured exhibitionism. The "Home" experience is more light-hearted for men than for women. Although there are some imitations of glamour poses, many of the Blokes' photographs are humorous – a man on a fishing boat holding a crab in front of his genitals, a man standing in front of a mounted fish that gapes up at his penis, and so on. Many men play games with costumes: the man wearing a top hat, bow tie and tuxedo jacket and nothing else; the man with the ribbon on his penis; the man in the cowboy hat and belt without pants, and so on. For women, humour is evident in the biogs, but is less available (or less utilized) *visually*, though more spontaneous genres, especially of the "show us your tits" or the caught-in-the-shower varieties, allow for spaces outside simple successes or failures of glamour emulation.

The Home Blokes editor repeated how much men loved showing off their penis, often lamenting the censorship rules that prevent them from showing it in all its glory: "A lot of them ring up and complain. 'You oughta see it when it's *really* up!'" According to the editors, men rarely regret the experience, while women sometimes do. Men often enjoy the recognition it brings them in their local community:

> I'll get a letter saying, "Everyone recognized me and they keep slapping me on the back going 'Hey, bloke! You're in *Picture* magazine!' I've made lots of friends since then!"

Men also frequently get a form of reflected prestige that comes from what Samantha described as "the fantasy of seeing their girlfriend nude in a magazine that other guys look at." This process, characterized by Eve Sedgwick (1985) as a triangular structure fundamental to patriarchies, is a familiar one: relations between men are secured by a symbolic or literal traffic of a woman (or feminized object).

Community formation is a central and deliberate part of these magazines' work. It involves first constructing a certain social formation (Anglo working-class culture) as ordinary, and then, second, refiguring this ordinariness as a form of heroism. As the editors say, *everyone* in *Picture* and *People* is a hero, a champion. "[B]e a hero and show us yer dial!" urges the editorial voice. Nudity's ambiguous association with both ordinary and godlike humanity makes it an ideal tool for this manoeuvre. The workings of traditional heroic nudity are here inverted. Whereas in classical times the heroes' nudity was the reflection of their already existing heroism, the Home People become heroes precisely because they are brave enough to go nude (rather like Lady Godiva). As in Peter Cattaneo's film *The Full Monty* (1997), it is the exposure precisely of their ordinariness that makes these working-class men and women heroic.

Refiguring the ordinary as heroic helps generate a sense of community, and indeed, there is in fact plenty of behind-the-scenes interaction between readers and editors.[34] This community has its limits, of course. The culture that the magazine confirms is white, working-class and masculinist. According to the editors, white working-class men like to see their world reflected back to them in these magazines. There are thus no Asian models; the issue of *People* with an Aboriginal centrefold was their worst-selling issue ever. And no matter how popular the Home Blokes Annual, or the one-off male centrefold allowed in

1999, no matter how many women want to see Home Blokes of the Week, the idea that these are predominantly men's magazines is (currently) final. Women readers are to be kept happy, but only in the margins, lest the heroic masculinity of these magazines be decentred and the sexual equality celebrated in these magazines be taken too far. But the pressure is on.

For the moment, though, it is clear that the social consequences of public female nudity are still potentially far more serious than those that attend male nudity, though again, the financial opportunities such occasions bring are far greater for women than men. Taking the plunge and baring all can be great fun but its impacts are not necessarily the same for men and women. One Bag Girl, when asked why she isn't showing her face, replies: "Because of where I work. I think I'd get into trouble." She is possibly right. Some years back the Queensland Attorney-General requested that a Justice of the Peace resign after she appeared as "Girl number six" in *Picture* (Williams 1997: 4). Some of the people we interviewed knew of others: the girl who had been sacked for showing pictures of herself as Home Girl to her female workmate; the man who sent in a photo of an ex-girlfriend, forging her signature and getting another woman to impersonate her over the phone when the magazine rang up to develop the biography. A previous editor reports having been phoned by lawyers, years after a woman's photograph appeared, who were wanting to use it as evidence against a woman fighting a custody battle for her children (Williams 1997). Samantha told us that the Home pages can't be used as weapons against the men, because they're proud to be on display: "It's a lot more light-hearted with the guys. There's a lot more sinister stuff going on with the girls." While this is a generalization, it's still the case that female nudity is potentially tainted with moral unfitness, and in a sexually unequal society, nudity can be used as a weapon, and photographs can become dangerous objects. The potential danger of nude images for women was acknowledged by a previous female editor of the Home Girls page in an admission that rather gives the lie to the idea of a friendly community of liberals: "I don't really know why the women do it . . . I know I wouldn't. Would you?" (Williams 1997: 4). A Home Girl we interviewed had had a great time, but had been puzzled by the reaction of some of her female colleagues, who had been unable to look her in the eye. For some Home Girls, regrets and dangers; for others, laughs and compliments. Individual experiences will always differ, but the historically more fraught meanings of female nudity help structure the conditions of possibility of these experiences.

It seems likely that the dangers associated with nudity being reported back to the workplace are more acute for women than for men. In 1994, a police-woman was suspended without pay ("at her request") and an internal police inquiry ordered after she posed naked for *Australian Penthouse* – under a pseudonym and with her profession altered. The editor of *Penthouse* explained why she had thought she could pose with impunity:

> She felt she could, because one of her former boyfriends, who is also a policeman, appeared nude in *Australian Women's Forum*. She felt that if he was allowed to model nude for a women's magazine, why shouldn't she do the same thing for a men's magazine? (Harvey 1994: 5)

Clearly, some people are allowed to be more ordinary than others.

Home is Where the Cam is: JenniCam

Baudrillard (1987: 19) once claimed that in postmodernity "the drama is acted out on the screens and nowhere else." Exaggerated as this claim may be, it nonetheless strikes a kind of symbolic chord, one that resonates quite widely as a postmodern fantasy-nightmare, explored in films like *Total Recall*, *The Truman Show*, *The Matrix* and *Ed TV*. While the popularity of such films attests to that nightmare's current seductiveness, it's not a fantasy most of us would want to live with all the time. The JenniCam website is, however, one woman's attempt to do something rather like that.

JenniCam was originally a black and white digital camera that posted live images from Jennifer Kaye Ringley's college dormitory room every three minutes to a select audience of in-the-know Net users. This camera was replaced some time later by a colour version (maintained by a friend on a borrowed server) that netcasted her life to an increasingly voracious (and mostly male) public.

Although the cam was located in Jenni's bedroom, nudity was not, at least initially, the feature of JenniCam, though one could always hit it lucky and see Jennifer changing or getting out of the shower. But the site gained global fame/notoriety when the originally incidental nudity in Jenni's life became more programmatic, climaxing (or perhaps not) in an attempt to netcast herself having sex, an attempt that failed mid-way as her server crashed under the strain of thousands of simultaneous log-ons. Now, Jennifer is in a new city, with a new server, and her services require an annual US$ 15 subscription to cover the cost of bandwidth. Those unwilling to pay the price can keep abreast of JKR via a free highlights page and a number of JenniCam tribute sites.

Jennifer's occasional nudity combines something of the attractions of both celebrity and homemade nudity. The paradox involved in rendering the homemade public and/or professional is delightfully encapsulated in the oxymoronic URL for JenniCam – http://www.boudoir.org. The Web did not bring into being the piquant idea of the public boudoir (which is after all a staple of fine art and erotica) but it has enormously amplified its scale. Engaging voyeuristically with Jennifer means subjecting yourself to the vicissitudes of the chase, getting up expectations, having them disappointed or unexpectedly (rather than programmatically) satisfied. The potential for boredom is, in fact, as much the point as any unexpected "hit," since it is an important part of the desired reality-effect. Back in the dorm days, Jenni would occasionally perform choreographed strip shows, but there was plenty of other, often dull, material – the "in-between bits" that, in fact, actually constitute a life. As a contemporary review put it:

> We see Jen doing homework, Jen on the phone, an empty room, and cute closeups of her new hedgehog Spree. We also see Jen watching TV and we get at least eight hours of darkness at night, just like real life. (Gliddon, "90 Degrees," website)

Real-time has its weird global effects though; Australian viewers discovered that the prime time of Jenni's life corresponded with the down-time of office life (the hottest events occurred between midday and 4p.m. weekdays, Australian time.) Antipodean good fortune notwithstanding, real-time voyeurism of this kind means working with the rhythms and temporalities of someone else's day and night. A poll on the JenniCam Tribute Site asks the question: "Do you ever feel *slighted* when Jennifer goes on vacation?"

The sense of clandestine pleasure vital to voyeurism is created partly through the technology Jenni chose – a series of regularly uploaded still images rather than a video camera. While this choice may or may not have been technologically driven (i.e. a question of bandwidth), an astute JenniCam fan noted its beneficial effects in amplifying the sense of furtiveness that is a key to the site's appeal (Gliddon, "Re: JenniCam," website). Another fan disagreed, arguing that it is the furtiveness of Jen *herself* that is the attraction, regardless of bandwidth (Fletcher, website). Either way, both fans are paying homage to the old truth that voyeurism relies not on full revelation but on a dialectic between revelation and concealment.

Concealment fuels the desire for greater revelation, as MacCannell's (1989) analysis of staged authenticity as a pursuit without end makes clear. Wearying of obviously public performances, the true fan becomes interested in that next, always retreating, "offstage" moment of their object of desire. This very modernist quest ties in with the postmodern tautology by which fame has become its own object. To return to the cynical terms of Daniel Boorstin (1971), Jenni could be seen as a "pseudo-event," "famous for being famous." Actually, Jenni herself says something quite similar: "I'm not a remarkable person. The interesting thing is not me, the interesting thing is the camera . . . Without the camera I probably would have been a nobody" (Hagenbaugh 1997). Unlike the Home Girls, whose "ordinariness" is precisely the condition of their momentary fame, JenniCam saves Jenni *from* ordinariness. Nonetheless, it celebrates her everydayness, since her broadcast life is intended to be neither exemplary nor allegorical (though it may become so, as in my reading of her as a woman of our times). JenniCam is the triumphant celebration of "form" over "content" to the point where form *becomes* a kind of meaning in itself. Thus it is only logical that Jenni and her camera should occasionally seem to have hybridized, the term "JenniCam" being used on the discussion sites to refer variously to the site, the technology and the star.[35]

If JenniCam fuses a life and a recording technology, this gives her choice of technology an almost ontological status, at least to aficionados:

> Jennifer Ringley is a FRAUD!!!! . . . Jennifer did not originate anything . . . there were cam-girls before her and there will be many more in the future. The only thing Jennifer had going for her was page design . . . and even that is looking tired compared to the newer girls pages. ("Re: JenniCam; Cybersaint," website)

JenniCam is the postmodern imperative to record the self taken to an extreme. Like many contemporary cultural forms, it mixes two fundamentally opposing but culturally important ideas of self: as an authenticity to be revealed and/or a performance to be created. It is not at all uncommon to see both of these models of selfhood conjoined or in uneasy relation, often within the same text. Nudity is available as a metaphor in both of these models. On the one hand, it figures as the ultimate sign of authenticity; Jenni undressing or having sex proves that this is "the real thing." But nudity also appears as self-conscious performance, as when Jenni strips for the camera. Over the years, the nature and meaning of Jenni's nudity has evolved:

> Where in the past the nudity was almost incidental, Jen now responded to her wider, mostly male audience, first by putting on impromptu, and then planned strip shows, which were distinguished by better camera work and more accurate and revealing lighting. (Gliddon, "What is JenniCam?", website)

The presence of the camera has its own effects, as the camera both reveals and produces the reality it claims to uncover.

As we have seen with many of the forms of nudity explored in this chapter, the recording of the self and the fame it brings have self-confirmatory, indeed therapeutic, dimensions. Like many of the Home Girls, Jenni claims that there have been personal benefits from having her life beamed to the world: she has met many friends and her self-image has improved. Fan pages have been constructed in her honour and she receives hundreds of emails every day.

But fame can also damage, most obviously in the form of lost privacy. This is played out in particularly strange ways in the JenniCam phenomenon, since

Jenni's fame lies precisely in her decision to abandon her privacy. This paradox becomes all the more bizarre the more one reads about JenniCam. It was, apparently, intended to be a "secret" site, and Jenni was furious at what she deemed a breach of trust by a computer magazine that unintentionally spilled this intimate global secret by reviewing the site. The story of the magazine's "breach" is now itself recorded on the Web, along with extracts from the unhappy email exchanges between Jenni and the editors who helped to make the site so popular that it had to close. As the extracts below make clear, Jenni, the woman who broadcast her life on the Web, nonetheless believed in privacy:

> I have always made sure to state clearly that the cam was a private address. Though you did not publish the address, the [review] article itself goes against the whole concept of privacy . . . [D]idn't it occur to you that a "private" page should remain private? (Ringley, quoted in Kidman, website)

The editor replied as follows:

> I'll be honest: no, it didn't. We are talking about a Web site. A Web site is by definition a *public* forum. Had you wanted a truly private page, you could have implemented intranet-style security . . . You chose not to. I can't quite see how *you* can connect a camera to a public forum and then claim that anyone who happens to look at it, or mention that it exists is breaching *your* privacy. (Kidman, website)

Along with the loss of privacy, the celebrity inevitably opens him/herself up for moral opprobrium. Jenni has been no exception, finding herself reproved not merely for her immodesty but for her "professionalization" (as well as for her technological outdatedness). We have already discussed how moral disapproval of female nudity is likely to be greater if there is money involved. This has been the case with Jenni's transition to "org." Jennifer has been keen to make it clear that she receives no benefit from the fee:

> I hope you understand how much I hate doing this. I feel like I'm letting everyone down. I feel like a traitor . . . If I had the thousand dollars to keep the site free, I would pay it – I want you to know that I'm not making a penny off this. The original plan was to take $8 for bandwidth, $2 for hardware upgrades, and $1.50 for me, I've opted not to take the money. As it stands now, we're dedicating $10 to bandwidth, $3 for hardware upgrades, and $2 for the Internet billing company. It seems fairer, and I don't want to make a profit from this. I want you to enjoy it. (Ringley, quoted in Gliddon, "What is JenniCam?", website)

This has not prevented online debate about Jenni's "morality;" one thread in an online JenniCam discussion forum was titled "JenniCam: Cybersaint or

Self-serving Trollop?" Thoroughly Postmodern Jenni she may be, but the choice of subject position offered her (saint or whore) is hardly new. While the moral logic is entirely familiar (her exposure is OK if it's free; blameworthy if not), it is interesting to note that this morality implies an ontology. Professionalizing the self is seen as de-authenticating it. Once Jennifer accepts money for the cam, she becomes less "real," condemned by one non-fan as a "fraud." This implicit ontology echoes one of the structuring ruptures of modernity: the split between home and work, such that paid work comes to be conceived of as a performance, inauthentic and alienated, while nonetheless, paradoxically, being the source of one's personal and social identity.

Finally, and familiarly, fame is seen to exact its price. Jenni's self-revelation is ironically seen to have corrupted that self, to the point where Jenni becomes, in the eyes of her erstwhile friend, technological adviser and keeper of the JenniCam archive, inauthentic to herself:

> I remember a really loveable, sweet girl named Jen who enjoyed having her pictures on the web. I remember the hard work I did for her . . . I'm not mad – I'm sad. I miss the old Jen, the girl who always had a friendly word, whose magical laugh could make my day. She's gone, probably for good, lost in the curious swamps of fame and – I devoutly hope – fortune. Well, here's how it all ends, in a chilly-cold note that contained not even a relieving touch of the Jen-flair and good humour I knew and loved, Jen has changed. I have changed, we all changed. Allow me to shed a tear.

The story ends when JenniCam – star, cyborg, corporation – finally copyrighted herself, and threatened to sue her own archivist:

> This message is to inform you that your web site which is located at http://207.1151.18.99/ contains material that [is] owned by and the exclusive property of JenniCAM.org - http://www.jennicam.org. This material is protected by copyright law.

Jenni's commingling of the "boudoir" and the "org" is certainly striking and in some sense exceptional. But on closer inspection, its remaking of public and private space is just one example of the many complex intersections, collapses and refurbishing of the public/private divide that constituted high modernity.

Conclusion: The Naked Truth

Clearly, although our ideas about identity, reality, authenticity and performance have undergone great changes in the past few decades, the metaphor of the naked truth has not had its day. The fundamental ambiguity of nakedness as a metaphor, and our social unease with it as an embodied state (the "unnaturalness" of the "state of nature") continue to make it an ideal vehicle for carrying contradictory ideas about truth and reality. According to the porn-maker Keith, the proliferation of sexualized images in the modern world has meant that the fantasy of unattainability has lost its power. Perhaps the new fantasy, he suggests, is one of *attainability*. I'd like to take this further by suggesting that sexual reality genres do not merely fetishize sex; they fetishize reality itself. Rawness can be as sexy as perfection, especially in a world still mostly bent on battering us with images of flawlessness. Nakedness, that sign of the raw, will surely continue to do battle with nudity, that sign of the ideal.

As reality genres continue to proliferate, we can only wonder whether nakedness will continue to bear this weight, or whether its richness will finally be exhausted under the increasing imperative to reveal all. My suspicion is that late-modern Westerners will be torn for a while longer yet between thinking of identity as an essence to be revealed and a performance to be carried out, and that nakedness, the world's oldest metaphor, will continue to be a vehicle through which we explore and live out this ambivalence.

Notes

1. For simplicity, I am using Baudrillard's (1987) term "simulacrum" as though it were a synonym for "image" or artifice. In fact, Baudrillard uses it more specifically (and more usefully) than this. He adapts Plato's term "simulacrum" to mean an imitation of an imitation. The endpoint of chains of simulacra is when the simulacrum ends up logically preceding the real. Take the example of pornography. Video porn might once, according to Baudrillard's logic, have been understandable as an imitation of reality – a photographic reproduction of people having sex. In a world dominated by the reproduction and circulation of such images, however, it is "real" sex that comes to imitate the imitation. People engaged in sex may well take as their models of behaviour the images that they have seen in porn. Baudrillard calls this process the precession of simulacra, whereby the "bad copy" comes to take logical precedence over, and eventually supplant, the real. Representations and images eventually come to alter reality itself. I have noted above that Baudrillard's concept relies on an ultimately unsustainable opposition between a brute reality and representations or images of that reality; despite this, it can usefully alert us to the effects of representations on everyday assumptions, expectations and practices.

2. This taxonomy is not meant to be exhaustive, but rather to help foreground issues of interest. For other taxonomies of nudity, see Toepfer (1996) and of course the medieval Christian taxonomy described in Chapter 2.

3. *Sartor Resartus* makes structural use of the metaphor implicit in the French term *sans-culottes*. The term referred first to the poorer Parisian republicans during the

French Revolution, who refused to wear the breeches of the aristocracy, wearing trousers instead. From this derivation, it can more generally mean an extreme republican or revolutionary. The *sans-culottes* were not, therefore, naked, but trousered. Still, the name (which means "without breeches") is open to a punning suggestion of nakedness. This is how Carlyle (1987) uses it, as an image for the revolutionariness of nakedness. Delacroix, too, turns the term into a visual pun: the *sans-culotte* in the left foreground of *Liberty Leading the People* is, literally, trouserless. Carlyle's thought, though, was always checked by a strongly conservative element (Hudson 1908: xiii).

4. The material in this section is drawn from an interview with Larry Pickering in 2000. I'd like to thank Larry Pickering for his generosity and insights.

5. This was not only an academic response. The following letter also plays with this idea:

> What a fuss about Liz and Phil overlooking the lake. Pity that so many were offended. An equally powerful statement could have been made had the artist used his own parents as models – nude, of course – and placed crowns on their heads. We'd have taken the point just as well. The anonymity of the models, with the real possibility of anatomical accuracy, would have enhanced the impact of the message – whatever it was. On the other hand, it might have proved a bit difficult to get his mum and dad to model in the nude. (Tibbals 1995)

Such a reading, based on the Freudian interpretation of monarchs and rulers as dream symbols for our parents (Freud 1963: 153), might help explain why throughout the incident, the Queen's body was depicted as in need of defence, as in two previous fracas in which two prime ministers (first Bob Hawke and then Paul Keating) put their hands on the royal back. These examples of inappropriate male touching of the maternal body – a body that should be sacrosanct, inviolate and untouchable – mapped bodily questions onto political ones; Hawke's and Keating's *faux pas* was popularly linked to their republicanism.

6. Melanie Klein's (1988) theory of human psychic life as characterized by ongoing psychical dramas of destruction and reparation seems apposite here. A Kleinian reading would see the naked Queen and Prince as having triggered fears about identity and belonging on both an individual and group level.

7. It is worth remembering that the Queen's nakedness could function as a symbol of vulnerability only in an era where public nudity is uncommon or shameful, and also when the body is taken as the property of a private individual. The monarch's body, for example, was not always understood only as the housing of his or her private soul. In court society, the king's body was also a prime site of the elaborate theatre that displayed the absoluteness of his rule, and so the "levée" (the morning ceremony in which the monarch arose naked and was formally dressed) was a public affair (Elias 1983: 84–5). The monarch's nakedness thus did not signify his/her ordinariness, nor was it vulnerable, obscene or individual. It was, rather, a site of the "intimate cementing of political relations" (Craik 1994: 12).

8. In literature, New Critics denounced such approaches as the "affective fallacy" (Wimsatt and Beardsley 1967).

9. For an account of how it is that somatophobia, misogyny and the reverence of bodily beauty, both male and female, could paradoxically coexist in Platonic thought, see Spelman (1982).

10. There are other discrepancies too, e.g. between the visual and literary evidence (McDonnell 1991: 184).

11. In republican Rome, *virtus* meant personal pre-eminence gained through "the true life" – that is, through deeds done on behalf of the state. *Virtus* was a noble and often military quality and was a form of pre-eminence that extended to one's family, ancestors and even unborn posterity. *Virtus* was achieved through public deeds, not private ones, and not through learning or commerce. *Virtus* was by definition unavailable to women, slaves, non-citizens or the lower orders.

12. Craig Cooper (1995) concludes that the tale is probably fictional, though it perhaps derives from a not impossible tactic: the parading before the jury of the "tragic victim," beating her breast and tearing at her gown in the manner of an Attic tragedy.

13. A contemporary example of the phallic, weapon-like breast would be the parodic oversized breasts worn in the film *Truth or Dare* by Madonna and her dancers (see Yalom 1997: 196).

14. Thanks to Penny Rossiter for this well-phrased observation. Of interest too is the fact not only that many women wrote to the newspapers condemning the MP, but also that the Minister Assisting the Prime Minister for the Status of Women also condemned the MP's action as an unwarranted privilege (Gray 2003).

15. There was a brief postscript to the war memorial controversy, sixty years later. An article in *Australian Women's Forum* (a women's counterpart to *Penthouse* and *Playboy*) on the growth in porn made specifically for women prominently featured a full-page photograph (repeated, indeed, one page later) titled "Orgasm After Civilization." The photograph depicted a bare-breasted woman, head thrown back, lifting herself as though after sex off the body of Hoff's prone soldier, with the rest of the war memorial interior clearly visible. This was a photograph clearly calculated to shock and upset, and it did.

16. The chiton was a tubular dress, sometimes belted, worn by well-to-do Athenians (Cohen 1997: 67–8). For a discussion of the metaphorical meanings of the slipped chiton in the European tradition, see Warner (1985: Chapter 12).

17. I have discussed this incident and the question of the strategic value of female nakedness for protestors in detail in Barcan (2002a).

18. When model Kate Fischer unashamedly put a price on her genital area, comedians had a field day:

> Sydney party girl Kate Fischer . . . has been an inspiration. In a recent interview, she outlined her game plan for exploiting her body parts with all the business acumen of a De Beers executive with a diamond mine in the Kimberley region. Referring to her role in *Sirens*, she said: "I didn't show my map of Tassie [female genital area] . . . Well, I can then sell it to *Playboy* for a hundred grand or so in a couple of years if no-one's ever seen it before."

"Isn't it great to see a gal putting something away for the future?" scoffed comedian Wendy Harmer (1995).

19. I have been unable to find the article to which Moskowitz and Li (2002) refer. The *Wall Street Journal* did include, however, a more equivocal discussion, in which they described IEG's efforts (and difficulties) in persuading mainstream investors to support the adult industry (Jung 2000).

20. Reports differ as to whether the US$ 741,000 was a joint sum or the amount each was to be paid.

21. This account of the progress of the case is drawn from newspaper sources and from a summary in Kleinhans' (2001) essay about the tape.

22. For a more detailed consideration of some of the homemade nudity and reality genres, see Barcan (2000, 2002b).

23. My use of inverted commas around "real" and "authentic" signals my post-structuralist conviction that these genres do not capture an unmediated reality. In the interests of readability, I do not always use inverted commas, but they should be taken as an unwritten part of the argument. Recognizing that even "reality" genres are discursively produced does not mean, of course, that they are to be understood as simply the same as more stylized genres.

24. The Polaroid used to be popular because it avoided the public nature of commercial photo development. According to one of our interviewees who worked in a suburban photo-lab, plenty of explicit material now comes through for commercial processing, and is treated liberally by most processors, unless acts involving children are depicted.

25. Laurence O'Toole (1999: xiv) claims that the pornographic magazine has become "a rather stagnant form," valued mainly because of its portability and its relative discreetness.

26. Cf. Jane Juffer (1998: 51): "On the one hand, computer consumption of porn is intensely private, occurring not only in the privacy of one's home (or cubicle/office at work) but also in the isolated, ephemeral interaction of user and screen. On the other hand, the consumption is intensely public, in that information proliferates and spreads to numerous sites, transgressing the physical boundaries that make other kinds of porn outlets, such as bookstores and theaters, much more easily identifiable and regulatable."

27. For a fuller account of the phenomenon of Home Girls, see Barcan (2000) and Albury (1997). Information used in this section is drawn from interviews with a number of editors and participants, whom I'd like to thank for sharing their views.

28. The editors we interviewed claim it arose spontaneously and not in imitation of something else, though one mentioned a column called "Readers' Wives" in a British magazine.

29. The current editor could recall, *in total*, one Asian man and a Fijian, though it is clear from the names of contributors that there are some non-Anglo Europeans.

30. *Picture*'s rates range from A$75 for a Bag Girl (girls who send in photos but ask for their head to be covered with a graphic of a brown paper bag), to A$150 for a Home Girl, A$500 for a Home Girl of the Week and A$3500 for Home Girl of the Year. Men are paid less than women. Every female "Homie" receives a free T-shirt emblazoned "100% All Australian Home Girl."

31. The editors described informal ways of defining an erection. The key is the angle of the dangle. Anything above 45 degrees counts as an erection. However, recent rulings by the office of Film and Literature Classification have decreed that if the penis touches the stomach it is an erection, which effectively outlaws many reclining male nude poses. The editor describes having had some difficulty making a determination in the case of a Home Bloke doing a handstand.

32. Currently, the Australian unrestricted category allows the display of the penis, provided it is not erect. Current regulations insist that in the case of full-frontal male nudity, the face must be shown. Headless shots of men (though not of women) are deemed by the classifiers to focus undue attention on the genital area and are thus not permitted in this category. This explains why the "Bag" option is not available to men. Nonetheless, the magazine, with its ongoing characterization of the ordinary person as hero, chooses to refigure this legal compulsion as a form of personal heroism: "We're not accepting those who are TOO CHICKEN to show their noggins."

33. Samantha was in general less scathing about the male participants, whom she saw as mostly in it for the money, though she did laugh at those who thought it would lead to a career in modelling.

34. The editors' descriptions of a whole apparatus of communication between magazine and readership (in the form of phone calls, letters, surveys, requests to be used as models) make it clear that there is a hidden traffic behind the scenes between readers and producers, and not just in the Home Pages. Readers develop favourite models and Homies, and fan cultures develop. Requests for the names and addresses of Home Girls became so frequent that each magazine now incorporates a feedback forum in which readers can write to their favourite Homie. The magazine then continues to act as conduit, passing on letters. As Samantha says, "Sometimes we feel like a dating service!" *Picture* has celebrated its first union between Home Bloke and female fan, producing the first "*Picture* babies" – two children and a third on the way when the editor last heard.

35. Moreover, the term "JenniCam" has become a link that often leads to porn sites and to sites selling illegal surveillance technologies (like hidden cameras and microphones).

Conclusion

In 1981, Ronald and Juliette Goldman published a study of the attitudes to nakedness and clothing of 838 children in Australia, England, North America and Sweden. The children were asked three questions concerning the necessity of clothing in a hypothetically warm climate. Their responses were rated according to Kohlberg's scale of moral reasoning.[1] The following is a selection of responses to the question of whether people should wear clothes, and why:

> You can't go round bare naked. You've got to wear bathers. It's rude, and people would laugh. (Australian boy, 7 years)

> My mom says you shouldn't do that. She says it's not right to go around with nothing on. (Australian girl, 7 years)

> Yes, you can't simply be all naked. This is not educated. (Swedish boy, 13 years)

> It's not nice. It wouldn't matter if there were only girls. If there were only boys they'd be rude about it. (English girl, 9 years)

> It's just normal to wear clothes. Everyone does. (North American girl, 11 years)

> It's self-respect, when you see natives running around with no clothes on, they don't know any better. We do. (North American boy, 13 years)

> Yes, because policemen might lock you up, and your father would give you a hiding. (English boy, 5 years)

> It's rude. You can go only to certain beaches so they can get tanned all over. They're showing all their personal things. It's got to be kept under control. (Australian boy, 15 years)

These short responses distil many of the themes of this book: the association of nudity with savagery, rudeness, danger and criminality; and the association of clothing with education, civilization, politeness, hygiene and gender propriety. The children's answers remind us, in miniature, of the *politics* of nudity and clothing, especially how easily nudity can be used to determine who is a "proper" kind of human person. Their answers allude to most of the fundamentals of the social contract: the need for rules and control, the fear of punishment, the power of norms, and the internalization of these social norms as unquestionable truths. The researchers found that the responses of the teenagers, in particular, reflected an "overwhelming conventional law and order morality" (Goldman and Goldman 1981: 84). The older children were the most aware of the need for conformity and of the social sanctions that would be faced if one breached norms (p. 183). What we *don't* hear in the children's responses (probably because the questions focused on why we *should* wear clothes) are any of the positive meanings of nudity – as purity, freedom, naturalness and truth. Such meanings are as important and longstanding as the negative ones, but they have come down to the modern West more as a metaphorical residue or an artistic standard than as a set of daily experiences.

Although the children's overwhelming approbation of clothing as either inherently or socially necessary would be shared by most citizens of the modern West, the Western philosophical and religious traditions have nonetheless had moments of suspicion towards clothing. The bedrock of this suspicion is the Adam and Eve myth, which imagines clothing as the result of a primal transgression. Clothing is thus ambiguous from the first, a sign simultaneously of the birth of human culture and of distance from God. So too is nudity, a sign both of the original purity, truth and naturalness of human beings and of their subsequent fall into sin. Clothing has become an ambiguous symbol of the ambiguous nature of fallen humanness itself, and nudity an ambiguous symbol both of innate purity and of the inevitability of its loss.

This book has focused on the Judeo-Christian tradition as a legacy of potential meanings of nudity. But in daily life, we meet nudity as a set of instances rather than as an abstract category. We make decisions about when and how to cover up, or what movies to let our children watch, or whether to get changed in the private cubicle or the public area of a changing-room. Some of these choices are made *for* us to such an extent that they do not represent a moment of conscious choice at all. Most of us do not decide *whether* to dress before going out, but *how*. When we do think about nudity, our response will vary greatly according to context. Our reaction to nudity may be nuanced ("That's not appropriate at the dinner table") or simple ("That's disgusting!").

Whatever choices or determinations we as individuals might make, it is clear that our culture provides us with a vast array of possible responses to nudity, ranging from disapprobation to romanticization. The rich philosophical, religious and artistic traditions of the West help structure our reactions to nudity and our bodily experiences of it. While in any given instance we as individuals might make a clear-cut judgement, our society as a whole is characterized by *ambivalence* towards nudity. This ambivalence is related to a host of others – ambivalence about the body itself, about sex, about the benefits of modern civilization and, deep down, about what it means to be a human, and about the place of humans in nature.

Ambivalence and Nature

In his study of the nude in art, Liam Hudson (1982: 9) claims that our prime psychological relation to our body is one of ambivalence: "Far from being an arbitrary physical lump onto which we project culturally determined values, [the body] positively demands of us responses that are contradictory, fissured." Hudson claims that ambivalence, equivocation, discrepancy and dissemblance are ubiquitous in human consciousness, and he sees the human characteristic of symbol-making as a response to such uncertainty. "In the face of irreconcilable conflict," he says, "we move spontaneously from the level of the literal to that of the symbol" (p. 41). The symbolic is the venue in which we can "explore our confusions, gain manageable excitement from them, and attempt their resolution at one remove" (p. 41). The body is itself a symbol – our first, our most malleable and our most fundamental symbol. Moreover, this symbol is uniquely ours and also shared with every human being on earth. It is inherently both personal and social. Hudson believes that the nude in art has a psychological function, namely, the containment of ambivalence about the body (p. 89).

Whether or not one accepts the proposition that ambivalence might be a universal human response to the body, it is certainly the case that it is one prevalent response to the question of human embodiment and nature. Modernity has shaped its own forms of ambivalence, based on conflicting ideologies of both human nature and nature more generally. The history of the West has been marked by both humanist admiration for humankind, the measure of all things, and abhorrence and disgust at humankind, the quintessence of dust, and the Western history of nudity has followed suit.

We may like or loathe our bodies, but most of us are not indifferent to them. Indeed, it is quite probable that many of us are ambivalent about them. Some form of ambivalence about the body may even be inevitable. After all, mind and body, body and self, are not one and the same. Even in societies not characterized by the radical conceptual splitting of mind from body typified by Cartesianism, there must still be some form of distinction between body and self. The body always exceeds our conscious control; there will always be some bodily processes that remain remote from our perception and consequently remain peripheral to our sense of identity.[2] And the ever-present shadow of the body's mortality means that the body is unlikely to be regarded without ambivalence, even within a spiritual or religious worldview.

The body is the most intimate and immediate of sites where we see our human identity intersect with the question of biology, and hence, ultimately, of nature. It is subject to the operations of biology and the environment, but Nature is, we know, a cultural idea, and a deep and complex one at that. The idea of nature as impersonal or amoral has frequently had to compete with a moral conception of nature as, variously, cruel, vengeful, the instrument of God, a benign force or a loving teacher.[3] Different ideas of nature have implied different conceptions of the place of humankind in nature. Today, we sometimes think of modern society as sadly distant from nature, but then we regard nature itself with ambivalence, as something to be transcended as well as idealized. Sometimes modern societies think of nature as something to rule over; at other times, nature is seen as a source of rules for *us* to follow. Sometimes we imagine humans as part of nature, at other times we do not.

Nature is, according to Raymond Williams, a term whose singleness masks the incredible complexity both of natural processes themselves and of nature as a cultural idea. Indeed, according to Williams (1976: 219), nature is "perhaps the most complex word in the language." Yet it has often been reduced to a singularity. Nature came to be personified as a single goddess very early in history, and the reduction of nature spirits and gods to a single Nature (be it a Mother Nature or a singular abstract "Nature") has been "surprisingly persistent" (p. 220). Historically, the emergence of a singular Nature parallels that of a monotheistic Christian God. The singularity of the term "nature" belies the wide, indeed opposing, range of meanings it has been able to carry. Nature has been "at once innocent, unprovided, sure, unsure, fruitful, destructive, a pure force and tainted and cursed" (p. 222). Williams points out that conceptions of nature have tended to parallel political changes, a parallel made possible by the idea that nature has "laws" and "rules." One of the most significant changes in the idea of nature was a shift over the eighteenth and nineteenth centuries to an understanding of nature as the opposite of anything made by man. The opposition between nature and society could work in two directions. Nature might be something we should transcend and override. (As Katharine Hepburn's character put it in John Huston's film *The African Queen* (1951), "Nature, Mr. Allnut, is what we are put into this world to rise above.") But Nature could also be imagined as a cure for a flawed society. In the Enlightenment, this took the form of the idea that "an obsolete or corrupt society [was] needing redemption and renewal;" in the Romantic period, it was an "artificial" or "mechanical" society that needed to learn from Nature (Williams 1976: 223). Nakedness in particular has had to bear the weight of being the bodily state considered most "natural." Little wonder, then, that nakedness has been subject to such contradictory moral loading.

This book has surveyed some of the major impacts of the Western heritage on the contemporary meanings of nakedness and on modern experiences of the nude body. It has shown how our beliefs and experiences have been marked by the complex cultural legacy of, among other things, the Judeo-Christian religious tradition, the Western philosophical lineage, and the European fine art tradition. Throughout, we saw that nakedness operates differently across the social spectrum. Gender is perhaps the most obvious site of the differential operation of nudity. There is nothing new in this: the nudity of men and women has always meant different things and has had to obey different social and cultural laws. We noted, for example, how the loftiest meanings of nudity were never fully available to women after the decline of the mother goddesses. Feminists, then, have a difficult relation to this complex tradition. They have lamented what they often see as its denigration or exploitation of the female body, and have noted the impossibility of unambiguous female nakedness in the shadow of this history. So, too, race has been a key determinant of the meanings of nudity, and continues to be so, at least if the responses of the children surveyed by the Goldmans are anything to go by. Rank and social class also greatly influence how nudity will be valued. The topless waitress receives none of the approbation of the Venus de Milo. Nor is art necessarily a clear guide to other social mores. Art and daily life are not simple mirrors of each other; what goes in the gallery or in literature by no means goes on the street.

Those who believe in the "naturalness" of the body and of sex might see the Western legacy as one primarily of loss, as Paul Ableman (1984) does in *The Banished Body*. Ableman sees Christianity as having ushered in a long era of alienation from the body:

> In Mark's Gospel, after Judas has kissed Jesus and thus delivered him to his enemies, Jesus is led away to judgement, crucifixion and the dawn of Christianity. All desert him except for a mysterious young man who "followed him with nothing but a linen cloth about his body; and they seized him, but he left the linen cloth and ran away naked." It is tempting to see in that anonymous youth, who makes such a fleeting appearance in history, a symbol of the body fleeing the dispensation to come. (Ableman 1984: 39–40)

But of course the nude body didn't flee completely – it cannot – and it was never a free body in the first place. But the dispensation that Ableman laments certainly did make of nudity something quite complex and contradictory, and it remains so even in modern times.

To conclude, I will sum up some of the key elements of the power of nudity as a cultural idea. First, it is a metaphor for both plenitude and lack, the all and the nothing of human existence and culture. Second, it is a metaphor for a degree-zero humanity, an enormously potent cultural fiction. Third, although its meanings are not restricted to the sexual, it is caught up in the understanding, experience and regulation of sex and gender. And fourth, the nude body resists being caught in the spotlight of any one of these "meanings" of nakedness. It is precisely the fact that the real naked body *cannot* be contained in any given moment by any one of these meanings that makes nudity a slippery, ambiguous, "dangerous" category, culturally speaking. We know it is dangerous because we see institutionalized attempts to contain it – laws, prohibitions, taboos – and because we *all* jostle with it in mundane and habitual ways, even in private. Perhaps we turn away from the person next to us in the changing-room; maybe we are undecided how revealing a swimming costume to buy; maybe we studiously avoid looking at a woman breastfeeding; or perhaps we decide to take the risk and go for a joyous skinny dip. Nudity, in public and in private, is a rich affair. Clearly, when you strip nakedness bare, there is more than meets the eye.

Notes

1. Lawrence Kohlberg (1981) divided reasoning into three stages (preconventional, conventional and postconventional), each of which was further divided into two stages. His scale is unashamedly progressivist. It privileges autonomous and principled reasoning over conventional, instrumental or conformist reasoning. Lower categories of moral reasoning are those that invoke the threat of punishment and obedience, and the stages progress through instrumental relativism (i.e. pragmatic reasoning) through law-and-order type responses, through to responses that show an understanding of the social contract. Kohlberg's scale culminates in "universal ethical principles" – those that arise from conscience and that recognize reciprocity and the equality of individuals (see Goldman and Goldman 1981: 172; Kohlberg 1981). The Goldmans found that Australian children consistently scored highest on postconventional thinking, even though Swedish children held the most liberal attitudes.

2. This is the argument made by phenomenologist Drew Leder (1990) in *The Absent Body* to explain the plausibility of Cartesianism. Not all parts of the body offer up much by way of perceptual data, and we often become aware of the body in *dys*function. Even allowing for the incredibly subtle forms of self-knowledge opened up by non-Western experts such as yogis, it still seems likely that there will always be something of the body that escapes conscious knowledge, control or perception.

3. For example:

> Nature is amoral – not immoral . . . [It] existed for eons before we arrived, didn't know we were coming, and doesn't give a damn about us. (Gould 1999: 195)

For an account of nature's amorality that nonetheless presents nature as a negligent female force (a bad mother) one cannot go past the following from David Hume:

> Look round this universe . . . The whole presents nothing but the idea of a blind nature, impregnated by a great vivifying principle, and pouring forth from her lap, without discernment or parental care, her maimed and abortive children. (Hume 1947: 211)

References

Abbott, Greg (1996) "Jessica Hustles Detractors." *Sydney Morning Herald* 21 April: 7.

Ableman, Paul (1984) *The Banished Body*. London: Sphere (orig. published as *The Anatomy of Nakedness*, 1982).

Albury, Katherine (1997) "Homie-Erotica: Heterosexual Female Desire in *The Picture*." *Media International Australia* 84 (May): 19–27.

Alford, C. Fred (1989) *Melanie Klein and Critical Social Theory: An Account of her Politics, Art, and Reason Based on her Psychoanalytic Theory*. New Haven, CT: Yale University Press.

"A Mother" (1883) Letter. *The Argus* [Melbourne] 18 May: 10.

Anon. (1965) "Barely African." *Sydney Morning Herald* 21 May: 2.

Anon. (1966) "Ballet Topless in New York." *Courier-Mail* [Brisbane] 18 November: 4.

Anon. (1990) "Nude Sisters Too Rude." *Blue Mountains Whisper* 10 (Nov.): 1–2.

Anon. (1993) "'Photo' Fails to Amuse Kennett." *Sydney Morning Herald* 3 August: 6.

Anon. (1994) "The Naked Truth." *Sun-Herald* [Sydney] 27 February: 144.

Anon. (1996) *The Atlanta Dream: A Photographic Tribute*. Special issue of *black+ white*, 2nd edn. Sydney: Studio Magazines.

Anon. (1997a) "AFI Award Winner Rachel Strips in Casino Protest." *Who Weekly* 26 May: 21.

Anon. (1997b) "Naked Prayer." *Sydney Morning Herald* 22 February: 2.

Anon. (2001) "VH1 Ranks '100 Most Shocking Moments in Rock and Roll' in Special Premiering May 21–25 at 10:00pm." *PR Newswire* 17 May.

Anon. (2003) "Let Them Wear Panties." *Sydney Morning Herald* 12–13 July:18.

Ashbee, Brian (1997) "Naked Pleasure." *Art Review* 49 (Sept.): 56–7.

Ashcroft, Bill, Gareth Griffiths, and Helen Tiffin (1998) *Key Concepts in Post-Colonial Studies*. London: Routledge.

Ashworth, Ron (1946) "Irresponsible Sex Relations Destroying Mankind." *Australian Sunbather* 1(3), no page numbers.

—— (1948) "Beauty in Naturism." *Australasian Sunbathing Quarterly Review* 1(1): 6–7.

Augustine (1986) *The Confessions of St Augustine*. Ed. Hal M. Helms. Orleans, MA: Paraclete Press.

—— (1998) *The City of God Against the Pagans*. Ed. and trans. R.W. Dyson. Cambridge: Cambridge University Press.

"A Woman" (1883) Letter. *The Argus* [Melbourne] 18 May: 10.

Ayto, John (1993) *Euphemisms: Over 3,000 Ways to Avoid Being Rude or Giving Offence*. London: Bloomsbury.

Bain, D.M. (1982) [Untitled]. *Liverpool Classic Monthly* 7(1): 7–10.

Baker, Lee D. (1998) *From Savage to Negro: Anthropology and the Construction of Race, 1896–1954*. Berkeley, CA: University of California Press.

Bakhtin, Mikhail (1984) *Rabelais and his World*. Trans. Hélène Iswolsky. Bloomington, IN: Indiana University Press.

Banks, Joseph (1998) *The Endeavour Journal of Joseph Banks: The Australian Journey*. Ed. Paul Breunton. Pymble (Sydney): Angus & Robertson/HarperCollins.

Barcan, Ruth (1999) "Privates in Public: The Space of the Urinal." In *Imagining Australian Space: Cultural Studies and Spatial Inquiry*. Nedlands, WA: University of Western Australia Press.

—— (2000) "Home on the Rage: Nudity, Celebrity, and Ordinariness in the Home Girls/Blokes Pages." *Continuum: Journal of Media and Cultural Studies* 14(2): 145–58.

—— (2001) "'The Moral Bath of Bodily Unconsciousness': Female Nudism, Bodily Exposure and the Gaze." *Continuum: Journal of Media and Cultural Studies* 15(3): 305–19.

—— (2002a) "Female Exposure and the Protesting Woman." *Cultural Studies Review* 8(2): 62–82.

—— (2002b) "In the Raw: "Home-Made" Porn and Reality Genres." *Journal of Mundane Behavior* 3(1) http://www.mundanebehavior.org

—— (2004) "'Regaining what Mankind has Lost through Civilisation': Early Nudism and Ambivalent Moderns." *Fashion Theory: The Journal of Dress, Body and Culture* 8(1): 1–20.

Barthes, Roland (1973) *Mythologies*. Trans. Annette Lavers. London: Paladin.

Bartky, Sandra Lee (1990) "Shame and Gender." *Femininity and Domination: Studies in the Phenomenology of Oppression*. New York: Routledge.

Bartlett, Alison (2002) "Scandalous Practices and Political Performances: Breastfeeding in the City." *Continuum: Journal of Media and Cultural Studies* 16(1): 111–21.

Bataille, Georges (1982 [1928]) *Story of the Eye, by Lord Auch*. Trans. Joachim Neugroschal. Harmondsworth: Penguin.

Baudrillard, Jean (1987) *The Evil Demon of Images*. Power Institute Publications no. 3, Sydney: Power Institute of Fine Arts.

Beaglehole, J.C. (1955) *The Journals of Captain James Cook on his Voyages of Discovery. Vol 1: The Voyage of the Endeavour 1768–1771*. Cambridge: Hakluyt Society/Cambridge University Press.

Benyon, E.W. (1995) Letter. *Sydney Morning Herald* 19 April: 16.

Berger, John (1972) *Ways of Seeing*. London: BBC and Penguin.

Bindrim, Paul (1968) "A Report on a Nude Marathon: The Effect of Physical Nudity Upon the Practice of Interaction in the Marathon Group." *Psychotherapy: Theory, Research and Practice* 5(3): 180–8.

Blessing, Jennifer (1997) "The Art(ifice) of Striptease: Gypsy Rose Lee and the Masquerade of Nudity." In *Modernism, Gender, and Culture: A Cultural Studies Approach*. Ed. Lisa Rado. New York: Garland, 1997.

Bloom, Harold (1986) Introduction. *Thomas Carlyle*. Ed. and introd. Harold Bloom. New York: Chelsea House.

Blumenberg, Hans (1998) "Die Metaphorik der 'nackten' Wahrheit." *Paradigmen zu einer Metaphorologie*. Frankfurt am Main: Suhrkamp.

Boileau, Jacques (1675) *De l'abus des nudités de gorge*. Brussels: François Foppens.

—— (1678) *A Just and Seasonable Reprehension of Breasts and Naked Shoulders Written by a Grave and Learned Papist*. Trans. Edward Cooke. London: Jonathan Edwin.

Bond, Kingsley G. (Rev.) (1964) "Topless Dresses and Morals." *People* 23 September: 13–14.

Bonfante, Larissa (1989) "Nudity as a Costume in Classical Art." *American Journal of Archaeology* 93(4): 543–70.

Bonner, Frances (1998) "Forgetting Linda: Women Cross-Dressing in Recent Cinema." *Continuum: Journal of Media and Cultural Studies* 12(3): 267–77.

Boorstin, Daniel J. (1971) *The Image: A Guide to Pseudo-events in America*. New York: Atheneum.

Bordo, Susan (1993a) "Reading the Male Body." *Michigan Quarterly Review* 32(4): 696–735.

—— (1993b) *Unbearable Weight: Feminism, Western Culture, and the Body*. Berkeley, CA: University of California Press.

Bourdieu, Pierre (1984) *Distinction: A Social Critique of the Judgement of Taste*. Trans. Richard Nice. Cambridge, MA: Harvard University Press.

Braidotti, Rosi (1994) *Nomadic Subjects: Embodiment and Sexual Difference in Contemporary Feminist Theory*. New York: Columbia University Press.

Breuer, Leslie F. and Martin S. Lindauer (1977) "Distancing Behavior in Relation to Statues in a Simulated Museum Setting." *Perceptual and Motor Skills* 45: 377–8.

Bronfen, Elisabeth (1992) *Over her Dead Body: Death, Femininity and the Aesthetic*. New York: Routledge.

Bryant, Clifton D. (1982) *Sexual Deviancy and Social Proscription: The Social Context of Carnal Behavior*. New York: Human Sciences.

Butler, Judith (1990) *Gender Trouble: Feminism and the Subversion of Identity*. New York: Routledge.

Button, James (1997) "Whatever it Takes for the Naked Truth." *The Age* [Melbourne] 10 May: 7.

Bynum, Caroline Walker (1991) "The Body of Christ in the Later Middle Ages: A Reply to Leo Steinberg." In *Fragmentation and Redemption: Essays on Gender and the Human Body in Medieval Religion*. New York: Zone.

Cameron, Deborah (1992) "Republic a Search for Identity." *Sydney Morning Herald* 20 February: 6.

Caputi, Jane (2001) "On the Lap of Necessity: A Mythic Reading of Teresa Brennan's Energetic Philosophy." *Hypatia* 16(2): 1–26.

Carlyle, Thomas (1987) *Sartor Resartus*. Ed. and introd. Kerry McSweeny and Peter Sabor. Oxford: Oxford University Press.

Carter, Angela (1982) *Nothing Sacred: Selected Writings*. London: Virago.

Cash, Stephanie (1994) "CIA Bars Nudity in Art Works." *Art in America* 82(3): 31.

Castles, Stephen, et al. (1992) *Mistaken Identity: Multiculturalism and the Demise of Nationalism in Australia*, 3rd edn. Sydney: Pluto Press.

Christ, Alice T. (1997) "The Masculine Ideal of 'The Race that Wears the Toga.'" *Art Journal* 56(2): 24–30.

Cixous, Hélène (1981) "Sorties." In *New French Feminisms: An Anthology*. Ed. and introd. Elaine Marks and Isabelle de Courtivron. New York: Schocken.

Clark, Kenneth (1956) *The Nude: A Study of Ideal Art*. Harmondsworth: Penguin.

Clarke, Magnus (1982) *Nudism in Australia: A First Study*. Deakin, Vic.: Deakin University Press.

Cockburn, Jon (1995) "Naked Royals." *Agenda* 43 (July): 43–5.

Cohen, Beth (1997) "Divesting the Female Breast of Clothes in Classical Sculpture." In *Naked Truths: Women, Sexuality, and Gender in Classical Art and Archaeology*. Ed. Ann Olga Koloski-Ostrow and Claire L. Lyons. London: Routledge.

Contractor, Aban (1995) "Some Grin and Others Bare it." *Canberra Times* 14 April: 2.

Cooper, Craig (1995) "Hyperides and the Trial of Phryne." *Phoenix* 49: 303–18.

Cooper, Emmanuel (1995) *Fully Exposed: The Male Nude in Photography*, 2nd edn. London: Routledge.

Cooper, Wendy (1971) *Hair: Sex Society Symbolism*. New York: Stein & Day.

Cosic, Miriam (1995) "Shock of the New: 'Mum' without her Clothes." *Sydney Morning Herald* 18 April: 15.

Craft-Fairchild, Catherine (1993) *Masquerade and Gender: Disguise and Female Identity in Eighteenth-Century Fictions by Women*. University Park, PA: Pennsylvania University Press.

Craik, Jennifer (1994) *The Face of Fashion: Cultural Studies in Fashion*. London: Routledge.

Crawley, Ernest (1965) "Nudity and Dress." In *Dress, Adornment, and the Social Order*. Ed. Mary Ellen Roach and Joanne Bubolz Eicher. New York: John Wiley.

Crowley, Nick (1998) "Hooray!" Letter. *Sydney Morning Herald* 7 March: 42.

Cruden, Alexander (1848) *A Complete Concordance to the Old and New Testament: Or, A Dictionary, and Alphabetical Index to the Bible in Two Parts*, 11th edn. London: Longman.

Dampier, William (n.d.) "Dampier's Voyage Round the World." In *Voyages Round the World* by Captain James Cook. Ed. D. Laing Purves. Edinburgh: W.P. Nimmo, Hay & Mitchell.

Danto, Arthur C. (1994) "Lucian Freud." *The Nation* 24 January: 100–4.

Darwin, Charles (1959 [1906]) *The Voyage of the Beagle*. Introd. H. Graham Cannon. London: J.M. Dent.

Delvecchio, Julie (1995) "By Royal Appointment." *Sydney Morning Herald* 28 December: 22.

Dentith, Simon (1995) *Bakhtinian Thought: An Introductory Reader*. London: Routledge.

Derrett, J. Duncan M. (1973) "Religious Hair." *Man* 8(1): 100–3.

Derrida, Jacques (1987) "Le Facteur de la vérité." In *The Post Card: From Socrates to Freud and Beyond*. Trans and introd. Alan Bass. Chicago: University of Chicago Press.

Descartes, René (1970) "Second Meditation. The Nature of the Human Mind: It is Better Known than the Body." In *Descartes: Philosophical Writings*. Ed. Elizabeth Anscombe and Peter Thomas Geach. London: Nelson's University Paperbacks.

Donne, John (1971) *The Complete English Poems*. Ed. A.J. Smith. Harmondsworth: Penguin.

Donoghue, Daniel (2002) *Lady Godiva: A Literary History of the Legend*. Oxford: Blackwell.

Douglas, Anna (1994) "Childhood: A Molotov Cocktail for our Time." *Women's Art Magazine* 59 (July/Aug.): 14–18.

Douglas, Jack D. and Paul K. Rasmussen, with Carol Ann Flanagan (1977) *The Nude Beach*. Beverly Hills, CA: Sage.

Douglas, Mary (1984 [1966]) *Purity and Danger: An Analysis of the Concepts of Pollution and Taboo*. London: Ark.

Dover, K.J. (1978) *Greek Homosexuality*. London: Duckworth.

Dovey, Jon (2000) *Freakshow: First Person Media and Factual Television*. London: Pluto Press.

Durkheim, Emile (1976 [1915]) *The Elementary Forms of the Religious Life*. Introd. Robert Nisbet. Trans. Joseph Ward Swain. London: George Allen & Unwin.

Dyer, Richard (1979) *Stars*. London: British Film Institute.

Edelman, Lee (1996) "Men's Room." In *Stud: Architectures of Masculinity*. Ed. Joel Sanders. New York: Princeton Architectural Press.

Ehrentheil, Otto F., Stanley J. Chase and Mary R. Hyde (1973) "Revealing and Body Display." *Archives of General Psychiatry* 29(3): 363–7.

El Guindi, Fadwa (1999) *Veil: Modesty, Privacy and Resistance*. Oxford: Berg.

Elias, Norbert (1983) *The Court Society*. Trans. Edmund Jephcott. Oxford: Basil Blackwell.

—— (1994) *The Civilizing Process: The History of Manners and State Formation and Civilization*. Trans. Edmund Jephcott. Oxford: Basil Blackwell.

Elkins, James (1996) *The Object Stares Back: On the Nature of Seeing*. New York: Simon & Schuster.

Elkins, Murray (1974) "The Significance of Streaking." *Medical Aspects of Human Sexuality* 8: 157–8.

Ellingson, Ter (2001) *The Myth of the Noble Savage*. Berkeley, CA: University of California Press.

Ellis, Havelock (1923) *Studies in the Psychology of Sex. Vol 4: Sexual Selection in Man*. Philadelphia, PA: F.A. Davis.

—— (1929) Introduction to Maurice Parmelee, *Nudism in Modern Life*. London: Noel Douglas.

—— (1937) "The Evolution of Modesty." In *Studies in the Psychology of Sex*. Vol. 1. New York: Random House.

Epictetus. (1995) *The Discourses of Epictetus*. Ed. Christopher Gil. London: J.M. Dent.

Evans, Louise (1999) "Who Came A-Watching Matildas Point to Success of their Naked Ambition." *Sydney Morning Herald* 1 December: 50.

Ewin, Joanne (1995) "Is PM Having Snigger?" Letter. *Canberra Times* 18 April: 12.

Exon, Neville (1995) "'Twas the Wrong Head Rolled." Letter. *Canberra Times* 18 April: 12.

Ewing, William A. (1994) *The Body: Photoworks of the Human Form*. London: Thames & Hudson.

Falconer-Flint, Dany (1992) "Verandahs." *Quadrant* 36(11): 69–72.

Falk, Pasi (1994) *The Consuming Body*. London: Sage.

Farouque, Farah (1995) "A Head Rolls in Ruckus Over Nude Sculpture." *The Age* 15 April: 1.

Featherstone, Mike (1991) "The Body in Consumer Culture." In *The Body: Social Process and Cultural Theory*. Ed. Mike Featherstone, Mike Hepworth, and Bryan S. Turner. London: Sage.

Feifer, M. (1985) *Going Places*. London: Macmillan.

Fisher, Seymour (1973) *Body Consciousness*. London: Fontana/Collins.

Foucault, Michel (1979) *Discipline and Punish: The Birth of the Prison*. Trans. Alan Sheridan. Harmondsworth: Penguin-Peregrine.

—— (1984 [1976]) *The History of Sexuality: An Introduction*. Trans. Robert Hurley. Harmondsworth: Penguin.

—— (1989 [1973]) *The Birth of the Clinic: An Archaeology of Medical Perception*. London: Routledge.

Fougerat de David de Lastours, [François] (1929) *Morale et nudité. Précédé de l'introduction à l'étude de l'insolation*. Paris: [Collections de la ligue] Vivre [M.K. de Mongeot].

France, Anatole (1909) *Penguin Island*. Trans. A.W. Evans. London: John Lane the Bodley Head.

Freedberg, David (1989) *The Power of Images: Studies in the History and Theory of Response*. Chicago: University of Chicago Press.

Freud, Sigmund (1953) *The Interpretation of Dreams*. In *The Standard Edition of the Complete Psychological Works of Sigmund Freud*. Ed. and trans. James Strachey, with Anna Freud. London: Hogarth Press and the Institute of Psycho-Analysis, Vol. 4.

—— (1963) "Symbolism in Dreams." Lecture 10 of *Introductory Lectures on Psycho-Analysis*. In *Standard Edition*, Vol. 15.

—— (1966) "Fetishism." In *The Standard Edition*, Vol. 21.

Frow, John (1995) "Private Parts: Body Organs in Global Trade." *UTS Review* 1(2): 84–100.

Fuller, Jacqueline (1995) "Ghostly Reminder of the Ugly Aussie." *Canberra Times* 17 April: 1.

Fulton, Christopher (1997) "The Boy Stripped Bare by his Elders: Art and Adolescence in Renaissance Florence." *Art Journal* 56(2): 31–40.

Gay, Jan (1933) *On Going Naked*. London: Noel Douglas.

Gelder, Ken, and Jane M. Jacobs (1998) *Uncanny Australia: Sacredness and Identity in a Postcolonial Nation*. Carlton South, Vic. Melbourne University Press.

Giblett, Rod (1996) *Postmodern Wetlands*. Edinburgh: Edinburgh University Press.

Gilman, Sander L. (1986) "Black Bodies, White Bodies: Toward an Iconography of Female Sexuality in Late Nineteenth-Century Art, Medicine, and Literature." In *"Race," Writing, and Difference*. Ed. Henry Louis Gates. Chicago: University of Chicago Press.

Gittleson, N., et al. (1978) "Victims of Indecent Exposure." *British Journal of Psychiatry* 132: 61–6.

Goffman, Erving (1965) "Attitudes and Rationalizations Regarding Body Exposure." In *Dress, Adornment, and the Social Order*. Ed. Mary Ellen Roach and Joanne Bubolz Eicher. New York: John Wiley.

Goldman, Ronald J. and Juliette D.G. Goldman (1981) "Children's Perceptions of Clothes and Nakedness: A Cross-National Study." *Genetic Psychology Monographs* 104(2): 163–85.

Goodson, Aileen (1991) *Therapy, Nudity and Joy: The Therapeutic Use of Nudity through the Ages from Ancient Ritual to Modern Psychology*. Los Angeles: Elysium Growth Press.

Goodwin, Sarah Webster and Elisabeth Bronfen (eds) (1993) *Death and Representation*. Baltimore, MD: Johns Hopkins University Press.

Gould, Stephen Jay (1999) *Rocks of Ages: Science and Religion in the Fullness of Life*. New York: Ballantine.

Graves, Douglas R. (1979) *Figure Painting in Oil*. New York: Watson Guptill.

Graves, Robert (1966) "The Naked and the Nude." In *Collected Poems 1965*. London: Cassell.

Gray, Darren (2003) "Breastfeeder was Wrong: Vanstone." *Sydney Morning Herald* 28 February: 4.

Greaves, B.C. (1995) Letter. *Sydney Morning Herald* 19 April: 16.

Grishin, Sasha (1998) *Garry Shead: Encounters with Royalty*. North Ryde, NSW: Craftsman House.

Grosz, Elizabeth (1994) *Volatile Bodies: Towards a Corporeal Feminism*. St Leonards, Vic. Allen & Unwin.

Guillois, Mina and André Guillois (1989) *L'Humour des nudistes . . . et des strip-teaseuses*. Alleur (Belgium): Marabout.

Gutting, Gary (ed.) (1994) *The Cambridge Companion to Foucault*. Cambridge: Cambridge University Press.

Hagenbaugh, Barbara (1997) "Users Turn On to Woman with Web Appeal." *Sydney Morning Herald* 20 September: 30.

Hanson, Karen (1993) "Dressing Down Dressing Up: The Philosophic Fear of Fashion." In *Aesthetics in Feminist Perspective*. Ed. Hilde Hein and Carolyn Korsmeyer. Bloomington, IN: Indiana State University.

Haraway, Donna J. (1991) "A Cyborg Manifesto: Science, Technology, and Socialist-Feminism in the Late Twentieth Century." In *Simians, Cyborgs, and Women: The Reinvention of Nature*. London: Free Association Books.

Harmer, Wendy (1995) "Naked Ambition." *Sydney Morning Herald Good Weekend* 30 September: 14.

Harris, John (1994) *One Blood: 200 Years of Aboriginal Encounter with Christianity: A Story of Hope*, 2nd edn. Sutherland, NSW: Albatross.

Harvey, Sandra (1994) "Policewoman Barely Makes Penthouse." *Sydney Morning Herald* 13 July: 5.

Heath, Stephen (1986) "Joan Rivière and the Masquerade." In *Formations of Fantasy*. Ed. Victor Burgin, James Donald, and Cora Kaplan. London: Methuen.

Hepworth, Mike and Mike Featherstone (1982) *Surviving Middle Age*. Oxford: Basil Blackwell.

Herodotus (1954) *The Histories*. Trans. and introd. Aubrey de Selincourt. Harmondsworth: Penguin.

Hershman, P. (1974) "Hair, Sex and Dirt." *Man* (n.s.) 9: 274–98.

Holder, R.W. (1995) *A Dictionary of Euphemisms*. Oxford: Oxford University Press.

Hollander, Anne (1993) *Seeing Through Clothes*. Berkeley, CA: University of California Press.

Howard, Seymour (1986) "Fig Leaf, Pudica, Nudity, and Other Revealing Concealments." *American Imago* 43(4): 289–93.

Hudson, Liam (1982) *Bodies of Knowledge: The Psychological Significance of the Nude in Art*. London: Weidenfeld & Nicolson.

Hudson, W[illiam] H[enry] (1908) Introduction to Thomas Carlyle, *Sartor Resartus [and] On Heroes and Hero Worship*. London: Dent.

Hume, David (1947) *Dialogues Concerning Natural Religion*, 2nd edn. Ed. and introd. Norman Kemp Smith. Indianapolis, IN: Bobbs-Merrill.

Irigaray, Luce (1985) *This Sex Which is Not One*. Trans. Catherine Porter with Carolyn Burke. Ithaca, NY: Cornell University Press.

—— (1993) *An Ethics of Sexual Difference*. Ithaca, NY: Cornell University Press.

Jackson, Jennifer (1995) "Nude for a Day." *Harper's Bazaar* April: 50.

Jeans, D.N. (1981) "The Making of the Anzac Memorial, Sydney: Towards a Secular Culture." *Australia 1938: A Bicentennial History Bulletin* 4 (Nov.): 48–60.

Johnson, Dirk (1996) "Students Still Sweat, They Just Don't Shower." *New York Times* 22 April: A1+.

Juffer, Jane (1998) *At Home with Pornography: Women, Sex, and Everyday Life*. New York: New York University Press.

Jung, Helen (2000) "It's Online, it's Profitable – but it's Porn." *Wall Street Journal* 9 February: NW4.

Keleman, Stanley (1981) *Your Body Speaks its Mind*. Berkeley, CA: Center Press.

Kenyon, Elizabeth du Mello (1989) "The Management of Exhibitionism in the Elderly: A Case Study." *Sexual and Marital Therapy* 4(1): 93–100.

Kierkegaard, Søren. (1958) *The Journals of Søren Kierkegaard: A Selection*. Ed. and trans. Alexander Dru. [n.p.]: Collins/Fontana.

—— (1960) *The Diary of Søren Kierkegaard*. Ed. Peter P. Rohde. New York: Philosophical Library.

Kilmer, M. (1982) "Genital Phobia and Depilation." *Journal of Hellenic Studies* 102: 104–12.

Kirby, Kathleen (1996) *Indifferent Boundaries: Spatial Concepts of Human Subjectivity*. New York: Guilford.

Klein, Melanie (1988) *Love, Guilt and Reparation and Other Works 1921–1945*. Introd. Hanna Segal. London: Virago.

Kleinhans, Chuck (2001) "Pamela Anderson on the Slippery Slope." In *The End of Cinema as We Know It: American Film in the Nineties*. Ed. Jon Lewis. New York: New York University Press.

Knight, Richard Payne (1957 [1786]) *A Discourse on the Worship of Priapus*. Rpt in *Sexual Symbolism: A History of Phallic Worship*. Introd. Ashley Montagu. New York: Julian Press.

Kohlberg, Lawrence (1981) *The Philosophy of Moral Development: Moral Stages and the Idea of Justice*. San Francisco, CA: Harper & Row.

Kramilius, Antanas V. (1995) "It Just Turns Australia into a Laughing-Stock." Letter. *Canberra Times* 18 April: 12.

Kristeva, Julia (1982) *Powers of Horror: An Essay on Abjection*. Trans. Leon S. Roudiez. New York: Columbia University Press.

Kronenfeld, Judy (1998) *King Lear and the Naked Truth: Rethinking the Language of Religion and Resistance*. Durham, NC: Duke University Press.

Kuhn, Annette (1985) *The Power of the Image: Essays on Representation and Sexuality*. London: Routledge & Kegan Paul.

Lacan, Jacques (1982) "The Meaning of the Phallus." In *Feminine Sexuality: Jacques Lacan and the École Freudienne*. Ed. Juliet Mitchell and Jacqueline Rose. London: Macmillan.

Lakoff, George and Mark Johnson (1980) *Metaphors We Live By*. Chicago: University of Chicago Press.

Lamb, Charles (1903) "A Complaint of the Decay of Beggars in the Metropolis." In *The Works of Charles and Mary Lamb. Vol. 2: Elia and the Last Essays of Elia*. Ed. E.V. Lucas. London: Methuen.

Lambdin, Thomas O. (trans.) (1996) "The Gospel of Thomas (II, 2)." In *The Nag Hammadi Library in English*, 4th edn. Ed. and trans. James M. Robinson. Leiden: E.J. Brill.

Langdon-Davies John (1928) *Lady Godiva: The Future of Nakedness*. New York: Harper.

Leach, E.R. (1958) "Magical Hair." *Journal of the Royal Anthropological Institute of Great Britain and Ireland* 88(2): 147–64.

Leder, Drew (1990) *The Absent Body*. Chicago: University of Chicago Press.

—— (1992) "A Tale of Two Bodies: The Cartesian Corpse and the Lived Body." In *The Body in Medical Thought and Practice*. Dordrecht: Kluwer.

Leigh, David, et al. (2002) "The National Crisis, Day 14." *Guardian* 14 December: 1+.

Lewis, Robin J. and Louis H. Janda (1988) "The Relationship between Adult Sexual Adjustment and Childhood Experiences Regarding Exposure to Nudity, Sleeping in the Parental Bed, and Parental Attitudes toward Sexuality." *Archives of Sexual Behavior* 17(4): 349–62.

Lovejoy, Arthur O. (1960) *Essays in the History of Ideas*. New York: Capricorn.

Lumby, Catharine (1997) "The Naked Truth: Fame is no Laugh." *Sydney Morning Herald* 18 July: 17.

MacCannell, Dean (1989 [1976]) *The Tourist: A New Theory of the Leisure Class*. New York: Schocken.

MacCary, W. Thomas (1982) "Naked Men as Women." In *Childlike Achilles: Ontogeny and Phylogeny in The Iliad*. New York: Columbia University Press.

McCrum, Robert, William Cran and Robert MacNeil (1986) *The Story of English*. London: Faber & Faber (BBC Books).

MacDonald, John M. (1973) *Indecent Exposure*. Springfield, IL: Charles C. Thomas.

McDonnell, Myles (1991) "The Introduction of Athletic Nudity: Thucydides, Plato, and the Vases." *Journal of Hellenic Studies* 8: 182–93.

McLuhan, Marshall (1997) "The Gutenberg Galaxy." In *Essential McLuhan*. Ed. Eric McLuhan and Frank Zingrone. London: Routledge.

Mainsbridge, B.N. (1995) Letter. *Sydney Morning Herald* 19 April: 16.

Mann, J.C. (1974) "*Gymnazo* in Thucydides i.6. 5–6." *Classical Review* 24: 177–8.

Mansfield, Nicholas (2000) *Subjectivity: Theories of the Self from Freud to Haraway*. St Leonards, Vic: Allen & Unwin.

Marshall, P. David (1997) *Celebrity and Power: Fame in Contemporary Culture*. Minneapolis, MN: University of Minnesota Press.

Marx, Jack (1997) "That Video." *Australian Style* 23: 46–7.

Marx, Karl (1988) *The Communist Manifesto*. Ed. Frederic L. Bender. New York: Norton.

Mason, Peter (1990) *Deconstructing America: Representations of the Other*. London: Routledge.

Massey, Doreen (1994) *Space, Place and Gender*. Oxford: Polity.

Maurstad, Tom (1998) "Nude on the Net: Celebrities are Unwilling Participants in Skin Trade." *Dallas Morning News* 6 December: 1C.

Mauss, Marcel (1973) "Techniques of the Body." *Economy and Society* 2(1): 70–88.

Mayrand, Robert T. (1968) "Nudists Have More Sexual Energy." *Modern Sunbathing Quarterly* 816 (Summer): 9–14.

Mercer, Kobena (1990) "Black Hair/Style Politics." In *Out There: Marginalization and Contemporary Culture*. Ed. Russell Ferguson et al. New York: New Museum of Contemporary Art, and Cambridge, MA: MIT Press.

Michaels, Eric (1990) *Unbecoming: An AIDS Diary*. Rose Bay: EmPress.

Miles, Margaret R. (1989) *Carnal Knowing: Female Nakedness and Religious Meaning in the Christian West*. Boston, MA: Beacon Press.

Miller, Derek (1974) "The Significance of Streaking." *Medical Aspects of Human Sexuality* 8: 158–9.

Montag, Warren (1997) "The Universalization of Whiteness: Racism and Enlightenment." In *Whiteness: A Critical Reader*. Ed. Mike Hill. New York: New York University Press.

Montalbano, F.J. (1967) "Nudity (in the Bible)." In *New Catholic Encylopedia*. New York: McGraw-Hill.

Morris, William and Mary Morris (1988) *Morris Dictionary of Word and Phrase Origins*, 2nd edn. New York: Harper & Row.

Moskowitz, Eric and David K. Li (2002) "He was Porn to Run: Internet Boss Flees Payment to Pamela and Tommy Lee." *New York Post* 15 December: 31.

Muir, Les and Connie Muir (1995) "Authorities are to Blame." Letter. *Canberra Times* 18 April: 12.

Mulvey, Laura (1975) "Visual Pleasure and Narrative Cinema." *Screen* 16(3): 6–18.

Mumford, Lewis (1944) *The Condition of Man*. London: Secker & Warburg.

Myers, Wayne A. (1989) "The Traumatic Element in the Typical Dream of Feeling Embarrassed at Being Naked." *Journal of the American Psychoanalytic Association* 37(1): 117–30.

Nadel, Henri (1929) *Devons-nous vivre nu? Tome II: La Nudité et la santé*. Paris: Éditions de Vivre.

Nead, Lynda (1992) *The Female Nude: Art, Obscenity and Sexuality*. London: Routledge.

Neaman, Judith S. and Carole G. Silver (1983) *A Dictionary of Euphemisms*. London: Unwin.

Nelson, Peter (1995) Letter. *Sydney Morning Herald* 19 April: 16.

Nietzsche, Friedrich (1973) *Beyond Good and Evil: Prelude to a Philosophy of the Future*. Trans. and introd. R.J. Hollingdale. Harmondsworth: Penguin.

Norman, Jean (1995) "Mr Smooth." *Sydney Morning Herald Good Weekend* 5 August: 25–6.

Norwood, C.E. (Rev.) (1933) *Nudism in England*. London: Noel Douglas.

O'Toole, Laurence (1999) *Pornocopia: Porn, Sex, Technology and Desire*, 2nd edn. London: Serpent's Tail.

Pagden, Anthony (1993) *European Encounters with the New World: From Renaissance to Romanticism*. New Haven, CT: Yale University Press.

Parmelee, Maurice (1929) *Nudism in Modern Life: The New Gymnosophy*. Introd. Havelock Ellis. London: Noel Douglas.

Pascal, Blaise (1961) *The Pensées*. Trans. and introd. J.M. Cohen. Harmondsworth: Penguin.

Pateman, Carole (1988) *The Sexual Contract*. Stanford, CA: Stanford University Press.

Perniola, Mario (1989) "Between Clothing and Nudity." Trans. Roger Friedman. In *Fragments for a History of the Human Body. Part Two*. Ed. Michel Feher, with Ramona Naddaff and Nadia Tazi. New York: Zone.

Plato (1955) *The Republic*. Trans. and introd. H.D.P. Lee. Harmondsworth: Penguin.

Pointon, Marcia (1993) "The Case of the Dirty Beau: Symmetry, Disorder and the Politics of Masculinity." In *The Body Imaged: The Human Form and Visual Culture Since the Renaissance*. Ed. Kathleen Adler and Marcia Pointon. Cambridge: Cambridge University Press.

Polinska, Wioleta (2000) "Dangerous Bodies: Women's Nakedness and Theology." *Journal of Feminist Studies in Religion* 16(1): 45–62.

Posner, Richard A. and Katherine B. Silbaugh (1996) *A Guide to America's Sex Laws*. Chicago: University of Chicago Press.

Poucel, Jean (1953) *Naturisme, ou la santé sans drogues*. Paris: J. Oliven (Limoges, Impr. de la Société Journaux et publications).

Probyn, Elspeth (1990) "New Traditionalism and Post-Feminism: TV Does the Home." *Screen* 31(2): 147–59.

Rabelais, François (n.d.) *The Five Books of Gargantua and Pantagruel*. Trans. J. LeClercq. New York: Modern Library.

Ramsey, G.G. (trans.) (1982) *Juvenal and Persius*. London: Heinemann.

Rhoads, John M. and Priscilla Day Boekelheide (1984–5) "Female Genital Exhibitionism." *Psychiatric Forum* 13(1): 1–6.

Rivière, Joan (1986) "Womanliness as Masquerade." In *Formations of Fantasy*. Ed. Victor Burgin, James Donald, and Cora Kaplan. London: Methuen.

Roberts, Neil (1995) "Tale of Two Men: Art or Outrage?" *Sydney Morning Herald* 17 April: 1.

Rotello, Gabriel (1996) "Rub a Dub Dub." *Advocate* 11 June: 80.

Rousseau, Jean-Jacques (1935) *The Confessions of Jean-Jacques Rousseau*. Trans. W. Conyngham Mallory. New York: Tudor.

Russell, John (1983) Letter. *The Argus* [Melbourne] 7 May: 8.

Safire, William (1996) "Half in Love with 'Full Frontal.'" *New York Times Magazine* 25 February: 30–1.

Salardenne, Roger (1931) *Le Nu intégrale chez les nudistes français*. Paris: Prima.

Savage, Tony (1995) "Sculptor is 'The Ugly Aussie.'" Letter. *Canberra Times* 18 April: 12.

Schama, Simon (1996) *Landscape and Memory*. London: Fontana.

Schapiro, Mark (1994) "The Fine Art of Sexual Harassment." *Harper's Magazine* July: 62–3.

Seccombe, Mike (ed.) (1995) "Kookaburra." *Sydney Morning Herald* 22 April: 36.

Sedgwick, Eve Kosofsky (1985) *Between Men: English Literature and Male Homosocial Desire*. New York: Columbia University Press.

Senchuk, Dennis M. (1985) "Innocence and Education." *Philosophical Studies in Education* (1985): 6–24.

Senior, John (1995) Letter. *Sydney Morning Herald* 19 April: 16.

Sharma, Arvind (1987) "Nudity." In *Encyclopedia of Religion*. Ed. Mircea Eliade. Vol. 11. New York: Macmillan.

Shulman, Ken (1994) "The Loincloth Legacy." *Artnews* 93(2): 20.

Silverman, Kaja (1986) "Fragments of a Fashionable Discourse." In *Studies in Entertainment: Critical Approaches to Mass Culture*. Ed. Tania Modleski. Bloomington, IN: Indiana University Press.

Silvester, John (1998) "Byrne Anguish over Sex Video." *Sun-Herald* [Sydney] 28 June: 13.

Slovenko, Ralph (1965) "A Panoramic View: Sexual Behavior and the Law." In *Sexual Behavior and the Law*. Ed. Ralph Slovenko. Springfield, IL: Charles C. Thomas.

Smedley, Audrey (1998) *Race in North America*. Boulder, CO: Westview Press.

Smith, Alison (1996) *The Victorian Nude: Sexuality, Morality and Art*. Manchester: Manchester University Press.

Smith, David (Sir) (1995) "Will Gareth Grovel Again?" Letter. *Canberra Times* 18 April: 12.

Smyth, Terry (1996) "The Naked Truth." *Sun-Herald* [Sydney] 8 September: Tempo 4–5.

Spelman, Elizabeth V. (1982) "Woman as Body: Ancient and Contemporary Views." *Feminist Studies* 8(1): 109–31.

Squires, Tony (1999) "Date with the Coy Division." *Sydney Morning Herald* 4 December: Spectrum 22.

Stanley, H.M. (1984) *Address to the Manchester Chamber of Commerce*. London: WM Clowes & Sons.

Steele, Valerie (1996) *Fetish: Fashion, Sex and Power*. Oxford: Oxford University Press.

Steinberg, Leo (1996) *The Sexuality of Christ in Renaissance Art and in Modern Oblivion*, 2nd edn. Chicago: University of Chicago Press.

Stratton, Jon (1998) *Race Daze: Australia in Identity Crisis*. Annandale, NSW: Pluto Press.

Stuart, Andrea (1996) *Showgirls*. London: Jonathan Cape.

Sturma, Michael (1995) "The Nubile Savage." *History Today* 45(4): 7–9.

Sturtevant, E.H. (1912) "*Gymnos* and *Nudus*." *American Journal of Philology* 33: 324–9.

Sussman, Stephen Allan (1977) "Body Disclosure and Self-Disclosure: Relating Two Modes of Interpersonal Encounter." *Journal of Clinical Psychology* 33(4): 1146–8.

Synnott, Anthony (1993) *The Body Social: Symbolism, Self and Society*. London: Routledge.

Taylor, Mandy (1995) Letter. *Sydney Morning Herald* 19 April: 16.

Thomas, Nicholas (1994) *Colonialism's Culture: Anthropology, Travel and Government*. Cambridge: Polity.

Thomson, Arthur (1964 [1929]) *A Handbook of Anatomy for Art Students*. New York: Dover.

Tibbals, Bill (1995) Letter. *Sydney Morning Herald* 19 April: 16.

Tickner, Lisa (1978) "The Body Politic: Female Sexuality and Women Artists Since 1970." *Art History* 1: 236–47.

Todorov, Tzvetan (1984) *The Conquest of America: The Question of the Other*. Trans. Richard Howard. New York: Harper & Row.

Toepfer, Karl (1996) "Nudity and Textuality in Postmodern Performance." *Performing Arts Journal* 18(3): 76–91.

—— (1997) *Empire of Ecstasy: Nudity and Movement in German Body Culture, 1910–1935*. Berkeley, CA: University of California Press.

Toolan, James M. (1974) "The Significance of Streaking." *Medical Aspects of Human Sexuality* 8: 152, 157.

Torgovnick, Marianna (1990) *Gone Primitive: Savage Intellects, Modern Lives*. Chicago: University of Chicago Press.

Townsend, Chris (1996) "A Picture of Innocence?" *History Today* 46(5): 8–11.

"T.P.I." (1883) Letter. *The Argus* [Melbourne] 24 May: 7.

Turner, Bryan S. (1996) *The Body and Society: Explorations in Social Theory*, 2nd edn. London: Sage.

Turner, Graeme (1994) *Making it National: Nationalism and Australian Popular Culture*. St Leonards, Vic: Allen & Unwin.

Urry, John (1990) *The Tourist Gaze: Leisure and Travel in Contemporary Societies*. London: Sage.

Vachet, Pierre (1949) *Connaissance de la vie sexuelle*. Fontenay-Saint-Père: Éditions Vivre d'abord.

Walker, Benjamin (1977) *Encyclopedia of Esoteric Man*. London: Routledge & Kegan Paul.

Walker, Susannah and Elizabeth Renkert (1997) "Dinner for 12." *marie claire* 25 (Sept.): 104+.

Walters, Margaret (1978) *The Male Nude: A New Perspective*. New York: Paddington Press.

Wark, McKenzie (1999) *Celebrities, Culture and Cyberspace: The Light on the Hill in a Postmodern World*. Annandale, NSW: Pluto Press.

Warner, Marina (1985) *Monuments and Maidens: The Allegory of the Female Form*. London: Weidenfeld and Nicolson.

Watson, Irene (1998) "Naked Peoples: Rules and Regulations." *Law/Text/Culture* 4(1): 1–17.

Welby, William (1934) *"Naked and Unashamed": Nudism from Six Points of View*. London: Thorsons.

Wheeler, Roy (1995) "Queen Shouldn't be Fair Game." Letter. *Canberra Times* 18 April: 12.

Williams, Raymond (1976) *Keywords: A Vocabulary of Culture and Society*. London: Fontana (Flamingo).

—— (1980) "Ideas of Nature." In *Problems in Materialism and Culture*. London: Verso.

Williams, Sue (1997) "Risky Business." *Sydney Morning Herald* 27 July: Tempo 4.

Willis, Susan (1991) "Work(ing) Out." In *A Primer for Daily Life*. London: Routledge.

Wilson, Alexander (1992) *The Culture of Nature: North American Landscape from Disney to the Exxon Valdez*. Cambridge, MA: Blackwell.

Wimsatt, W.K. and Monroe C. Beardsley (1967) "The Affective Fallacy." In W. K. Wimsatt, *The Verbal Icon: Studies in the Meaning of Poetry*. Lexington, KY: University of Kentucky Press.

Wolff, Janet (1990) *Feminine Sentences: Essays on Women and Culture*. Berkeley, CA: University of California Press.

Woolf, Virginia (1977) *Orlando*. Frogmore, Htds: Granada.

Woolmington, Jean (ed. and introd.) (1988) *Aborigines in Colonial Society: 1788–1850. From "Noble Savage" to "Rural Pest,"* 2nd edn. Armidale, NSW: University of New England.

Wortley, Richard (1976) *A Pictorial History of Striptease: 100 Years of Undressing to Music*. London: Octopus.

Wright, T. (1995) "Not Freedom of Expression." Letter. *Canberra Times* 18 April: 12.

Yalom, Marilyn (1997) *A History of the Breast*. New York: Alfred A. Knopf.

Young, Iris Marion (1990) "Women Recovering our Clothes." In *Throwing like a Girl and Other Essays in Feminist Philosophy and Social Theory*. Bloomington, IN: Indiana University Press.

Websites

Davis-Floyd, Robbie, *Birth as an American Rite of Passage*. Designed for the Web by Ed Goldberg. http://www.birthpsychology.com/messages

Dennis, David, "A Note from Jen's Lawyers." JenniCam site. Accessed 25 May 1999. http://www.boudoir.org

Eros Foundation, http://www.eros.com.au

Fake Name, "Re: Ohio State Rugby Players Doff Shirts." Online posting. 5 Nov. 1999. alt.nudism.moderated. Accessed 9 Nov. 1999. alt-nudism-moderated@moderators.isc.org

Fletcher, "Re: JenniCam; Cybersaint or Self-Serving Trollop?" Online posting. 2 Aug. 1997. Accessed 25 May 1999. *apcmag*. http://apcmag.com

Gliddon, Josh, "90 Degrees from Everywhere/JenniCam." Online posting. 6 Feb. 1997. Accessed 25 May 1999. *apcmag*. http://apcmag.com

—— "What is JenniCam? A Short History." Online posting. 24 July 1997. Accessed 25 May 1999. *apcmag*. http://apcmag.com

—— "Re: JenniCam; Cybersaint or Self-Serving Trollop?" Online posting. 1 Aug. 1997. Accessed 25 May 1999. *apcmag*. http://apcmag.com

Hargreaves, Geoff, "Re: The Great Piano-Leg Mystery." Online posting. 20 Apr. 1994. Victoria 19th-Century British Culture & Society. Accessed 21 Sept. 2000. http://www.indiana.edu/~victoria/discussion.html

Kidman, Angus, "Privacy and Punishment: An Email Conversation." Online posting. 24 July 1997. Accessed 25 May 1999. *apcmag*. http://apcmag.com

Mike, "Neighbors Complaining About My 4-Year Old Going Topless." Online posting. 17 Oct. 1999. alt.nudism.moderated. Accessed 19 Oct. 1999. alt-nudism-moderated@moderators.isc.org

"Re: JenniCam; Cybersaint or Self-Serving Trollop?" Online posting. 25 Dec. 1997. Accessed 25 May 1999. *apcmag*. http://apcmag.com

The Rec.Nude Legal FAQ, rev. 7/9/99. Accessed 14 Oct. 1999. http://www-hep.phys.cmu.edu/~brahm/legal.html

Robinson, B.A., "Nudity in the Bible." Accessed 7 Sept. 2000. http://www.religioustolerance.org/nu_bibl.htm

"Them Modest Highschoolers." Online discussion. 17 Oct. 1999+. alt.nudism.moderated. Accessed 19 Oct. 1999. alt-nudism-moderated@moderators.isc.org

"L'Utopie." Accessed Sept. 2000. http://cancres.free.fr/documents/exposes/utopie.htm

Index

metaphor, 7, 57, 139, 156
  see also clothing – as metaphor; nudity –
    as metaphor
metaphysics
  Greek, *see* nudity – in the Greek
    tradition
  Hebrew, *see* nudity – in the Judaic
    tradition
  Platonic, *see* Plato
  Western, 12, 37
Miles, Margaret, 5, 25, 30, 36–52 passim,
    77, 80, 106, 108–9, 117–18, 126–7, 138,
    195, 227–8, 235–6, 248–9
misogyny, 44, 192–3, 248–9
  in Christianity, 63, 87, 108–9
missionaries, 158
models
  artists', 34
  female, 34, 109
  male, 39
  photographic, 26, 41, 45, 265
  pornographic, 243–4
  relationship between artist and model,
    42–3
modernity, 1, 63, 272
  see also shame – rise of in modernity
  as nostalgic, 61, 136, 161, 165, 255
    see also ambivalence – about
      modernity
modesty, 55, 74n11, 111, 176
  modesty poses, 18
    see also fig leaf.
morality, 1, 47, 77, 82, 93, 103, 109, 116,
    242–4, 271–2
Mulvey, Laura, 41

nakedness, *see* nudity
naked truth, the, 48–9, 62, 89, 97–106
  see also Nuda Veritas
naked vs. nude
  distinction in fine art, 30–47, 126, 145
    see also Berger, John, Clark, Kenneth
  feminist responses to, 36–47
    see also Nead, Lynda
  etymology of, 32–3, 74n17, 74n18
nature, 14, 33, 55, 281–2, 284n3
  see also ambivalence – about nature;
    animality

belief in "naturalness," 30, 97, 282
  see also nudity – "naturalness" of
sex and nature, 115, 172–3
vs. culture, 13–15, 31, 141, 154, 282
  see also humanness – separation from
    nature
naturism, *see* nudism
Nead, Lynda, 37, 39, 46, 71
Nietzsche, Friedrich, 59, 75n23, 76n29
Nuda Veritas, 102
  see also naked truth
nude, the, 4, 20, 26, 30–2, 33–46 passim,
    60–1, 71, 105–6, 109, 14–14–5, 150,
    262, 281
  feminist treatment of, 5, 41, 111–12
  male, 34
    see also nudity – heroic
nudism, 3, 5, 46, 54, 88–9, 91, 97–8, 133,
    140n6, 166–81, 231–2
  see also magazines – nudist
  and anti-materialism, 84
  and body image, 170–1
  and freedom, 94, 169
  and men, 110
  and sex, 114–15, 172–9
  and sexuality, 173, 177, 180–1
  and voyeurism, 178–81
  and women, 94, 172–3, 175–6, 178–80,
    204n33
  as a critique of modernity, 167
  as a lifestyle, 84, 169–71
  as exhibitionism, 178–9
  as medical practice, 84, 167, 174–5
  as political practice, 84, 168–71
  as scientific and rational, 167, 175
  as social deviance, 166–81
  as utopian, 167
  Ashworth, Ron, 27, 115, 172–3
  Christian, 20, 167, 169
  contemporary, 169–71
  early, 166–9, 173–6
  in Australia, 26–7, 166
  in France, 166–9, 174
  in Germany, 166–8, 174, 203n25
  in the UK, 166–7, 175
  in the US, 176
  Internet groups, 92, 241
  Koch, Adolf, 168

Index

  see also Adam and Eve
in the Greek tradition, 7–8, 12, 36–7,
  81–3, 98, 113–14
in the Judaic tradition, 7–8, 12, 81, 83,
  113–14
in theatrical performance, 21–2, 53
  see also striptease
magical powers of, 110, 182–4, 190–5,
  204n35, 205n39
male, 110, 182–91, 227–8
  see also flashing; nudity – heroic
  in groups, 118–90
  see also streaking
medieval taxonomy of, 80–1, 89, 153,
  158, 181
negative meanings of, 106–138, 244–8
of indigenous peoples, 154–65
  see also Aborigines
of Jesus Christ, 228
  imitations of, 235–6
  in Renaissance painting, 69–70, 228
of monarchs, 215, 219–26, 274n7
of politicians, 103, 215–18, 233
positive meanings of, 83–106, 242–4
ritual, 53
satirical, 212–26
social consequences of, 267–8
  see also nudity – criminality
studies of, 4–7
  see also breasts, clothing, *Emperor's
    New Clothes*, genitals, Godiva, Lady,
    naked truth, nudism, penis

objectification, 41–3, 114, 237, 262
Ohio State University women's rugby team,
  241
Olympic Games, 237–9
ordinariness, 212, 241–3, 253, 264, 269–79
  see also nudity – homemade

paedophilia, 91–2, 130, 140n6
Pascal, Blaise, 100–1
Paul, St, 25, 56, 74n10, 76n28
Peeping Tom, 89, 229
penis, 17, 20, 104, 141n19, 184–7, 191,
  222, 232
  erection, 73n4, 108, 140n13, 141n23,
    186, 263, 266, 277n31, 277n32

phallus worship, 182–4, 204n34
  vs. phallus, 184–5, 191
  see also fig leaf; flashing; nudity – of Jesus
    Christ
performance, 53–4, 260
  see also identity – as performance; nudity
    – in theatrical performance; striptease
performativity, *see* Butler, Judith
Perniola, Mario, 7, 12, 19, 76n28, 78, 81,
  98–9, 113–14, 119–20, 123, 139
perversion, *see* exhibitionism, flashing,
  streaking
philosophy, 23, 53, 58
photography, 102, 237–9
  see also images
  anthropological, 151, 163
  as identity work, *see* identity – individual
  erotic, 26, 45, 54, 111, 253, 258
  glamour, 249–51
  of children, 91–3, 135
  Polaroid, 253, 276n24
Phryne, trial of, 229
Pickering, Larry, 215–18
Plato, 49, 81, 183
  importance of vision to, 81, 99, 117
  on femininity, 36, 117, 275n9
  on relation between body and soul, 36,
    56, 75n27, 86–7, 117, 141n17, 227,
    275n9
  theory of Forms, 98
pornography, 41, 111, 119–20, 209
  effects of, 112
  for women, 260–2
  influence on depilation, 28–9
  Internet, 246, 254–5
  magazines, *see* magazines – pornographic
  reality porn, 251–72
  see also sex videos – stolen
postfeminism, 242, 244
postmodernity, 129–30, 255, 268
post-structuralism, 24, 49, 52, 105, 155,
  252, 260
Praxiteles, 18, 82, 229
Prince Charles, 217, 218
Prince Philip, 219–26
privacy, 85, 245–8, 270–1
  blurring of public and private, 95, 241,
    253, 256–7, 276n26
  see also JenniCam

Dandy Gilver and a
Deadly Measure
of Brimstone